# PASCAL

## PROGRAM DEVELOPMENT WITH TEN INSTRUCTION PASCAL SUBSET (TIPS) AND STANDARD PASCAL

Prentice-Hall Software Series
Brian W. Kernighan, Advisor

# PASCAL

## PROGRAM DEVELOPMENT WITH TEN INSTRUCTION PASCAL SUBSET (TIPS) AND STANDARD PASCAL

MICHAEL KENNEDY
MARTIN B. SOLOMON
*University of Kentucky*

PRENTICE-HALL, INC.
Englewood Cliffs, New Jersey 07632

*Library of Congress Cataloging in Publication Data*

Kennedy, Michael   (date)
      PASCAL: program development with ten instruction
PASCAL subset (TIPS) and standard PASCAL.

      (Prentice-Hall software series)
      Includes index.
      1. PASCAL (Computer program language)   I. Solomon,
Martin B.  II. Title.  III. Series.
QA76.73.P2K46         001.64'24         81-5150
ISBN 0-13-652735-3          AACR2

© 1982 by Prentice-Hall, Inc., Englewood Cliffs, NJ 07632

Printed in the United States of America

10  9  8  7  6  5  4  3  2  1

*Editorial/production supervision: Nancy Milnamow*
*Cover design: Edgar Blakeney*
*Manufacturing buyer: Gordon Osbourne*

Prentice-Hall International, Inc., *London*
Prentice-Hall of Australia Pty. Limited, *Sydney*
Prentice-Hall of Canada, Ltd., *Toronto*
Prentice-Hall of India Private Limited, *New Delhi*
Prentice-Hall of Japan, Inc., *Tokyo*
Prentice-Hall of Southeast Asia Pte. Ltd., *Singapore*
Whitehall Books Limited, *Wellington, New Zealand*

*For:*

**Evan Kennedy**      **Elizabeth Solomon**

**Heather Kennedy**      **Michaelle Solomon**

**Blaise Pascal** (1623-1662) contributed to projective geometry by his work in conics, made significant contributions to probability theory, and invented the adding machine.

**Charles Babbage** (1792—1871) originated the modern electronic computer by designing its mechanical forerunner, the analytical engine.

**George Boole** (1815—1864) published *Mathematical Analysis of Logic,* which marked the founding of the discipline of Boolean algebra.

**Niklaus Wirth** authored *Systematic Programming* and developed the computer language PASCAL.

The primary intent of this book is to create in beginning students an ability to solve problems through development of PASCAL language programs. The approach used herein is different from many texts which purport to produce the same result. We teach a few elements with considerable rigor and precision (our casual approach notwithstanding) and also teach the methods of synthesis of those elements which result in the production of good programs. We generate a climate in which the synthesis will be learned as the student uses the elements and the methods of integration, and we present only those tools which tend to keep the student out of trouble.

We believe that students learn and synthesize foremost by thinking and doing (once they understand the elements and understand the methods for integrating); they learn next best by interacting with a teacher who is responsive to their questions and can discern their misunderstandings; and they learn least well by reading "case histories" which are, really, artifacts of someone else's thought processes as that person went through the synthesis. Programming, program development, and certainly problem solving is a creative activity--not a mimicking activity. You will find this text short on long examples. Nothing would be easier than to fill a text with "realistic" examples--but such examples contribute little to the learning process.

Our approach may leave us open to the criticism that this is primarily a book about program statements. It isn't, as we believe will be obvious by the integrative skills of the readers, provided they work the Lab Problems and Exercises. In general, we lead students along a path which causes them to integrate what they know.

When we introduced the "teaching subset" approach in 1970 with TEN STATEMENT FORTRAN (TSF) we felt obliged to defend the concept of selecting a sparse subset of the language and coercing students to use only that subset while learning program development. After the successes of that language and PL/ZERO, and the informal emulation of the approach by other texts, we felt that the days of inundating the beginning student with mounds of information about a computer language were over. We were appalled, therefore, to see introductory textbooks on PASCAL opening with a

descriptive treatment of the sundry data types. Surely the
wide offering of data types is the nicest feature of PASCAL.
And, just as surely, those data types have no place in the
opening month cf a course on program development. Students
must first learn what an algorithm is and how tc implement
it. We take up data structures when the student has the
programming sophistiction to know the contribution they can
make to problem solving.


## A Guide to Course Crganization

    Prior to the beginning of the course, the instructor
should be aware of both the rationale behind this book and
of the pedagogical devices we use.

    The book is modular. Thus the instructor has the
opportunity to design his own course depending on what he or
she feels is important. The text consists of seven parts:


## PART I--THE TEN INSTRUCTION PASCAI SUBSET (TIPS)

    By studying this Part the student learns a basic, but
complete, language for structured programming. Covered are
elements of the language, input, output, computation, built-
in functions, selection, iteration, user-written procedures,
and arrays. We use the term "instruction" loosely to
include declarations, statements, and built-in procedures.
The ten instructions are; PROGRAM, PROCEDURE (without
parameters), VAR (REAL and INTEGER), READ, WRITFLN,
assignment, IF-THEN-ELSE, WHILE-DC, FOR-DO, and the user-
written-procedure call. The delimiters BEGIN and END are
used to form compound statements. The student uses the
subset to solve more than a dozen easy laboratory problems
which are imbedded in the text. The ideas of the well-
structured program, hierarchical program development, and
readable program format are introduced early and amplified
throughout Part I.


## PART II--SCLVING PROBLEMS BY DEVELOPING PROGRAMS

    In this Part the student is taught a formal approach for
program development. We call it the Program Development
Scroll and the pullout sheet at the back of the text shows
its application to a particular problem. Part II introduces
no new language features. What it does include are sections

on debugging and testing, somewhat harder laboratory problems, and an exhaustive checklist (Problem Solving with a Computer--Reprise) for program development and implementation.


## PART III--PASCAL DATA STRUCTURES

In this Part, we shift from TIPS to PASCAL. (We capitalize the language name PASCAL to differentiate it from the man's name.) We introduce the remaining scalar types, CHAR and BOOLEAN, the user-defined scalar types and the subrange types. Then we turn to discussion of the remaining structured types: SET, RECORD, and FILE. The Part concludes with a section on list processing with pointer variables. The student is referred to Laboratory Problems (in Part VI) for practice.


## PART IV--PASCAL PROGRAM STRUCTURES

The most important discussion in this Part is of user-written procedures and functions with parameters. (We introduce user-written PROCEDUREs in PART I to help the student comprehend the idea of program modularity without the complexity of parameters.) Also included is material on the use of the case statement, go-to escapes from decision and looping structures, and recursive procedures. Again there are pointers to relevant Lab Problems.


## PART V--MODULES ON COMPUTERS AND COMPUTING

This Part includes material deemed to be important to the beginning programmer. Subjects include information about computer architecture, the compiling process, microcomputers, terminals, keypunches, flowcharting, number systems and bases, numerical considerations in computing, and a brief history of the computing field. The sections are independent and the instructor may choose when and whether to introduce them.


## PART VI--LABORATORY PROBLEMS

Thirty-eight Laboratory Problems were included in Parts I and II. Another twenty-three, on math, science, and business topics, are included here primarily for use with Parts III, IV, and V.

PART VII--APPENDICES

   The Appendices include the reference material the
student needs: elements of the language (reserved words,
special identifiers, functions, procedures, operators),
error messages, and answers to questions and exercises.
Also included are the PASCAL syntax diagrams (with the
solely hierarchical or self-recursive ones arranged
hierarchically and the rest arranged alphabetically).  There
are two more Appendices which, because they are on a fold
out, actually appear after the index.  On one side is a
sample Program Development Scroll keyed to Part II.  The
second is a "family tree" of all the PASCAL data types.


Aids to Learning

   Throughout the text we include numerous shaded
boxes such as this one.  The boxes contain material
on algorithm design, good programming practice,
testing, debugging, documentation, readable-program
format and other non-syntax related matters.  The
shaded boxes are our way of including "semantic"
material at appropriate points in the text but
allowing the student to differentiate it from the
rules--i.e., the "grammatic" material.  You might
encourage your students to go through the complete
text towards the end of the course just to reread
all the shaded boxes.

   You will find a certain amount of text enclosed by
boxes such as this one.  This is reference material
which will be useful when it is encountered, and perhaps
later.  **In some instances this material is to be
provided by the instructor; blanks are left for the
student to complete.  Perhaps you will want to leaf
through the text and notice those reference blocks which
relate to a particular microcomputer, terminal, or
version of PASCAL which may require you to provide the
student with some specific information.**

   We use flowcharts primarily as a pedagogical tool, not
as a program design tool.

One additional teaching device which may not be obvious
from a quick examination of the text is that the style
progresses slowly and subtly from patient hand holding
towards the sort of treatment one might find in a humane
reference manual.  We feel that part of the process of
educating people who are going to do programming is to get
them ready for the real world in which writers and vendors
and manufacturers present them with a cursory description of
a new product, feature, or technique, and leave it to them
to integrate its use into their own situation.  Again, it is
the working of the Lab Problems which provides the
comprehension.


A Suggested Syllabus Outline

There are many ways to use this text; the authors
recommend that you consider the following:

Initially assign Part I up to Computation, requiring
that Lab Problems 00 and 01 be worked as quickly as
possible.  Concurrently assign Module 2, 3, or 4 (depending
on whether your course uses microcomputers, remote
terminals, or a card-oriented batch system) and provide the
additional information required for using your particular
computer system.  Immediately assign Lab Problems 02 and 03
and take up Computation.  The results from Lab Problem 03
introduce the concept of IF-THEN-ELSE so it is best if that
problem is completed before the topic of selection is taken
up.  Cover the rest of Part I at fairly high speed.
Sometime during Part I assign the reading of Module 1 (Some
Fundamentals of a Computer System).

We strongly suggest that the student be required to work
most or all Laboratory Problems in Part I.  Particularly
integral to the progression of learning in Part I are Lab
Problems 00, 01, 02, 03, 04, 06, 07, 08, 09, (11, 12 or 13),
and 14 (if you choose to take up multi-dimensional arrays.)
The Lab Problems in Part I are simple.  Good students will
be able to do them instantly; poorer students will be able
to do them; all students will have the confidence which
comes from repeatedly attacking and solving problems.

During the time Part II (Program Development) is covered
we recommend that no new language features be introduced.
You might assign some of the other Modules as you wish
during this time (number systems, numerical considerations,
history of computing) since they will not interfere with the
learning of program development with the TIPS language.

Problems of varying degrees of difficulty and on a wide
variety of subjects appear in Parts II and VI; we feel a
student should work several of those in the later portions
of the course or should solve other problems of your choice.
You can provide such data in such a manner as seems
appropriate for your computer configuration.

Part III (PASCAL Data Structures) and Part IV (PASCAL
Program Structures) may then be covered and Lab Problems
from Part VI or from your own store used to drive home the
points.


## Suggested Program Format

The indentation and comment format we suggest is
probably best explicated by example:

```
(* PROGRAM DESCRIPTION *)
PROGRAM heading (INPUT,OUTPUT);
    VAR
        AA: (* USE OF AA *) REAL;
        BB: (* DESCRIPTION OF BB *) REAL;
        CC: (* SOMETHING ABOUT CC *) INTEGER;
    PROCEDURE heading;
        BEGIN (* name of procedure *)
        statements in procedure
        END; (* name of procedure *)
    BEGIN (* MAIN *)
    statements;
    IF condition THEN
        statement
    ELSE
        BEGIN
        statements
        END;
(* SECTION SEPARATING COMMENT *)
    WHILE condition DO
        BEGIN
        statement; (* STATEMENT SPECIFIC COMMENT *)
        FOR i := b TO e DO
            BEGIN
            statements
            END
        END
    END.  (* MAIN *)
```

You may notice that we are parsimonious with indentation. We don't indent after a BEGIN because the BEGIN is already indented. In general, indentation when it is not necessary causes the program to become jumbled up on the right side of the page--and that hardly increases readability.

We have examined the various indentation techniques and have settled on our own. In our scheme, the IF is paired with the ELSE regardless of whether simple or compound statements are involved. The condition to be tested is bracketed by IF and THEN on the same line. (The same applies to the WHILE--DO and the FOR--DO.) Our feeling is that most indentation schemes run into trouble because they attempt to pair the THEN and ELSE and then have to treat simple and compound statements after the THEN or ELSE differently or indent excessively. We are aware that our approach won't sit well with everyone and we invite you to prescribe a different one for your students if you wish. After all, the more important consideration here is that indenting be done to improve readability of programs.

We don't indent comments which describe general sections of the program because (1) a person should be able to read down the comments in a straight vertical column to find what he or she wants, and (2) a perfectly good cue as to "level" is the indentation of the statements themselves, and (3) the greater the degree of indentation the shorter the comment (unless you are willing to use multiple lines which creates other problems of readability).

## Acknowledgements

Many people and organizations provided information, inspiration, and assistance; without them the effort would not have been successful. Some of them are:

Jean Feraca, Lynda Kennedy and Patty Marshall our human text editors, who outwitted EDGAR, our machine text editor, and, using the SCRIPT language, produced the camera-ready copy.

Pat Thomson, who proofread the entire book twice, worked all the exercises, tested all PASCAL programs and program segments, and contributed in numerous other ways.

J.W. Atwood, Sir George Williams University, Montreal,
    Canada, who contributed several of the more interesting
    laboratory problems.

Harriet F. Schulz, formerly of IBM, who contributed to the
    section on Problem Solving with a Computer--Reprise.

Thaddeus Curtz, Former Chairman, Department of Computer
    Science, University of Kentucky, who contributed to
    Problem Solving with a Computer, Reprise.

Forbes Lewis, Chairman of Computer Science at the University
    of Kentucky, who said the right thing at the right time
    to initiate this project.

Wendy Jacobson, Department of Landscape Architecture,
    University of Guelph, Ontario, who said the right thing
    at the right time to sustain the effort.

A.C.R. Newbery, Department of Computer Science, University
    of Kentucky, whose straightforward presentation of
    numerical pitfalls in computing inspired Module 7.

Michal Howard, who read the work from the point of view of a
    student.

Francie Newbery, who worked the exercises in Part I.

Steve Cline, Nancy Milnamow, Paulette Cristie, and Chris
    Prince of Prentice-Hall for putting up with us.

The anonymous reviewers who battered our egos, but bettered
    our book.

Apple Computer Company, Cupertino, California, for the loan
    of an APPLE II Plus with the University of California at
    San Diego (UCSD) PASCAL compiler and operating system.

M & R Enterprises, Sunvale, California, for the loan of a
    SUP'R'TERMINAL board for our APPLE computer.

Ron Parker and Barry Burman of North Carolina Educational
    Computing Services who loaned the software which enabled
    our APPLE to elegantly communicate with the Triangle
    Universities Computation Center.

Springer-Verlag Publishers, for permission to use reference
    material from the PASCAL User Manual and Report, 2nd
    Edition, by Kathleen Jensen and Niklaus Wirth.

The Computation Center at the University of North Carolina,
    Chapel Hill, for some of the material on how to use a
    remote terminal.

TABLE OF CONTENTS

# part I

# THE TEN INSTRUCTION
# PASCAL SUBSET
# (TIPS)

# INTRODUCTION

You are off on an exciting adventure: you are about to
learn how to use an electronic device to increase your
mental ability.  Within a few weeks you will understand the
most central and fundamental concepts of a field which is
transforming our society.  Further, you'll have a tool to
use in solving problems you encounter.

Whether you'll find the process of learning about
automated information handlers, which is what computers
really are, difficult or easy depends on several things:
your background, your interest, perhaps your "natural
ability," and the time you spend with the subject.  Our goal
in writing this book is to make the process both as easy and
as enjoyable as possible.

Many centuries ago we humans learned that we could put
together natural substances and materials to increase our
physical strength and power; we became tool-making animals.
And many years ago we learned that we could devise tools
that were quite complex, at least in concept.  These tools
we called machines.  By combining these machines we made
other machines which operated automatically; we merely
supervised their performance.  Now we have learned to
construct devices which increase our mental ability.  They
do many of the chores we commonly associate with thinking
or, at least, "figuring."  These latest machines are called
computers because they were originally developed to do
arithmetic computation.

An early use of computing equipment was, as is true with
many inventions, to aid our ability to make war.  The close
of World War II saw modern computer development well on its
way.  Since that time the amount of information a computer
can remember and the speed with which it can process that
information has increased thousands of times.  This
tremendous increase in power was accompanied by an
associated increase in complexity.  As with other automatic
machines, however, much of this complexity went toward
making the machine itself easier to use.

One of the outgrowths of this tendency toward
"simplicity through complexity," is the development of
artificial languages used by people to communicate with
computers.  Each type or brand of computer has what is

called a <u>machine language</u>: a (usually) complicated set of
instructions which tells the machine to do simple things
such as add two numbers together.  Instructing, or
<u>programming</u>, a computer to do things, even easy things, in
its machine or "natural" language is quite tedious.
Therefore artificial languages were developed so that the
computer itself could be told to translate the artificial
language instructions into its own language and obey those
instructions to solve problems.

Many artificial languages for computers exist today.
One major, recently developed language is called PASCAL.  It
is a sophisticated language, named for the mathematician,
Blaise Pascal, inventor of the adding machine.  The language
<u>PASCAL</u> was designed by a computer scientist named Niklaus
Wirth, to enable students to learn "programming as a
systematic discipline."  PASCAL is not just a beginner's
language, however.  It is powerful and can be used with many
brands and models of computers.  Further, if you learn
PASCAL you will have learned most of the important features
which are common to all the major computer languages.
PASCAL is a "high level language"--meaning that its
structure and use is the sort that humans can use quickly
and easily; it is closer to English and math than to
"computerese."

Learning all of PASCAL is quite a task.  One of PASCAL's
features, though, is that you need to know only a small part
of it to be able to program a computer to solve many, many
problems.  Part I of this text describes, in detail, ten
instructions of the  PASCAL language; we call this portion
of the PASCAL language the <u>Ten Instruction PASCAL Subset</u> or
<u>TIPS</u>.

For every different brand and model computer, a special
program, called a compiler (or interpreter), must be
developed to translate the artificial language, say TIPS or
PASCAL, into the computer's own language.

To summarize the jargon, then:

<u>PASCAL</u> is the language which you are about to learn,

<u>TIPS</u> is a small part of PASCAL which you can begin using
      immediately to learn the fundamentals of problem solving
      by computer, and

A **compiler** is a computer program which translates the TIPS or PASCAL program into the machine language of the computer you are using.

## Structuring Programs for People

With this book we will do more than simply explore the grammar (syntax) of the PASCAL language. Learning the mechanics of a language is only the first step to learning the language. The primary reason to use a computer (and by implication, to learn a computer language with which you can instruct the computer) is to solve problems. But it turns out that there is much more to using a computer well than just writing instructions which tell the computer how to solve a particular problem. The programs you will learn to write will have a "structure" beyond what the computer itself demands. The structure will allow your computer instructions or programs to be easily read, understood, modified, and corrected, if necessary, by people. For many years it was tacitly assumed that if a programmer wrote programs which made the machine do what it was supposed to do, he or she had written a good program. The fact that the programmer couldn't go back to the program three months later and easily figure out what he or she had done was accepted as unfortunate but inevitable. Then people began to realize that if the programmer followed a few uniform rules in preparing the program in the first place, it would be easier to understand and clearer to everyone. The computing world is still reverberating from the shock of this revelation.

Throughout this book we will use shaded boxes such as this one to give you additional information. Much of this extra information is advice on how to become really good at instructing the computer. We include in the boxes ideas on good programming practice, ways to keep things from going wrong, ways to test programs, and other things we feel are important but which are not involved in your learning the fundamentals of PASCAL.

To use a parallel from another field--learning a foreign language such as French--the unshaded parts of the text give you the syntax or structure and the shaded material helps you learn to use the language idiomatically or with facility.

In the beginning we will solve problems which deal with numbers, but later we will deal with problems whose only restrictions are that they must be couched in terms of symbols. To solve any problem on a computer we must approach the task in a systematic way. The next section indicates how this might be done.

If you want to use a computer you must learn to be precise. You cannot communicate with a computer by hand waving and mumbling. A computer can be of service only if it is instructed carefully and according to preset rules. The following steps outline the procedure for using a computer to solve a problem. In each step precision is the watchword.

1. Formulate the problem. It is not enough to have a fuzzy idea of the sorts of answers desired for a final solution. A major advantage of using a computer to solve a problem is that one is forced to define the problem precisely.

   In this context you must determine if the problem is computer-solvable. A question such as "What is the best strategy to assure that our country will not run out of energy?" is not one which yields easily to computer solution. On the other hand, "What is 28 times 3?" is solvable by computer but is decidedly more trouble to do on a machine than by other means. In between there are many problems which are efficiently solvable by machine. Knowing which problems are computable and which are not is one difference between the creative computer user and the technician.

2. Decide on a method for solving the problem. This is where the human skill comes in. Most problems can be solved in more than one way on a computer. It is usually up to the person instructing the computer, called a programmer, to choose a particular method. Such a method--a step-by-step procedure for solving a problem--is called an algorithm.

3. On a sheet of paper write an informal but accurate description of the algorithm. Part of this informal description may involve a flowchart. A flowchart is a two-dimensional diagram which describes the algorithm in detail. Flowcharting techniques are discussed in Module 5. We will sometimes use flowcharts in the text to describe algorithms to you. In actually designing an algorithm, a flowchart may be useful, but there are better, more general, ways; we will describe them in Part II.

4. Using the informal algorithm description as a guide, write the computer instructions. Writing these instructions is one of the easier parts of the process, but it must be done with care. A part of this book describes instructions which may be used to tell the computer how to proceed in order to follow an algorithm. These instructions govern the computer's three main activities: input of data, manipulation of numbers and symbols according to the algorithm, and output of the answers wanted. A sequence of instructions which governs a computer's activities in this way is called a program.

5. Assemble the information the computer is to use as input or data in solving the problem. A single item of information, such as a number, is called a datum. The program that was previously written in Step 4 determines the order in which the computer will take in the data. The programmer must be certain, then, that he or she has precisely assembled the correct number of data and that they are in the proper order.

6. Prepare the written program and the assembled data so that they are in machine-readable form. Depending on the computer equipment you are using, this will mean either (a) typing the program and data into a microcomputer using a typewriter-like keyboard, or (b) typing the same information into a large computer using a remote terminal keyboard, or (c) preparing a data processing card for each line of the program and cards for the data. Microcomputers are discussed in Module 2, Remote Terminals are discussed in Module 3, and the data processing card and keypunch are discussed in Module 4.

---

In this course you will be using

( ) a microcomputer   (Read Module 2)

( ) a remote terminal  (Read Module 3)

( ) a card-based system (Read Module 4)


The equipment is designated as:_____

_____.

---

7.  Submit the machine-readable form of the program and a
    set of test data to the computer.  When the program is
    executed by the computer a <u>listing</u> will usually be
    generated on paper or on a TV-like "screen" called a
    <u>Cathode</u> <u>Ray</u> <u>Tube</u> or <u>CRT</u>.  The listing will consist of
    the program instructions and the answers or results.
    Analyze the results carefully for errors.

8.  If no answers are produced, or if the answers are
    incorrect, at least one error has been made in at least
    one of the previous steps.  The action which must be
    taken depends, of course, on the nature of the error(s).
    The process of finding and correcting errors is called
    <u>debugging</u>.

    It is vastly superior to do steps 1 through 7 carefully
    enough so that debugging isn't necessary.  It is also
    much more satisfying to do something right the first
    time.  But since all programmers make errors, we have
    included a section in Part II on program debugging for
    use later in the course.  Your computer may supply you
    with an <u>error code</u>, which is a number indicating which
    error has been made.  To understand the error code look
    in either Appendix E or on a separate code sheet which
    your instructor may supply.

9.  Prepare <u>documentation</u> describing what the program does,
    how to use it, what its limitations are, who wrote it,
    and other informational items.  This step actually
    should be part of almost all of the preceding steps.
    You should not wait until last to begin it, though it
    cannot be completed until the others are finished.

10. Use the program.  If you are satisfied that the program
    is correct, your actual data are accurate, and the
    documentation is complete, run "<u>production</u>" with your
    program.

    There is nothing magical about computers.  Most answers
that a computer can arrive at could also be arrived at by a
human if he lived long enough, had enough pencils, and
paper, etc.  (See Note 1; notes for each Part are at the end
of that Part.)  What's important to remember is that,
regardless of the speed at which a computation is done, the
process is a straightforward, one-step-at-a-time, matter.

    Now consider a simple problem: calculate x as a/b + 1.5,
where a and b are known.  We will show steps 3 through 7 of

the process described above.  First you see a flowchart.
This flowchart depicts an algorithm for reading two numbers
into a computer, dividing the first by the second, adding
1.5 to the quotient, and printing the result.

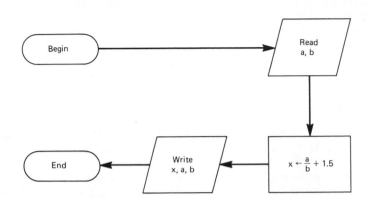

Below is a complete TIPS program, written on a <u>coding</u>
<u>form</u>, although lined paper works just as well.  Here the
programmer decided to call the program by the name "EASY".
The coding form below contains the TIPS <u>program</u> (those lines
shown without shading), the <u>data</u> (shown with light shading),
and some <u>control</u> <u>commands</u> (shown with dark shading), which
are not part of the TIPS program at all but rather give the
computer information about the person running the program,
the program itself, and the data.  The control commands are
for a version of PASCAL developed by the University of
Waterloo, Ontario, Canada.

```
                                    COLUMNS
1  2  3  4  5  6  7  8  9 10 11 12 13 14 15 16 17 18 19 20 21 22 23 24 25 26 27 28 29 30 31 32 33 34 35 36 37 38 39 40 41 42 43

//JOBNAME   JOB   5500-50001,,'STUDENT NAME'
/*PASSWORD       SECRET
//STEPI EXEC  WPASCAL,REGION=200K
PROGRAM EASY (INPUT,OUTPUT);
     VAR
        A:REAL;
        B:REAL;
        X:REAL;
     BEGIN
     READ (A,B);
     X:=A/B+1.5;
     WRITELN (X:10:2,  A:10:2,  B:10:2)
     END.
%EOF
     55.0      11.0
/*
```

(line numbers to the left: 1→ PROGRAM EASY (INPUT,OUTPUT); 2→ VAR 3→ A:REAL; 4→ B:REAL; 5→ X:REAL; 6→ BEGIN 7→ READ (A,B); 8→ X:=A/B+1.5; 9→ WRITELN (X:10:2, A:10:2, B:10:2) 10→ END.)

Refer now to the numbers to the left of the program.
They are there to identify the lines of the program and are
not part of the program itself.  Line number 1:

                PROGRAM EASY (INPUT, OUTPUT);

heads the program.  This heading gives the PROGRAM a name
("EASY") and also tells the computer that it should prepare
to receive input and to generate output.

   Lines 2 through 5 tell the computer that the identifiers
A, B, and X are variable names or variables which stand for
numbers and will be assigned numerical values once the
program is underway.  Several types of variables are allowed
in PASCAL but only two types will be used in TIPS.  The
first of these is REAL; using this word tells the machine
that A, B, and X can take on values which are real numbers
(in a mathematical sense) such as 55.4 or -0.2 or 95.0.

   Line 6 marks the BEGINning of the action part of the
TIPS program.  Notice that the word BEGIN is not followed by
a semicolon as were the previous three lines.  (Putting

semicolons in the correct places is often a large factor in whether a TIPS program is correct.)

Line 7 tells the computer to use its input device to read data. When the computer executes this instruction (much as a soldier might execute an order) it will take in two numbers from the data you provide. The first number will be associated with (stored in) the variable A. Where will the second datum be stored?

Line 8 tells the machine to divide the number stored in the memory location A by the number stored in memory location B and to add 1.5 to the result. This quantity will then be stored in memory location X.

Line 9 instructs the machine to write out, in order, the numbers stored in location X, then A, then B. We are interested primarily in the value stored in X, of course, but it is good practice to print out the numbers we put in as well. The ":10" following each variable tells the computer to write out the entire number within 10 horizontal spaces. The ":2" in each case tells the machine to write the number with 2 digits to the right of the decimal point.

Line 10 signals the END of the program. Notice that it is terminated by a period.

After the program, data, and control commands have all been written on the coding form in the appropriate order, the information on the form is typed on a terminal or microcomputer keyboard or is transferred to data processing cards by use of a device called a keypunch.

Each line of the coding form becomes one punched card or one line on the computer terminal. If cards were used, the resulting card deck would appear as shown below.

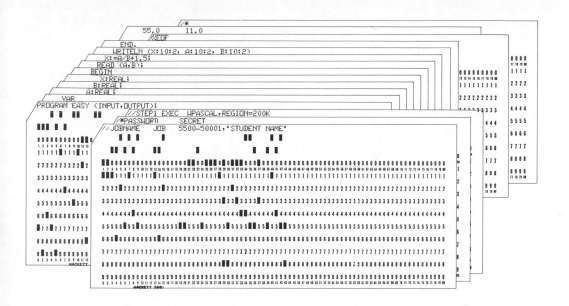

This deck would be submitted to the computer. The
computer would produce a listing of all the instructions.
This listing, when printed out on paper, is sometimes called
<u>ha</u><u>rd</u> <u>copy</u>, and is shown next.

WATERLOO PASCAL -- ( OS, SO/1/21 ): UNIVERSITY OF KENTUCKY

```
 1  |   PROGRAM EASY (INPUT,OUTPUT);
 2  |      VAR
 3  |         A:REAL;
 4  |         B:REAL;
 5  |         X:REAL;
 6  |      BEGIN
 7  |      READ (A,B);
 8  |      X:=A/B+1.5;
 9  |      WRITELN (X:10:2, A:10:2, B:10:2)
10  |      END.
11  |   %EOF
```
Execution begins...
```
      6.50      55.00       11.00
```

...execution ends
11 lines; no diagnostics

If a computer terminal were used, the equivalent information would appear typed or on a CRT. Regardless of whether the input came from cards or terminal, the values for X, A, and B would be output.

You may have noticed that different lines of the program start at different distances from the left margin. This practice, called _indentation_, is not a requirement of the computer or of PASCAL syntax. The computer would accept the PROGRAM EASY if it were written:
PROGRAM EASY (INPUT, OUTPUT); VAR A: REAL; B: REAL; X: REAL; BEGIN READ (A,B); X := A/B+1.5; WRITELN (X:10:2,A:10:2,B:10:2) END.

But the program is much easier to read if every line expresses a separate step and if the lines are indented to show their relationships. We say the left margin is position one; we start the word PROGRAM there. We indent the word VAR 4 spaces, and the variables it declares 4 more spaces (to position 9.) The BEGIN keyword is "unindented" to position 5 and the instructions which follow also start in that position. As we introduce new instructions we will tell you how we think they ought to be indented to provide readability.

To practice the mechanics of running jobs on a computer, keypunch or type in this job, calling it Lab Problem 00. Your instructor will provide you with details regarding the particular information needed to use the computer you have available. There is a blank in the section entitled "The Package: Program, Data, and Control Commands" for you to write in the appropriate control commands.

Without looking back, try to draw the flowchart for the problem in the space below. (The problem was to read in two numbers, divide the first by the second, add 1.5 to the quotient, and print the resulting number.)

Sometime in your elementary school years you were probably taught that "Now you are big boys and girls, so you can use pen or ball point instead of pencil." Well, there aren't any big boys and girls when it comes to taking the first shot at a flowchart or program. Use a pencil with an eraser so that you don't end up with a product that has more scratched out than written in.

## Characters

The most basic elements of TIPS are characters. There are many permissible characters. Typically, they are:

| | |
|---|---|
| 26 Alphabetic Characters: | A B C D E F G H I J K L M<br>N O P Q R S T U V W X Y Z |
| 10 Arabic Digits: | 0 1 2 3 4 5 6 7 8 9 |
| Characters such as:<br>(The character set available will be different<br>on different machines.) | + - = < . |

Note that we have shown only capital letters used as alphabetic characters; these are the only ones which may be keypunched using a standard keypunch machine. Computer terminals, however, will usually allow the input of lower case alphabetic characters and they may work in TIPS; ask your instructor.

Because different computers and computer terminals vary in the characters that they allow, we provide a table (below) of the elementary characters which are allowed in TIPS (and in standard PASCAL). In case you must use substitute characters in your situation, write the substitute characters to the left of the characters below.

| | | | | |
|---|---|---|---|---|
| [ ] | + plus | | [ ] | ( left parenthesis |
| [ ] | - minus | | [ ] | ) right parenthesis |
| [ ] | * asterisk (times) | | [ ] | [ left bracket |
| [ ] | / slash (divide) | | [ ] | ] right bracket |
| [ ] | = equals | | [ ] | { left brace |
| [ ] | > greater than | | [ ] | } right brace |
| [ ] | < less than | | [ ] | : colon |
| [ ] | , comma | | [ ] | ; semicolon |
| [ ] | . decimal point | | [ ] | ' single quote |
| [ ] | ↑ up arrow | | [ ] | blank |

Every TIPS program is composed of rearrangements and repetitions of the elementary characters.

## Special Symbols

The special characters above, when used in TIPS, are called **special symbols**. There are five other special symbols formed by <u>concatenating</u> (placing together in order) basic symbols. No blanks are allowed between the two characters. Some versions of PASCAL use different symbols than those shown below. If yours does, write them in the box below.

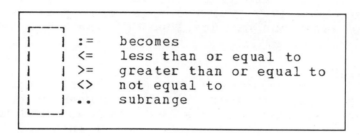

```
  ┌───┐
  │   │   :=   becomes
  │   │   <=   less than or equal to
  │   │   >=   greater than or equal to
  │   │   <>   not equal to
  │   │   ..   subrange
  └───┘
```

## Identifiers

An identifier in TIPS is a name. An identifier is either a single letter or a single letter followed by one or more letters or digits. For example, the variables A, B, and X in the sample program were identifiers. An identifier in TIPS can have a length of up to 8 characters. (Some versions of PASCAL allow much longer identifiers but look for differences only in the first eight.

(In the system you are using, up to ___ characters are

allowed and (all) (only the first ___) are considered.)

The choice of an identifier by the programmer is arbitrary. Identifiers have many uses in TIPS. For example, they can identify programs (as "EASY" did) and they can stand for numbers (as did "A", "B", and "X" in the sample program).

Some examples of identifiers are:

```
X17          A           OPENER         SIGMA
PAUL         EASY        NETPAY         ABC123
```

Sometimes in the early part of this text we will use
nonsense identifiers so as not to confuse you.  To
emphasize the fact that the construction of variable
names is arbitrary, we might call the sum of X and Y
by the name GERTA instead of SUMXY.  Some students
might mistake SUMXY for a command; GERTA, probably
not.  When you write programs, however, "Do as we
say, not as we do."  Use the most meaningful
variable names you can develop.

## Syntax Diagrams

A syntax diagram is a graphic description or definition
of an element in TIPS.  Here is the syntax diagram for an
identifier.

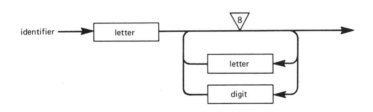

where a letter is defined as

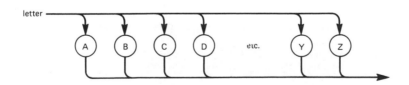

and a digit is defined as

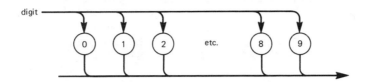

    In a syntax diagram a letter, digit, special symbol or
delimiter word is shown in a circle (or rounded box) but any
element which is defined in another syntax diagram is shown
in a square box.  If a triangle is used on a path, it
indicates the maximum number of times the path may be
traversed.


## Exercises

    (Appendix D contains the answers to exercises and
questions in this book.)

Which of the following are invalid identifiers in TIPS?
Why?

    a.   MAKING
    b.   ALL
    c.   243
    d.   THREE3
    e.   EA SY
    f.   NETPAYDUEAFTERALLTAXESANDDEDUCTIONS
    g.   =+
    h.   ANSWER
    i.   A = B


## Delimiter Words (Reserved Words)

    Delimiter words (reserved words), like the identifiers
just discussed, are also strings of alphabetic characters.
But, whereas identifiers are created arbitrarily by the
programmer, delimiter words have specific spelling and

purpose. Delimiter words are those words which have special meaning in the TIPS language. By analogy, delimiter words in TIPS are words like SIT, STAY, HEEL, and ROLLOVER in a well trained dog's vocabulary. (A <u>delimiter</u> is a character or sequence of characters used to separate other sequences of characters.)

Reserved words may not be used as identifiers. **RESERVED WORDS MAY NOT BE USED AS IDENTIFIERS!** OK? OK.

There are 35 delimiter words (reserved words) in TIPS (and PASCAL.) They are:

| | | | |
|---|---|---|---|
| AND | END | NIL | SET |
| ARRAY | FILE | NOT | -THEN |
| BEGIN | FOR | OF | TO |
| CASE | FUNCTION | OR | TYPE |
| CONST | GOTO | PACKED | UNTIL |
| DIV | -IF | PROCEDURE | VAR |
| DO | IN | PROGRAM | -WHILE |
| DOWNTO | LABEL | RECORD | WITH |
| -ELSE | MOD | -REPEAT | |

In addition to the reserved words there are other <u>special identifiers</u> in TIPS (and PASCAL) which you should probably not use as identifiers. These are words such as READ and WRITELN which you may use as identifiers but which lose their original meaning to TIPS (or PASCAL) if you do. The only ones which are used in TIPS are

| | | | |
|---|---|---|---|
| ABS | INPUT | READ | SQR |
| ARCTAN | INTEGER | REAL | SQRT |
| COS | LN | ROUND | TRUNC |
| EXP | OUTPUT | SIN | WRITELN |

You should also not use a PROGRAM name as a variable name in that PROGRAM.

## Exercise

Make a list of all the delimiter words used in Lab Problem 00.

What follows is a discussion of the components of a TIPS
program made up of the elements that we discussed
previously.

## The PROGRAM Header

The PROGRAM header names the program and tells how the
program will communicate with its environment.  In TIPS
programs this communication is almost always accomplished by
input coming from outside the computer and output being
displayed by the computer.  As a normal convention, these
are called the INPUT file and the OUTPUT file.  So the
header for a program named GEORGE would be:

        PROGRAM GEORGE (INPUT,OUTPUT);

There are uses for programs without input, but they are
rare, so in the normal case you will include both.  Some
implementations of TIPS (and PASCAL) require that you use
the identifier OUTPUT in the header.  Notice that a
semicolon follows the PROGRAM header.

## Declarations

Declarations give the computer information about the
program itself and the data the computer is to manipulate
under the control of the program.  The declaration section
is always the first part of the program.  It starts after
the program header and ends before a BEGIN in the TIPS
program.  Each declaration is followed by a semicolon.  For
example,

        VAR
            SHOES: REAL;
            SOCKS: REAL;

The declaration section precedes the other part of the TIPS
program which instructs the computer to take action.  This
"other part" of the program is composed of statements.

## Statements

Statements are the major elements which make up the action part of TIPS programs. Each statement is a sequence of the permissible basic elements. A TIPS statement instructs the computer to perform some action.

The data forms have been declared in the preceding section of the program. Now the actions which are to take place--the manipulations of the data themselves--are prescribed by statements. An example of a statement is

$$X := A/B+1.5$$

The action is: calculate the value of A/B+1.5 (given that A and B have previously been defined to have values) and store the number which results as the value of the variable X.

Because the definition of a statement can be confusing we may as well confuse you at the outset. The following are both true:

1. The action part of a TIPS program always consists of a single statement followed by a period.

2. The action part of a TIPS program may consist of many statements. They are separated by semicolons.

And how can the same thing be made up of exactly one statement and yet many statements as well? The answer to this seeming paradox is that a statement can contain other statements. A syntax diagram for a TIPS statement (including only those that you've studied so far) is:

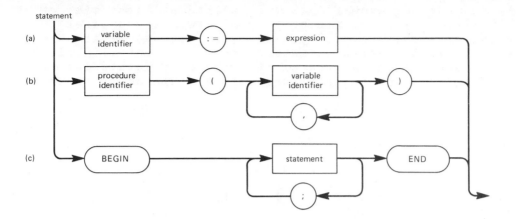

This diagram says a statement can consist of three different things: the form (a) (variable := expression) is exemplified by

        X := A/B+1.5

You have seen two examples of the form (b)

        READ (A,B)
        WRITELN (X,A,B)

The procedure identifiers built into TIPS are READ and WRITELN.

    Form (c) is the clue to our paradox.  A statement can consist of the word BEGIN followed by a statement which may be followed either by the word END or by a semicolon and another statement.  This construction is called a compound statement and will be very important later in solving more complicated problems.  (A definition which contains itself (e.g., the definition of "statement" contains "statement") is called a recursive definition.)


Blanks

    In general, blank spaces are unimportant in TIPS statements; blanks may be used to improve the readability of a statement for us, but the computer usually ignores them.

Blanks <u>must</u> <u>not</u> appear, however, within an identifier or
delimiter words. Blanks <u>must</u> appear before and after
delimiter words when no special symbol separates them from
other delimiter words or identifiers. A blank is implied
after each line of a program; therefore an identifier or
delimiter may not begin on one line and end on the next.


<u>Numbers</u>

TIPS is a language designed basically to perform
numerical computations. It is not surprising, therefore,
that numbers play a large role in the TIPS language.

The form of numbers used by TIPS consists simply of
arabic digits which may (or may not) contain a decimal point
and/or algebraic sign. The decimal point, if used, must be
somewhere within the number but not the first or last
character of it. Thus 0.0 is legal but 0. and .0 are not.
If no decimal point appears in the number, the decimal point
is assumed to be after the rightmost digit. If the number
is positive, a preceding plus sign is optional. If the
number is negative, it must begin with a minus sign. No
commas or blanks may appear anywhere within the number.
Again, the admissible characters in numbers are: plus or
minus sign, any of the arabic digits 0 through 9, and a
single decimal point. (We will see shortly that the
alphabetic character E may also be used in the construction
of numbers.)

Some valid TIPS numbers are:

```
0
0.5
-0.6
1111110000000.00000
50000000000000000000000000.0
0.00000000000000000005
-66.6666
+54
126
```

The syntax diagram for numbers such as those above is:

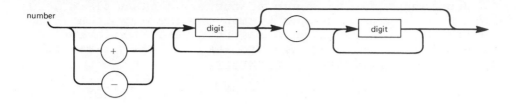

There are limits to the <u>range</u> (the magnitude, or scale)
that numbers can take on, but the limits are so large that
they need not be considered just now.

The concern at this point is with the number of
<u>significant digits</u> which the programmer will use in doing a
calculation. Your instructor should tell you the number to
write in the box below.

When using your computer, the programmer is only

guaranteed that the _____ most significant digits

will be used in a computation.

Thus, while there is no practical limit to the number of
digits a programmer may supply in a number, and no practical
limits to the size of the number, there is a distinct
restriction on the number of digits which will be considered
by the computer when performing a computation.  We
illustrate the restrictions relating to the number of
significant digits by presenting two columns of numbers
below.  The left column shows numbers which the programmer
might provide to the computer.  The right column shows a
number that the computer might use in its calculations,
assuming that six significant digits will be retained.  The
loss of significance should be obvious.

| If the programmer specifies | The computer might use |
|---|---|
| 1.234567 | 1.23457 |
| 0.000333444555 | 0.000333444 |
| 112233445566.0 | 112233000000.0 |
| -0.1000001 | -0.100000 |
| -0.1000009 | -0.100001 |
| 40000.02 | 40000.0 |

A programmer may make use of numbers in two places. If the programmer puts a number within the program in a TIPS statement (an example of this is the number 1.5 in the statement X := A/B+1.5 in Lab Problem 00), the number is called an internal datum or constant.

If the programmer supplies numbers which follow the program (an example of this was the card following the program in Lab Problem 00 which contained the numbers 55 and 11), then these numbers are referred to as external data.

Whether numbers are used as internal or external data, they have the same form and restrictions as to decimal points, arabic digits, and algebraic sign.


## Comments

Declarations and statements are comprised of characters which are arranged in such a way as to "make sense" to the computer. Comments are also comprised of characters but are intended, instead, to "make sense" to the humans who look at the program listing.

A comment does not instruct the computer to do anything. It is simply a device by which information for human understanding can be placed before, within, and after the instructions to the machine. The comments, along with the actual computer statements, are printed out on the program listing.

To place a comment in a program, the programmer places a { before any sequence of characters and a } after them. (In many implementations of TIPS and PASCAL, the curly brackets (called braces) are interchangeable with (* and *). This is because some terminals do not have braces on the keyboard. We will use this latter form of the delimiters.) Comments can be inserted before, within, or after instructions. Actually, comments may be placed anywhere that a blank is allowed in a TIPS program. The syntax diagram is:

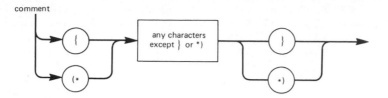

comment

For example,

```
COLUMNS
(* COMMENTS HELP PEOPLE UNDERSTAND PROGRAMS *)
```

To see comments in a program, we rewrite Lab Problem 00.

```
COLUMNS
(* PROGRAM TO SOLVE LABORATORY PROBLEM ZERO *)
(* WRITTEN BY SAM M. STUDENT IN DECEMBER, 1982
   AT THE UNIVERSITY OF KENTUCKY *)
PROGRAM EASY (INPUT, OUTPUT);
    VAR
        A: (* THE NUMERATOR *); REAL;
        B: (* THE DENOMONATOR *) REAL;
        X: (* THE RESULT *) REAL;
    BEGIN
(* INPUT SECTION *)
    READ (A, B);
(* COMPUTATION SECTION *)
    X := A/B + 1.5;
(* OUTPUT SECTION *)
    WRITELN (X:10:2, A:10:2, B:10:2)
    END.
```

The comments which describe a set of statements in the program should begin at the left margin. In this way your eye can just read down the comments and comprehend the action part of the program.

We suggest that the comment which describes each variable be placed after the colon and before the type identifier.

The computer, of course, is not concerned with the comments in a program. The machine simply prints them out dutifully to adorn the program listing. You could make an analogy between comments and the printing that a keypunch does at the top of a card. After all, computers don't need that printing either; they "read" the holes in the card.

Try punching a program sometime with the keypunch print switch turned off, or typing on the keyboard of a video tube with the brightness turned off. You'll get an immediate dose of what it is like to try to figure out an unfamiliar or stale program which doesn't have any comments.

## Exercises

(Appendix D contains the answers to exercises and questions in this book.)

1. Which of the following are invalid TIPS numbers? Why?

   a. 234.567
   b. -17
   c. 123 456
   d. 0.000003
   e. 63*45
   f. A32
   g. 1.000.01
   h. +-1.000000045
   i. 1234.56789
   j. 1/2
   k. 345,678

   l. .2
   m. 15.
   n. 0.
   o. .0
   p. 32,767

2.  Which of the following are keywords?

|          |          |          |
|----------|----------|----------|
| READING  | WRITING  | PROGRAM  |
| END      | IF       | TRY      |
| NOT      | QUIT     | DIV      |

Now you have been exposed to the basic elements of TIPS.
You know that characters go together to make up identifiers,
delimiter words, and data; that these elements together with
more characters are used to make up statements and
declarations; and, finally, that these elements, with
comments, go together to make up a TIPS program.  The art of
programming involves arranging these elements so that the
finished program instructs a computer to do your bidding.
You must have a very clear idea of what you want to do--so
clear that you could explain it, step by step, to a very
literal-minded person--before you can make use of a
computer.  And even with a good understanding of your
problem you must know a language that the computer can take
instructions in.  We would be less than honest if we didn't
admit that, despite these prerequisites, there is sometimes
a lot of head scratching, fist banging, and muttering before
the final product emerges.

A computer usually solves a problem by engaging in three
main activities:

1. It calls for and accepts data (in TIPS these data
   are always in the form of numbers),

2. It manipulates those data according to the program
   that is used (such as addition, multiplication,
   etc.), thereby producing information.

3. It writes out the information.

We refer to these activities or processes as input,
computation, and output.  Numbering them 1, 2, and 3 does
not imply, for example, that all the input must be done
before all the computation, but simply that, in general,
input precedes computation, which precedes output.

We now turn our attention to the specific instructions
in TIPS that make it possible to do virtually any numerical
problem amenable to computer solution.  These instructions
fit into the general framework of a program:

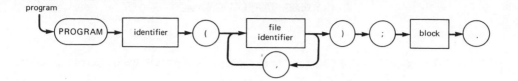

The block of the TIPS program is described in the next section.

## Exercise

Examine the syntax diagram above and relate its parts to the program EASY. Identify the block of EASY.

The block of a TIPS program consists of two sections

1) declaration portion
2) action portion

In TIPS, the declaration section consists only of
"declaring" to the computer the names of all variables which
are going to be used for REAL (or, later, INTEGER) numbers.
The syntax diagram of the instruction which does this is:

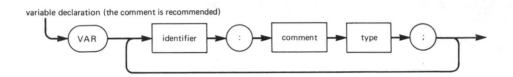

In our sample program the declaration of variable names was
done by:

```
VAR
     A: (* THE NUMERATOR OF THE FRACTION *) REAL;
     B: (* THE DENOMINATOR OF THE FRACTION *) REAL;
     X: (* THE FINAL RESULT *) REAL;
```

> The comments are not required. But it is a
> very good idea to use a comment on that same line to
> tell what the variable actually means. Notice that
> the suggested format of the VAR declaration makes it
> easy to read and understand.

In general, when we use identifiers to stand for values
in a program, we call them <u>variable names</u> or, more simply,
<u>variables</u>.

**There may be only one VAR instruction in a TIPS PROGRAM.
All the variables in a program must be declared.** The word
REAL indicates to the machine that the variables declared
are to be of the REAL variety. A REAL variable is one that

can accommodate numbers with a decimal point and digits to the left and right of that decimal point. (An INTEGER variable is one which holds only whole numbers. INTEGERS will be covered shortly.)

## Exercise

Suppose you wished to write a program which needed four variables and you decided to use the names PIG, COW, HORSE, and DUCK. The program name you've selected is ORWELL. How would the program begin? Don't forget the semicolons!

### How Long Should Identifiers Be?

There's no good answer to this question. Or rather, there are several good answers, depending on who's doing the answering. Some programming languages, including some versions of PASCAL, allow 31-character variable names. Some languages support only two-character variable names. Long variable names make the program longer, and muck up expressions to the point that you can't see what is going on. Short variable names are remarkably hard to connect with their meanings after a little time has passed. Our best advice is to develop a style in terms of naming variables. You might take the word(s) involved and leave out the vowels. (E.g., TTLPPLTN for Total Population, SCLSCRTYNMBR for Social Security Number.) Or you might use a commonly associated acronym or abbreviation, such as SSN for Social Security Number.

Whatever you do, for each identifier, if the name does not obviously describe the variable, then describe it in a comment in the program. If you want to describe it more fully then put the full description in the documentation and a short description in a comment. It is also a good idea to include a comment telling about the documentation and where it might be found.

One of the basic functions of the computer is to call for data and assign the data values to variables in the program.  In TIPS, this is done with a statement whose syntax form is

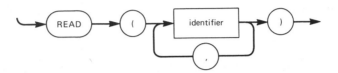

**Any variables used in the action part of a program must have been previously declared in the VAR instruction.**

Basically, a computer operates by taking in an entire program--in our case an entire TIPS program--memorizing it completely, and then beginning to obey the commands, or statements, one at a time, starting at the beginning of the program and going "south," (that is, towards the end). Thus, when the computer encounters a statement, as it did in the sample program, which says

| COLUMNS | | | | | | | | | | | | | | | | | | | | | | | | | | | | | | | | | | | | | | | | | |
|1|2|3|4|5|6|7|8|9|10|11|12|13|14|15|16|17|18|19|20|21|22|23|24|25|26|27|28|29|30|31|32|33|34|35|36|37|38|39|40|41|42|
| | |R|E|A|D| |(|A|,|B|)| | | | | | | | | | | | | | | | | | | | | | | | | | | | | | |

it is essentially being told to find the first two numbers in the data and to associate the first one with the variable A and the second one with B.

Another way to say this is that the first datum is "stored in" A and the second one is "stored in" B; we'll make this idea that a variable is a location in which a number is stored more concrete shortly.  If, later in the program, a second READ statement were executed, such as

then the third datum supplied after the program would be
stored in "C" and the fourth would be stored in "A".  What
would happen to the first datum, which had previously been
stored in "A"?  It would simply be "lost," that is, not
remembered by the computer any longer.  In effect, the
fourth datum would take its place.

    The designers of a computer language usually attempt to
use delimiter words which are English words that convey
meaning to the operations the computer is going to perform.
Thus, the READ statement instructs the computer to "fetch"
values from the list of data and assign those values, in
order, to the variable names which appear within the
parentheses.

    How should the data be arranged so that the program can
bring them into the computer's memory associated with the
correct variable name?  The only really important things are
that the order of the external data following the program be
the same as the order in which the program calls for them,
and that the data are separated by one or more blanks.  Each
number (datum) should, of course, be keypunched or typed
without blank spaces between its digits (i.e.,
contiguously).

---

On your system the data may lie anywhere on the

line or card, from position 1 to position _____.

---

    In summary, then, the READ statement in TIPS instructs
the computer to take data from a card or typed line and
transfer the data into the computer's memory.  Each variable
name which appears within the parentheses in the READ
statement is to be associated with a number on a data card
or data line.  Each variable name in the READ statement is,
by this method, defined (or redefined) to have a value.

    It is important to understand the distinction between
the VAR instruction and the READ statement.  Though they
both mention variable names in the body of the statement,
the VAR instruction merely tells the computer that the

programmer intends to use certain names to stand for
numbers; the READ statement tells the computer that a name
is to stand for a <u>particular</u> number whose value will be
supplied by the card reader or keyboard.  That is, the VAR
instruction <u>declares</u> that certain variable names are to be
used and the READ statement <u>defines</u> the value(s) of the
variable(s).


Exercise

    Assume four numbers were punched on a data card which
was ready to be read by the computer and the computer
executed the statement

        READ (CAT,CAT,CAT,DOG)


If the data card contained 5.4   6.0   -777.2   0.0098, what
number would be associated with CAT after the execution of
the statement?   With DOG?

We stated earlier that one of the main activities of a computer is writing out information. One way it can do this is on what is called a line printer. Conceptually, a line printer is a typewriter that can print lines of up to, usually, 132 characters long. Another property of the garden-variety line printer is that it goes at high speed, usually printing between 600 and 2000 lines per minute. Try that on your portable typewriter.

The instruction which produces output on the line printer (or the printer or CRT on your terminal) is a built-in procedure statement called WRITELN. WRITELN tells the machine to WRITE A LINE and prepare itself to write another. (There is also a procedure WRITE. It operates the same as WRITELN except that WRITE does not complete an output line each time it is used.) The syntax of WRITELN is:

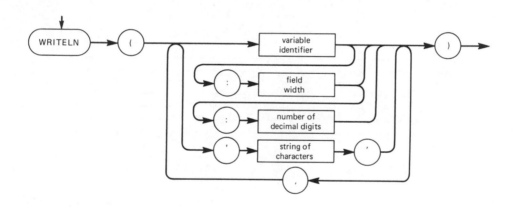

That is, WRITELN can produce output of two sorts of things:

1. variables whose values are to be printed, such as A, CAT, X. (A field width may be specified; if it is, the number of decimal digits may be specified. These concepts will be explained shortly.)

2. sequences of characters called <u>character strings</u> which are enclosed between apostrophes or single quote marks. Examples are:

```
' X='
' '
' THE BANK BALANCE IS:'
' HAPPY BIRTHDAY ABIE BABY'
' ANY CHARACTERS ARE PERMISSIBLE IN CHARACTER STRINGS'
```

We look first at the use of WRITELN statements to put
out the values of the variables.


## Writing Values of Variables

The WRITELN statement operates very much like the READ
statement except that it is used to transfer information out
of the machine rather than in.  And while the READ statement
defines a variable as having a certain numerical value, the
WRITELN statement lets the outside world know what the value
of a given variable is.  The value of the variable in
computer memory is not disturbed or changed by this writing-
out process.

If we write the statement

```
                                   COLUMNS
1 2 3 4 5 6 7 8 9 10 11 12 13 14 15 16 17 18 19 20 21 22 23 24 25 26 27 28 29 30 31 32 33 34 35 36 37 38 39 40 41 42


     WRITELN (AMK:12:4, KRK:6:1)

```

the computer will write out the values associated with AMK
and KRK.  Suppose AMK was -5.3 and KRK was 15.333.  AMK
would be printed out in a twelve-position field with four
digits to the right of the decimal and five blank spaces.

        bbbbb-5.3000

where b stands for a blank space.  Notice that the decimal
point and the minus sign each occupy one position in the
field.  The blank spaces are all to the left of the actual
number (we call these leading blanks); numbers so printed
are called right-adjusted or right-justified in the field.
TIPS numbers are always written out right-adjusted.  How
would you guess that KRK would be printed out?

In general, the specification for printing out a datum is

        datum:width:precision

where width and precision are positive whole numbers. The number "width" indicates the number of characters in the field and should be large enough to include:

(a) at least one leading blank,
(b) a minus sign if there is one,
(c) number of digits to the left of the decimal point,
(d) the decimal point itself,
(e) number of digits to the right of the decimal point.

By using the same field width in successive WRITELN statements you can arrange the numbers in columns.

The number "precision" should provide for the appropriate number of digits to the right of the decimal point. You should try to arrange it so that the total number of significant digits is not greater than the number the machine is capable of using in its computations.

As you can see from the syntax diagram, you may specify either (a) just the variable, (b) just the variable and the field width, or (c) the variable, field width, and number of decimal digits. You should always use a field width great enough to assure that the numbers do not run together.

If you do not specify a field width and precision the computer will provide you with the complete number--although not necessarily in the best format. If you specify an insufficient number of decimal digits, the computer will ignore you and provide sufficient space.

Consider the following program, data, and control commands to be run with a PASCAL 8000 compiler (a version of PASCAL distributed by the Australian Atomic Energy Commission):

## COLUMNS

| 1 | 2 | 3 | 4 | 5 | 6 | 7 | 8 | 9 | 10 | 11 | 12 | 13 | 14 | 15 | 16 | 17 | 18 | 19 | 20 | 21 | 22 | 23 | 24 | 25 | 26 | 27 | 28 | 29 | 30 | 31 | 32 | 33 | 34 | 35 | 36 | 37 | 38 | 39 | 40 | 41 | 42 |
|---|---|---|---|---|---|---|---|---|---|---|---|---|---|---|---|---|---|---|---|---|---|---|---|---|---|---|---|---|---|---|---|---|---|---|---|---|---|---|---|---|---|

```
//JØBNAME  JØB  1234-56789,'PUPIL, PETE'
/*PASSWØRD      SECRET
//       EXEC PASGØ
//CMPI DD *
(* NØNSENSE INPUT AND ØUTPUT *)
PRØGRAM EXAMPLE (INPUT,ØUTPUT);
    VAR
        ABC: (* *) REAL;
        TØT: (* *) REAL;
        GGG: (* *) REAL;
    BEGIN
    READ (GGG,ABC);
    READ (TØT);
    WRITELN (TØT,GGG);
    WRITELN (GGG,ABC)
    END.
$PASOBJI
    0.883127
            41              -169.99
```

This program prints two lines of information: the values associated with TOT and GGG on the first line and the values associated with, again, GGG and ABC on the second line. And we would reasonably expect the two lines to appear as:

```
41                      0.883127
0.883127                -169.99
```

Because we did not specify a field width or number of decimal digits, the computer may print the numbers "scientifically" instead of "reasonably." That is, each positive number may appear as a number between 1.00000 and 9.99999 times ten raised to some power. For example, the number 678.923 could be represented as 6.78923 times $10^2$. In this case the computer would write out 6.78923E+02, where the "E" denotes, "ten raised to the power of." Therefore, 6.78923E+02 means 6.78923 times $10^2$. One might also interpret the number following the E as the number of

decimal places the decimal point should be moved <u>to the</u>
<u>right</u> to represent the number in "reasonable" form.  If the
algebraic sign following the E is negative, then the decimal
point should be moved to the left.  In the example above,
the output of our computer program might actually appear as:

```
4.10000E+01          8.83127E-01
8.83127E-01         -1.69990E+02
```

```
+-------------------------------------------+
|                                           |
|      If you do not specify the field      |
|                                           |
|  width or number of decimal digits the    |
|                                           |
|  computer will assume values.  Your       |
|                                           |
|  computer will assume _____ for the    |
|                                           |
|  field width and _____ for the number  |
|                                           |
|  of decimal digits.                       |
|                                           |
+-------------------------------------------+
```

## <u>Writing Character Strings</u>

Character strings are groups of characters placed in a
TIPS program WRITELN statement to provide alphabetic
information on the output listing.  The printed or displayed
characters can be used to identify numeric values or for
other purposes.  For example, the statements

```
WRITELN (' THESE VALUES WERE ON THE FIRST CARD');
WRITELN (X:5:1, Y:7:4, Z:4:1)
```

would produce

```
THESE VALUES WERE ON THE FIRST CARD
   1.0 2.0000 3.0
```

assuming the values of X, Y, and Z were 1, 2, and 3,
respectively.

Notice that the character string is enclosed in single
quote marks in the WRITELN statement. But when the
characters are printed during the execution of the program
they appear without the quotes. It is, of course, the quote
marks which allow the computer to understand that what is to
be printed is a character string rather than a variable
value. For example,

        WRITELN (' ABCDEF')

will result in the printing of

            ABCDEF

whereas

        WRITELN (ABCDEF)

would cause the value associated with a variable named
ABCDEF to be printed.

        We make two further points before we leave the
discussion of character strings in WRITELN instructions.

        First, to provide a space between a number followed by a
character string (and also for another reason which will
appear later), you should always leave at least one blank
space between the beginning quote mark and the first
character of the string you want printed. That is, you
should say:

            ' X IS ODD'  rather than  'X IS ODD'.

        Second, if you want an apostrophe to appear in the
character string itself, you put in two in succession: E.g.,

            'IT ISN''T NEAT BUT IT WORKS'

        When using an <u>interactive</u> program (one that
operates on a terminal or microcomputer while you
type in the data) it is a good idea to write out a
character string to prompt yourself (or whomever
else may run the program) to put in the correct
data. For a well-worn example, you might insert the
statement

WRITELN (' ENTER THE NUMERATOR AND DENOMINATOR');

just before the READ (A,B) statement in Lab Problem 00.

Incidentally, to produce a blank line on your output use the word WRITELN by itself without parentheses.  For example:

        WRITELN


## Exercises

1.  How would the computer represent the following numbers in E notation?

        666.666       -7.1       0.0003

2.  How would you interpret the following numbers?

        5.500000E-03        -5.500000E+03

3.  If Q contains the number 6.5, R contains 100.25, and S contains 0.25, what values are printed by

        a.  WRITELN (Q)
        b.  WRITELN (Q,R,S,S)

4.  What statement would you write to provide a blank line between two lines of output?  That is, how could you instruct the printer to double space?

5.  What is the difference between (a) a comment and (b) a character string in a WRITELN statement?

6.  Examine the syntax diagram for WRITELN.  Then write an instruction to produce the single line which prints the value of the variable EXER along with descriptive information as shown below

    THE WEIGHT MUST BE 35.2 OR WE'RE IN TROUBLE!

    using the fact that the variable EXER contains 3.52003E+01.

   Solving a problem with TIPS requires a TIPS program,
some control commands, and (usually) some data.  Lab Problem
00, which contained all three of these elements, is again
shown below with the TIPS instructions unshaded, the data
lightly shaded, and the control commands darkly shaded.

```
                                    COLUMNS
 1 2 3 4 5 6 7 8 9 10 11 12 13 14 15 16 17 18 19 20 21 22 23 24 25 26 27 28 29 30 31 32 33 34 35 36 37 38 39 40 41 42 43

    //JOBNAME    JOB     5500-50001,'STUDENT NAME'
    /*PASSWORD        SECRET
    //STEP1 EXEC   WPASCAL,REGION=200K
 1→ PROGRAM EASY (INPUT,OUTPUT);
 2→    VAR
 3→       A:REAL;
 4→       B:REAL;
 5→       X:REAL;
 6→    BEGIN
 7→    READ (A,B);
 8→    X:=A/B+1.5;
 9→    WRITELN (X:10:2,  A:10:2,  B:10:2)
10→    END.
    %EOF
        55.0       11.0
    /*
```

## Program

   In TIPS a program is a sequence of instructions of the
types previously discussed: PROGRAM, VAR, READ, and WRITELN
plus six others soon to be introduced in detail.  The
program always begins with a PROGRAM header and ends with
END.  Only TIPS instructions and comments may lie between
PROGRAM and END.

## External Data

In TIPS 'external data' refers to the numbers which will be brought into the computer's memory by use of the READ statement. The program dictates the order in which the numbers are to be typed in or punched on the data cards. The first READ statement encountered in the program will attempt to bring in (or read: pronounced reed, not red.) one or more numbers. Each number should consist of one or more digits and be free of internal blank spaces. There should be at least one blank space between the numbers. The second READ statement executed will bring in a second group of numbers, etc., until all the data are read.

All of the program precedes all of the data. In simplified explanation, the computer learns all of what it is to do--that is, it memorizes the entire program--and then begins READing the numbers with which to do the job. **Thus the order of cards or lines is: all the program, then all the data.**

## Control Commands

In addition to the program and data, control commands are necessary to run a TIPS program. These commands give information to the computer such as: the name of the person running the job, the student or account number, the course number, the problem number, etc. A control command also separates the program and the data. Control commands vary from computer to computer.

In the blanks below you may write the control commands which will be used in your particular situation. Several lines have been left before the program, before the data, and at the end, though certainly not all of these will be used.

If you are using a microcomputer or a terminal, you will issue the control commands as you type, edit, and run your program. Refer to Modules 2 and 3.

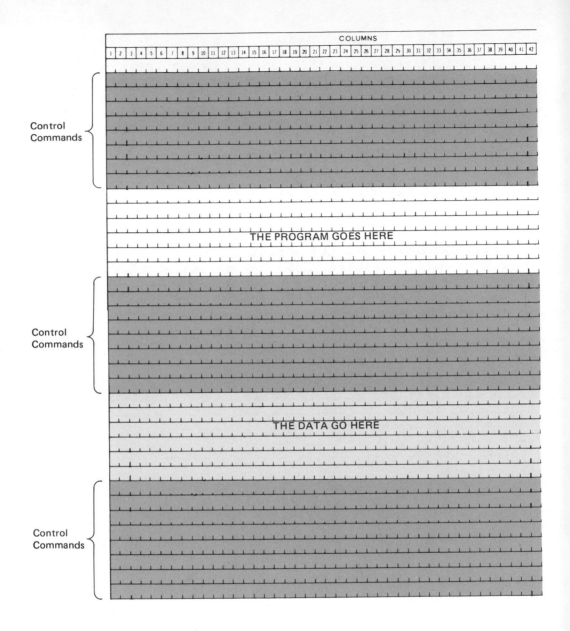

The Package: Program, Data, Control Commands

Write and run a TIPS program to read in five numbers and write them out in the opposite order from which they appeared as data.  Print out the input data.  Identify the output with character strings produced by WRITELN statements.

Draw a flowchart in the space below before writing the TIPS program.  (Module 5 discusses flowcharting in detail.)

If you make an error in a computer program, the machine _may_ tell you about it by printing an error message on the output listing.  (A list of the error codes and related messages is contained in Appendix E.  Your instructor may, however, supply you with a list for your particular compiler.  If she or he does, use that list instead.)  With very rare exceptions, any program which produces error messages must be corrected and rerun.  Programs which contain warning messages usually should be corrected, although your instructor may tell you that some warning messages will be allowed on your listing or terminal.

Clearly, if computers could only read in data and print them out again, they would not have made the impact on society that they have. Computers have other powers and these center around the second of the three major activities we discussed above: input, computation, and output.

Computation simply means to combine numbers according to a set of rules. For example, if a programmer declared the variables AA, BB, CC and DD and defined the variables AA, BB, and CC with a READ statement to have certain values, he or she could then write the statement

```
                                    COLUMNS
 1 2 3 4 5 6 7 8 9 10 11 12 13 14 15 16 17 18 19 20 21 22 23 24 25 26 27 28 29 30 31 32 33 34 35 36 37 38 39 40 41 42



    DD := AA - BB + CC
```

This would compute the value of the number that AA stands for, minus the value of the number that BB stands for, plus the value of the number that CC stands for. This resulting number is used to define the value of DD. (We sometimes say that the value is stored in DD). DD could be written out on the computer's printer or display device. DD could also be used in later computations because now, in addition to having been declared, it is also defined to have a value.

Other examples of statements which cause computation are

a.      TRY := (B+C)/D

b.      TOT := 10*GGG-HHH/III

c.      TEST := HUG-UGH

d.      X := MCA

The four statements above are examples of the _assignment_ statement. Unlike the other instruction types studied so far, it has no keyword associated with it; only an := symbol, which means "is replaced by," or "becomes," provides a clue to its identity.  Before a complete description of the assignment statement is presented, we turn to a discussion of its most interesting part: the <u>arithmetic</u> <u>expression</u>, the portion on the right side of the := symbol.


<u>Arithmetic</u> <u>Expressions</u> (<u>Instructor</u>: <u>Please</u> <u>See</u> <u>Note</u> <u>2</u>.)

An <u>arithmetic expression</u> in TIPS is a combination of variables, internal data (constants), parentheses, and operators which, when processed according to the rules of arithmetic, produces a single, numerical result.  The characters to the right of the := symbol in an arithmetic assignment statement comprise an expression.  The expressions in the four examples immediately above were

a.        (B+C)/D

b.        10*GGG-HHH/III

c.        HUG-UGH

d.        MCA

An arithmetic expression can also consist of a single variable or internal datum, as in the last case, MCA.

An <u>arithmetic</u> <u>operator</u> denotes multiplication, division, addition, or subtraction as shown below:

* means multiply
    B times C is written as B*C

/ means divide
    B divided by C is written as B/C

+ means add
    B plus C is written as B+C

- means subtract
    B minus C is written as B-C


Although arithmetic expressions in TIPS are similar to those in algebra, there are some differences:

1. There is no exponentiation as such. Expressions such as A³ are not allowed. There are ways to evaluate any algebraic expression despite the fact that a direct mechanism for exponentiation is not available. For example, A² can be expressed as A*A. (Note: some of the more complicated expressions involving exponentiation will have to wait until the discussion of logarithmic and exponential functions and/or iteration.)

2. The multiplication operator must always be present when multiplication is intended. You cannot say BC when you mean B*C. The computer would interpret BC as simply another variable name.

3. Division is indicated by use of the "/" symbol rather than the traditional

numerator
denominator

form. This limitation occurs because TIPS statements are simply strings of characters, one after another in a line with no possibility of elevating any character. Thus one may not make use of the technique used in algebra of placing operands (constants and variables in an arithmetic expression) on different levels of the line. So the expression

TOTALS
NUMBER

would be represented as

TOTALS/NUMBER

Order of Computation

The order of computation in TIPS expressions is much the same as in algebra; computations are performed in a priority sequence which may be viewed in the following way:

First: Quantities within parentheses are computed. If there are parentheses within parentheses the innermost pair contains the computation to be done first.  The order of computation of quantities within parentheses or in the absence of parentheses depends on the following priorities.

Second:  Multiplication and division operations are done; neither takes priority over the other.  If more than one such operation exists, the <u>leftmost</u> is done first and the process proceeds from left to right.

Third:  Addition and subtraction take place.  Neither takes precedence over the other.  As in multiplication and division, the leftmost operation is done first and processing proceeds from left to right.


<u>Exercises</u>:

1.  What is the value of each expression if A=2, B=3, C=4, and D=1?

    a.   A*B                      g.   A*C*A
    b.   C-B*A                    h.   (A*C)*A
    c.   (C-B)*A                  i.   A/C/2
    d.   A*B+C/2                  j.   A/(C/2)
    e.   (A*B+C)/2               k.   A+B/D+C
    f.   A+B*C-C*B               l.   (A+B)/(D+C)

2.  Write TIPS expressions for each algebraic expression below where w, x, y, and z are variables.

    a.   w + x - y              b.   w - x²
    c.   w • x - y              d.   w - xy
    e.   w - xy + z             f.   wxy + z

    g.   $\dfrac{w}{z} + x$      h.   w - x - z

    i.   $\dfrac{w}{y} + \dfrac{x}{z}$      j.   $\dfrac{w}{x} \bullet \dfrac{1}{z}$

    k.   $\dfrac{w + x}{y + z}$      l.   $w - \dfrac{xy}{2}$

3.  What is the value of each expression below if B=1, C=2, D=3, E=4, and BC=5?

    a.  B+E/C                   f.  B-(E+C)/BC
    b.  E+D*E*E                 g.  B-(E+C)/(B*C)
    c.  BC+D                    h.  BC*D/(C+D)
    d.  B-E*C/BC                i.  E-E*E
    e.  (E-E+C)/BC              j.  B+0.5-BC*(C*C*C)

4.  Which of the following are invalid expressions if BB=2, CC=3, DD=4 and no other variable names are allowed?

    a.  EB+CC*DD
    b.  B*B+CC
    c.  EB+*CC
    d.  BB+CC**DD
    e.  EB(CC+DD)
    f.  BB-CC+DD*3

## Three Frequent Difficulties with Expressions

Some sample expressions are now presented which illustrate difficulties which beginning programmers frequently encounter. It is extremely important to understand these difficulties, because errors in writing expressions usually are not detected by the computer as are some other types of errors; errors involving expressions just result in wrong answers.

Difficulty Number One: The programmer fails to use parentheses when other than the natural hierarchy of operations is desired. For example, suppose you want to write a TIPS expression to compute (a-b) divided by (c-d). What you should write is (A-B)/(C-D) but you fail to include parentheses, and you write A-B/C-D, which is interpreted as (a) minus (b/c) minus (d).

As another example, A/B*C is sometimes written to mean

$$\frac{A}{B \bullet C}$$

when it really means

$$\frac{A \bullet C}{B}$$

To write the TIPS equivalent of A divided by the product of B times C you should write A/(B*C).

When asked to evaluate a root of a quadratic equation, a novice programmer will frequently leave out a necessary set of parentheses. One correct TIPS representation of

$$x = \frac{-b \pm \sqrt{b^2 - 4ac}}{2a}$$

is (-B+SQRT(B*B-4*A*C))/(2*A), from which no set of parentheses can be omitted without producing an incorrect result. ("SQRT" takes the square root of a non-negative number within the parentheses following it; more about that later.) You should make use of parentheses whenever you are in the slightest doubt about the order of evaluation of an expression.

Difficulty Number Two: A programmer wants to multiply two variables and writes their names without using the multiplication sign between them. For example, he writes XY when he means X*Y. Or X(Y+Z) is written to mean X*(Y+Z).

Difficulty Number Three: A programmer places two operators in sequence without an intervening parenthesis such as A/-B, when what is meant is A/(-B).

In one sense a programmer can make two kinds of errors in writing computer language programs: errors in syntax and errors in semantics. As an example, let's look at an analogue with another language, English, and assume that a child has been given kale, which he dislikes, for supper. If he says, "I don't want no kale," he has made a syntactic error--an error in form. On the other hand, if he says, "I don't want any spinach," he has made a semantic error--an error in meaning.

Computers frequently catch syntactic errors that programmers make. Usually, the machine issues

some sort of cryptic (or even rude) message, such as
those found in Appendix E.  But computers don't
catch semantic errors.  Errors in meaning are as
easy to make, harder to find, and may be more
devastating if allowed to go undetected.

## Assignment Statements

The first method you studied for defining the value of a
variable was the READ statement.  The second method is the
assignment statement; it has the syntax

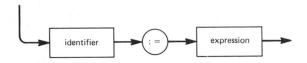

where we have defined "expression" in the previous section.
The symbol

        :=

is called the replacement or assignment operator.

For example, let a program begin:

```
PROGRAM EXPO (INPUT,OUTPUT);
    VAR
        A: (* COMMENT *) REAL;
        B: (* COMMENT *) REAL;
        C: (* COMMENT *) REAL;
    BEGIN
    A := 5;
    B := 7;
    C := A + B
```

In each of the last three statements the characters to
the right of the := symbol constitute an arithmetic
expression; a variable lies to the left of the := symbol.
The first two of these statements define A as 5 and B as 7.
The last statement in the program segment defines C to have
the value of 12.  This last statement does not affect the
values already assigned to A and B.  However, if later in
the program the statement

```
A := C*C
```

were encountered, the variable A would be redefined as 144 and the old value of A that was first assigned (namely, 5) would be erased.

An assignment statement **always** assigns the value just computed to the variable named on the left side, erasing the previous value, if any. The values of variables which appear only on the right side are unaffected.

> When checking a program over prior to submitting it to a computer, a good procedure is to examine every variable in each arithmetic expression to be certain that it has been previously defined.

## The Assignment Operator

The ":" in the symbol ":=" indicates that the assignment operator does not mean "equals" in the algebraic sense. Rather, the symbol denotes a transfer operation to be carried out by the computer. First, the value of the expression to the right of the symbol is computed. It is mandatory that each variable appearing on the <u>right</u> side of := symbol be defined before the assignment statement in which it appears is executed by the program; that is, each variable on the right hand side must have already been given a value, normally by a READ statement or by a previous assignment statement.

Second, the variable on the left of the := symbol is defined (or redefined) to have the value of the expression just computed. The := symbol therefore means "becomes" or "is replaced by" when it appears in the TIPS program.

To illustrate that the := symbol in TIPS means "becomes" rather than "equals," consider the statement

```
B := B+2
```

This <u>does</u> <u>not</u> <u>imply</u> <u>that</u> B <u>is</u> <u>equal</u> <u>to</u> <u>itself</u> <u>plus</u> <u>two</u>. Finding a numerical value of B which would make this mathematically true would be difficult. B := B+2 is an operation, not an equation. Suppose B were 7. Then

```
B := B+2
```

merely instructs the computer to

1.  Compute the value of the expression by adding B and
    2 (which will produce 9) and

2.  Redefine the value of the variable to the left of
    the := symbol, namely B, as the value of the
    expression, namely 9.

Thus, the effect of the statement is simply to increase
by two the value B had before the execution of the
statement.

Question: What value would AZ have after the following
statements were executed?

```
AZ := 3;
AZ := (AZ+AZ)*AZ
```

## Exercises

1.  What is the value of R in each assignment statement
    below if A=1, B=2, C=3, D=4, AB=5, and X=6?

    a.  R := A+B*C*2
    b.  R := (A+B*C)*2
    c.  R := AB+B*C
    d.  R := AB/D
    e.  R := C*(D+AB)
    f.  R := B+C+D*AB
    g.  R := A*X*X+B*X+C

Computers are fast, but there is no point in
wasting their power.  For a simple example, if you
need to calculate the value of

$$ax^2+bx+c$$

rewrite it as

$$(ax+b)x+c$$

The first case requires three multiplications and
two additions.  In the second case you save a
multiplication.  And, for most machines,

multiplications and divisions take about 10 to 200 times as long as additions. This is normally not important unless a very large number of multiplications can be saved.

Could you extend the above example to any polynomial of arbitrarily high order? How many multiplications would you save?

2.  What value is printed by the statements below?

```
A := 3;
B := 5;
C := A/B;
C := C+1;
WRITELN (C)
```

3.  Variable A contains some number, say "a". Likewise B contains "b". Write TIPS statements to put "a" into B and "b" into A. In other words, interchange the values in A and B.

4.  To convert a Fahrenheit temperature to the equivalent Celsius value you subtract 32 and multiply by 5/9. Write a complete TIPS program to do this. Then check your program "by hand" (this is called a desk check) with the following temperatures:

212, 32, 98.6, 5, 9, 0, -0, -40, -459.688

In a long or involved calculation, make it a point to insert output statements at points along the way so that you can check intermediate results. There is very little to be saved by using one very long arithmetic expression over using two or three shorter ones. And there is much to be lost. Compute intermediate results and print them out.

Write a program to find the sum and the average of four numbers. Assume that a data card or line containing the four numbers will be provided at the time the program will be run on the computer and that you do not know what specific numbers will be used. Your program should print out the input data as well as the answer. Draw a flowchart in the space below before you write the program.

As you become more experienced in computing you will realize that there are so many things to do that it is easy to make mistakes. Over the years some commentary on human endeavor in complex matters (which computing certainly is) has developed in the form of "laws". While they are meant to be humorous, they contain more fact than fiction. The best known are Murphy's Laws, three of which are:

1. Nothing is as easy as it looks.

2. Everything takes longer than you expect.

3. If anything can go wrong, it will--at the worst possible moment.

You can succeed only if you are careful, diligent, and thorough.

Find the area of the geometric figure shown below.

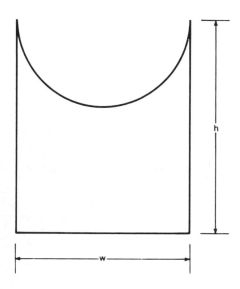

Follow the steps outlined in the section, "Problem Solving with a Computer." Examine the flowchart on the next page to determine if it does indeed indicate a solution to the problem. What is the general method of attack on the problem? What are the meanings of r and s? Run the program twice using the two sets of data below. Hand check the results.

|              | HEIGHTS | WIDTHS |
|--------------|---------|--------|
| Data Set One | 25.0    | 10.0   |
| Data Set Two | 5.0     | 20.0   |

     Some programmers assume that if the program produces answers rather than error messages, the answers are correct. They frequently aren't. Don't allow yourself the false sense of security of such assumptions--always check your answers for correctness.

If the answers are wrong, the problem might be in <u>any</u> of the steps outlined in Problem Solving with a Computer. If something should appear incorrect in Lab 03, be sure you examine each step separately.

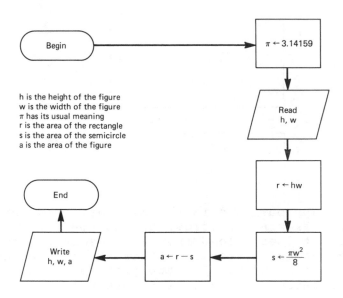

Begin

$\pi \leftarrow 3.14159$

h is the height of the figure
w is the width of the figure
$\pi$ has its usual meaning
r is the area of the rectangle
s is the area of the semicircle
a is the area of the figure

Read
h, w

End

$r \leftarrow hw$

Write
h, w, a

$a \leftarrow r - s$

$s \leftarrow \dfrac{\pi w^2}{8}$

A TIPS program which corresponds to the flowchart could be written as follows. Notice that every variable is declared and defined to have a numeric value. (Note also that a statement extending too long for a line may be continued on the next line).

```
(* CALCULATE AREA OF GEOMETRIC FIGURE *)
PROGRAM LAB03 (INPUT, OUTPUT);
    VAR
        HEIGHT: (* VERTICAL DIMENSION *) REAL;
        WIDTH: (* HORIZONTAL DIMENSION *) REAL;
        PI: (* USUAL MEANING *) REAL;
        RAREA: (* AREA OF ENCLOSING RECTANGLE *) REAL;
        SAREA: (* AREA OF SEMICIRCLE *) REAL;
        AREA: (* THE RESULT *) REAL;
    BEGIN
    PI := 3.14159;
    READ (HEIGHT, WIDTH);
    RAREA := HEIGHT * WIDTH;
    SAREA := PI*WIDTH*WIDTH/8.0;
    AREA := RAREA-SAREA;
    WRITELN (' INPUT VALUES: ',HEIGHT,WIDTH,
        ' AREA=',AREA)
    END.
```

Write programs so they print out the input data as well as the answers. Thus, in this example, the height and width of the figure are made part of the output. There are two good reasons: First, it enables a person examining the output to determine which problem has been solved. You can imagine that a piece of paper with only a single answer on it might leave some question as to what numbers went together to produce the solution. Secondly, if the correct numbers are printed out in the correct order, you have reasonable assurance that they went in properly.

While the flowchart and the program have some similarities, there are also some differences:

1.  The flowchart employs single character names which are described under the begin block. The program, on the other hand, uses multiple character names. At the risk of belaboring the obvious, the names HEIGHT and WIDTH have no intrinsic meaning to the

computer; COW and CLOD could have been used as well. But humans (the programmer and perhaps the employer) must understand the program too. And that's easier if the names bear some relation to the problem being solved.

2. Algebraic notation is used in the flowchart boxes containing computation.

3. The replacement operator is a short arrow pointing to the left in the flowchart whereas the := symbol is used in the program.

4. The flowchart makes no attempt to observe the rules of grammar of TIPS.

5. A begin block begins a flowchart; the directly corresponding statement in TIPS is the first BEGIN delimiter. The flowchart is terminated by an end block which corresponds to the "END." delimiter in TIPS.

One reason for these differences is that a flowchart is a description of an algorithm which could be implemented by using pencil and paper, a pocket or desk calculator, or a computer. Thus the flowchart should make sense to anyone familiar with flowcharting conventions; those who are unfamiliar with TIPS programming should not be excluded. A person writing a flowchart should resist the temptation to write the statements of any computer language, including TIPS, in the flowchart boxes.

## Rationale

Well, how were the results from Laboratory Problem 03?
Embarrassing?  How could you have calculated a negative
number for the area using the height and width of Data Set
Two?  Because the algorithm  called for subtracting a
semicircle from a rectangle--an approach which works fine
provided the height is greater than or equal to half the
width; otherwise the program, and the programmer, are in big
trouble.  Did you realize that the numbers  you were putting
in implied a degenerate figure which looks like this:

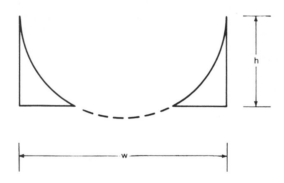

Of course, you could examine the data and decide whether
this was the case.  But that brings up an interesting
question: could the computer examine the data and decide
whether the result would be meaningful?  The answer is yes!
In fact, the real power of a modern computer lies in its
ability to make decisions and take appropriate action.  The
specifics of the decision and the computer's subsequent
action must be spelled out by the programmer.  The flowchart
on the next page will illustrate the exact nature of the
decision to be made and the action taken subsequent to the
decision.  The terms used here are the same as in the
original flowchart of the problem.

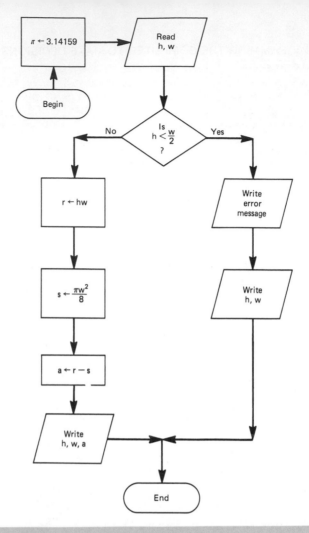

We tried to lead you into the trap of the
geometric figure with the negative area.  Who would
expect a textbook to be so underhanded?  Moral:
don't trust anybody's data or suggested solutions.
Design algorithms and write programs defensively!

## Compound Statements

The above flowchart contains a major, startling
difference from the ones we have looked at so far: at the
diamond shaped box the computer makes a decision about which
way to go.  The flowchart will be translated into a TIPS
program, which is a sequence of statements, one after

another.  Normally, statements are executed in their
physical order, that is, the order in which they appear in
the program.  However, as the flowchart implies, when the
computer makes a decision it must be able to select between
different sets of instructions, thereby interrupting the
normal sequence.  The order in which the computer actually
executes statements is called the logical order.

It is clear that some mechanism for skipping over some
statements and executing others is needed.  Depending on the
values of the variables "h" and "w," the program should
either execute the sequence of statements

```
RAREA := HEIGHT*WIDTH;
SAREA := PI*WIDTH*WIDTH/8.0;
AREA := RAREA-SAREA;
WRITELN (' INPUT VALUES: ', HEIGHT,WIDTH,
    ' AREA=',AREA)
```

or should execute a sequence of statements which tells of
the error

```
WRITELN (' YOU BLEW IT - FIGURE IS DEGENERATE');
WRITELN (' WIDTH=',WIDTH,' HEIGHT=',HEIGHT)
```

What are the components of a mechanism which would allow
this either-or condition to come about?

First, we need a method which will allow a sequence of
statements to be treated as a group.  We do this by
surrounding or encasing them between two delimiter words.
You've met them before: BEGIN and END.

So if we want a sequence of statements treated all
together, we simply precede it by BEGIN and follow it by
END.  An example looks like this:

```
BEGIN
RAREA := HEIGHT*WIDTH;
SAREA := PI*WIDTH*WIDTH/8.0;
AREA := RAREA-SAREA;
WRITELN (' INPUT VALUES: ', HEIGHT,WIDTH,
    ' AREA=',AREA)
END
```

But doesn't the END keyword end the whole program?  No,
not if it doesn't correspond to the first BEGIN keyword in
the program, and not if it isn't followed by a period.  One

might think of the BEGIN delimiter as a kind of left parenthesis and the END delimiter as the balancing right parenthesis. Just as you can have parentheses within parentheses you can have a BEGIN-END within another BEGIN-END. **A semicolon is never used immediately before an END keyword.**

A sequence of statements encased in a BEGIN-END pair is called a compound statement. What is the other compound statement which is appropriate in this example of the degenerate figure?

So we have a technique for binding together a sequence of statements which is either to be executed as a group or skipped as a group. What now is the mechanism for actually determining which group is to be executed and which is to be skipped? A new statement is involved here: IF-THEN-ELSE.

## The IF-THEN-ELSE Statement

Remember the diamond-shaped block in the revised flowchart for Lab Problem 03?

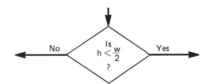

Here is how the IF-THEN-ELSE statement (we'll usually call it the IF statement from now on) would implement that diamond-shaped block. We show it together with the two statement groups it selects between:

```
IF HEIGHT<WIDTH/2.0 THEN
     BEGIN
     WRITELN (' YOU BLEW IT--FIGURE IS DEGENERATE');
     WRITELN (' WIDTH  ',WIDTH,'  HEIGHT  ',HEIGHT)
     END
ELSE
     BEGIN
     RAREA := HEIGHT*WIDTH;
     SAREA := PI*WIDTH*WIDTH/8.0;
     AREA := RAREA-SAREA;
     WRITELN (' INPUT VALUES H AND W:',HEIGHT,WIDTH,
         ' AREA IS ',AREA)
     END
```

This IF statement says: IF the HEIGHT is less than half the WIDTH, THEN execute only the compound statement which prints out the error message.  Otherwise (ELSE), execute only the compound statement which does the computation of AREA and prints out the answer.

Make sure you understand how the IF statement works in this example.  Now examine the syntax diagram of the IF statement:

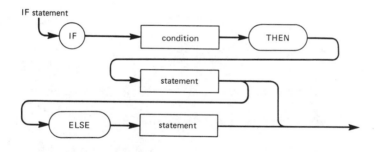

IF, THEN, and ELSE are delimiter words. You are already familiar with a statement.  What is a condition?

It is an entity which may be either true or false--nothing else.  In TIPS a condition compares two expressions, which represent two numbers, and becomes true or false depending upon the values of the numbers and the comparison operator which joins them.  The syntax diagram of the condition is: (See Note 3.)

condition

expression → comparison operator → expression

You are already familiar with expressions (constants, variables, operators, and parentheses) which translate into numbers during the execution of a program. There are six comparison operators:

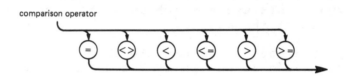

comparison operator

= <> < <= > >=

which have the following meanings:

    = (equal)     < (less than)     > (greater than)

    <> (not equal)  <= (less than     >= (greater than
                  or equal to)         or equal to)

In summary then, the first line of the IF statement says:

    IF some-true-or-false-condition THEN

The remainder of the syntax diagram shows two statements--either may be simple or compound--and the keyword ELSE. Notice that there are no semicolons within the IF statement except those which occur within the compound statements.

When you use the IF-THEN-ELSE statement you <u>alter the flow of control</u> of the computer program. Study the IF statement carefully! Understand it fully before you proceed!

## Simplifications of the Decision-Making Structure

The decision-making form that we showed in the example is the most general one you will need to use. Basically the issue was whether to execute one set of statements while skipping another or vice versa. We might illustrate this by a flowchart and corresponding program skeleton.

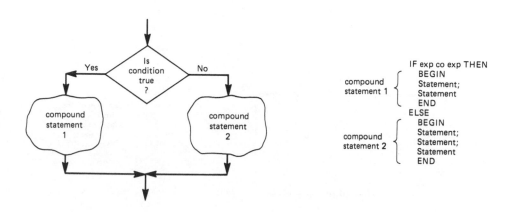

But things could be simpler. Suppose one (cr both) of the statement sequences consisted of a single statement. Then we could omit one (or both) BEGIN-END pairs. In general,

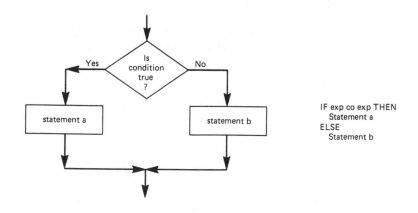

Another simplification occurs if the program logic does not require the use of the ELSE clause at all. Notice that the syntax diagram allows for this. Suppose, for example, we wish the computer to execute a group of statements (or a single statement) if a condition is true and skip them (it) otherwise. In this case there is no balancing sequence of statements to execute if the condition is false and to skip otherwise. The flowchart and the program would look like this:

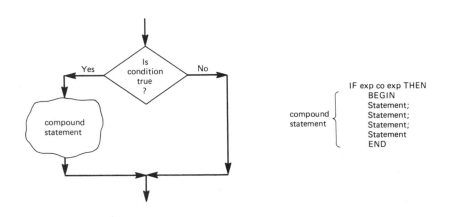

When the statement sequence is a single statement, the BEGIN-END pair may be omitted. For example:

```
IF ASSETS>DEBTS THEN
    WRITELN (' SOLVENT')
```

If you put a semicolon within an IF statement where it doesn't belong all kinds of interesting and unhappy things can happen. For example, if you write

```
IF PROFIT >= 0.0 THEN
    WRITELN (' PROFIT=',PROFIT);
ELSE
    WRITELN (' LOSS=',PROFIT)
```

the semicolon after the first WRITELN statement concludes the IF statement. Therefore PASCAL thinks that the ELSE begins a new (and illegal) statement. Remember that a semicolon can <u>never</u> come immediately before an ELSE! Remember that a semicolon can <u>never never</u> precede an ELSE!

TIPS statements can begin in any position of
the line or in any card column.  For readability,
however, it is wise to indent some lines to show the
relationships among the statements.  We suggest the
following:

Put "IF condition THEN" on one line.  Indent
all lines of the following statement or compound
statement by 4 spaces.  Put the ELSE keyword on a
line by itself in vertical alignment with the IF
keyword.  Again, indent all lines of the following
statement or compound statement by 4 spaces.  For
example,

```
A := 3;
B := 5;
C := 10;
IF C>A THEN
    A := A+5;
IF A<>C THEN
    BEGIN
    B := B+3;
    WRITELN (A,B,C)
    END
ELSE
    WRITELN (C,B,A);
A := B+C
    •
    •
    •
```

## Exercises

'1.  Given that A=5, B=3, and C=1, determine whether each
     of the following is true or false:

```
a.    A*A <= A*B
b.    A*A = A*B + 10*C
c.    A > B
d.    A*B*2 >= B*10
```

2.  Which of the following statements are invalid?

```
a.  IF ABLE IS GREATER THAN BAKER THEN
        X := 0;
b.  IF Q = P THEN
        WRITELN (Q);
```

Programming the Computer to Make Decisions          71

```
        c.   IF R => S THEN
                X := 0;
```

3.   What are the two different uses for the = character
     in TIPS?

4.   What would be printed?

```
     A := 4;
     B := 3;
     C := 6;
     IF C< (A+B)  THEN
         WRITELN (' C IS LITTLE')
     ELSE
         WRITELN (' C IS BIG');
```

5.   Suppose that you have two data: the first number is
     either a Fahrenheit or Celsius temperature; the
     second number is a code: 3 if the temperature is
     Celsius and 6 if Fahrenheit.  Write a program to
     read these two data and convert the temperature
     value to the other scale.  Title the results so that
     a person seeing the output understands it.  If the
     code is in error, that is if it is not a 3 or 6,
     print "ERROR IN CODE..ERROR VALUE IS x"

6.   What would be printed?

```
     A := 3;
     B := 5;
     C := 10;
     IF C > A THEN
         A := A + 5;
     IF A <> C THEN
         BEGIN
         B := B + 3;
         WRITELN (' A, B, AND C ARE ',A,B,C)
         END
     ELSE
         WRITELN (' C, B, AND A ARE ',C,B,A)
```

## Nested IF Statements; The Affair of the Dangling ELSE

    Many problems demand that a selection structure be inside
another selection.
There is
no real difficulty if each IF statement contains the

ELSE keyword.
A potential problem
occurs if, however, you have one IF statement within another and
only one has an ELSE clause.  For example,

```
A := 1;
B := 1;
IF A <> 1 THEN
IF B <> 1 THEN
WRITELN (' THIS WON'T BE PRINTED')
ELSE
WRITELN (' BUT WILL THIS BE PRINTED?')
```

To ask the question another way, is the ELSE keyword paired
with the first IF or the second IF?

And to ask it still another way, does it mean:

```
A := 1;
B := 1;
IF A <> 1 THEN
    BEGIN
    IF B <> 1 THEN
        WRITELN (' THIS WON'T BE PRINTED')
    ELSE
        WRITELN (' THIS WON'T BE PRINTED EITHER')
    END
```

or does it mean

```
A := 1;
B := 1;
IF A <> 1 THEN
    BEGIN
    IF B <> 1 THEN
        WRITELN (' THIS WON'T BE PRINTED')
    END
ELSE
    WRITELN (' THIS WILL BE PRINTED')
```

**The answer is: an ELSE keyword is paired with the
immediately preceding IF keyword which is unpaired.**  So if
you have a nest of ten IF statements with only seven ELSE
keywords, the first three IF statements from the top won't
have ELSE keywords associated with them, assuming you don't
change things with BEGIN--END pairs.  In the program above,
nothing will be printed at all.  That is, the first
arrangement above is correct and the second one is not;
since A is equal to 1, both WRITELN statements are skipped.

Which brings us to the ultimate conclusion: just as you should use extra parentheses in an expression when you aren't sure about how the computer will do the evaluation, you should use BEGIN--END pairs to "parenthesize" IF--THEN or IF--THEN--ELSE statements you are unsure of.

Incidentally, it may happen that you want to take no action if a condition is true but to take action if it is false. Then you could write:

```
IF A=0 THEN
      (* NULL STATEMENT *)
ELSE
      WRITELN (A)
```

This is possible because a blank by itself is considered to be a statement (see the syntax diagram for statements on the back of the fold-out at the end of the book). The inclusion of the comment announcing the null statement is present only for the sanity of anyone trying to read the program. Nevertheless, such a statement is hard to read and is considered poor form.

## Exercises

Write IF statements which correspond to each of the following flowcharts.

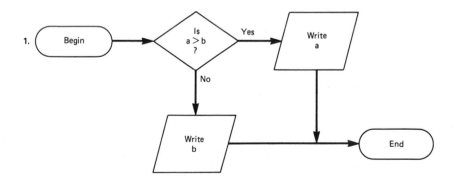

2.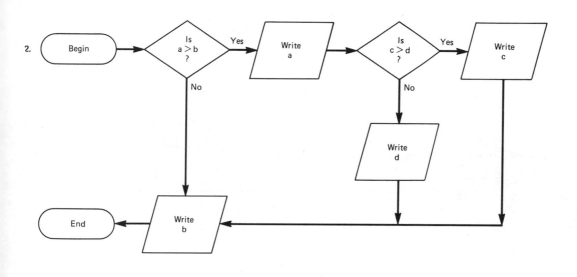

3.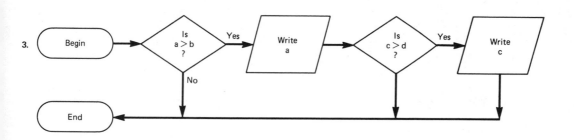

4.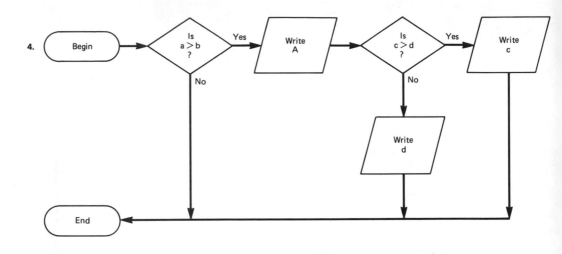

5.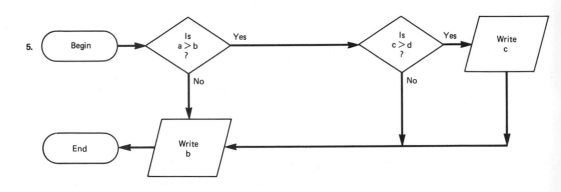

Programming the Computer to Make Decisions

**6.**

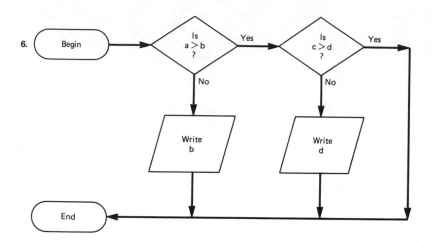

Begin

Is
a > b
?

Yes

No

Is
c > d
?

Yes

No

Write
b

Write
d

End

Prepare the Revised Lab Problem 03 for the computer; call it LABORATORY PROBLEM 04 and, again, run it twice using the data for Lab 03. Do you like the results better?

A frequent difficulty with computer programs is that they will work with one set of data but not with another because different data direct the execution of the program through different paths. When testing a program it is imperative that you keep in mind the ways in which different data will affect the action of the program and to attempt to check out all possibilities. Part II of this text discusses various aspects of testing and debugging programs and following the various paths of execution.

ARITHMETIC FUNCTIONS

There are several arithmetic functions, like square root, which are used so frequently that they are available in PASCAL.  To obtain use of these functions a programmer simply writes a special identifier to denote the name of the function wanted in an arithmetic expression, and after the function name, includes the value, (called the argument), that is to be used in its calculation.  This argument must be enclosed in parentheses.  The method for invoking a standard function is to place

        functionname(argument)

in an arithmetic expression; the value of the function is calculated and that value is used in the expression.  The argument of the function may itself be a constant, variable, or even an expression which may involve other functions.

    For example, to add the value of ERC to the square root of YYY we could write the expression:

        ERC+SQRT(YYY)

where SQRT is the TIPS name for the square root function. This expression could be part of an assignment statement:

        ZZZ := ERC+SQRT(YYY)

    We now expand the definition of an arithmetic expression to be a combination of variables, internal data (constants), parentheses, operators, and functions which, when processed according to the rules of arithmetic, produces a single, numerical result.

    If you are not familiar with trigonometric or transcendental functions, or have forgotten them, some of what follows will not be meaningful.  But don't worry; we make very little use of these functions in this book.

    The arithmetic functions provided for the programmer's convenience in TIPS (and PASCAL) are:

|              |        |      |
|--------------|--------|------|
| absolute value | called | ABS  |
| square       | called | SQR  |
| square root  | called | SQRT |
| e to the x power | called | EXP |

```
natural logarithm (base e)    called    LN
trigonometric sine            called    SIN
trigonometric cosine          called    COS
trigonometric arctangent      called    ARCTAN
```

Each of the functions is explained below.

The ABS function provides the absolute value (or the positive value) of the argument. That is, the absolute value of 6 is 6. The absolute value of -6 is 6.

The SQR function provides the squared value of the argument. That is, SQR(-2.5) is 6.25.

The SQRT function provides the positive square root of the argument; the argument must be either positive or zero.

The EXP function produces Euler's constant, "e" (2.71828....) raised to the power specified by the argument. That is, EXP(4.5) means: 2.71828 raised to the 4.5 power.

The LN function provides the logarithm to the base "e" of the argument; the argument must be positive.

(Sometimes you want the logarithm of a number to the base "10" rather than base "e". So you might write

```
INVLNTEN := 1.0/LN(10.0)
    •
    •
LNBSTENX := LN(X)*INVLNTEN
```

By imitating this method, logarithms to any base may be found.)

The argument for the SIN or COS function is a variable, constant, or expression which represents, in radians, the angle for which the SIN or COS is wanted. For example, if you wrote the statement

```
X := COS (3.14159)
```

the result stored in X would be -1.0. To convert an angle in degrees to one in radians, you multiply it by pi (3.14159) and divide by 180.0.

The ARCTAN function (the inverse tangent) returns an angle, in radians, whose tangent is the argument. The

angle, returned by the ARCTAN function will lie between
-pi/2 and pi/2.  (All 12 trigometric and inverse trigometric
functions can be formed with the sin, cos and inverse
tangent).  To convert an angle in degrees to one in radians,
you multiply it by pi and divide by 180.0

As an example of the generality and flexibility of
functions, consider

        AAA := BBB*SQRT(CCC+444/SIN(EEE))

It is a valid TIPS expression.  What does it say?

The names of the functions are not among the reserved
keywords.  That means you may declare them for use as
variable names.  However, if you do use a function name as a
variable name, then you cannot use that function in that
program.  Appendix B contains a list of all the functions
available in TIPS and PASCAL.


## Exercises

1.  If A = 1, B = 2, C = 3, D = 4, E = 0.5, then what is
    the value of F in the statements below?

        a.    F := SQRT(D*4)
        b.    F := SQRT(D-B*2)
        c.    F := ABS(E-SQR(D))
        d.    F := A+B/E*SQRT(B*B*B)
        e.    F := SQRT(A-B-C)

2.  Which statements below are constructed improperly?

        a.    F := SQRT(A,B)
        b.    F := SQRT(A*B)
        c.    F := SQRT ABS(A-B)
        d.    F := SQRT OF C

3.  What value is printed by the statements below?

        A := 3;
        B := 9;
        C := A*B;
        C := C*C;
        C := SQRT(C)
        WRITELN(C)

The two roots of ax²+bx+c=0 can be computed by means of the formula:

$$x = \frac{-b \pm \sqrt{b^2 - 4ac}}{2a}$$

Use the computer to find the roots where a, b, and c are read in as data. If the roots are not complex (that is, b²-4ac is positive or zero) and if "a" does not equal zero, write out a, b, c and each of the roots. If the roots are complex or if "a" equals zero, simply print a, b, and c. Identify all numeric output by using alphabetic character strings. Use comments in the program so that another person can tell who wrote it, when, etc. Also use comments to identify sections of the program code.

Here's an awful thought for those of you who are expecting the computer to catch your syntax errors. You don't know all of the TIPS language--much less the PASCAL language of which it is a part. Thus you might write a syntactically incorrect statement which correctly commands the computer to do something by use of a language feature that you don't know about. Two results: no error message and wrong answers. In this way a large and powerful computer language is like a Swiss Army knife with thirty blades: if you misuse one feature you may cut yourself on another. Moral: get the syntax right on your own--program carefully!

Computers are capable of executing many thousands of
TIPS statements each second.  With the knowledge you have
acquired so far you would be hard pressed to conceive of a
program which would require more than a fraction of a second
of computer time.  You also probably wonder how you can
effectively use a computer, since, in the length of time it
takes you to write a TIPS statement, you probably could have
done the job some other way.  But you know that computers
are indeed useful and you perhaps know that some computer
programs require minutes or even hours to complete their
tasks.  What's the trick?

The answer to this riddle is that the computer has the
ability to execute a single sequence of instructions as many
times as the programmer wants.  When you give a program to a
computer it remembers the entire thing.  This makes it
possible for the computer to execute parts of the program
repeatedly.  We illustrate how this can be useful by showing
a flowchart of an algorithm which produces the square root
of each positive integer whose root is less than 20.

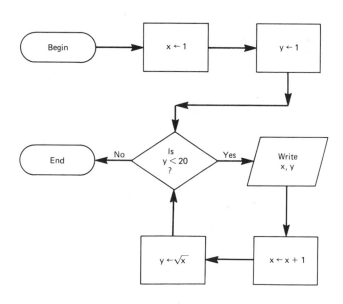

This flowchart has only six boxes (excluding Begin and End); each of these represents a simple operation. Still, you should spend several minutes examining the flowchart. Be sure that you understand the function of each box and the overall scheme of the algorithm. Don't be concerned that you couldn't write the TIPS statements which would implement the algorithm. It isn't possible for you to do so with the material presented to you so far.

The surprising feature of the flowchart--the feature which distinguishes it from those presented before--is the sneaky way the path of control loops back on itself, resulting in the repeated execution of four boxes. How many times is each of the six boxes executed?

To implement this algorithm requires another TIPS statement. Here is the complete program:

```
    (* WRITE ALL POSITIVE WHOLE NUMBERS WHOSE SQUARE
        ROOTS ARE LESS THAN 20 *)
    PROGRAM DOSQRT (OUTPUT);
        VAR
            X: (* EACH BASE NUMBER *) REAL;
            Y: (* EACH SQUARE ROOT *) REAL;
        BEGIN
        X := 1.0;
        Y := 1.0;
        WRITELN (' THE BASE IS', ' THE SQUARE ROOT IS');
        WHILE Y<20 DO
            BEGIN
            WRITELN (X:11:1, Y:19:5);
            X := X+1.0;
            Y := SQRT (X)
            END;
        WRITELN (' JOB FINISHED')
        END.
```

Here you see another major use for binding consecutive statements together into a group; it allows us to program the computer to repeatedly execute that sequence of statements. This repeated execution is called <u>looping</u> or <u>iteration</u>. Notice that in the program above X is incremented by one each time through the loop. After executing all of the statements between the BEGIN-END after the WHILE, the computer loops back to the WHILE statement to check the relationship between Y and 20. When this happens and Y is equal to or greater than 20, the loop is terminated and the first statement after the BEGIN-END group is

executed next: in this case a statement which prints a
message.

The syntax diagram for the WHILE-DO statement is:

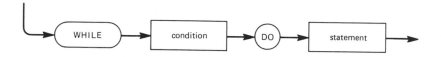

The contained statement, of course, can be either simple or
compound.  The idea of the WHILE statement is:

       WHILE condition is true DO

          a simple or compound statement

   When the WHILE statement is encountered during the
execution of a program, the truth or falsity of the logical
expression, which will involve the values of variables, is
determined by the computer.  If the condition is false, the
statement, whether simple or compound, will be skipped.  If
the condition is true, the following statement will be
executed.  Then the condition following the word WHILE is
rechecked and the result of the rechecking dictates, again,
whether the following statement is to be skipped or
executed.

   If the condition is true before the WHILE-DO is
encountered, then something within the statement must occur
to make the condition false at some time in the future, or
the program will be trapped in an "endless loop."  For
example, the statements

       X := 1;
       WHILE X>0 DO
          WRITELN (' WHAT? ME WORRY?')

would leave the computer printing the mad refrain down
through the endless corridors of time, were it not for a
computer operator, or timer, which would finally terminate
the program.

   What was it in the square root program which ultimately
terminated the loop?

## Compound Conditions

So far, all the logical expressions we have used have
been composed of two arithmetic expressions joined by a
comparison operator.  There are, however, logical operators
which join logical expressions to form logical results.  The
three logical operators, in order of their priority, are

```
NOT
AND
OR
```

The meanings of the logical operators are similar to
their meanings in everyday English usage.  As an example of
the use of the AND logical operator, we can write:

```
IF (P>5.0) AND (Q=7.0) THEN
    WRITELN (' TRUE')
```

This statement says: if P is greater than five AND also
Q is equal to seven, then print "TRUE".

P>5.0 is either true or false for a given value of P; we
say that P>5.0 has truth value.  Likewise Q=7.0 has truth
value.  Any expression with truth value is a logical
expression and any two logical expressions can be joined by
a logical operator to form another logical expression.  The
logical operator which joins the expressions in the example
is the "AND".

If we had written

```
IF (P>5.0) OR (Q=7.0) THEN
```

the statement following THEN would have been executed if
either P was greater than five or Q was equal to seven, or
if both were true.

The logical operator NOT simply changes the truth value
of any logical expression it precedes.  For example, if P is
such that

```
P>5.0
```

is false, then

        NOT(P>5.0)

is true.

    NOT may precede any logical expression even if the NOT
is preceded by another logical operator.  For example,

        WHILE (P>5) OR (NOT (Q=7)) DO statement

    The following is a list of all operators studied thus
far; the closer an operator is to the top of the list the
higher its priority is during the evaluation of an
expression.  Operators on the same line have equal
priorities and are considered from left to right.  In the
absence of parentheses which dictate the order in which
operations are performed, the priorities below will.  (See
Note 4.)

```
┌─────────────────────────────────┐
│  NOT                            │
│                                 │
│  *   /   AND                    │
│                                 │
│  +   -   OR                     │
│                                 │
│  >   >=  <   <=  =  <>           │
└─────────────────────────────────┘
```

    Because the logical operators are of higher precedence
than the comparison operators (> >= < <= = <>), expressions
containing both comparison and logical operators must
utilize parentheses for proper evaluation.  For example

        IF P>7 AND Q=7 THEN

would try to "AND" 7 and Q--which is nonsense.  Therefore we
must write

        IF (P>7) AND (Q=7) THEN

    The logical operators are really much easier to master
than the arithmetic operators, but most people have quite a
few years' headstart on the latter.  Here we give the rules
for the three logical operators.  To decipher the tables
below let T stand for a logical expression which has the
value TRUE and F stand for an expression which has the value
FALSE.

```
NOT T is F
NOT F is T

T AND T is T
T AND F is F
F AND T is F
F AND F is F

T OR T is T
T OR F is T
F OR T is T
F OR F is F
```

## Exercises

1. Which statements below will cause "yes" (in some language) to be printed?  Assume P=7 and Q=7.

```
a.  IF P>5 THEN
        WRITELN (' YES')
b.  IF NOT (P>5) THEN
        WRITELN (' YA')
c.  IF NOT ((P>5) OR (Q=7)) THEN
        WRITELN (' JA')
d.  IF (P=Q) OR (Q=P-2) THEN
        WRITELN (' SI')
e.  IF (P>5) OR (Q=7) THEN
        WRITELN (' YEAH')
f.  IF (P>5) AND (Q=6) THEN
        WRITELN (' OUI')
g.  IF (P>5) OR (Q=6) AND (Q=P) THEN
        WRITELN (' HAI')
```

2. What is printed in each segment?

```
a.   K := 0;            b.   K := 3;
     J := 7;                 WHILE K<20 DO
     WHILE J>0 DO                K := K-4;
         BEGIN              WRITELN (K)
         K := K+1;
         J := J-1
         END;
     WRITELN (K,J)
```

(requires knowledge of elementary trigonometry)


    An airport manager has asked you to prepare a table to
determine the height of clouds above the airport.  The
airport is equipped with a powerful light mounted so as to
shine vertically on the bottom of the cloud layer and a
device for measuring the angle between the horizontal and
the spot on the bottom of the cloud.  Use comments to make
the program listing more readable; use WRITELN with
character strings to identify the computer output.  (If you
have difficulty analyzing the problem, there is a hint in
Appendix D.)

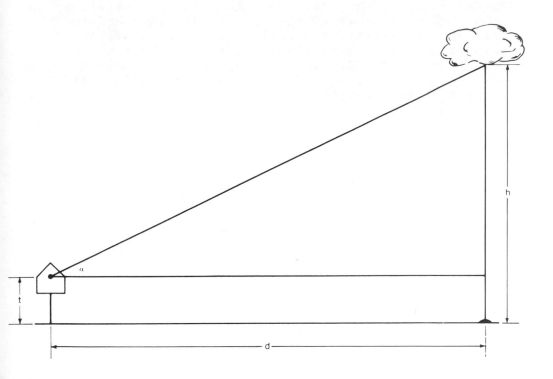

In the diagram above, the tower height above the ground,
t, is 61.2 meters and the distance from the tower to the
light, d, is 4107.6 meters.  Print out a two column table
where the first column is the angle in degrees and the
second column is the corresponding cloud height, h.  Start
at 0 degrees and increase by 1/2 degree increments until
either a maximum cloud height of 40,000 meters, or a maximum
angle of 75 degrees, is attained.

One measure of the quality of a computer
program is the extent to which it can be applied to
a wide variety of problems--that is, the degree to
which it is general.  (Clearly there are some
advantages to specialized programs as well;
otherwise the goal we should be seeking is a single
giant computer program which everyone used for every
problem.  No one has seriously suggested that--yet.)
One way which frequently leads to greater generality
in programs is to avoid the use of constants and to
read in all quantities as data.  Attempt to write
this Lab Problem without any constants.  Then check
your program for any numerical digits.  There is a
good chance that you used a constant or two in spite
of your attempt not to.

Thus far we have dealt with one kind of numerical quantity: the REAL (floating point) number.  If we wanted a variable name to stand for a REAL number we would write an instruction such as

```
VAR
     VARNAME: (* WHAT IT IS USED FOR *) REAL;
```

This would allow the variable name VARNAME to take on a wide range of values such as

```
0.0   -1.23456    1.23456E+40    1.23456E-40
```

Having this capability is quite useful and probably most programming used to solve scientific problems uses REAL numbers most of the time.  One might imagine that the name floating-point comes from the fact that the decimal point could "float" anywhere within a large string of digits.  For example, the number 1.23456E+40 is

```
12345600000000000000000000000000000000000.0
```

And the number 1.23456E-40 is

```
0.000000000000000000000000000000000000000123456
```

```
┌─────────────────────────────────────────────────────┐
│  The range of REAL numbers on your computer is        │
│                                                       │
│  _____to_____             │
└─────────────────────────────────────────────────────┘
```

With numbers of such range it is much more economical for the computer to remember the number as two parts: a mantissa (e.g.,1.23456) and an exponent (e.g.,40 or -40). However, when some arithmetic operations such as addition are done on these numbers, the decimal points must be aligned, the operation performed, and then the answer converted to the mantissa-exponent form.  This business of unconverting and reconverting REAL numbers takes some extra time.

Thus a second kind of number is available in TIPS: INTEGER. INTEGER numbers have a smaller range--considerably smaller, in fact--but can be manipulated much more quickly than REAL numbers; further, arithmetic on INTEGER numbers can be done exactly--a statement that cannot be made about REAL numbers. (See Module 7.)

The INTEGER number is <u>assumed</u> to have a decimal point at its extreme right.

```
+------------------------------------------------------------+
|                                                            |
|     The range of INTEGER numbers for your machine is       |
|                                                            |
|   _____to_____              |
|                                                            |
+------------------------------------------------------------+
```

In general, a programmer should use INTEGER variables whenever he or she wants a number without a fractional part and which lies within the INTEGER number range. Examples of quantities which could be represented by INTEGER numbers are:

1.  A count of the number of times a loop is executed.

2.  A number indicating a number of discrete objects, such as automobiles or people.

Examples of INTEGER numbers are

        12345    -7777777    -9    0    35

To declare an INTEGER variable we would simply continue the VAR instruction:

```
        VAR
            R1: (* A REAL VARIABLE *) REAL;
            R2: (* ANOTHER REAL VARIABLE *) REAL;
            SAM: (* AN INTEGER VARIABLE *) INTEGER;
            CCUNT: (* ANOTHER INTEGER VARIABLE *) INTEGER;
```

When you write out an INTEGER variable, like SAM above, you may simply say WRITELN (SAM) or you may specify a field width, e.g., WRITELN (SAM:12). Of course you don't specify a precision field because there are no decimal digits. No decimal point will be printed. INTEGER variables (or even

INTEGER expressions) may also be used to prescribe the field
width and precision in WRITELN instructions.  If COUNT is an
INTEGER with the value 12 then the instruction
WRITELN(SAM:COUNT) would cause the same action as the
instruction WRITELN(SAM:12).

> In general, arithmetic involving INTEGER
> variables is faster.  So when only whole numbers are
> required, using INTEGER variables can decrease the
> duration of program runs.  When INTEGER and REAL
> variables (or constants) are both employed in an
> expression, the INTEGER variables are first
> converted to REAL values and only then are used in
> computation.  In some types of problems this can
> significantly degrade program performance.

## Division of INTEGER Numbers

If two numbers which do not have fractional parts, that
is, integers, are added, subtracted, or multiplied, the
resulting number is also an integer.  However, if one
integer is divided by another the result may not
mathematically be an integer.  For example, if five is
divided by two the mathematical result is two and a
half--clearly not an integer.  But if you are working with
integers, you may want your results expressed in terms of
integers.

You may remember, from your elementary school years,
that there is a type of division operation between integers
which produces integer results.  Does

$$
\begin{array}{r}
6 \\
3)\overline{22} \\
\underline{18} \\
\text{Remainder } \quad 4
\end{array}
$$

bring back any memories?  To make this happen in TIPS you
use two keyword operators: DIV and MOD.

DIV produces the division of a dividend (the first quantity) by a divisor (the second quantity), yielding an integer quotient; any fractional part is dropped.

MOD produces the remainder from dividing a dividend by a divisor.  For example:

```
(* HOW MANY SCHOOL BUSES CAN WE COMPLETELY FILL
       WITH CHILDREN AND HOW MANY CHILDREN
              WILL BE LEFT OVER? *)
PROGRAM FIELDTRP (OUTPUT);
    VAR
        CHILDREN: (* TOTAL NUMBER OF CHILDREN *) INTEGER;
        BUSSEATS: (* NUMBER OF SEATS ON EACH BUS *) INTEGER;
        FULLBUS: (* NUMBER OF FULL SCHOOL BUSES *) INTEGER;
        LEFTKIDS: (* NUMBER OF CHILDREN REMAINING
                      AFTER FILLING THE BUSES *) INTEGER;
    BEGIN
    CHILDREN := 360;
    BUSSEATS := 50;
    FULLBUS := CHILDREN DIV BUSSEATS;
    LEFTKIDS := CHILDREN MOD BUSSEATS;
    WRITELN (FULLBUS, LEFTKIDS)
    END.
```

would print out 7 and 10.

On the matter of algebraic signs:

> A DIV B is positive if A and B are of like signs; it is negative otherwise.

> A MOD B has the same sign as A.

The regular division sign "/" is allowed when one integer quantity is to be divided by another, but the result is a REAL number, complete with any fractional part.  The arithmetic operators for INTEGERS, then, in the order of their evaluation, are

| First | * | / | DIV | MOD |
|---|---|---|---|---|
| Second | + | - | | |

## Exercise

Write the statements to convert the contents of the variable
SECS, which contains a number of seconds, to hours, minutes
and seconds.  That is, if SECS contained 3662 then the
answer would be 1 hour, 1 minute and 2 seconds.

For the time being, for every variable you use
in a program you must make the choice between
INTEGER or REAL.  As time goes on you will learn
more about this choice.  For the present you might
keep the following in mind:

1.   In deciding whether a variable should be typed
     INTEGER or REAL, a major issue is
     whether the number which the variable is to
     stand for could ever need to possess a
     fractional part.  If so, REAL must be used.

2.   If the value of the number might possibly be
     too large (or too small) to fit into an
     INTEGER variable, REAL must be used.

3.   The eight standard functions you've studied in
     TIPS produce REAL results when their arguments
     are REAL or INTEGER.  However, ABS and SQR
     will produce INTEGER results if their arguments
     are INTEGER.

4.   INTEGER and REAL variables may take
     different amounts of space in the machine.

     In your machine they (do) (do not) (may).

5.   There are statements, some of which will be
     introduced later, which require the use of
     INTEGER numbers.

6.   If a variable represents an integer but is
     going to be used frequently in expressions
     with REAL variables it should probably be
     declared REAL.

7.   INTEGER variables and constants are usually
     handled much more quickly by the computer.
     In the absence of any reason to the contrary,
     then, INTEGER is preferable.

# Functions and Operations Between REAL and INTEGER Numbers

If an operation takes place between a REAL number and an INTEGER number, the result of that operation is considered to be REAL. Thus, an expression which contains one or more REAL numbers is considered to be a REAL expression.

A variable declared as INTEGER cannot hold a fractional part of a number. It is therefore illegal to set an INTEGER variable equal to a REAL expression. The statements below would cause an error:

```
VAR X:(* COMMENT *)REAL;
    I:(* COMMENT *)INTEGER;
BEGIN
X := 3.8;
I := X+6;
WRITELN (I)
```

Adding an INTEGER to a REAL creates no problem: the result is simply REAL. But the attempt to store the value 9.8 in I does create an error: the 0.8 cannot be held in I.

All of the eight functions previously presented may have REAL or INTEGER expressions as arguments. However, two of them, ABS and SQR, return INTEGER values when the argument is INTEGER.

Further, there are two more functions in TIPS which accept a REAL argument but produce an INTEGER result. TRUNC (a REAL expression) drops the fractional part completely. That is, TRUNC (-84.7) produces -84 as the INTEGER value. ROUND (a REAL expression) produces the INTEGER value which is the closest whole number. Thus ROUND (-84.7) produces -85 as the INTEGER value.

## Exercise

If X, Y, and Z are declared as

```
VAR
    X: (* COMMENT *)REAL;
    Y: (* COMMENT *)REAL;
    Z: (* COMMENT *)INTEGER;
```

what values are printed by

```
a.   X := 3.7;              b.   X := 100.5;
     Y := 4.9;                   Y := 1.4;
     Z := TRUNC(X+Y);            Z := ROUND(X+Y);
     WRITELN (Z)                 WRITELN (Z)
```

## Mixed Mode

In the olden days, a decade or so ago, programmers could not mix INTEGER and REAL numbers in expressions in high level (TIPS-like) languages. "Mixed mode" was one of the most common errors in expressions. If you wanted to add J (an INTEGER number) to X (a REAL number), and if you wrote

        X+J

you might get an error message. You could correct it by converting the INTEGER value of J to an equivalent REAL value, say RLJ, by writing

        RLJ := J

then you could write

        X+RLJ

and it would be accepted.

Things are different now. Mode mixing has gone underground. Instead of causing an error message, mode mixing simply makes things take longer, in the compilation and/or the execution of a program, because the computer must convert each INTEGER number to REAL before it can do the indicated operation on all of them.

This story has two morals: (1) try to do arithmetic operations exclusively on numbers of the same type, especially if many operations are concerned, as within a highly iterative loop (this is important only if a very large number of computations are to be performed; otherwise the difference is trivial); and (2) when you do mix modes, be sure you understand what the results are going to be.

The need for a particular kind of loop, called a "counted loop," shows up frequently in programming. To illustrate it we change the example of the loop which printed square roots. Suppose the number of times the loop was to be executed was known to the computer before the loop was entered. For example, instead of wanting the square roots of all numbers whose roots were less than 20, say we simply wanted the square roots of the first 500 integers. The defining flowchart might look like this:

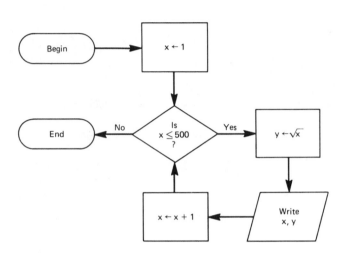

We could program this as:

```
(*CALCULATE THE SQUARE ROOTS OF THE FIRST 500 INTEGERS *)
PROGRAM LOOP1 (OUTPUT);
    VAR
        I: (* LOOP INDEX AND SQRT ARGUMENT *) INTEGER;
        Y: (* THE SQUARE ROOT *) REAL;
    BEGIN
    I := 1;
    WHILE I <= 500 DO
        BEGIN
        Y := SQRT(I);
        WRITELN (I,Y);
        I := I+1
        END
    END.
```

In every counted loop three specific operations must take place.  First, we _initialize the indexing variable_.  In other words, we must give the variable which is going to do the counting a beginning value.  The box in the above flowchart which makes this happen is

```
┌─────────────┐
│             │
│   x ← 1     │
│             │
└─────────────┘
```

A second function is _testing the indexing variable against the ending value_.  In our flowchart the following box performed this function:

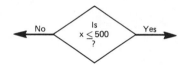

Thirdly, we need to _increment the indexing variable_.  That, of course, is done by

```
┌─────────────┐
│             │
│  x ← x + 1  │
│             │
└─────────────┘
```

We can combine these three flowchart boxes into one.  So:

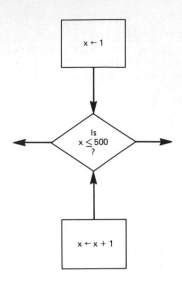

becomes

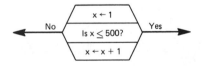

(See Note 5.)

Now, what's so great about that? Well, it just so happens that there is a single statement in TIPS to implement it. It looks like this:

        FOR I := 1 TO 500 DO

Now our program can be rewritten as

```
(* SQRT CALCULATING PROGRAM USING FOR--DO *)
PROGRAM LOOP2 (OUTPUT);
    VAR
        I: (* SAME AS BEFORE *) INTEGER;
        Y: (* SAME AS BEFORE *) REAL;
    BEGIN
    FOR I := 1 TO 500 DO
        BEGIN
        Y := SQRT(I);
        WRITELN (I,Y)
        END
    END.
```

The advantage of the FOR--DO over the WHILE--DO is that the initialization and incrementation of the index variable are taken care of automatically and the testing is simplified.

The syntax of the FOR-DO statement is

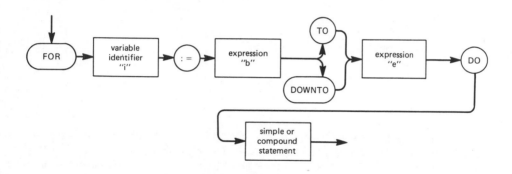

where i is an INTEGER variable name and b and e are the beginning and ending values used to count the loops. **In TIPS the quantities b and e must be INTEGER constants, variables or expressions.**

The FOR-DO statement (using the TO keyword rather than DOWNTO) basically assigns a progression of values to the variable i of the type INTEGER. The first time through the loop the value assigned is the value of the expression "b"; the next value is b+1; the next value is b+2; this continues until the value assigned is greater than the value of the expression "e". Then the statement (or statement sequence) is skipped and the program continues below it.

Two simple illustrations will make it clear to you what happens both with the TO keyword and the DOWNTO keyword. Suppose LOWNUM and HIGHNUM have been declared INTEGER and given the values 5 and 9, respectively. Then, assuming COUNTVAR is an integer variable also, this statement

```
FOR COUNTVAR := LOWNUM TO HIGHNUM DO
    WRITELN (COUNTVAR)
```

would produce the output:

```
5
6
7
8
9
```

The statement

```
FOR COUNTVAR := HIGHNUM DOWNTO LOWNUM DO
    WRITELN (COUNTVAR)
```

would produce

```
9
8
7
6
5
```

Two special cases can also be disposed of by example. First, suppose b is equal to e. In the cases above, if LOWNUM and HIGHNUM were both -18 then both statements would print just one number. What would it be?

The other special case occurs if, say, the TO keyword is used and the expression e is less than the expression b. For example,

```
FOR I := 10 TO 5 DO
    WRITELN (I)
```

In this case WRITELN is never executed and nothing is printed. An identical effect would be produced by

```
FOR I := 5 DOWNTO 10 DO
    WRITELN (I)
```

## Exercise

Suppose you have 10 pairs of numbers. Of each pair, the
first is a number which is either a Fahrenheit or Celsius
temperature. The second is a code (3 if the temperature is
on the Celsius scale and 6 if it is on the Fahrenheit
scale). Write a program to read these data and convert each
temperature to the other scale. Title the results so that a
person reading the output would understand it. If there is
an error in the code (that is is the code is not a 3 or 6),
print an error message for that pair.

## Exponentiation with Looping and Functions

TIPS and PASCAL have no exponentiation operator. That
is, there is no operator to automatically calculate
something like SOMEVAR to the 5.2 power or ANYVAR to the PWR
power.

Basically you have three choices of a technique,
depending partly whether the exponent you want to use is
INTEGER or REAL.

(1) If the exponent is INTEGER, and not too large, you
can simply do the exponentiation directly in an expression.
If you want, for example, AVAR to the fourth power you may
just say:

```
RESULT := AVAR*AVAR*AVAR*AVAR
```

(2) If the exponent is INTEGER, and moderately large,
you could do the exponentiation in a FOR--DO loop. For
example, BVAR to the 19th power:

```
RESULT := BVAR;
FOR I := 2 TO 19 DO
    RESULT := RESULT*BVAR
```

(There are cleverer ways to do this; how might you easily
compute BVAR to the 16th power?)

(3) If the exponent is not an integer in the
mathematical sense then you would have to use logarithms.
To take CVAR to the 3.6 power you could write:

```
RESULT := EXP(3.6*LN(CVAR))
```

Some versions of PASCAL have implemented exponentiation. In those versions, the exponentiation operator is normally two consecutive asterisks **.

> Good programming requires intense concentration. Keep in mind that you want the program to work correctly the first time and that, without care, you may make one or more mistakes in every single line of program. Continually ask yourself if each line is correct during the programming process. Be alert and convinced that you can write correct programs.

Use the computer to find the average of m numbers where
m is a quantity which may vary from problem to problem.   To
do this problem supply m+1 data values.   The first value
should be the number m.   The remaining values should each be
one of the numbers to be averaged.   One possible flowchart
for the problem appears below:

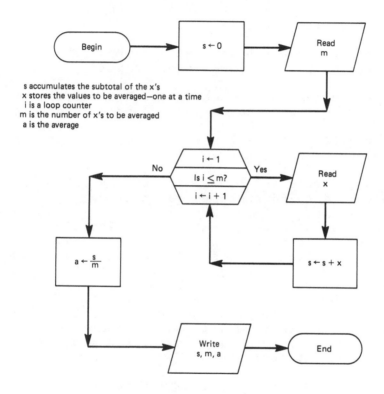

If you do not understand why this flowchart will result
in S becoming the sum of the m values, you might pretend you
are the computer and follow the flowchart through a simple
exercise.   You could use the data

        4
        3.2
        4.8
        5.1
        10.9

to see if you can get the answer: 6.0

To aid you in understanding the process which takes place when a computer executes a program, we now introduce a computer in schematic form. In many essential ways this computer bears a strong resemblance to present, actual computers. Our schematic computer has card input and line printer output but the principle would be the same for a terminal or microcomputer. We show this computer as being composed of four major parts:

1.  Storage, where the program and the numbers to be operated upon are remembered or held;

2.  A device for reading cards and transferring the numbers on those cards into computer storage;

3.  A printing device upon which the computer can write numbers from its storage;

4.  An arithmetic and comparison unit which performs calculation and compares quantities.

The schematic storage is composed of locations or "boxes" which can contain either instructions (TIP statements) or decimal numbers. Actually, when a program is stored in a computer's memory it consists of the machine's own language instructions and numbers in binary form. (See Module 6.) It gets these instructions by transforming into machine language the TIPS program which it has been given. For simplicity, however, we will show the storage containing the TIPS program statements instead of the equivalent machine language instructions.

To illustrate what takes place inside the computer we will write a program which would follow the flowchart of Lab Problem 07.

```
(* SCHEMATIC COMPUTER DEMONSTRATION *)
PROGRAM FINDMEAN (INPUT, OUTPUT);
    VAR
        S: (* ACCUMULATES THE SUBTOTAL OF THE X'S *) REAL;
        M: (* THE NUMBER OF X'S TO BE AVERAGED *) INTEGER;
        I: (* A LOOP INDEX *) INTEGER;
        X: (* EACH NUMBER TO BE INCLUDED IN THE AVERAGE *) REAL;
        A: (* THE AVERAGE OF ALL THE X'S *) REAL;
    BEGIN
    S := 0.0;
    READ (M);
    FOR I := 1 TO M DO
        BEGIN
        READ (X);
        S := S+X
        END;
    A := S/M;
    WRITELN (S,M,A)
    END.
```

After the TIPS program has been placed in computer
storage but before it has been executed, a representation of
storage might look like this:

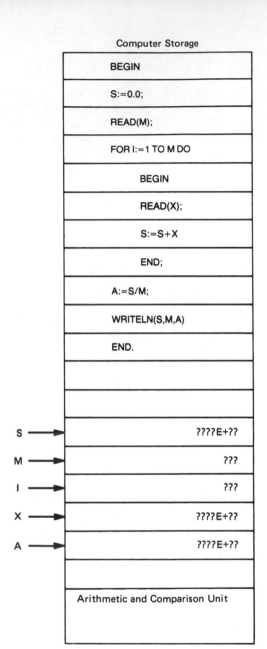

Computer Storage

| |
|---|
| BEGIN |
| S:=0.0; |
| READ(M); |
| FOR I:=1 TO M DO |
| BEGIN |
| READ(X); |
| S:=S+X |
| END; |
| A:=S/M; |
| WRITELN(S,M,A) |
| END. |

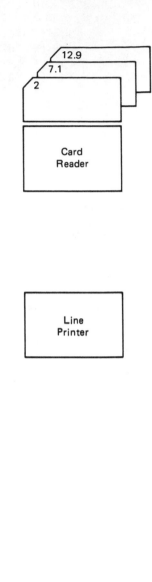

12.9
7.1
2

Card Reader

Line Printer

S ⟶ ????E+??
M ⟶ ???
I ⟶ ???
X ⟶ ????E+??
A ⟶ ????E+??

Arithmetic and Comparison Unit

Here only the statements and delimiters which are actually used during the execution of the program are shown; these statements are called the <u>executable</u> statements. The PROGRAM header is used basically to tell the computer that a TIPS program is on its way and that the computer must prepare to communicate with the outside world by use of its

INPUT and OUTPUT files.   The PROGRAM header is not executed
as part of the program.   The VAR instruction, likewise, is
not shown again, since its function is to tell the computer
that it must make room for the variables X, S, A, I, and M.
Notice that while there are spaces available for these five
variables--that is, the variables have been declared and the
computer expects to use them--the variables themselves
initially contain unusable quantities (garbage, we genteely
call it) indicated by ?.????E+?? for REAL numbers or ??? for
INTEGERs.

   The program will now be run schematically.   An arrow

will indicate the particular instruction being executed and
the rest of the schematic will show the effect.   Carefully
examine each of the following 15 steps in the execution of
this program.   If you completely understand the process, you
probably comprehend programming as we have discussed it so
far.

1. The PROGRAM begins.

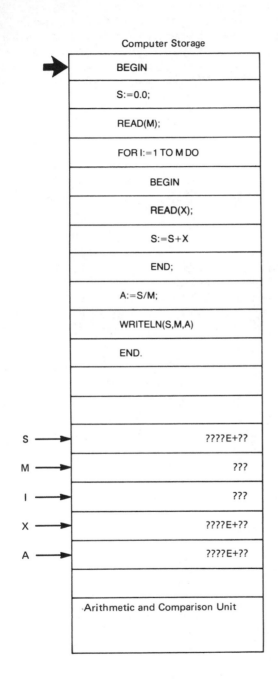

Computer Storage

| |
|---|
| BEGIN |
| S:=0.0; |
| READ(M); |
| FOR I:=1 TO M DO |
| BEGIN |
| READ(X); |
| S:=S+X |
| END; |
| A:=S/M; |
| WRITELN(S,M,A) |
| END. |

S → ????E+??
M → ???
I → ???
X → ????E+??
A → ????E+??

Arithmetic and Comparison Unit

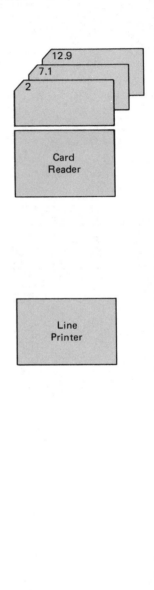

12.9
7.1
2

Card
Reader

Line
Printer

2.  Garbage is erased from S and replaced by zero.

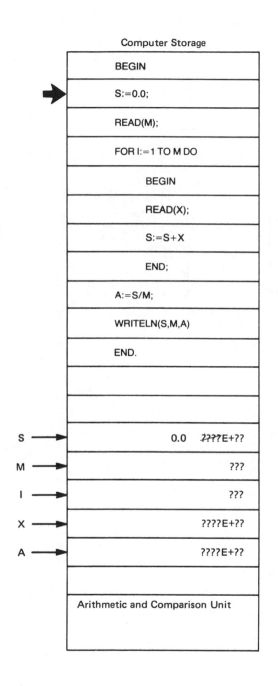

Computer Storage

| BEGIN |
| S:=0.0; |
| READ(M); |
| FOR I:=1 TO M DO |
| BEGIN |
| READ(X); |
| S:=S+X |
| END; |
| A:=S/M; |
| WRITELN(S,M,A) |
| END. |

S →    0.0    ????E+??

M →    ???

I →    ???

X →    ????E+??

A →    ????E+??

Arithmetic and Comparison Unit

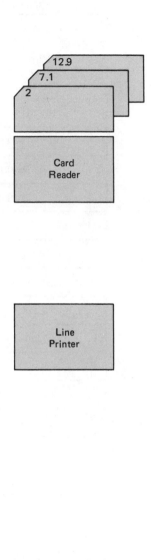

12.9
7.1
2

Card
Reader

Line
Printer

3. The first data card is read by the card reader and the number on that card, 2, replaces the garbage in location M.

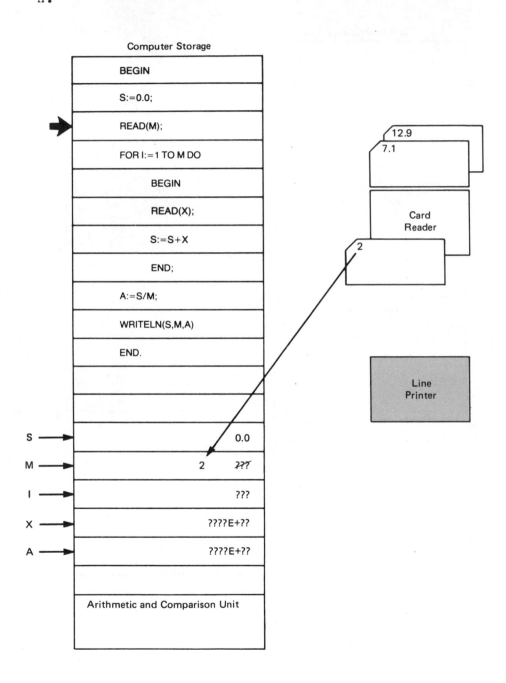

Computer Storage

| |
|---|
| BEGIN |
| S:=0.0; |
| READ(M); |
| FOR I:=1 TO M DO |
| BEGIN |
| READ(X); |
| S:=S+X |
| END; |
| A:=S/M; |
| WRITELN(S,M,A) |
| END. |

12.9
7.1

Card Reader

2

Line Printer

S → 0.0
M → 2 ~~???~~
I → ???
X → ????E+??
A → ????E+??

Arithmetic and Comparison Unit

A Schematic Computer

4.  Garbage is erased from location I and is replaced by the
    value 1.  The value in I is checked against the value in
    M.  (Notice the Arithmetic and Comparison Unit.)  The
    program continues in sequence.

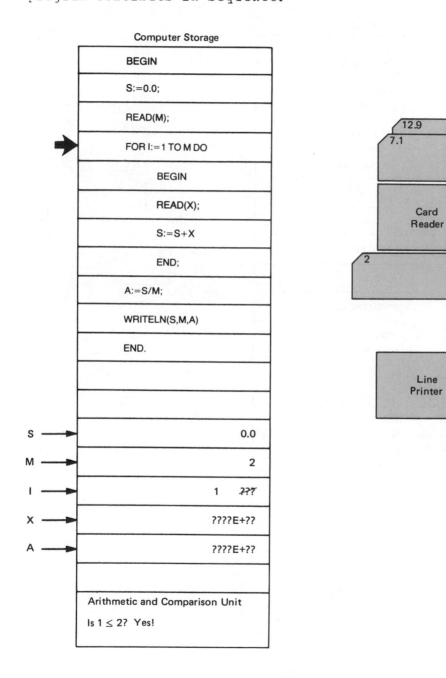

Computer Storage

| |
|---|
| **BEGIN** |
| S:=0.0; |
| READ(M); |
| FOR I:=1 TO M DO |
| BEGIN |
| READ(X); |
| S:=S+X |
| END; |
| A:=S/M; |
| WRITELN(S,M,A) |
| END. |

S → 0.0

M → 2

I → 1  ~~???~~

X → ????E+??

A → ????E+??

Arithmetic and Comparison Unit

Is 1 ≤ 2?  Yes!

12.9
7.1

Card
Reader

2

Line
Printer

5.  The BEGIN keyword is reached, which indicates that a compound statement is beginning.

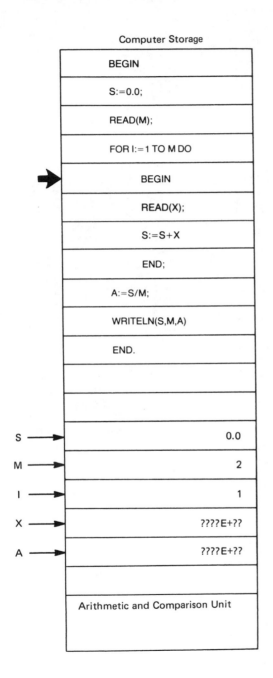

Computer Storage

| |
|---|
| BEGIN |
| S:=0.0; |
| READ(M); |
| FOR I:=1 TO M DO |
| BEGIN |
| READ(X); |
| S:=S+X |
| END; |
| A:=S/M; |
| WRITELN(S,M,A) |
| END. |
| |
| |

S ———▶ 0.0
M ———▶ 2
I ———▶ 1
X ———▶ ????E+??
A ———▶ ????E+??

Arithmetic and Comparison Unit

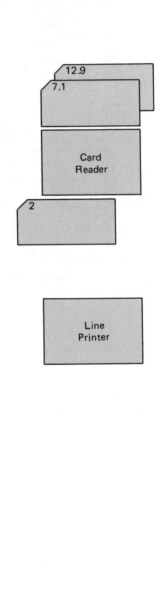

12.9
7.1

Card
Reader

2

Line
Printer

6. The second datum (the first value in the list to be averaged) is read by the card reader and that number replaces the garbage in location X.

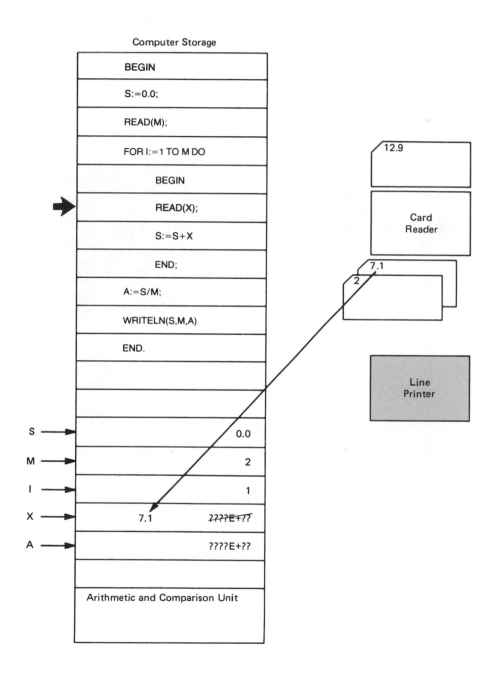

Computer Storage

| |
|---|
| BEGIN |
| S:=0.0; |
| READ(M); |
| FOR I:=1 TO M DO |
| BEGIN |
| READ(X); |
| S:=S+X |
| END; |
| A:=S/M; |
| WRITELN(S,M,A) |
| END. |

12.9

Card Reader

7.1

2

Line Printer

Arithmetic and Comparison Unit

7. The values in locations S and X are added together and the result replaces the value previously stored in S. (Notice the Arithmetic and Comparison Unit.)

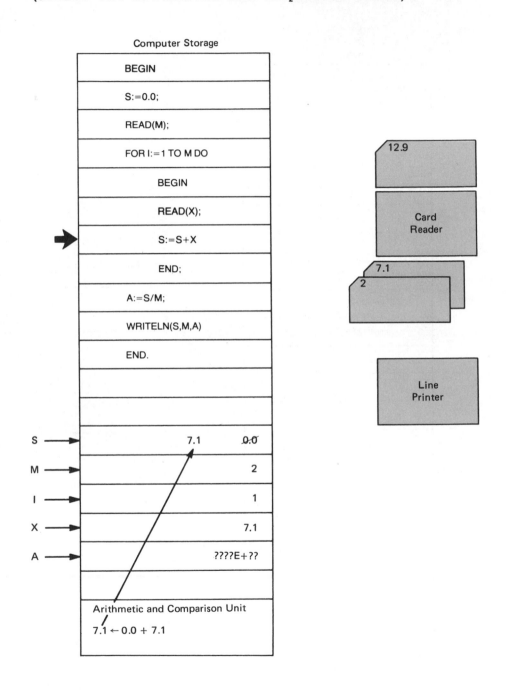

Computer Storage

| |
|---|
| BEGIN |
| S:=0.0; |
| READ(M); |
| FOR I:=1 TO M DO |
| BEGIN |
| READ(X); |
| S:=S+X |
| END; |
| A:=S/M; |
| WRITELN(S,M,A) |
| END. |

12.9

Card Reader

7.1
2

Line Printer

S   7.1   0.0
M   2
I   1
X   7.1
A   ????E+??

Arithmetic and Comparison Unit

7.1 ← 0.0 + 7.1

8. Because the END of the (compound) statement has been reached, the value 1 is added to the value in I and the result stored back in I. The value in I is compared with the value in M. Control transfers back to the beginning of the compound statement following the FOR-DO.

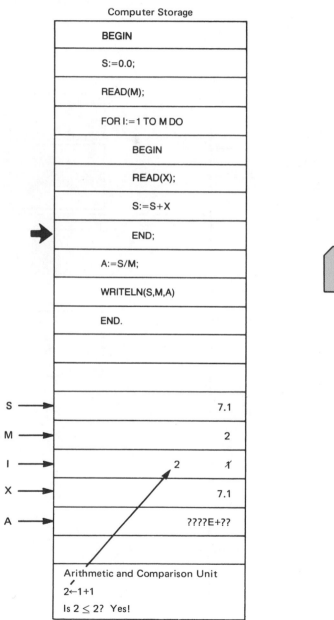

Computer Storage

| BEGIN |
| S:=0.0; |
| READ(M); |
| FOR I:=1 TO M DO |
| BEGIN |
| READ(X); |
| S:=S+X |
| END; |
| A:=S/M; |
| WRITELN(S,M,A) |
| END. |

S → 7.1
M → 2
I → 2  1̸
X → 7.1
A → ????E+??

Arithmetic and Comparison Unit
2←1+1
Is 2 ≤ 2? Yes!

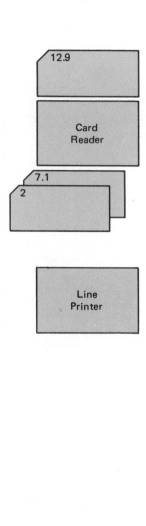

12.9

Card Reader

7.1
2

Line Printer

9. A BEGIN keyword is reached again which indicates that a block of instructions (the compound statement) is beginning.

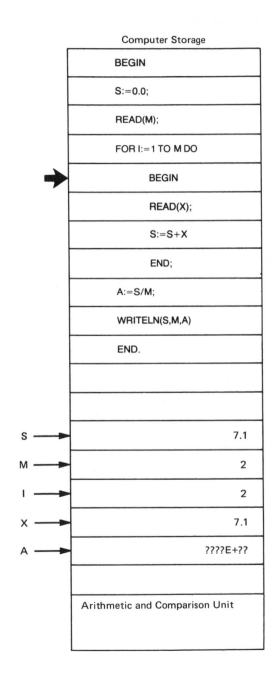

Computer Storage

| |
|---|
| BEGIN |
| S:=0.0; |
| READ(M); |
| FOR I:=1 TO M DO |
| BEGIN |
| READ(X); |
| S:=S+X |
| END; |
| A:=S/M; |
| WRITELN(S,M,A) |
| END. |

| | |
|---|---|
| S → | 7.1 |
| M → | 2 |
| I → | 2 |
| X → | 7.1 |
| A → | ????E+?? |

Arithmetic and Comparison Unit

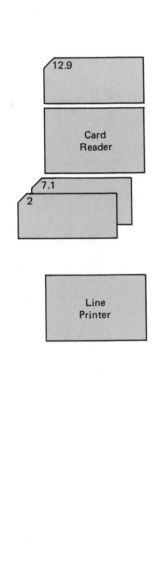

12.9

Card Reader

7.1

2

Line Printer

10. The third datum is read and transferred to location X, where it replaces the value previously stored there.

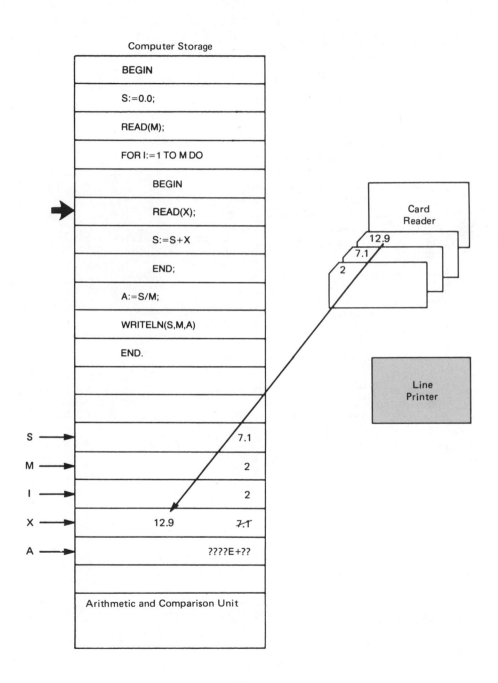

Computer Storage

| |
|---|
| BEGIN |
| S:=0.0; |
| READ(M); |
| FOR I:=1 TO M DO |
| BEGIN |
| READ(X); |
| S:=S+X |
| END; |
| A:=S/M; |
| WRITELN(S,M,A) |
| END. |

Card Reader

12.9
7.1
2

Line Printer

S → 7.1
M → 2
I → 2
X → 12.9   7.1
A → ????E+??

Arithmetic and Comparison Unit

**11.**  S is increased by X.

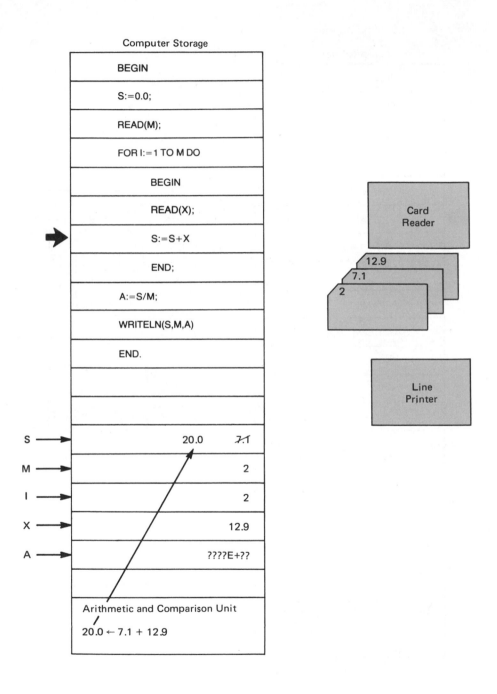

Computer Storage

| |
|---|
| BEGIN |
| S:=0.0; |
| READ(M); |
| FOR I:=1 TO M DO |
| BEGIN |
| READ(X); |
| S:=S+X |
| END; |
| A:=S/M; |
| WRITELN(S,M,A) |
| END. |

S → 20.0  ~~7.1~~
M → 2
I → 2
X → 12.9
A → ????E+??

Arithmetic and Comparison Unit

20.0 ← 7.1 + 12.9

Card Reader

12.9
7.1
2

Line Printer

12. I is increased by 1. I is tested against M. The program continues in sequence; the sequence of statements under the FOR--DO is <u>not</u> repeated.

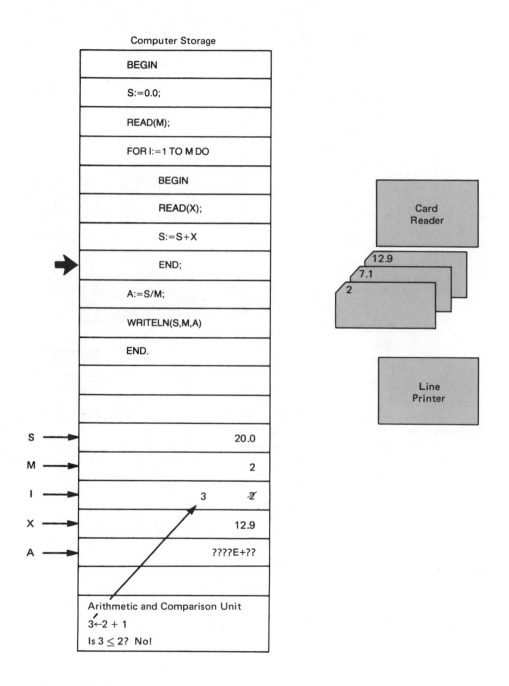

Computer Storage

| BEGIN |
| S:=0.0; |
| READ(M); |
| FOR I:=1 TO M DO |
| BEGIN |
| READ(X); |
| S:=S+X |
| END; |
| A:=S/M; |
| WRITELN(S,M,A) |
| END. |

Card Reader

12.9
7.1
2

Line Printer

S → 20.0
M → 2
I → 3 ~~2~~
X → 12.9
A → ????E+??

Arithmetic and Comparison Unit
3←2 + 1
Is 3 ≤ 2? No!

13. The quotient S over M is computed and the result is stored in A.

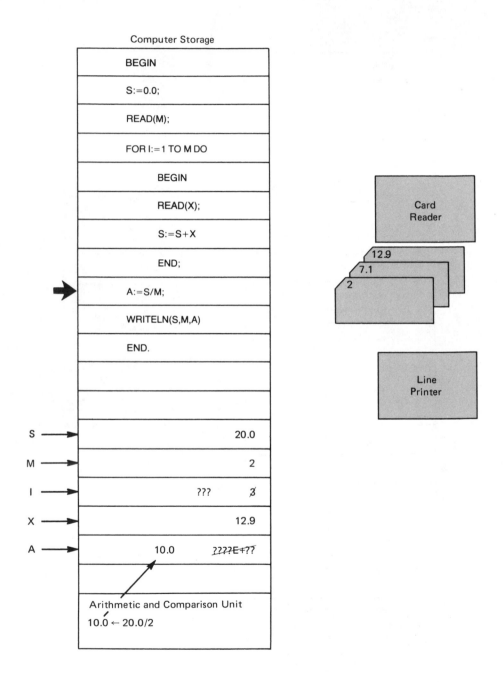

Computer Storage

| |
|---|
| BEGIN |
| S:=0.0; |
| READ(M); |
| FOR I:=1 TO M DO |
| BEGIN |
| READ(X); |
| S:=S+X |
| END; |
| A:=S/M; |
| WRITELN(S,M,A) |
| END. |

➤ A:=S/M;

Card Reader

12.9
7.1
2

Line Printer

S ⟶ 20.0

M ⟶ 2

I ⟶ ??? 3̸

X ⟶ 12.9

A ⟶ 10.0 ????E+??

Arithmetic and Comparison Unit
10.0 ← 20.0/2

14.  The values of S, M, and A are printed.

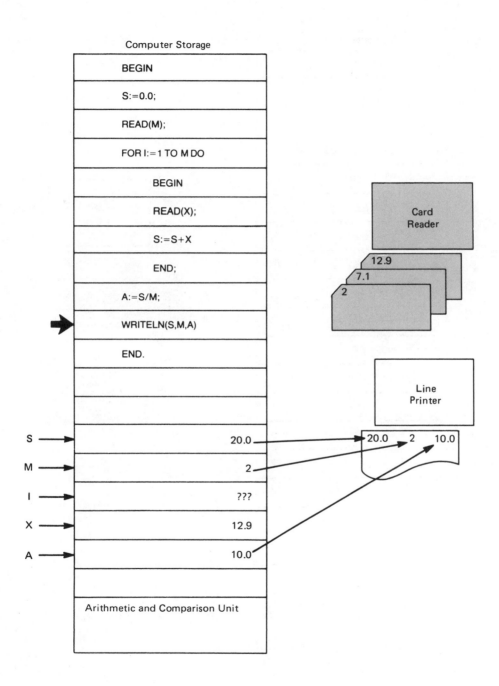

Computer Storage

| |
|---|
| BEGIN |
| S:=0.0; |
| READ(M); |
| FOR I:=1 TO M DO |
| BEGIN |
| READ(X); |
| S:=S+X |
| END; |
| A:=S/M; |
| WRITELN(S,M,A) |
| END. |

Card Reader

12.9
7.1
2

Line Printer

20.0   2   10.0

S → 20.0
M → 2
I → ???
X → 12.9
A → 10.0

Arithmetic and Comparison Unit

15.  The program terminates.

Computer Storage

| |
|---|
| BEGIN |
| S:=0.0; |
| READ(M); |
| FOR I:=1 TO M DO |
| BEGIN |
| READ(X); |
| S:=S+X |
| END; |
| A:=S/M; |
| WRITELN(S,M,A) |
| ➡ END. |
| |
| |

| | | |
|---|---|---|
| S ➡ | ? | 20.0 |
| M ➡ | ? | 2 |
| I ➡ | ? | ??? |
| X ➡ | ? | 12.9 |
| A ➡ | ? | 10.0 |
| | | |

Arithmetic and Comparison Unit

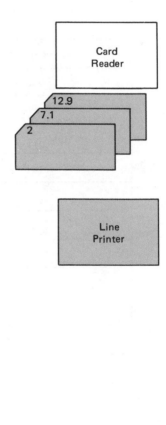

Card Reader

12.9
7.1
2

Line Printer

A Schematic Computer

When you put a statement in a loop, it is
usually going to be executed more than once--in some
loops it will be executed many, many times.  So you
should be careful that you aren't repeatedly doing
something within the loop that could be done
outside.  For a trivial example, say you want to
write a loop to find the sum of the sines of the
angles whose values, in degrees, are 0,1,2,...89.

Don't write

```
      SUMSINE := 0;
      FOR I := 0 TO 89 DO
          BEGIN
          SINE := SIN(I*3.14159/180.0);
          SUMSINE := SUMSINE+SINE
          END;
      WRITELN (SUMSINE)
```

but compute outside of the loop that part of the
arithmetic that doesn't change, e.g.,

```
      SUMSINE := 0;
      DEGTORAD := 3.14159/180.0;
      FOR I := 0 TO 89 DO
          BEGIN
          SINE := SIN(I*DEGTORAD);
          SUMSINE := SUMSINE+SINE
          END;
      WRITELN (SUMSINE)
```

Some people would suggest that you ought to
compute pi divided by 180.0 independently of the
computer program and put it in as a constant; we
wouldn't.  Computers do arithmetic faster and,
usually, with greater accuracy than do people.

Problems to be solved can be described in several ways. Also, the algorithms which depict the step-by-step method for solving these problems can take several forms. In this section we will show, through examples, some of the descriptions you are likely to encounter and use.

Suppose we want to find the sum of the series

$$1 + x + x^2 + x^3 + \ldots$$

where x is a real number which is greater than zero but less than one. Under these conditions it is clear that each term (for example, $x^2$ or $x^3$) of the series will be smaller than the one before it. For example, if x is 0.2 then $x^2$ is 0.04 and $x^3$ 0.0016, etc. Suppose we will accept as a solution to our problem the sum of all the terms which are greater than one thousandth. We could desribe the solution to this problem in several ways.

## A Mathematical Description

Given

$$0 < x < 1$$

find

$$\Sigma x^n$$

such that each term is > 0.001 and n = 0,1,2,3,...

## A Narrative Description

Obtain the value of x for which the series sum is desired. Check the value to see if it lies within the proper range, zero to one. If not, complain and quit. Otherwise, begin adding terms together, starting with 1,

Algorithms: Descriptions

then x, then x² and continue until a term with value less
than or equal to one-thousandth is found.  Write the value
of x and the sum computed.


## A One-Dimensional-Step-by-Step Description

Here we present another description which appears
narrative in form but which actually describes steps which,
when followed, lead to a solution of the problem.  The term
"one-dimensional" is used to indicate that any given step
either precedes or follows any other step, much as any point
on a one-dimensional line precedes or follows any other
point.

1.  Obtain the value of "x" for which the series sum is
    desired.

2.  If x<=0 or x>=1 then do step 2a and skip step 3 and
    its substeps.

    2a.  Write out only the value of "x" and indicate
         that it is not in the proper range.

3.  Otherwise, do steps 3a, 3b, 3c, and 3d.

    3a.  Let a symbol "s" take on (stand for) the value
         one.

    3b.  Let a symbol "t" take on the value of "x".

    3c.  As long as "t" is greater than 0.001, do steps
         3c1 and 3c2 repeatedly.

         3c1. Let "s" take on a new value which is its
              old value plus "t".

         3c2. Assign a new value to "t" which
              is its old value multiplied by x.
              (For example, if t is x³, then t becomes
              t•x, or x⁴).

    3d.  Write out the value of "x" and the value of "s"
         which has been computed.

4.  Consider the process finished.

Note that the Step-by-Step Description of the problem is longer and more complicated than the narrative one. While it may seem more complex, it is also more explicit. It is this move toward greater explicitness which allows you to design programs. The Step-by-Step Description depicts an algorithm for solving the problem, whereas the Narrative Description and the Mathematical Description do not.

## A Two-Dimensional Flowchart Description

In writing out a description of an algorithm, it is sometimes useful to consider a two-dimensional description of the solution. One form of a two-dimensional description is the flow diagram or flowchart. Its advantages over the one-dimensional description include the arbitrary placement of the various steps on a sheet of paper and the freedom from having to number or name various steps. A flowchart description also permits easy addition or deletion of steps without affecting the order of other steps. This makes it useful during the preliminary planning of the algorithm.

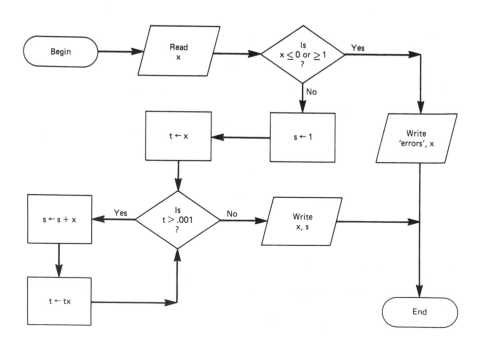

## A Second One-Dimensional Description

For some programmers it seems easiest to conceive of a solution to a problem in terms of the narrative or mathematical description, then draw a flowchart description for the more logically difficult parts, and finally devise a step-by-step description which is the computer program for the solution to the problem.  Here we show a program which sums the series.

```
(* PROGRAM TO SUM A SERIES *)
PROGRAM SUMSER (INPUT, OUTPUT);
    VAR
        X: (* BASE OF SERIES *) REAL;
        S: (* PARTIAL SUM OF THE SERIES *) REAL;
        T: (* EACH COMPUTED TERM *) REAL;
    BEGIN
(* READ X, CHECK IF IN RANGE *)
    READ (X);
    IF (X<=0) OR (X>=1) THEN
        WRITELN (' ERROR',X)
    ELSE
(* INITIALIZE S AND T *)
        BEGIN
        S := 1;
        T := X;
(* COMPUTE SERIES SUM *)
        WHILE T>0.001 DO
            BEGIN
            S := S+T;
            T := T*X
            END;
(* WRITE X AND SERIES SUM S *)
        WRITELN (X,S)
        END
    END.
```

Notice that parentheses are required in the IF-THEN-ELSE statement above.  Why?  Because logical operators AND and OR are of a higher priority than the comparison operators! This is unlike other computer languages such as PL/ONE or FORTRAN.

For purposes of this discussion we put forth the idea of an entity which we call an _operation_. We represent it by a rectangular box. It has exactly one entrance and exactly one exit.

Now we define a second entity which we call a _decision_. It is a computer step which may direct the path of control that the computer takes in either of two ways. We represent the decision as a diamond shaped box with one entrance and two exits.

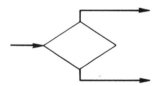

Now we look at three ways in which operation and decision entities can be arranged. We call these arrangements _logic-control structures_ or just _structures_.

The first structure is called _sequencing_ or _then_. We show it as:

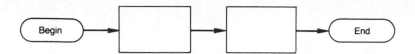

The meaning is that operations will take place one after another, in the sequence in which they are written. The structure has exactly one entrance and one exit.

The second structure involves two operations and a decision connected in this way:

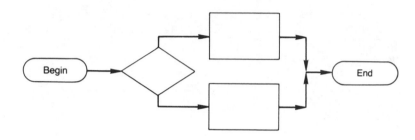

Here a condition is checked for truth or falsity based on the values of variables in the machine. Depending on the outcome of the check, one or the other of two possible operations is selected. (Either, but not both, of the operations might be absent.) Control then passes to the exit. This structure is called selection or if-then-else. It has one entrance and one exit.

The third structure also involves the decision element. Again, two possible paths of execution exist within the structure. One of them goes to the exit but the other loops back so that statements which may have already been executed may be reexecuted. This structure is called iteration or while-do.

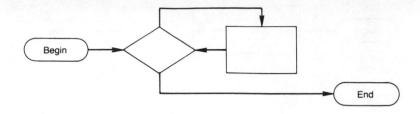

Again, there is one entrance and one exit; any set of
flowchart boxes with one entrance and one exit depicts what
is called a proper algorithm.

Now let's go back to the rectangular operation box and
define it. It can be several things.

1. The operation box could represent a single computer
   instruction such as READ, arithmetic assignment, or
   WRITELN.

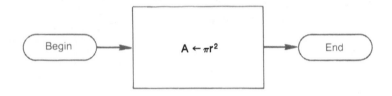

$$A \leftarrow \pi r^2$$

2. The operation box can represent any of the three
   structures, since each of them has but one entrance
   and one exit.

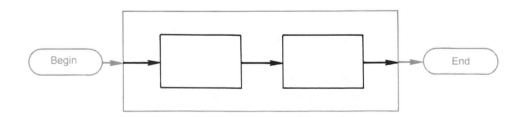

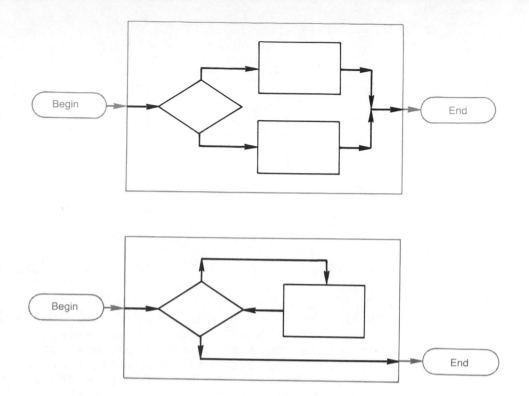

3.  The operation box can represent <u>combinations</u> of any
    of the three structures.  There are two ways to
    combine structures: linking and nesting.

    Linking: a structure may follow another structure.
             Thus the exit of one structure becomes
             the entrance of another.  Linking is, in
             fact, just the sequence logic-control
             structure.  For example, here is
             selection followed by iteration.

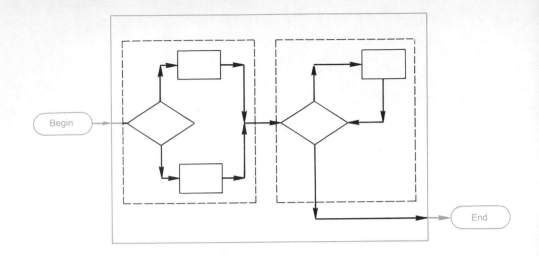

Nesting: a structure can be contained within another
structure.  This is true because every
structure contains an operation box and an
operation box can contain a structure.  For
example, here a sequence structure and an
iteration structure are contained in a
selection structure.

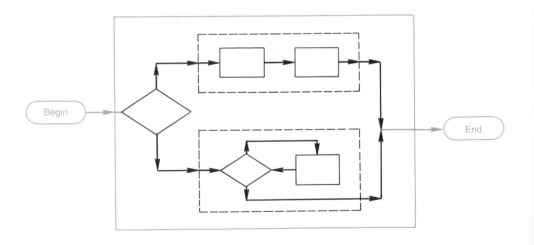

4. An operation box can represent an entire algorithm or computer program. Such a program is made up, then, of only the three basic logic-control structures combined according to linking and nesting.

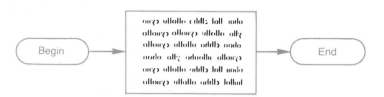

## Repeated Refinement

You have already discovered that designing an algorithm is not always a simple process. Furthermore, as more complex problems are dealt with, the difficulty increases dramatically. The best approach to the design of complex algorithms is to first write a very general (but accurate) representation of the algorithm. Flowchart language works well to illustrate the design process as we will show you shortly. The Program Development Scroll, which will be presented in Part II, is a more practical and effective technique for algorithm design. With either approach the idea is to repeatedly refine the algorithm description until a program emerges.

As an example of repeated refinement, consider a solution to the following problem:

A card contains three numbers refered to as K, A, and B. Write a TIPS program to instruct a computer to read the card and take the following action:

If K is one then multiply A by B and print the product.

If K is two then subtract B from A and print the difference.

If K is three then evaluate the series

$$(A+B) + (A+B)^2 + (A+B)^3 + (A+B)^4 + \ldots$$

Add terms to the series until the absolute value of an individual term becomes less than .001.

We begin with the most basic possible flowchart:

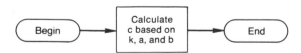

The next step in design of a more specific algorithm might be to represent the operation box above by a sequence of operation boxes:

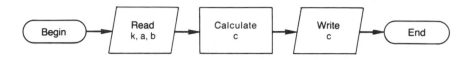

Now we refine the flowchart description again so that it includes more detail and becomes more like a form which could be programmed in TIPS. We do this here by applying the concept of nesting to the middle box. We will let that box represent a selection structure which contains another selection structure. This might produce:

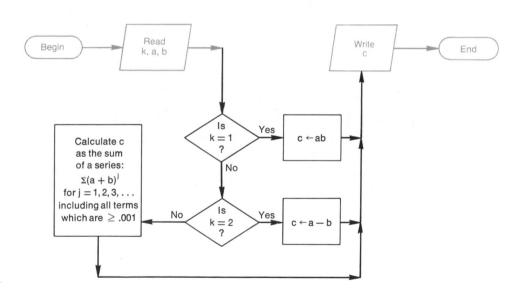

We are now closer to having an algorithm which can be implemented as a TIPS program. But there is more to do. We again apply "nesting," this time to the box which computes "c" as the sum of the series.

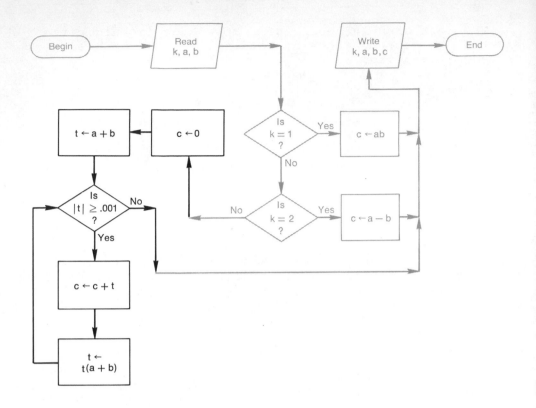

Using this technique of <u>repeated refinement</u> (which is
sometimes called <u>top-down design</u> or <u>stepwise refinement</u>) we
have arrived at an algorithm which is sufficiently detailed
to be programmed in TIPS, as shown below.

```
(* STEPWISE REFINEMENT EXAMPLE: FINAL PROGRAM *)
PROGRAM ABC (INPUT, OUTPUT);
    VAR
        K: (* INDICATES IF C IS TO BE A*B, A-B, OR THE SUM OF
            A SERIES PREVIOUSLY DESCRIBED. K IS 1, 2 OR 3
            RESPECTIVELY. *) INTEGER;
        A: (* INPUT VARIABLE *) REAL;
        B: (* INPUT VARIABLE *) REAL;
        C: (* THE RESULT--SEE DESCRIPTION OF K ABOVE *) REAL;
        T: (* EACH COMPUTED TERM OF THE SERIES *) REAL;
    BEGIN
    READ (K,A,B);
    IF K=1 THEN
        C := A*B
    ELSE
        IF K=2 THEN
            C := A-B
        ELSE
            BEGIN
            C := 0.0;
            T := A+B;
            WHILE ABS(T)>=0.001 DO
                BEGIN
                C := C+T;
                T := T*(A+B)
                END
            END;
    WRITELN (K,A,B,C)
    END.
```

You need to be careful to make sure each BEGIN has a
matching END, just as you need to be careful to use a right
parenthesis to balance each left parenthesis in an
expression. When you are reading over a program, pencil in
hand, it helps to draw brackets linking each BEGIN-END pair
as shown above. These brackets may form "nests" and should
pair delimiters which are in vertical alignment. The
brackets must never cross.

Repeated refinement, then, is a process for designing an
algorithm. This process proceeds from the most general
description of the algorithm to a detailed, particular
one--which is a TIPS (or other computer-language) program.

## Auxiliary Variables

There is a slight complication in using only the three basic logic-control structures: more variables may be needed to make the algorithm work. And since the instructions we have provided for you to use in TIPS allow only the three basic structures, you need to know that a difficulty might arise and that it can be easily solved by what we call auxiliary variables.

Basically, an auxiliary variable is a variable which has nothing to do with your problem as such but one which tells a later portion of the program what occurred in an earlier portion. We illustrate with a flowchart schematic and explanation:

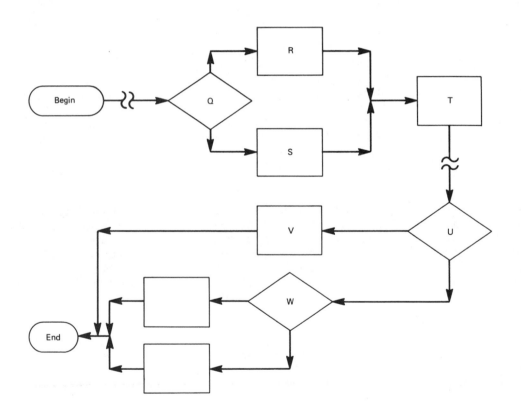

Here a decision based on a condition Q is made early in the program. Based on the decision, one of two control

paths are possible, resulting in operation R or S; the paths
of control rejoin at operation T.  Now another decision
based on condition U is made, which again separates the
paths of control.  One path simply leads to an operation V
but the other leads to a decision, W, which is based partly
on whether operation R or operation S was previously
selected.  There are several ways to attack this problem but
one of the simplest is to use an auxiliary variable (e.g.,
AUXVAR) which is set, say, to zero by operation R if the
path of control goes that way, and is set to one if the path
of control goes through operation S.  Then the decision W
can be made, based partly on the value of AUXVAR.  The sole
function of AUXVAR was to reveal the earlier path of
control.

The above is but one of the instances when
variables can be used as indicators of the previous path of
control.  We won't give you an example because whatever we
chose would probably not be appropriate for your future
experience.  But you should know that variables can aid in
selecting the path of control through a program when it is
in execution.  (Later we will describe a new variable type,
BOOLEAN, which is particularly useful as an auxiliary
variable.)


## Algorithm Design in Summary

Several ideas are central to the design of algorithms
and computer programs:

First is that there are three basic logic-control
    structures: sequence, selection, and iteration.

Second is the idea of a proper algorithm: a sequence of
    steps or statements such that the sequence has only one
    entrance and one exit.  Each of the three structures is
    a proper algorithm.

Third, structures can be combined by linking, because each
    structure is a proper algorithm.

Fourth is the idea that any structure can contain any other
    structure and that the process of putting structures
    within structures can be continued indefinitely.  You
    can imagine a while-do containing a while-do containing
    a while-do. . . .  It's sort of like a TV set showing a
    picture of itself showing a picture of itself showing,

etc. Combining structures in this way is called
<u>nesting</u>.

Fifth, that <u>any</u> algorithm that can be run on a computer can
be expressed by combinations of the three basic logic-
control structures, aided, perhaps, by the use of
auxiliary variables.

Sixth, that the best way to design an algorithm is to begin
with a single operation (which is an accurate but
undetailed description of the algorithm) and then to
repeatedly refine the algorithm by combining structures
using linking and nesting.

The program in the immediately preceding section might
not work at all if it gets bad data.  For example, if K=3
and if A and B add to one or more (or -1 or less), there's
trouble ahead.  Furthermore, the program doesn't actually
check to see if K is only 1, 2, or 3.  Another criticism is
that the program does not identify what it prints out.  And
if K is 3, the sum A+B is formed every time through the
loop, when another technique might prevent all those
additions.  Finally, the program could certainly be more
useful if any number of sets of K, A, and B could be run,
one after another.  Modify the flowchart and the program so
that they are immune to these criticisms.  Then run the
resulting program with enough data so that all paths of
execution through the algorithm are explored.  Hand check
the results.

The fact that a human, given enough time, could
arrive at any answer that a computer can generate
does not mean that a human can solve any problem a
computer can.  Sometimes temporal considerations are
a part of the problem.  The numbers which tell the
rockets on a space ship what to do after the first
stage of the rocket separates cannot take ten
minutes for a human to compute.  If more than a
second or so is required, a satellite may be falling
into the Indian Ocean.

Flowcharting an algorithm gives the programmer one advantage: it allows her or him to work out the logic in a relatively free environment. When working with the flowchart language a programmer can attack the problem without the constraints of writing correct TIPS syntax. Furthermore, he or she can use blocks to specify operations which might later become many TIPS statements but which, for the moment, may be considered a single entity. Suppose a programmer has drawn the flowchart below. Each of the four rectangular boxes, let us say, consists of about a dozen instructions in TIPS. The diamond-shaped boxes are decisions of the if-then-else variety. The flowchart is a correct representation of what the progrmmer wants to do; also, as a whole, it depicts a proper algorithm: one with one entrance and one exit. However, it is not made up solely of the three structures we have discussed previously. Furthermore, it is not, in its present state, programmable in TIPS. We call an algorithm which does not meet these requirements "<u>unstructured</u>." What is it about the flowchart which makes it unstructured?

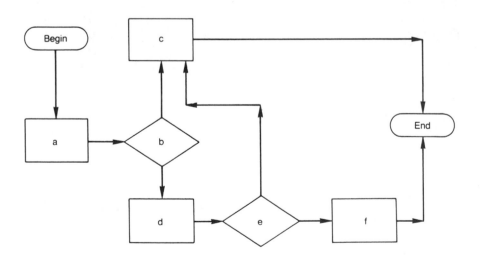

We have stated that any algorithm can be reduced to combinations of the three structures, so a flowchart must exist which performs the task, meets the structure requirements, and is programmable in TIPS.   Here is one which is satisfactory on all three counts:

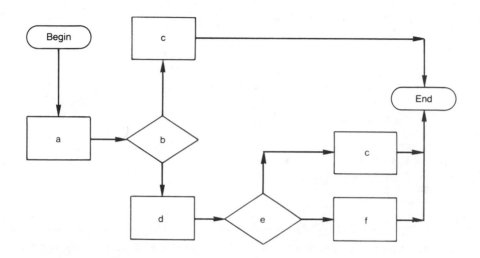

The clear disadvantage of this flowchart is that box c, which represents about a dozen statements, occurs more than once.   This would mean more TIPS statements, more cards or lines, and more computer storage used for the program--not a very efficient situation.

Here is the outline of a program which follows the flowchart above.   Study the flowchart and program outline below until you understand how they are equivalent.

```
(* STRUCTURED PROGRAM WITH REDUNDANT STATEMENTS *)
PROGRAM PGM (INPUT, OUTPUT);
    VAR
        what have you
    BEGIN
    statements in box a
    IF condition in box b THEN
        BEGIN
        statements in box c
        END
    ELSE
        BEGIN
        statements in box d
        IF condition in box e THEN
            BEGIN
            statements in box c (again)
            END
        ELSE
            BEGIN
            statements in box f
            END
        END
    END.
```

Fortunately, a mechanism exists which frees us from
duplicating sequences of statements, such as those in box c,
within a program.  In flowchart language this feature is
called a procedure.  (In computing terminology there exist
many synonyms for the word procedure.  Some of them are:
subprogram, subroutine, and module.)  We might depict it as
follows:

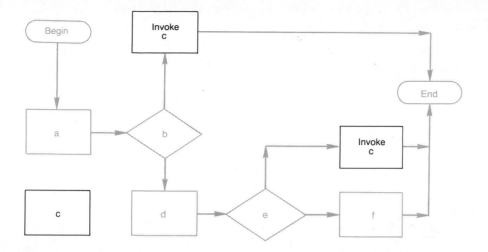

Here we show box c off to the side, seemingly by itself. Where box c appeared in the flowchart we substituted a box which simply <u>invokes</u> or <u>calls</u> box c.  When represented in this fashion, the statements in box c can be executed when, and only when, invoked by the main program, since there is no direct path of control to box c.  Also implicit in this flowchart is the idea that the statements in box c need only be written once.  Box c constitutes a procedure.

In TIPS, a set of instructions which constitute a procedure is headed by the delimiter word <u>PROCEDURE</u>.  (See Note 6.)  Essentially, we take the statements which would be in box c and declare them to be a separate entity within the program.  We have given the PROCEDURE the arbitrary name BOXC.

Here is an outline of a TIPS program which follows the flowchart which contains the procedure.

```
(* STRUCTURED PROGRAM WITH BOXC PROCEDURE *)
PROGRAM MAINPGM (INPUT,OUTPUT);
    VAR
        what have you
    PROCEDURE BOXC;
        BEGIN
        statements in box c
        END;
    BEGIN
    statements in box a
    IF condition in box b THEN
        BOXC
    ELSE
        BEGIN
        statements in box d
        IF condition in box e THEN
            BOXC
        ELSE
            BEGIN
            statements in box f
            END
        END
    END.
```

Important points:

1.   The statements in box c are encased between a BEGIN and an END.  Further, they are preceded by the keyword PROCEDURE and, in that heading, given a name: BOXC.  Thus, except for the fact that PROCEDURE is used instead of PROGRAM, the entity we have called BOXC appears very much like a TIPS program.  What other difference do you see in the heading?

2.   A PROCEDURE must be placed in the declarations section of a PROGRAM and before the action section which starts with the keyword BEGIN.  Specifically, in a TIPS program, it comes immediately <u>after</u> the VAR declarations.  A PROCEDURE is really a declaration of something which is going to be used in the PROGRAM.  So it belongs in the declarations section.

3.   The procedure named BOXC is completely included within the PROGRAM named MAINPGM.

4.   A TIPS statement,

    BOXC

appears in MAINPGM at the points where the sequence of
statements in box c would have been encountered if the
PROCEDURE were not available.

   5.   The statements in box c occur only once rather than
twice, as would be required if PROCEDUREs were not
available.

   The diagram below shows how a PROCEDURE is utilized.
The solid arrows show the transfer of control which takes
place when the PROCEDURE is used for the first time.   The
dashed arrows show its use a second time.

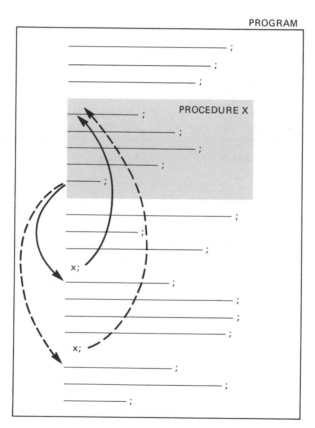

   The diagram above is intended to show that the PROCEDURE
can be _invoked_ (or brought into action) at any point in the
PROGRAM, and that control will be returned _to the point of
invocation_ after the PROCEDURE has completed execution.

## PROCEDURE Example

Suppose that in a program we want to calculate the
factorials of various integers at different points during
the execution of the program.  N factorial is defined as

$$N! = N*(N-1)*(N-2)*...*1$$
Also $0! = 1! = 1$

For example,

$$4! = 4*3*2*1 = 24$$
$$6! = 6*5*4*3*2*1 = 720$$

Consider the following PROGRAM:

```
(* PROGRAM TO INVOKE FACTORIAL PROCEDURE *)
PROGRAM DRIVER (INPUT, OUTPUT);
    VAR
        X: (* FACTORIAL OF X WANTED HERE AND THERE *)INTEGE
        K: (* A COUNTER USED IN PROCEDURE FACT *) INTEGER;
        ANS: (* THE COMPUTED FACTORIAL *) INTEGER;
(* THE PROCEDURE TO COMPUTE FACTORIALS *)
    PROCEDURE FACT;
        BEGIN (* PROC FACT *)
        ANS := 1;
        FOR K := 2 TO X DO
            ANS := ANS*K
        END; (* PROC FACT *)

    BEGIN (* PROGRAM DRIVER *)
    •
    •
    X := 5;
    FACT;
    WRITELN (X,ANS);
    •
    •
    X := 3;
    FACT;
    WRITELN (X,ANS);
    •
    •
    X := 0;
    FACT;
    WRITELN (X,ANS);
    •
    END. (* PROGRAM DRIVER *)
```

There are three important points.  First, we write one
sequence of statements to compute the factorial and put the
sequence of statements together in a PROCEDURE named FACT.
The PROCEDURE goes in the declaration section of the
PROGRAM.  The PROCEDURE is composed of a compound statement
which ends with "END;".

Second, each mention of FACT in the main PROGRAM causes
execution of the statements contained in the PROCEDURE named
FACT.  Upon termination of the PROCEDURE FACT, the statement
directly following the invoking statement is executed and
processing continues sequentially from that point.

Third, all variable values declared in the PROGRAM may
be used in the PROCEDURE.  We say these variables are "known
to" the PROCEDURE.

The values printed by the program above would be:

    5    120
    3    6
    0    1

> Notice that in the PROGRAM and PROCEDURE above
> we use comments after each major BEGIN and END
> delimiter to identify the particular segment.
> That's a good idea.  Why, if you start that in these
> early days of your programming career you may never
> misplace an END delimiter!

## Nested PROCEDUREs

An PROCEDURE may be nested within another PROCEDURE.
Thus, a PROGRAM might invoke a PROCEDURE named A which
might, in turn, invoke a PROCEDURE named B.  The PROGRAM
could not legitimately invoke PROCEDURE B directly.

When a PROCEDURE is within another PROCEDURE, the inner
PROCEDURE bears the same resemblance to the outer one as the
outer one does to the PROGRAM.  A skeleton of a PROGRAM with
three PROCEDUREs might look like this.

```
(* NESTED PROCEDURES EXAMPLE *)
PROGRAM NESTPROC (INPUT, OUTPUT);
    VAR
        variables
    PROCEDURE A;
        PROCEDURE B;
            BEGIN (* PROC B *)
            statements in procedure B
            END; (* PROC B *)

        BEGIN (* PROC A *)
        statements in procedure A including
            invocations of procedure B
        END; (* PROC A *)

    PROCEDURE C;
        BEGIN (* PROC C *)
        statements in procedure C
        END; (* PROC C *)

    BEGIN (* MAIN PROGRAM *)
    statements in main program including
    invocation of procedures A and C but not B.
    END. (* MAIN PROGRAM *)
```

A moment's reflection will convince you that
PROCEDUREs can aid in the design of algorithms and
the construction of programs.  The statements in a
PROCEDURE can be considered a combination of the
three structures nested within the operation box
which invokes the PROCEDURE.  Thus, PROCEDUREs
promote good algorithm design, because they promote
thinking in terms of repeated refinement.

Programming by extensive use of PROCEDUREs is
called modular programming, and it facilitates
designing algorithms "from the top down."
PROCEDUREs, therefore, are not merely for situations
in which program statements might have to be written
two or three times, but are useful whenever a set of
structures or statements constitute a "logical
piece" of a program.

Assume you have "m" physical objects, all different and distinguishable from one another.  You want to know how many possible different subsets consisting of "j" objects exist if a subset is formed by choosing once from the "m" objects.

For example, if m=5 and j=3, you can make up any of ten different subsets of objects.  If we designate the m objects by the letters A, B, C, D, and E, the ten possible subsets are ABC, ABD, ABE, ACD, ACE, ADE, BCD, BCE, BDE, and CDE. (The order of the objects makes no difference; CBA is considered the same as ABC.)

The formula which tells the number of subsets in the general case is

$$\frac{m!}{j!\,(m-j)!}$$

Verify that this formula produces 10 if m=5 and j=3.

Write an internal PROCEDURE which will calculate the number of combinations of "m things taken j at a time" by the formula above.  Your internal PROCEDURE should contain an internal PROCEDURE to calculate factorials.

Test your programming by writing a calling PROGRAM (such a program is called a driver) which will read several pairs of m and j and print the desired results.  Make sure the program works for special cases (e.g., m=j=1) and sounds the alarm for impossible situations (e.g., j>m).  Use comments throughout.

## <u>Summary</u> <u>of</u> <u>TIPS</u> <u>Operators</u> (<u>in</u> <u>Order</u> <u>of</u> <u>Priority</u>)

```
NOT

*   /   DIV   MOD   AND

+   -   OR

>   >=   <   <=   =   <>
```

## <u>Summary</u> <u>of</u> <u>Semicolon</u> <u>Placement</u>

The placement of semicolons in PASCAL programs may have initially confused you. There is, however, a pattern. The semicolon is used <u>only</u> to separate statements or instructions. That is, the semicolon <u>does</u> <u>not</u> <u>terminate</u> statements or instructions; it separates adjacent ones. This rule, and the syntax diagrams, define the placement of semicolons. You can check you program also by the statements below.

A semicolon always follows a PROGRAM or PROCEDURE instruction.

A semicolon always follows each REAL or INTEGER keyword.

A semicolon never immediately precedes an END or ELSE.

A semicolon never directly follows a BEGIN, THEN, DO, or ELSE.

A semicolon normally follows an END unless:

    a. the END is the termination of the program (in which case the END is followed by a period),

    b. the END is directly followed by another END, or

    c. the END immediately precedes an ELSE.

## Summary of Indenting

Indenting is used only to make a program more readable by humans. There is no black art about it. Whatever best supports the comprehension of the readers is the way it ought to be.

What follows is the indenting scheme used in this book. We believe that it is a good scheme; but many people indent differently and they probably believe their schemes to be superior. Be that as it may--be sure to use some systematic indenting scheme--that is what is really important.

The PROGRAM header should begin in column one as should most comments except those explaining the usage of each variable.

Each indentation is four columns to the right of the last one.

The word VAR begins in column 5.

The name of each variable being declared begins in column 9.

The first BEGIN and PROCEDURE starts in column 5 unless they are within another PROCEDURE.

Do not indent after a BEGIN.

Each END starts in the same column as the corresponding BEGIN.

Indent four spaces after each IF, FOR, WHILE, ELSE.

When writing an IF statement, write the IF-condition-THEN on the same line, if possible. Then on the next line indent the statement which is to be executed if the condition is true. Then, on a line by itself and directly under the IF, write the ELSE, if there is one. Then on the next line indent four spaces and start the statement to be executed if the condition is false. An example of this is:

```
IF X = Y THEN
    WRITELN (' THE VALUES ARE EQUAL')
ELSE
    WRITELN ( ' THE VALUES ARE UNEQUAL')
```

By indenting this way, if a BEGIN block follows the THEN
it can be indented just as any other instruction.  For
example

```
IF  X = Y THEN
        BEGIN
        WATER := SQRT (WELL) ;
        WRITELN (' THE VALUES ARE EQUAL')
        END
    ELSE
        WRITELN ( ' THE VALUES ARE UNEQUAL')
```

## Using Comments

Use comments in your programs to describe such things as:

The explanation of the program purpose and methods

The names and organizations of the programmers

The date the program was finished

Notation for each time the program is revised

The meaning and use of each variable in the program

The meaning and use of each PROCEDURE

Any deviation from the normal practices used in solving
this problem

The existence of null statements

## Headings and Declarations

    (1)   PROGRAM name (INPUT, OUTPUT);

    (2)   VAR identifier: REAL;

             identifier: INTEGER;

    (3)   PROCEDURE name;

## Statements

    (4)   READ

    (5)   WRITELN

    (6)   variable := expression

    (7)   IF-THEN-ELSE

    (8)   WHILE--DO

    (9)   FOR--DO

    (10)  name (to invoke PROCEDURE "name")

(Compound Statements are formed by the delimiter words BEGIN and END.)

Write a TIPS program to instruct the computer to read any three numbers which might be in any order and to print them in ascending order. Draw a flowchart in the space below before you attempt to write the program.

If this problem appears too trivial, try it with ten numbers instead of only three.

If you tried to do the sorting problem (Lab Problem 10) with ten numbers, you probably gave up.  Another example of a problem for which our present knowledge does not seem sufficient is the following:

> Write a general program to read several values--the exact number specified by the data--and simply print these values in reverse order.  In other words, do Lab Problem 01 again, using a varying number of values instead of exactly five.

These examples illustrate that there is a class of problems for which scalar variables are really inadequate.


## The Variable Concept Expanded

The facility in TIPS which allows the solution of such problems is based on an expansion of the concept of a variable.  Heretofore, a variable name has represented only a single value at any one time during the execution of a program; we call such a variable a scalar variable.  We now introduce a feature which makes the variable concept much more powerful: we allow a single variable to stand for an entire sequence of values.  We call such a variable a subscripted variable, a vector variable, or a one-dimensional array.

Here's an example of using a variable name to stand for a single location in memory and contain a single numerical value:

        GOAT
```
 -354.8
```

Now we will gain the ability to use the name GOAT to stand instead for several locations in memory and, hence, for several values.  Each of the boxes holding a number is called an element, a cell, or a member of the array.

```
GOAT
┌─────────┐
│  -88.8  │
├─────────┤
│  55.0   │
├─────────┤
│   0.0   │
├─────────┤
│  11.0   │
└─────────┘
```

A question immediately arises: if one variable name
stands for several values, how does the programmer instruct
the computer regarding the particular value to be used, say,
in a calculation?  The solution lies in "attaching" an
INTEGER number, called a <u>subscript</u>, to the variable name.
The subscript, which appears in square brackets after the
variable name, uniquely identifies each member of the
sequence or array.  In this case the programmer instructs
the computer to identify each value in the array as follows:

```
GOAT
┌─────────┐
│  -88.8  │   GOAT[ 1 ]
├─────────┤
│  55.0   │   GOAT[ 2 ]
├─────────┤
│   0.0   │   GOAT[ 3 ]
├─────────┤
│  11.0   │   GOAT[ 4 ]
└─────────┘
```

Then, if the programmer wanted to construct an
expression to instruct the computer to divide the second
number in the array by the fourth and add 1.5 to the result,
he could write:

        X := GOAT[ 2 ]/GOAT[ 4 ] + 1.5

This would result in a value for the expression of

        55/11.0 + 1.5 which is 6.5.

The name "subscripted variable" comes from the fact that
these variables are used to represent quantities that, in
mathematics, are written as

$$X_i$$

where X is the variable name and i is called a subscript.
Incidentally, square brackets are not found on some
keyboards.  Most PASCAL versions allow the alternate forms
(. and .) to be equivalent to [ and ] respectively.
Therefore you could write X[3] or X(.3.) and they would mean
the same thing.

In summary, we have expanded the variable concept to
allow a variable name to take on the form:

        variable[subscript]

where "variable" is an identifier obeying the rules set up
for scalar variable names and "subscript" is an INTEGER
number.

## Using Subscripted Variables

How do subscripted variables allow us to deal with
problems which were not easily solvable with scalar
variables?  If we declare an array EXAMPLE of eight
locations as follows:

        VAR
            EXAMPLE: ARRAY [1..8] OF REAL;

we set up in the machine's memory

EXAMPLE

| | |
|---|---|
| ?.?????E+?? | EXAMPLE[1] |
| ?.?????E+?? | EXAMPLE[2] |
| ?.?????E+?? | EXAMPLE[3] |
| ?.?????E+?? | EXAMPLE[4] |
| ?.?????E+?? | EXAMPLE[5] |
| ?.?????E+?? | EXAMPLE[6] |
| ?.?????E+?? | EXAMPLE[7] |
| ?.?????E+?? | EXAMPLE[8] |

If the program executes the statement

READ (EXAMPLE [2])

this results in the reading of a number, say −31.3, which replaces the garbage in EXAMPLE [2] thusly:

EXAMPLE

| | |
|---|---|
| ?.?????E+?? | EXAMPLE[1] |
| −3.13000E+01 | EXAMPLE[2] |
| ?.?????E+?? | EXAMPLE[3] |
| ?.?????E+?? | EXAMPLE[4] |
| ?.?????E+?? | EXAMPLE[5] |
| ?.?????E+?? | EXAMPLE[6] |
| ?.?????E+?? | EXAMPLE[7] |
| ?.?????E+?? | EXAMPLE[8] |

This, in itself, offers no advantage over the use of scalar variables. However, we specified only that a subscript was a <u>number</u>; we did not say that the subscript had to be a <u>constant</u>. In fact, the power of using subscripted variables lies in using subscripts which are not constants but are themselves variables, or, even, arithmetic expressions.

As an example of the use of a variable as a subscript, observe that we could perform precisely the same operation as

        READ (EXAMPLE[2])

by writing a pair of statements

        SUBK := 2;
        READ (EXAMPLE[SUBK])

Even this only hints at the power which we now have. **The fact that we can use variable names as subscripts allows us, in effect, to calculate a portion of a variable name.** Suppose, for example, we wished to place zeros in all eight locations of the array EXAMPLE. We could write:

        FOR X33 := 1 TO 8 DO
            EXAMPLE[X33] := 0.0

Here, the storage location referenced in the statement

        EXAMPLE[X33] := 0.0

would be EXAMPLE [1] the first time through the loop, EXAMPLE [2] the second time through, EXAMPLE [3] the third time through, etc. So zeros would be placed in all eight locations. Please study the above example carefully until you understand it thoroughly.

## Exercise

Suppose that the following values are stored in memory:

| | |
|---|---|
| X[1] | 0.0 |
| X[2] | 0.0 |
| X[3] | 3.0 |
| X[4] | 45.0 |
| X[5] | 0.0 |
| LAMB | 2 |
| NAT | 4 |

If the assignment statement X[LAMB] := 234.0 were executed, what changes in memory would result?  Since LAMB contains the value two, X[LAMB] refers to the second location in the sequence of locations called X (in other words, X[2], and therefore the value in X[2] would be changed from 0.0 to 234.0.  What happens if the assignment statement X[NAT]=X[NAT]+LAMB is executed?  Since NAT contains the value four, this statement says: Add the contents of LAMB to the contents of X[4].  The value 45.0 in X[4] is changed to 47.0.  What value is stored in X[3] by the statement

$$X[3] := X[LAMB]+X[NAT]+LAMB+NAT?$$

## Declaration of Subscripted Variables

In order to take advantage of this new facility the programmer must use a declaration within the VAR instruction.  To declare the array GOAT used previously, the programmer would have written:

COLUMNS

| 1 | 2 | 3 | 4 | 5 | 6 | 7 | 8 | 9 | 10 | 11 | 12 | 13 | 14 | 15 | 16 | 17 | 18 | 19 | 20 | 21 | 22 | 23 | 24 | 25 | 26 | 27 | 28 | 29 | 30 | 31 | 32 | 33 | 34 | 35 | 36 | 37 | 38 | 39 | 40 | 41 | 42 | 43 | 44 | 45 |
|---|---|---|---|---|---|---|---|---|----|----|----|----|----|----|----|----|----|----|----|----|----|----|----|----|----|----|----|----|----|----|----|----|----|----|----|----|----|----|----|----|----|----|----|----|

```
     VAR
          GOAT: (* HERD *) ARRAY[1..4] OF REAL;
```

This instruction tells the computer that the variable name GOAT is to stand for several locations. The first location will be referred to as GOAT [1], the last as GOAT [4], and the intervening locations are to be numbered consecutively GOAT [2] and GOAT [3].

The numbers in the VAR declaration indicating the lowest and highest subscripts <u>must</u> <u>be</u> <u>constants</u>. The reason is that the computer must know during the <u>translation</u> or <u>compilation</u> of the program, what variable names to expect and how many locations are to be devoted to each. **PASCAL does not allow you to indicate the number of locations to be used for an array with a variable.** For example,

```
     VAR
          X: ARRAY [1..M] OF REAL;
```

is illegal.

If the declaration

```
VAR
     ABCD: (* COMMENT *) ARRAY [0..5] OF INTEGER;
```

appeared in a program it would declare an array of <u>six</u> locations as follows:

| | |
|---|---|
| ??? | ABCD[ 0 ] |
| ??? | ABCD[ 1 ] |
| ??? | ABCD[ 2 ] |
| ??? | ABCD[ 3 ] |
| ??? | ABCD[ 4 ] |
| ??? | ABCD[ 5 ] |

As with scalar variables, the declaration of a variable does
not define the values to be placed in the various locations;
thus we show each location containing garbage or unusable
(undefined) information.  Defining the values associated
with variables, either scalar or subscripted, must be
performed with a READ statement or an assignment statement.


Exercises

1.  Write the instruction necessary to declare a scalar
    variable EXER and a subscripted variable CISE of 100
    locations numbered CISE [1] through CISE [100].

2.  Which of the following instructions are invalid?
    Why?

    VAR
        a. A: ARRAY [I..J] OF INTEGER;
        b. A: ARRAY [1..3] OF REAL;
        c. QUICK: (-10..10) OF REAL;
        d. DEAD: [25] OF INTEGER;
        e. ABLE: ARRAY [1..2] REAL;
        f. ABLE(4)  := 10.0;

3.  Why is the following group of instructions in error?

        VAR X: ARRAY [1..100] OF REAL;
        BEGIN
        X[0] := 24.5

4.  How many locations would be reserved by the
    following instruction?  What are they?

        VAR

RULEONE: ARRAY [-6..0] OF REAL;

## A Sample Problem

Now we turn back to the problem of writing a program which will read in several values--the exact number of which will be determined by the data--and print these values in reverse order. We will stipulate that there will be no more than 10 values, though there may be fewer. The number of values to be read is to be the first number in the data and will be called M in the program.

A complete program which would perform this feat is shown here:

```
(* READ IN VALUES, PRINT IN OPPOSITE ORDER *)
PROGRAM PRTREV (INPUT, OUTPUT);
    VAR
        M: (* NUMBER OF VALUES *) INTEGER;
        N: (* A FOR--DO INDEX *) INTEGER;
        K: (* A FOR--DO INDEX *) INTEGER;
        VALS: (* STORES ALL VALUES *) ARRAY [1..10] OF REAL;
    BEGIN
    READ (M);
    FOR K := 1 TO M DO
        READ (VALS[K]);
    FOR N := M DOWNTO 1 DO
        WRITELN (VALS[N])
    END.
```

In this program we used K as the subscript and loop index in the first loop. In the second loop we used N. We could have used K in the second loop but we want to illustrate a concept: at the time a statement containing a subscripted variable is executed, the particular variable which stands for the subscripting number is unimportant; the value of the subscript is important.

```
        READ (VALS[3])
```

and
```
        K := 3;
        READ (VALS[K])
```

and
```
        N := 3;
        READ (VALS[N])
```

each perform the same function.  To re-emphasize:  **whenever a program refers to an element of a subscripted array, the quantity in square brackets must either be an INTEGER constant, a variable which has previously been defined to have an INTEGER value, or an expression which has an INTEGER value.**

To show the technique used when writing flowcharts containing subscripted variables we present a flowchart depicting the algorithm followed by the above program.   The character V is used to stand for the variable VALS.

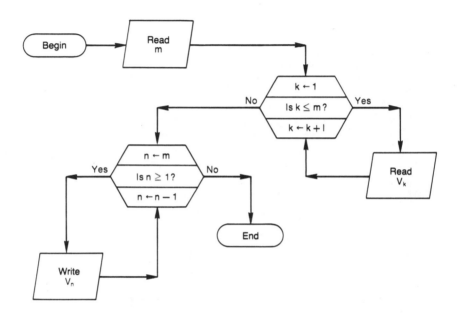

If the previous example is not clear, construct a schematic computer on a sheet of paper.  Draw a box (or column) for M, K, N and 10 boxes for VALS.  Run through the program with the following data:

        6
        18.5
        7.3
        −1.2
        5.5
        100.
        0.

Subscripted Variables

References to variables in an array usually require more time during the execution of a computer program than do references to scalar variables. If you are evaluating an expression which involves more than one or two references to a subscripted variable, it may be prudent to substitute a dummy variable. For example,

```
FOR I := 1 TO N DO
     A[I] := A[I]+SIN(A[I]-LN(A[I]))/A[I]
```

could be rewritten as

```
FOR I := 1 TO N DO
     BEGIN
     B := A[I];
     A[I] := B+SIN(B-LN(B))/B
     END
```

and execution time might be reduced. We say "might" because some compilers (usually called optimizing compilers) are smart enough to substitute, in effect, the dummy variable B. If speed is an issue for a program you write you probably would want to test this feature.

## Exercises

1.  If X[1]=2, X[2]=4, and X[3]=6.5, then what value is printed by the statements below?

    ```
    K := 1;
    L := 3;
    S := 0;
    S := S+X[K]+X[L];
    K := K+1;
    S := S+X[K];
    L := L-2;
    S := S+X[L];
    WRITELN (S)
    ```

2.  If Y[1]=10, Y[2]=4, Y[3]=3.5, and Y[4]=0.5, then what value is printed by the statements below?

    ```
    MAD := 1;
    TOT := 0;
    WHILE MAD<=4 DO
         BEGIN
    ```

Subscripted Variables                           169

```
          TOT := TOT+Y[MAD];
          MAD := MAD+2
          END;
     S := TOT/Y[1];
     S := S+Y[MAD-1];
     S := S+SQRT(Y[MAD-3]);
     WRITELN (S)
```

3.   Assume that L = 4, KK = 3, and MMM = 2.   What member
     of TEST is referred to in each of the following?

          TEST[L]        TEST[L + KK - 3]
          TEST[4]        TEST[KK * MMM - L DIV MMM]


## Subscripted Variables--When to Use Them

    When does a programmer use a subscripted variable?  It's
not easy to generalize, but you should keep in mind the
basic ability you have when using a subscripted variable: to
allow the calculation of part of the variable name so as to
make it unneccesary to name each variable explicitly at the
time the program is written.  If you have an aggregate of
data which consists of different numbers but which has some
common theme, you should consider representing it with a
subscripted variable.  For example, several thousand license
numbers of cars in a particular county might be candidates
for elements of a subscripted variable.

    Use of a subscripted variable or array is not without
its price, however.  Arrays take up memory space and time is
required to calculate each subscript.  If you have an
aggregate of data, you should ask yourself at least one
question before deciding that a subscripted array is
appropriate:  does the problem require that all of these
data be available to the program at any one time or would it
be possible to hold only one or two at a time and get the
same job done?  If the problem is such that the first datum
could be read in, processed, replaced with the second,
processed, etc., then a subscripted variable is not
appropriate.


## Use of Data as Subscripts

    As another example of the use of subscripts consider the
following problem.  A programmer is given a deck of cards
which represent votes for candidates in an election.  Each

card, except the last, is punched with a single digit (1, 2, 3 or 4) indicating a single vote for candidate 1, 2, 3 or 4. The last card is punched with the value -100 and is present simply to indicate the end of the data deck. The programmer is told to write a program which will count the number of cards punched with a 1, the number of cards punched with a 2, etc.

If he or she were doing the job by hand a person might designate four areas on a piece of paper as 1, 2, 3, 4 and begin looking at the cards, one at a time, making marks in the appropriate areas of the paper. After looking at all the cards, the number of marks in the "1" area would represent the number of "1" cards, etc.

The technique we will use with the computer is not much different. Instead of four areas on a piece of paper we will use a subscripted variable, NVOTES, which will represent four locations in a machine. The machine will initialize the four areas by putting zeros in each. The computer will then read each card and "make a mark" by adding a 1 to the appropriate location. If, for example, a card contains a 3, then NVOTES [3] will be increased by 1. At the termination of the card-reading phase, the machine will simply print out the values of the four locations as our answers. A program to use this method is shown below.

```
(* TALLY VOTES OF FOUR CANDIDATES *)
    PROGRAM VOTEPGM (INPUT, OUTPUT);
        VAR
            I: (* WHILE-DO INDEX *) INTEGER;
            SUB: (* THE CANDIDATE NUMBER OF EACH VOTE *) INTEGER
            LAST: (* A SWITCH THAT BECOMES 1
                    WHEN THE END OF DECK IS REACHED *) INTEGER;
            NVOTES: (* THE TALLY *) ARRAY [1..4] OF INTEGER;
        BEGIN
(* ERASE THE SLATE *)
        FOR I := 1 TO 4 DO
            NVOTES[I] := 0;
(* SET SWITCH *)
        LAST := 0;
        WHILE LAST = 0 DO
            BEGIN
(* GET VOTE *)
            READ (SUB);
(* CHECK FOR TRIP VALUE *)
            IF SUB = -100 THEN
                LAST := 1
            ELSE
(* TALLY VOTE *)
                NVOTES[SUB] := NVOTES[SUB] + 1
            END;
(* OUTPUT RESULTS *)
            WRITELN (' CANDIDATE',' NUMBER OF VOTES');
            FOR I := 1 TO 4 DO
                WRITELN (I:10, NVOTES [I]:15)
        END.
```

This program reads a number and uses that number as a
subscript.  If you have difficulty understanding the
program, go through it using the following sample data:

```
        3
        4
        3
        1
        -100
```

What results should be printed using these sample data?
In the above program why were the four elements of NVOTES
initially set to zero?  Why was SUB not initially set to
zero?

When you use a datum as subscript you must be very sure that it lies within the proper range. If, by accident or input error, a value were read by the above program which contained the number 5, either an incorrect answer would result or the program would end abnormally with an error message. Think about what could be done by the programmer to prevent this situation, since erroneous data are not at all uncommon.

This program also illustrates a variation on looping technique. Here again, the data determined the number of times the input loop was executed. But instead of prescribing the number in advance, the data contained a _trip_ value (-100) which, when sensed, terminated the input loop. A trip value should be one which could not possibly be a data value. Negative 100 is certainly safe in this case--what politician would allow himself to be so designated?

## Exercise

Write a program which will convert an undetermined number of integer Fahrenheit temperatures into Celsius temperatures. Each temperature to convert is between -40 and 212 degrees Fahrenheit. Your program should read in a Fahrenheit value, check it to see if it is in range (if not, print an error message and skip this value), and then call a PROCEDURE to do the conversion. Each Celsius temperature you produce should be averaged with the previous one calculated (if any) and the average printed. Since you may be required to calculate a given value many times, the following approach should be used: the first time your PROCEDURE is called, convert all Fahrenheit values between -40 and 212 and store the results in an array. Thereafter, you simply use the input value as an index into the array. This method is termed a table-lookup technique.

As a programmer, you may frequently be required to understand a program you did not write or, perhaps even more often, why a program you did write doesn't work. It helps in some instances to pretend you are the computer and ask yourself, "How might I do this if I were a literal-minded idiot?" The

answer to this question is:  the same way the
computer does, one step at a time.

     If you yourself act as the computer,
designating boxes (or columns) as locations in your
memory and entering and crossing off numbers as
dictated by the program, it is difficult not to
understand how the program works.  If this seems to
be a degrading way to learn a concept, keep in mind
that understanding subscripted variables is
difficult for many people.  Under these conditions,
any learning method that works is appropriate.  Once
the concept is established, programming with
subscripted variables turns out to be remarkably
easy.

Write a TIPS program which will read in "m" numbers, where m is specified by the data but is not more than 200. For each of these m numbers print out the number itself and, beside it, the value of the difference between the number and the average of all the numbers. Draw a flowchart in the space below before writing the program. Test your program with data. Hand check the results.

No computer program should ever be used to solve real problems without first having test data processed for which the programmer already knows the correct answers. All large computer programs initially contain programming errors; some very large programs have contained bugs which were not detected for years. It is ideal to test each possible logical path through a program. For big, complex programs this is impossible. But it is important for the programmer to create test problems which exercise as many different logic paths as are reasonably possible. These tests should include not only typical data but atypical values as well, such as might be produced by erroneous input data.

The formula for the standard deviation of a set of values is as follows:

$$\hat{\sigma} = \sqrt{\dfrac{\sum\limits_{i=1}^{n} (x_i - \bar{x})^2}{n-1}}$$

where the symbols are as defined in the flowchart below (See Note 7.)

Use the computer to find the average and the standard deviation of a set of n scores.

Suppose that a program which you write contains an expression involving division. Could the denominator ever be zero? Under what circumstances? Should some type of test be programmed to check for a zero divisor before the division takes place?

A program desk check is a careful examination of a program before you submit it to the machine. When you desk check your program, look at each subscript and ask yourself: under what conditions could this value be less than the lower limit or greater than the upper limit specified by the VAR declaration? Subscripts which are out of the appropriate range are a common occurrence and a major source of errors in computer programs. Using an IF statement to be sure a subscript is in range is not a bad idea at all. Also, your compiler may have an option which automatically checks all subscripts--but that uses a lot of computer time.

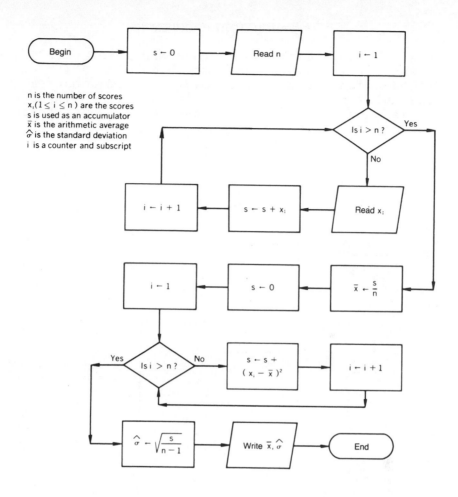

Begin → s ← 0 → Read n → i ← 1

n is the number of scores
$x_i (1 \le i \le n)$ are the scores
s is used as an accumulator
$\bar{x}$ is the arithmetic average
$\hat{\sigma}$ is the standard deviation
i is a counter and subscript

Is i > n? — Yes
No
i ← i + 1 ← s ← s + x; ← Read x;

i ← 1 ← s ← 0 ← $\bar{x} \leftarrow \dfrac{s}{n}$

Yes — Is i > n? — No — $s \leftarrow s + (x_i - \bar{x})^2$ → i ← i + 1

$\hat{\sigma} \leftarrow \sqrt{\dfrac{s}{n-1}}$ → Write $\bar{x}, \hat{\sigma}$ → End

Use the computer to sort m numbers into ascending order
using the sorting algorithm described below.   The algorithm
is called a "bubble sort"; it exchanges adjacent pairs of
numbers until the entire set is in order.   No input or
output is shown; determine how the method works before you
program it (See Note 7.)

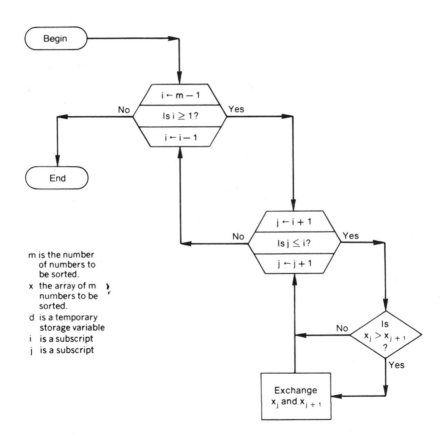

m is the number
  of numbers to
  be sorted.
x  the array of m
  numbers to be
  sorted.
d  is a temporary
  storage variable
i  is a subscript
j  is a subscript

By now you can see the value of using subscripted variables for applications which require the storage of sets of data of similar types, such as the scores of several students on an exam.  Storing these data in an array allows great flexibility in performing arithmetic on and obtaining statistics from such data.

It happens frequently, however, that simply numbering the locations of an array consecutively from a low number to a higher one is not always the most convenient way to deal with the data.  Imagine, for example, a class of four students, each of whom took three exams during the term. This means we would be dealing with twelve numbers.  We could declare an array of these twelve numbers as

VAR GRADES: ARRAY[ 1..12 ] OF REAL;

which might appear as:

| GRADES | Exam | Student |
|---|---|---|
| GRADES[ 1 ] | 1 | 1 |
| GRADES[ 2 ] | 1 | 2 |
| GRADES[ 3 ] | 1 | 3 |
| GRADES[ 4 ] | 1 | 4 |
| GRADES[ 5 ] | 2 | 1 |
| GRADES[ 6 ] | 2 | 2 |
| GRADES[ 7 ] | 2 | 3 |
| GRADES[ 8 ] | 2 | 4 |
| GRADES[ 9 ] | 3 | 1 |
| GRADES[ 10 ] | 3 | 2 |
| GRADES[ 11 ] | 3 | 3 |
| GRADES[ 12 ] | 3 | 4 |

Here GRADES[1] would be the grade of the 1st student on the 1st exam, GRADES[2] would be the grade of the 2nd student on the 1st exam, and so on.  If we wanted the average of all students on all exams we could simply add them together and divide by 12.  But what if we wanted the average of each student or the average on each exam?  Then we have to do some thinking.  Which elements or cells relate to the third student?  Which relate to the second exam?  We would have to contrive some scheme so that we could reference each variable if we knew the exam number (1,2, or 3) and the student number (1, 2, 3 or 4).  It's not too hard, actually. You can verify that if I is the exam number and J is the student number, then the proper subscript value, K, is given by the formula

$$K := (I-1)*NS+J$$

where NS is the number of students.  For example, the grade on the 2nd exam by the 3rd student is found in cell 7.

But there is a simpler way to think of these 12 data. Conceptualize them in "two-dimensional" fashion as three sets of four numbers each (or four sets of three numbers each).  Graphically, we might depict such a representation as:

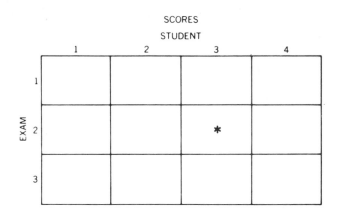

Here, for example, we would store the grade made on the second exam by the third student in the box marked *.

If we imagine the graphical representation above as an array in the machine, extending our concept of the subscripted variable a bit, we might call the location with the * by the name SCORES[2,3]. Isn't that a more meaningful description of the grade on the second exam by the third student than GRADES [7]?

To declare a variable which would have twelve locations known as SCORES[1,1], SCORES[1,2], SCORES[1,3], SCORES[1,4], SCORES[2,1], ..., SCORES [3,4], the programmer would write

```
        VAR
            SCORES: ARRAY[1..3,1..4] OF REAL;
```

An array declared in this way is called a doubly subscripted variable, a matrix variable, or a two-dimensional array. Each time such a variable name is used it is appended with two subscripts, separated by a comma. The first of these indicates the row number and the second indicates the column number.

All the rules which applied to singly subscripted variables apply here.

Use of doubly subscripted variables is not much more difficult than singly subscripted variables. Consider an example using the array SCORES declared above. Here is a set of statements which would read in twelve numbers and define each member of the array SCORES.

```
        PROGRAM EXAMS (INPUT, OUTPUT);
            VAR
                I: (* THE ROW INDEX *) INTEGER;
                J: (* THE COLUMN INDEX *) INTEGER;
                SCORES: (* THE EXAM SCORE MATRIX *)
                    ARRAY [1..3,1..4] OF REAL;
            BEGIN
            FOR I := 1 TO 3 DO
                FOR J := 1 TO 4 DO
                    READ (SCORES [I,J]);
                    •
                    •
                    •
```

The operation of the program segment involves a "loop within a loop" which, in flowchart language, might look like this:

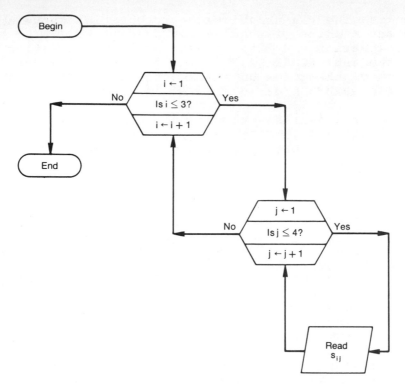

If you carefully follow the above algorithm through, you see that I and J take on the successive values:

| I | J |
|---|---|
| 1 | 1 |
| 1 | 2 |
| 1 | 3 |
| 1 | 4 |
| 2 | 1 |
| 2 | 2 |
| 2 | 3 |
| 2 | 4 |
| 3 | 1 |
| 3 | 2 |
| 3 | 3 |
| 3 | 4 |

which is, of course, what is desired.

If you are satisfied that you understand how the statements above read values into the proper locations, we

will now consider a slightly more complicated problem:
assuming that twelve locations are already defined, instruct
the computer to find the sum of scores for each student.
That is, we want four sums.  The first represents the sum of
the three numbers in the first column, etc.  How might these
four sums be stored?  (If your answer is: in a singly
subscripted variable, give yourself ten points.)  Let us
declare the variable STUDENT:

```
VAR
     STUDENT: (*COMMENT*) ARRAY[ 1..4] OF REAL;
```

Now we could write the statements to form the sums.  When we
were adding up several numbers in a loop using scalar
variables we used a statement

```
S := S+X
```

to accumulate the values of X.  Clearly such a procedure
worked only because we defined S to be zero before we began
the addition process.

    In our present problem we are faced with a similar
situation.  Now we must define four accumulators to have the
value zero.  We can simply write:

```
FOR I := 1 TO 4 DO
    STUDENT[ I ] := 0.0
```

    With this piece of housekeeping done we write the
statements to actually form the four sums.  As in reading
numbers into the two-dimensional array, this process
requires one loop <u>nested</u> inside another.  In this example we
will consider the scores in column-wise order.  (When we
read them in before, we operated on them in a row-wise
order.)

```
FOR J := 1 TO 4 DO
    FOR I := 1 TO 3 DO
        STUDENT[ J ] := STUDENT[ J ] + SCORES[ I,J ]
```

    At the conclusion of this set of statements each value
in the array will have been added into the appropriate
accumulator; the singly subscripted array STUDENT could now
be printed out to give the column sums.

    Question: if we had operated on SCORES in row-wise
order, would we have computed the same answer for the values
of STUDENT[ 1 ], STUDENT[ 2 ], etc.?  In other words, would

```
FOR I := 1 TO 3 DO
     FOR J := 1 TO 4 DO
          STUDENT[J] := STUDENT[J]+SCORES[I,J]
```

produce the same result?

The TIPS language does not limit construction of arrays
to only one or two dimensions.  There is considerable
capability for multi-dimensional arrays.  Of course, as the
number of elements in arrays increases, the amount of
computer storage used grows also.  Therefore, in fact, very
large, multi-dimensional arrays are not practical.

To illustrate the declaration of a five-dimensional
array, we could write

```
     VAR
          X: ARRAY[1..5,1..28,1..20,1..9,1..10] OF REAL;
```

This instruction attempts to reserve an array of five
dimensions which contains a total of 252,000 variable
locations, an amount not normally available to programmers.

---

The number of dimensions for arrays

allowed in your machine is _____.

---

## Summary of Rules for Subscripted Variables

Now you should have a general view of subscripted
variables, how they are declared, how they are used, and
what they mean.  A summary of the rules governing
subscripted variables follows:

1.   Subscripted variables must be declared once and only
     once using the single VAR instruction in the
     program.  The standard form of the declaration is:

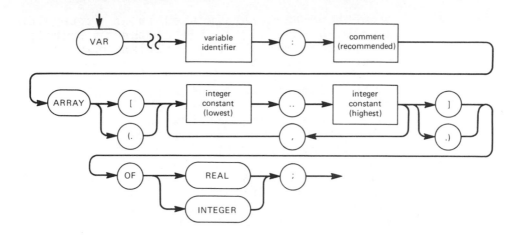

where "variable" is an identifier; "lowest" and
"highest" are two <u>integer</u> <u>constants</u> <u>written</u> <u>as</u>
<u>sequences</u> <u>of</u> <u>digits</u> <u>without</u> <u>decimal</u> <u>points</u> which
designate the smallest and largest subscripts which
may be used in conjunction with the variable.
Variables or expressions may not be used for
"lowest" or "highest" in the VAR declaration here.
The constants used here are not subscripts; they are
memory reservation quantities.  Do not confuse a
subscript, which may be a constant, a variable or an
arithmetic expression, with the reservation quantity
in a VAR declaration.

The number of variable locations reserved in memory
for the variable is

        highest minus lowest plus one

This rule applies whether either or both designators
are negative.  The locations reserved by the VAR
instruction will be numbered consecutively,
beginning with the lowest.

2.   Declaration of a subscripted variable does not
     define the value of any of its entries.  The
     programmer may not assume that subscripted variable
     locations contain zeros when they are declared.  If
     zeros are desired in the array, the programmer must
     put them there.

3. If an element of an array is used in an expression (for example, on the right side of the := symbol) or in a WRITELN statement, two quantities must have been previously defined:

   a. The value of the subscript.

   b. The value of the particular location in the array referred to by the subscript.

   If a single element of an array appears in a READLN statement or to the left of the := symbol in an assignment statement, the value of the subscript must have been previously defined.

4. Subscripts are INTEGER quantities, since they refer to discrete, separate locations in the computer's memory. That is, there is no such location as

   WOOPS[ 12.8345 ]

   Thus subscripts in TIPS must be of type INTEGER.

5. A subscript may be any valid INTEGER arithmetic expression. The value of any subscript, whether a constant, variable or expression, must lie between the values "lowest" and "highest" inclusive. That is, a variable declared as

   VAR RULEFIVE: ARRAY [ 1..44 ] OF REAL;

   could not be subscripted with any constant, variable or expression whose value was less than 1 or greater than 44.

6. The name chosen by the programmer as a subscripted variable name must conform to the same rules for name choice as scalar variables.

7. A programmer must not declare a scalar variable and a subscripted variable by the same name. A variable name, whether scalar or subscripted, may appear only once in the VAR declaration of a program and it must not be the same as the PROGRAM or PROCEDURE name.

8. A subscript is not a variable! A subscript is a number. You may use a constant to stand for that

number or you may use a variable or expression to
stand for that number, but the subscript itself, at
the time a program is executed, is a number.


## Exercises

What, if anything, is wrong with in the following?

a. VAR
        B,C,D[ 1..100 ]: INTEGER;

b. VAR
        PAY: ARRAY [I..J] OF REAL;

c. VAR
        PAY: ARRAY [ 10..20 ] OF REAL;
    BEGIN
    PAY[ 1 ] := 0;

d. VAR
        PAY: ARRAY [ 10..20 ] OF REAL;
        K: INTEGER;
    BEGIN
    K := 15;
    PAY[ K ] := 0;

e. VAR
        PAY: ARRAY [ 10..20,5..55] OF REAL;
        K: INTEGER;
    BEGIN
    K := 15;
    PAY[ K ] := 0;

f. VAR
        PAY: ARRAY [ 10..20,5..55] OF REAL;
        K: INTEGER;
    BEGIN
    K := 15;
    PAY[ K,K*2 ] := 0;

Based on the previous example with the array SCORES, write a complete program which will find and print the average of the scores of each student, the average of the scores made on each of the three tests, and the average of all students on all tests.  Supply data for the problem and check the results.  Draw a flowchart in the space below before writing the program.  Use comments in your program.

Before you run a set of test data, work out the answers you expect the computer to produce.  It is too easy to be prejudiced toward the answers your program produces if you wait until after the run to work out the test results.  Besides, you will probably learn something about your problem by actually getting your hands dirty with some data.

In some senses a program, with a computer executing its instructions, can be considered as a "black box" into which data flow and out of which output and answers come. By calling the program a "black box," it is suggested that the user of such a program need not know how the program does what it does in order to be able to use it. The user needs only know what inputs the program expects and what outputs it produces.

There are several difficulties with the idea expressed above. So many, in fact, that the entire process of computer programming is undergoing radical change. We illustrate these difficulties by first asking questions.

1.  Does the program really work correctly in every instance? How can the correctness of the program be shown without an analysis of how it does what it does? Is showing that the program produces correct results in a set of "test cases" sufficient proof of its correctness?

2.  If the program is found to contain an error, can it be fixed without unreasonable effort by the person who wrote it--especially if he or she hasn't looked at it in some time?

3.  Suppose the person who wrote the program is not available to make repairs? Can someone else do it?

4.  Is there enough information written down about--or within--the program so that a person who doesn't know how it works can use it effectively?

5.  Suppose that some large information-handling task needs to be done and we decide to do it by having several people participate in the writing of a large computer program. If programmers are people who simply produce "black boxes," can we be assured that the resulting composite program will work correctly?

6.  Programs are usually written by people for other people (students for teachers, employees for employers, etc.). Can the person bearing the general responsibility for the program's correctness examine the program and, with no more than a reasonable effort, follow the program's logic? Can he or she understand the algorithm, or, if

the person knows the algorithm, can he or she determine if it has been correctly implemented?

All these questions suggest that there is more to programming than simply producing a "working" program.

In the late 1960's serious proposals began to be advanced regarding the structure of programs, primarily to respond to the difficulties reflected by these questions. Some of the techniques used have come to be called, brilliantly enough, structured programming. In this text we have repeatedly made reference to good programming practice --remember all those shaded boxes. Structured programming might be considered another extension of that idea.


Fractured Programming

The vast majority of programs which have been written since the electronic computer came of age are bad. (With our value judgement "bad" we will tip our hats to the idea expressed among humanists that there are no bad people--only people who sometimes do bad things. Maybe that's a good idea, but programs don't have feelings, so we will call a program which does bad things, ever, a bad program.)

A bad program may be bad in several ways:

1.  It is incorrect. It does not solve the problem it was intended to solve.

2.  It is poorly documented. Thus a person who has a problem similar to the one that the program purports to solve has difficulty using the program.

3.  It is untrustworthy. It may be correct, but no demonstration of its correctness is presented, so a person using it or relying on its results has no asssurance that the answers it produces are right.

4.  It is difficult to understand and therefore difficult to modify if the situation or circumstances change; furthermore, it is difficult to fix if an error is discovered.

Bad programs are the product of a process which we call fractured programming. It is fractured programming which has produced the image which society quite correctly has of the whole computing industry.  **If we were engineers our bridges would fall down more often than they stayed up.** Programmers have paid tacit homage to the preposterous belief that a program was good if it obeyed the syntactic rules of the language and produced the correct answers.  For an industry that has moved as quickly as the automated information-handling industry has, it's been pretty slow to realize that this idea is absurd.

The results of this realization, however belated, have been many and varied.  Some of the words associated with the desire to divorce ourselves from fractured programming are: structured programming, modular programming, good programming practice, top down development, proving program correctness, and GOTO-less programming.

## Structured Programming: Canonical Forms

Structured programming means different things to different people.  But most who talk about structured programming can agree that a few basic ideas are always involved.  We look at these ideas first and then proceed to other matters which some call structured programming and others call by other names such as modular programming or good programming practice.

The first core idea is that every algorithm can be expressed in terms of the three basic (sometimes called canonical) composition rules we discussed before: sequence (then), selection (if-then-else), and iteration (while-do).

The sequence structure is included primarily to indicate the basic progression by which algorithmic problem solving takes place.

The selection structure is based on the idea that a test is made during the execution of a program and the result dictates either of two paths which later join and exit from the structure together.

The third form, iteration, indicates that a test is made and, depending on the result of the test, an immediate exit from the structure is made, or a set of statements is executed and then the condition is retested.  The set of statements at some time modify the condition being tested or the loop will continue indefinitely.

Each of the forms has but one entrance and one exit. There is a mathematical proof that any algorithm which has but one entrance and one exit (we have previously called this a proper algorithm) can be expressed by using only these three structures combined by linking and nesting.

The three canonical forms, plus the concept of invoking procedures form the basis of structured, modular, and sensible programming.

## North-to-South Programming

There is nothing particularly magic about the canonical forms. But the fact that all proper algorithms can be represented using only combinations of them suggests that some sort of common denominator for the order of program statements has been found. Future benefits may accrue if programs are written using the canonical forms; it is impossible to predict how far-reaching the results will be-- maybe fundamental changes in the ways programs are written, or computers writing programs themselves or . . .

But there is an immediate advantage in using the canonical forms and PROCEDUREs that is recognized by the "leading edge" of the programming community. That advantage is that programs become much more readable. The canonical forms make the logical order of the statements (the dynamic order, the order of execution) more like the physical order (the static order, the order of compilation).

This means that you can read a program from "north to south" when you are trying to understand what it does. There can be no wild transfers of control to distant parts of the program unless the canonical form (or structure) containing the branch extends that far and encompasses everything in between. And there can't be too many of these far-ranging structures, because, given any two structures, either (1) one follows the other or (2) one contains the other--they may not overlap.

The effect of this congruence, however rough, between physical order and logical order produces a simplifying effect similar to that which occurs, on another subject, when the base of the number system (say, base 10) is the same as the base of the measuring system (say, metric). While in a theoretical sense the answers may turn out the

same whichever measuring system is used, in a practical
sense the ease with which the process occurs is
substantially increased.


## Systematic Program Development

This section ends PART I in which you have learned the
complete TIPS language plus a good bit about the structure,
format, and characteristics of good programs.  But while you
know the ingredients of good programs you probably don't as
yet really know how to go about putting them together.  At
the moment it seems difficult enough just to get a program
which will make the machine do what you want it to do.
Building programs which are also well commented, well
structured, readable, properly indented, and so forth may
seem like an extra burden.

The truth of the matter is that developing a good
program to solve a problem is easier than quickly putting
together the instructions for a not-so-good program.  In
PART II of the book we concentrate completely on the subject
of the systematic development of programs in the TIPS
language.  We won't add any new language features.  For the
most part, we will be synthesizing material you are already
familiar with.  By the time you have studied PART II and
worked some of the Laboratory Problems there, you'll know
how to produce first-rate programs.

Notes usually provide additional information for the instructor; the student can, for the most part, ignore them. In some instances they explain why certain simplifications are being used in the teaching of the language. Notes occasionally assume previous knowledge of the language.

Note 1: Although it may be that an answer is required so quickly that there isn't time for a person to calculate it.

Note 2: PASCAL has a number of syntax diagrams which define an expression. We consider them too formal to be of much use to the beginning student. We rely instead on the student's understanding of an algebraic expression. The formal diagrams (expression, simple expression, term and factor) appear on in Appendix F for those who are interested.

Note 3: We introduce the concepts of condition, comparison operator, and logical operator for pedagogical reasons; they are not defined in standard PASCAL. Our comparison operators are the same as the PASCAL relational opeators, less the "IN" operator; our logical operators are those that are normally used when evaluating Boolean expressions.

Note 4: FORTRAN and PL/ONE programmers beware: PASCAL has different priorities for the arithmetic and logical operators than those which might be familiar to you.

Note 5: The hexagonal block is not a generally recognized flowchart symbol; its usefulness overrides its lack of official sanction.

Note 6: PROCEDURES in TIPS have no arguments.

Note 7: The algorithms employed in Lab Problems 12 and 13 are not particularly efficient or effective; they do, however, serve to illustrate the use of subscripted variables and allow the solution of fairly complicated problems in a straightforward manner.

# part II

# PROGRAM DEVELOPMENT

Once a computer program is correctly written, the problem it addresses is essentially solved.  Only time, money for the computer, correct data, and the will of the program owner are required to get the answers.

Therefore, the real issue of concern is: how do you get from the description of a particular problem to a TIPS program which tells the machine how to solve the problem. Well, we can't tell you exactly.  Nor can anyone else because designing an algorithm to solve a problem is just that: designing.  And a design process cannot be specified completely in advance.  If it could -- that is, if it were reducible to an algorithm -- then the world wouldn't need programmers.  We could just program a computer to write its own programs.

We can help you learn the fundamentals of the design process, suggest some ways to stay out of trouble, give you examples and trial problems, show you how to organize your thinking, and wish you luck.

In this Part of the text we will not take up any new language features or instructions.  Rather, we will help you learn to develop computer programs from problem statements. We will show you examples and help you solve problems using the TIPS language.  Let's look at the requirements of the job and the tools available to get it done.


## Requirements

1.  A problem which is precisely defined and understood.

2.  A TIPS program which will instruct the machine to solve the problem.

3.  A TIPS program which can easily be read, understood, corrected, and modified by you or someone else familiar with TIPS or PASCAL.

4.  Some sort of guarantee, absolute or partial, that the program will solve the problem.

1.  Your ability to reason and comprehend.

2.  Knowledge of the TIPS language.

3.  The idea of repeated refinement (sometimes called "hierarchical development" or "top down design").

4.  The three logic-control structures: sequence, selection, and iteration.

5.  The concept of PROCEDUREs --to aid in breaking the program down into parts, or modules, related in a hierarchical structure.

6.  Flowcharting technique to deal with the more difficult logical issues which arise.

7.  Comments in the program listing.

8.  Formatting (indentation) of the program statements.

Integrating the use of all these tools to produce a program is something that, up to this point in the history of computing, is rarely done or taught.  It's talked about a lot, but some major tools are generally omitted when an actual method for program development is suggested.  We now present an integrating mechanism which will allow you to begin with the hierarchical development idea at the beginning and arrive at a complete, fully commented and formatted TIPS (or PASCAL) program as a result.  It does not require that you write and rewrite the program as the development takes place.

The mechanism for aiding the design process is called a Program Development Scroll. It begins with a problem statement and ends with a working, tested, readable and well-structured program. Program development, despite the protestations and wishes of many in the computer science community, is a rather individual exercise (although the component parts of a large program may be developed by many individuals). It depends not only on the nature of the problem to be solved, but on the nature of the problem solver as well. We suggest you study the Program Development Scroll technique, and decide if it, or some modification of it, will help you program a computer effectively.

A Program Development Scroll begins as simply a blank piece of paper some twenty-five to fifty (or more) centimeters (10 - 20 inches) deep and very wide. An actual scroll would be rolled but you can cash in on its primary virtue, i.e., continuity, by using fanfold computer printout paper. A Program Development Scroll is "cartooned" on the next two pages. Understanding it completely will come with the following section in which we tackle a sample problem .

# PROGRAM DEVELOPMENT SCROLL

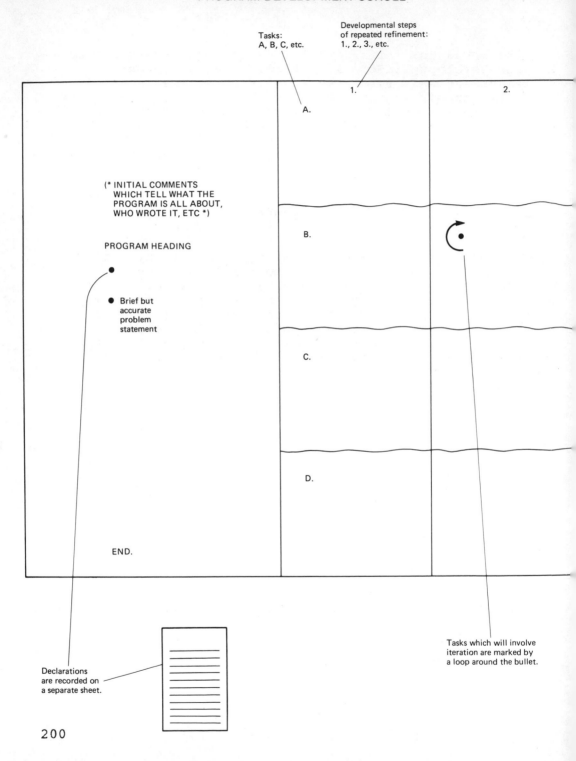

Tasks:
A, B, C, etc.

Developmental steps
of repeated refinement:
1., 2., 3., etc.

1.

2.

A.

(* INITIAL COMMENTS
WHICH TELL WHAT THE
PROGRAM IS ALL ABOUT,
WHO WROTE IT, ETC *)

PROGRAM HEADING

● Brief but
   accurate
   problem
   statement

B.

C.

D.

END.

Declarations
are recorded on
a separate sheet.

Tasks which will involve
iteration are marked by
a loop around the bullet.

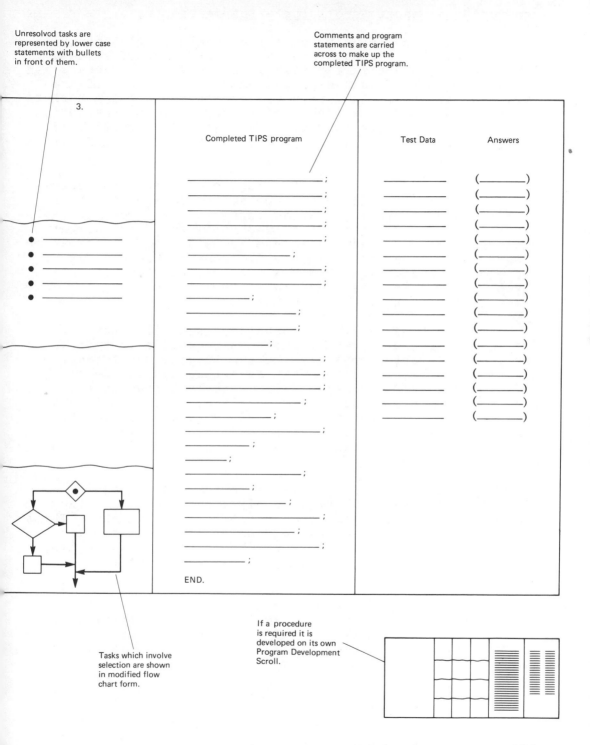

Unresolved tasks are
represented by lower case
statements with bullets
in front of them.

Comments and program
statements are carried
across to make up the
completed TIPS program.

3.

Completed TIPS program

Test Data          Answers

END.

Tasks which involve
selection are shown
in modified flow
chart form.

If a procedure
is required it is
developed on its own
Program Development
Scroll.

# Program Development Scroll for a Sample Problem

Let's take a sample problem and develop a TIPS program
to solve it. Here's the problem: Given a set of values,
find the median ("middle") value. One way to begin this is
to sort the set of values from lowest to highest. If the
number of values is odd, then the median is just the number
in the middle. If the number of values is even, the median
is the average of the two middle values. For example, if
the values are 8, 5.5, -31, 0, and 3, the median is 3. What
is the median of 6, 3, 2, and 1?

We now describe to you the program development process
which underlies the **fold-out page at the back of the book.**
We begin in the upper left-hand corner where a comment which
describes the problem to be solved appears. This comment
will be carried ultimately across the width of the scroll to
describe the final program itself. Beneath the comment is
the program heading PROGRAM FINDMEDN (INPUT, OUTPUT); which
gives the program a name and tells how the program
communicates with its environment.

Following the heading information is a brief but
completely accurate problem statement. Notice that it is
preceded by a dot or bullet. On the Program Development
Scroll, a bullet indicates that something has not been
resolved into TIPS program steps. The last item in this
leftmost column is "END." which optimistically heralds the
completion of the program. The "END." keyword, like the
initial comment and the program heading, will ultimately be
carried  directly across to the right to form part of the
completed program.

Next, we break this problem into tasks A through F.
Different problems will require different numbers of tasks.
Deciding on the tasks is usually something of an art. These
tasks, when put together, should solve the whole problem.
They should be sequential. They should break the problem
along sensible lines. And they should address the difficult
issues of the problem.

We will use a number of steps to refine this problem
into a program. We number these "refinements" horizontally
1, 2, 3, etc. across the top of the scroll. Each task (or
subproblem) will not necessarily reach the same level of
refinement in each step.

## Remarks on the Sample Program Development Scroll

(Refer to the Sample Program Development Scroll--that's the fold-out sheet at the back of the book--while reading this section.)  Also refer to the Declarations at the end of this section.


Task  A--Refinement 1

>    A clear first step.  We don't say what values, or how to get them into the machine, because we are doing the simplest breakdown of the problem.  There is time enough later to refine this step.


Task  B--Refinement 1

>    There are other ways to determine the median (e.g., pair the highest and lowest; pair the next highest and next lowest, etc.) but we've decided to use the sorting approach.  This kind of decision on method should precede the start of the Program Development Scroll.


Task  C--Refinement 1

>    It probably isn't a very big deal to determine if the number of values is odd or even but it is a vital part of getting the answer.  We will give the number of values the name NUMBER and make it an INTEGER quantity.  We record this fact here and also on a separate declaration sheet in the form it will appear in the TIPS program.


Task  D--Refinement 1

>    Here we've obviously thought about the problem a little more.  The idea of the index or position of the middle value implies that an array will probably be used to store the sorted numbers.

## Task E--Refinement 1

The answer to the problem is a single number which
we decide to call MEDIAN. It is not restricted to
an integer value so we make it REAL. We also record
it on the declaration sheet.

## Task F--Refinement 1

We will have to write out the value of the median
and, we suspect, some other values as well. What
these other outputs are will have to await future
refinement steps. It is important not to get bogged
down in details at this point. The first stage of
refinement is to break the problem into some
manageable steps without much detail. Concentrate
on a sequence of single statements, each of which is
a general, but accurate, description of something
which must be done.

## Task A--Refinement 2

We decide to define the number of values in the
list, NUMBER, by reading it in. Here we write the
first actual TIPS instruction: READ (NUMBER) Notice
that we don't put a semicolon after it. Semicolons
can only be inserted later when we know that they
are appropriate. We also decide to use an array,
VALUES, to store the values and declare it to have
50 elements. We will call this maximum value (50)
MAXIMUM. (The CONST declaration, which formalizes
and improves on this method, is covered in Part
III.) Notice that we will use a variable to denote
the value 50 whenever we can. If in the future we
want to change this problem to handle 100 or 1000
values, fewer changes will be required.

## Task B--Refinement 2

We can write a comment here because we know sorting
is a necessary step. This comment will be
incorporated into the program as will all comments
and program statements written on the Program
Development Scroll. Our uncertainty about exactly
how we are going to sort the array shouldn't slow us
down. An accurate comment seldom hurts.

Task C--Refinement 2

   Here we are dealing with the issue of finding out
   whether NUMBER is odd or even. We aren't making
   much progress. That's okay. Each task is
   different; each refinement is different. The
   important thing is to deal with each task each time
   through the refinement process.


Task D--Refinement 2

   Here we have decided to calculate a single value,
   MIDDLE, which will represent the "middle" of the
   array. We will have to figure out how to calculate
   it soon, but just knowing we have to do it and
   getting a comment down about it is progress.


Task E--Refinement 2

   Since we know the array name, the middle value index
   name, and the name of the median we can state a
   description of the solution using those names.


Task F--Refinement 2

   Now we have made a decision as to some of the output
   We will print the sorted list, which will require a
   looping structure so we use a circular arrow around
   the bullet. We will print some indication of
   whether the number of values in the list, NUMBER, is
   odd or even because we sense a potential for trouble
   if we get it wrong. And, of course, we will write
   out the median value, MEDIAN.


Task A--Refinement 3

   A little warning bell in our brain tells us that the
   program could fail if NUMBER isn't in the proper
   range. So we plan here to put in a check. The
   small diamond around the bullet indicates that a
   decision will be required at that point. We also
   write the instructions to get the array VALUES into
   the machine. Again, the clockwise arrow around the
   bullet indicates that a looping structure will be
   required to perform the function.

## Task B--Refinement 3

We decide to write a separate procedure to sort the
array VALUES. To include it in this program would
produce more than a page of instructions--something
we want to avoid. So we will borrow it from another
source or develop it as a procedure in its own
right, with a Program Development Scroll of its own.


## Task C--Refinement 3

We review the text on TIPS and realize that we can
use the MOD operator to determine whether NUMBER is
odd or even.


## Tasks D & E--Refinement 3

Here we feel the need of a flowchart because some
decision-making logic is involved. We can put the
flowchart directly on the Program Development
Scroll. **Or, if we need more room, we can use a
separate sheet for the flowcharts, and simply note
the sheet number on the Program Development Scroll.**

If NUMBER is odd then NUMBER DIV 2 + 1 is the
position of the middle value of the list and the
median is just that value. If NUMBER is even then
NUMBER DIV 2 is the position of the first of the two
middle values. Then MEDIAN is the average of that
value and the next one.

We've combined Tasks D and E. Sometimes it makes
more sense to let two tasks collapse into one. Here
we've established a path of control through the
algorithm based on the oddness or evenness of NUMBER
and it's better to go ahead and calculate the median
before bringing the two paths of control back
together again.


## Task F--Refinement 3

We now can write the statements to output VALUES,
NUMBER, and MIDDLE, so that we can check the inputs
and intermediate calculations in the problem. And
we output the value of MEDIAN. But we still haven't

figured out the odd-even indicator so we aren't
quite ready to write the statement even though we
know what we want to say.

## Task A--Refinement 4

More progress on input.

## Task B--Refinement 4

We have decided to name the sorting routine
SORTARRY, for "sort array."  We still have to write
the routine.

## Task C--Refinement 4

We decide on a way to indicate whether NUMBER is odd
or even: we define a variable ODDNMBR to indicate
the existence of a middle value.  If there is a
middle value, ODDNMBR will be set to 1; otherwise it
will be set to 0 (zero).  A comment tells the story.
ODDNMBR will be an integer.  (An alternative
approach, Boolean switches, will be covered in Part
III.)

## Tasks D & E--Refinement 4

We take a shot at transforming the flowchart into
TIPS program instructions.

## Task F--Refinement 4

This takes care of getting the odd-even indicator,
ODDNMBR, written out.  For the final program we will
bring all the previously constructed TIPS statements
and comments over from the previous refinements.

## Task A--Refinement 5

We write the "NUMBER in range" statements as

```
IF (NUMBER<1) OR (NUMBER>MAXIMUM) THEN
    WRITELN (' ERROR. NUMBER=',NUMBER)
ELSE
```

We include the ELSE clause because, if NUMBER is not
in range, we don't want to continue with the rest of
the program. Now all the input statements and
comments are ready. We just have to bring them over
from the previous refinements, add in the
appropriate semicolons, BEGIN's and END's. We defer
that until we are sure the whole program is ready.


Task B--Refinement 5

All we have to do is say SORTARRY to invoke the
routine. And yes, we still have to write it. But
now we know the approach (TIPS Lab Problem 13).
We'll write the procedure SORTARRY on a separate
program development scroll.


Task C--Refinement 5

Well, that's certainly a master stroke. The value
of ODDNMBR can be set just by noticing that it is
NUMBER MOD 2. We would cross out the TIPS
instructions in Task C--Refinement 4.


Tasks D & E--Refinement 5

Did we really write that mess in Refinement 4?
Rewrite! We will correct indentation!


Task F--Refinement 5

No more statements with bullets to resolve. We're
done here.


Tasks A,B,C,D,E & F--Refinement 6

Now it's all together. All program statements and
comments which have been previously written appear
here now with perhaps an improvement or two. We add
delimiters (such as BEGIN and END) and punctuation

```
```

(i.e., semicolons) to link the elements together. We clean up any indentation problems, make sure everything is in the right order--and we've got the completed program. We moved from a problem statement to a completed program in six refinement steps.

Some people might argue that the comment in Task A - Refinement 2 resembles the program statement there too much and that you should leave the comment out. You can listen to these arguments. But don't heed them. There are essentially two ways to read a good program listing: (1) read the comments to get a general idea of what's going on and what the various sections of the program are, and (2) read the programmer's instructions to the machine itself to find out, in detail, how a portion of the problem was solved. If the comment and the program statement happen to say the same thing, it's acceptable. Leaving out a pertinent comment might not be. The comments and the program steps are two different descriptions of the algorithm. One is for people, the other is for the machine. Each section -- the comment and the TIPS instructions -- should describe separately what is happening in the program.

Now that you've read this section straight through, go back and read it in a different order. First look at Task A, Refinements 1, 2, 3, 4, 5, 6; then Task B, Refinements 1, 2, 3, 4, 5, 6; Task C, etc.

```
Declarations for Sample Program Development Scroll

VAR
    I      : (* INDEX COUNTER *)                INTEGER;
    MAXIMUM: (* MAXIMUM NUMBER OF VALUES *)     INTEGER;
    MEDIAN : (* VALUE TO BE FOUND *)            REAL;
    MIDDLE : (* INDEX OF MIDDLE NUMBER *)       INTEGER;
    NUMBER : (* THE NUMBER OF NUMBERS *)        INTEGER;
    ODDNMBR: (* TO INDICATE ODD OR EVEN *)      INTEGER;
    VALUES : (* SET OF VALUES *)ARRAY [1..50] OF REAL;
```

## Testing the Sample Program

We are not, of course, finished. Not even when we write the routine SORTARRY and put the whole thing into the computer.

**We must carefully test the program!  We must do our best to break it, to try to make it fail.**

So we show a "seventh refinement": a set of test data. Our first attempts can be small. We try with three numbers--after we've figured out the answers by other means first. Then we try those three numbers in different orders, since the program's working depends on sorting the numbers. Then try it with negative numbers. Now, since the program operates differently on an even number of values than an odd number, try several sets of four values, with different signs and orders.

Now try the program at its limits: one value, zero values, fifty values, fifty-one values. Will it produce a value of zero for the median with both even and odd lists? Will it work on integers, on real numbers, on E-form numbers?

One thing you have probably decided with all this testing is that the program should be designed to read in several sets of data rather than having to be rerun for each data set. Make this modification to the program and run it, with a lot of test data.

When testing an algorithm for correctness, "boundary-line" examples of the problem can often prove that the algorithm is incorrect. For example, boundary definitions of the median algorithm would involve a problem with only one value (NUMBER=1) or the maximum values (NUMBER=50).

Showing <u>program</u> <u>correctness</u> is why we perform testing
and debugging (the process of finding "bugs" or mistakes).
Testing is a necessary (but not sufficient) process for
arriving at a belief that a program is correct.  Put more
pessimistically by one of the acknowledged authorities in
the field: program testing can be used to show the presence
of bugs but never their absence.  Nevertheless, testing is
worth doing, and it is important.  Showing the presence of
bugs is a worthwhile endeavor.  A program can only have so
many bugs--though that can be a lot--and every one you find
means there is one fewer.  The more extensive and creative
your testing is, the higher your probability of finding all
of the bugs.  Secondly, while you can never be sure that
there aren't any bugs in a program, if you've done careful
testing, you begin to develop this confidence that "by
George, this thing might be OK."  After all, no one
guarantees that the sun will rise every day, but observation
suggests....

Testing should be an integral part of programming;
debugging, you hope, won't be.  Write your programs
carefully, test each part separately to the extent that you
can.  Consider any errors which show up as a serious attack
on your quality as a programmer.  Ask why they happened.
More time is spent debugging programs than is spent writing
them in the first place.  That's an awful statistic.  And
the reason for it is that many programmers are careless and
do not plan ahead.  A prevalent attitude seems to be: some
errors are inevitable--why worry?

The most important thing about testing, bar none, is the
will to do it.  It really does take fortitude, not to
mention time and thought, to try to find fault with
something you have just created.  If you are dedicated to
really doing a good job of testing, half the battle is won.

The volume of test data can initially be small.  Since
small amounts of carefully conceived data can detect many
errors, early program testing with large amounts of data is
normally wasteful.

Much has been written about testing.  The procedures are
different depending on the application and on the potential
weak spots.  What follows are thoughts which you might find

appropriate. One is to let the machine do some of the testing for you. Don't overlook the possibility that you can use the computer to generate test data for you.

It is important to develop several sets of test data. Start with a small set for which you know the answers. If your program handles that satisfactorily, go on to more stringent data. If the program seems to do well when it is being given good input, try data which will exercise some of the error-checking capabilities. Will it tell you what's wrong? Will it blissfully pretend that a zero by zero matrix is fine? Or that a 28-foot tall person is okay?

It seems surprising that a program can pass many artificial tests, no matter how punishing, and can fail with the real data that are supposedly correct, polished, and well-behaved. Surprising, but it happens. Part of your test data should be real data for which you know the answers. Whether the data you use are real or artificial, you should calculate the answers ahead of time and then compare them with the computer's results. If you get the program output and then try to verify the results by hand, the chances are that you'll succeed--even if the computer's answers are wrong.

One innovative technique for program testing, if you have the ego for it, is game testing. The procedure goes like this: you write the most idiot-proof program you can (that is, you write the program so that any improper data will be detected by the program). Then give the program to a person who has agreed to test it for you. He or she may not alter the program, but may subject it to the most punishing tests which can be devised. He or she attempts to break the program by giving it bad data, misreading your documentation, misinterpreting the results, etc. If your opponent is bright and dedicated to the project, and the process continues with you modifying the program each time he or she finds a bug or weak spot, ultimately you will have a sturdy program.

Finally, don't let anything the least bit peculiar slip by without an explanation. "Inconsequential" errors have a way of developing into full blown disasters at the most awkward times. There is really no such thing as a "small" error or a "little" bug in a program. A computer program is made up of a finite number of discrete symbols: either they are all there in the proper order or they are not. Program correctness is a binary matter: it either exists or it doesn't.

## Why Bugs?

"An ounce of prevention is worth a pound of cure." This trite expression is nowhere truer than in the field of computer programming.

Debugging is a difficult thing to talk about because so much of what you do to make things right depends on what you did wrong in the first place. Trying to think about where you were least careful in the programming process frequently provides a clue regarding the source of the problem(s).

We could take the hard line and simply exhort you not to make any mistakes, but, having made one ourselves once, we understand that it can happenn. So we follow here with some general thoughts about debugging and avoiding the need for it.

## The "Throw It at the Machine" Syndrome

There is a tendency to write a computer program quickly, enter it quickly, and run it. The rationale is that "the computer can debug it for me." The computer can find syntactical errors in statements and find some coarse errors in logic such as use of undeclared variables. But these are the errors which are relatively easy to catch anyway. What the computer cannot do is find most errors in logic--if you said X:=A+B when you meant X:=A-B or IF D=E rather than IF D<E.

There are two major ways to find logic errors. One is to run the program with data--test data, that is--and notice that the answers are wrong. But if you are in such a rush to get "on the air" with your program, the chances are poor that you'll carefully check it with test data. A second approach is to review the program carefully without a computer in the picture--to sit at a desk with a small set of sample data and carefully step through the algorithm. This should be done at both the program development stage and with the printed program listing. For difficult sections of logic the "how would I follow this algorithm if I were an idiot?" approach works quite nicely. Define a schematic computer on paper and, with pencil in hand, go through the logic.

The person who simply sets up a program in a hurry and tosses it at the computer is wasting both machine time and human time. Much more time will be spent debugging such a program than would have been spent in doing it right the first time. Add to all this the amazing satisfaction you feel when a complicated program works the first time, and you have several powerful arguments for careful desk checking of logic, syntax, data, and all keypunched material.

You will sometimes believe that you know exactly why a computer program fails, but be cautious. It often happens that one symptom has a variety of possible causes. Picking the first possible cause that comes to mind often results in a blind-alley, so be careful to consider other alternatives than the first one suspected.

## The "Data-Naiveness" Syndrome

A frequent source of difficulty in programming centers around the use of invalid or incorrect data. It is important for programmers to know the valid values of data, especially during the design phase of program development. Printing all input data (echoing) is often a good idea, especially in the development phase of programming. In this manner, you document the data that was input to the program so that you can check the logic of the program unambiguously. You can write:

```
READ (X,Y,Z);
WRITELN(X,Y,Z)
```

This will read data values for X, Y, and Z, and also print those values at the time of input.

If you echo the input data values, they will be available for later inspection and verification. There is no substitute for knowing which values went in.

There exists in the programming profession what might be called the "data naiveness" syndrome. This is a belief that whoever produces the data for input into a computer program will insure that these data are correct. It isn't usually so.

The programmer must assume that any possible data-garbage might be used as input to a program simply because people are error-prone no matter how much they try to be accurate. The program which blindly uses input data for

subscript purposes, for example, will not execute properly
some day--when invalid input is presented. Notice we say
"when" and not "if".

Therefore, it is necessary to imbed various data tests
into most computer programs. PASCAL contains features to
aid in some of these areas, but most must be invented by the
programmer, based on the specific assumptions and possible
values of the data involved.

For example, we might know the minimum and maximum
values of certain data; if so, we can test for data
validity. Suppose that we are writing a payroll program and
we know that the value of hourly wage should never exceed
$10 and should never be less than $3.30; in such a case, we
could test the incoming data values for these limits.

However, if we do this, we must carefully document the
restrictions so that when the company changes the minimum
and maximum values of the hourly wage, someone will be able
to quickly and accurately change the program. Or better yet,
these validity limits might be input each time as data.

## The "One-More-Bug" Syndrome

Most computer programmers are hard-working, clever
people who have a great deal of self-confidence in their
ability. It is difficult, early in their careers, for them
to believe that they make many mistakes.

Consequently, when a program does not operate properly, a
common thought is that there is "a" bug. In reality, there
may be many errors remaining. This results in finding what
appears to be "the" bug, rerunning, finding "the" bug,
rerunning, etc. It is a good bet that, if an error exists,
more than one error exists. So take a thorough look at
other program statements even after "the" bug has been
located.

## The "It-Cannot-Be-I" Syndrome

Prevalent in beginning programmers, at one time or
another, is the belief that the machine must have made an
error. Since programming logic can be complex and subtle,
programming errors do not usually pop out of the page.
Because the programmer has been so intensely involved in the
logic of the program, a mistake can often be overlooked many

times.  Therefore, after pouring over the logic dozens (or
even hundreds) of times without seeing an error, the
"natural" conclusion is that someone else (but no one else
has been involved) or something else (aha, the computer) has
committed an error.  In truth, though, almost all errors are
due to bad data or incorrect programs because most computers
are designed to check themselves; they usually report to the
operator or simply stop if a computer malfunction occurs.

Frequently a person completely unfamiliar with the
program under development can rather quickly spot errors
which the programmer has passed over many times before.  An
undefined variable can produce different symptoms on
different runs effectively reinforcing the It-Cannot-Be I
Syndrome.

## The "Now It's Finished for All Time" Myth

Most computer programs are similar to living organisms:
they either change or die.  When designing a computer
program, the programmer can begin to imagine what types of
changes may be reasonably expected in the future.  With this
in mind, the program can be designed to accommodate future
change more easily.  For example, instead of using the same
constant in many different statements, a variable which is
defined  early  in  the program or read as data can be used.
Then, if that value is to change, one program or data change
will be required rather than a change to each of the many
statements using that constant.  This approach also protects
against overlooking one or more statements using that
constant.

Centralizing input and output is also beneficial in
coping with change and in reducing errors introduced by
change.  If all input is grouped together within a program,
then changes to input data types or numbers of variables can
be more easily and effectively handled.

After six months (sometimes six days) of not working
with a particular program, the programmer forgets some of
the logic and subtle aspects of a program.  Comments
imbedded into the program can help refresh a poor
remembrance.

## The "Quick and Dirty" Syndrome

It is sometimes said that proper planning through testing and documentation is unnecessary for a particular project, because the computer program will only be used one time.  People who say this are usually wrong on two counts: Almost all programs which are originally intended to be used once are eventually used over and over.  And, proper planning is necessary to help insure program correctness. After all, who wants incorrect output--even if the program will really be run only once.

## Growing Pains

A major source of programming errors is changing program objectives or specifications during program development. When changes are needed after a program is partially written, programmers must either begin again or start patching and inserting new logic into existing logic.  While the former approach may often be superior, it is seldom feasible.  Therefore programs often become nightmares because program functions are changed without proper care. Proper indentation of statements suffers particularly.  The use of well documented logic can minimize the adverse impact of change; the continuing creation and revision of documented logic forces the programmer to more carefully define the initial program and set forth the precise changes when program modification is needed.

## Debugging Aids in PASCAL

PASCAL provides a wide range of error messages to help you know what went wrong.  In particular, they tell you if you attempt to use a variable you haven't defined (that's probably "Mistake Number 1" on the Programmer's Top Thirty) and if you attempt to use an illegal subscript.  PASCAL error messages are safety devices--good to have when you need them, bad to develop a dependency on.  Each time you get an error message you should think seriously about why it happened.  Then make changes in the way you produce programs to reduce the probability that it will happen again.  You might even start a log of "Goofs I Have Made."  A year of writing down your programming goofs would probably make quite a good programmer out of you.  (You will find the PASCAL error messages in Appendix E.)

Several laboratory problems follow which you can work
using the TIPS language.  For each problem you work
construct a Program Development Scroll.  Test each one with
data you devise.


\* \* \* \* \* \* \* \* \* \* \* \* \* \* \* \* \* \* \* \* \* \* \* \* \* \* \* \* \* \*


LABORATORY PROBLEM 15 - Calculating Factorials

Problem: Calculate the factorials for the integers 1 through
    10.

Procedure: N factorial is represented as N!, and is
    calculated as N•(N-1)•(N-2) ... •1

    For example,

        6 factorial=6!=6•5•4•3•2•1

    and

        4 factorial=4!=4•3•2•1


Input: None


Output: Print out in tabular form each integer (1-10) and
    its factorial value.


        1       1
        2       2
        3       6
        4      24
        etc.

LABORATORY PROBLEM 16 - Calculating Square Roots

Problem: Compute a square root of a REAL positive number.

Procedure: The square root of S can be computed by using an
    algorithm based on the formula

        newx = (0.5) • (oldx + S/oldx)

This method utilizes an iteration process.  A starting value
of oldx is arbitrarily selected and is used to compute newx.
This computed value, newx, will be more nearly equal to a
true square root of S than was the arbitrarily selected
oldx.  We can compute a still better estimate of a square
root of S by replacing the value of oldx with that of newx
and recomputing newx.  This process may be repeated as many
times as we wish in order to give improved estimates of the
square root of S.

As an example, let's look at the process for S=25.  If 2 is
used as a starting estimate, then the process converges
toward 5.

    1st approximation:   newx=0.5•(2+25/2)=7.25
    2nd approximation:   newx=0.5•(7.25+25/7.25)=5.35
    3rd approximation:   newx=0.5•(5.35+25/5.35)=5.01

Terminate the iterative procedure when the absolute value of
the difference between two successive estimates is less than
some positive number, say, one ten-thousandth.

Input: Find a square root of each of the following three
    numbers: 16.0, 73.315 and 0.0025.  (If a negative
    starting point is given, the process will converge to
    the negative square root; if a zero starting point is
    given, the process will, of course, fail.)

Output: Print the value of S, the final value of newx, and
    the square root of S found by using the SQRT function.

LABORATORY PROBLEM 17 - The $24 Question

Background: The proceeds of money invested in a bank for one
    year are

        P[1]=Amount•[1+r]

    where r is the annual interest rate.  The value after
    the second year is

        P[2]=P[1]•[1+r]

    This process is known as compounding interest on an
    annual basis.  The bank computes the interest and rounds
    it to the nearest cent at the end of each year.


Speculation: It is widely reported that in 1626 Peter
    Minuit, the Governor of the Dutch West India Company,
    bought Manhattan Island from Indians for $24 worth of
    trinkets.


Problem: Write a computer program to compute the proceeds of
    $24 if it were invested in a bank in 1626 at 6 percent
    interest compounded yearly and held until this year.  If
    the Indians had so invested the $24, do you think they
    would have enough money now to repurchase Manhattan at
    its current value?  (Note: assume that no interest
    accrues for either this year or 1626.)



* * * * * * * * * * * * * * * * * * * * * * * * * * * * * * *



LABORATORY PROBLEM 18 - Prime Numbers

Problem: Write a program to print the prime numbers between
    2 and 100 inclusive.  Use the FOR statement.

Comment: A prime number is an integer greater than 1 which
    cannot be divided by any positive integer (except itself
    and 1) without yielding a fractional part.  The first
    few primes are 2, 3, 5, 7, 11, 13, and 17.

LABORATORY PROBLEM 19 - Loop Exercise

Problem: Write a program to implement the following
    flowchart.   If each execution of the output box results
    in a single line, how many lines should it print?   Use a
    value for n which is less than or equal to 7.

    Print each pair of digits (i and j) as close as possible
    to each other.   Does the resulting sequence of digit
    pairs when viewed as a single two-digit number, suggest
    anything about the construction of a base (n+1) number
    system?   Refer to Module 6.

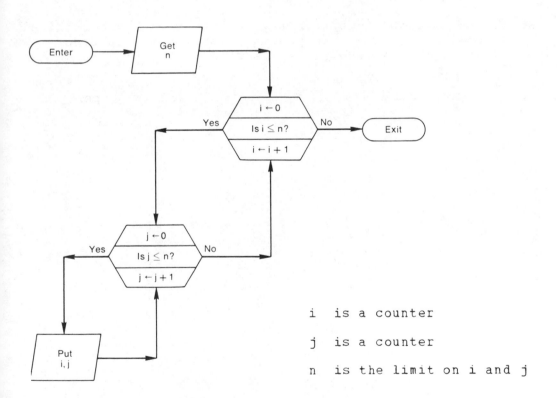

i   is a counter

j   is a counter

n   is the limit on i and j

LABORATORY PROBLEM 20 - Lowest Terms Fractions

Problem: Given a pair of numbers which represent the
     numerator and denominator of a fraction, write a
     procedure to reduce the fraction to its lowest terms.
     (A fraction is in lowest terms if there does not exist
     any prime number which can be divided wholly into both
     numerator and denominator.)  Write a calling program
     which reads inputs and prints answers.

Input: A numerator in columns 1-2 and a denominator in
     columns 4-5.

Output:  original numerator
         original denominator
         integral portion of answer
         new numerator
         new denominator

Note: The original numerator may be larger than the original
     denominator.  Also the program should print an error
     message if the denominator is zero.

LABORATORY PROBLEM 21 - Random Number Generation

Problem: Many computer applications require the use of
    random numbers.  Uniformly distributed random numbers
    all have the same probability of occurrence in the same
    manner that the different faces of a die all have
    equally probable chances of occurrence.  The power
    residue method of random number generation is quite
    popular.  It consists of computing

$$M[i+1] = M[i] \bullet L$$

    where M[i] is the ith random number, M[i+1] is the next
    random number and L is a constant multiplier.  This
    generator will produce random numbers from a rectangular
    distribution, i.e., one in which each number has the
    same chance of occurrence.

    To construct a generator, choose M[0] so that it is not
    divisible by 2 or 5.  Choose as a constant multiplier an
    integer of the form L=200t±r, where t is any integer and
    r is any of the values:

    3,11,13,19,21,27,37,53,61,67,69,77,83,91

    A value of L close to 10 raised to the D/2 power is a
    good choice, where D is the number of digits that the
    computer can hold in one word.  The low order one or two
    digits produced by this method are not random.
    Therefore, do not use the two low order digits in the
    random number, but retain them for computation of the
    next random number.

    Using the above method, write a program that will
    generate 100 random digits; count the frequency with
    which each digit occurs.  Then perform a chi-square test
    to determine if the numbers generated are sufficiently
    random.

Procedure: So that each program produces identical answers,
    use M[0] = 28437 and L = 52283 [INTEGER].  Produce a
    series of 100 random digits by using the digit in the
    ten thousands position of each M[i].  Do not use
    subscripted variables to produce these random numbers;
    use simple [scalar] variables instead.  Count the number
    of 0,1,2,3,4,5,6,7,8 and 9's generated.  Select the
    first random digit from M[1], not M[0].  (Although we
    show subscript terminology for the values of M, you do

not need a subscripted variable because only one or two
values of M are needed at any one time).
   When all random digits have been generated and
counted, compute the value of chi-square from the
formula:

$$\sum_{i=0}^{9} (o[i]-e[i])^2/e[i]$$

where o[i] is the number of times the digit i occurred
and e[i] is the number of times the digit i was expected
to occur (10 in this case).  A value of chi-square less
than 2.7 or greater than 19.0 would indicate that the
numbers generated are not truly random for this
particular problem.

Input: None.

Output: Write a table showing the digits 0-9 and the
   frequency with which each occurred.  Also print the
   value of chi-square.

LABORATORY PROBLEM 22 - Function Exercise

Problem: Calculate the value of r for 4 sets of data.

$$r = 16.781 \bullet COS(2 \bullet pi) \bullet (x + (y + 1.667))^i$$

Procedure: Read the following sets of values:

Input:

| set | x | y | i |
|-----|-----|-----|-----|
| 1 | 77.538 | -1.0 | 2 |
| 2 | -0.3862 | 0.125E-07 | 6.2 |
| 3 | 12.5E13 | -52.0 | -3.3 |
| 4 | 2.56E-2 | 0.0735E06 | 5 |

Output: If y+1.667≥0, print x, y, i and r.  If y+1.667<0, do
not attempt to calculate r, unless i is a mathematically
integer value, in which case do the exponentiation by
iteration; instead print x, y, and i.  An attempt to
calculate A raised to the B if A is negative will result
in an error condition if B is not an integer.

Note: Use 3.14159 for the value of pi.

LABORATORY PROBLEM 23 - Evaluation of e to the x power

Problem: We wish to find the value of e to the x power,
where e is Euler's constant, and e to the x power =

$$1 + (x/1!) + (x^2/2!) + (x^3/3!) + \ldots$$

Procedure: Note that each term can easily be calculated from
the preceding one.  For example:

1st term = $x^0/0!$ = 1

2nd term = $x^1/1!$  = $(x^0/0!)(x/1)$ = (1st term)  (x/1)

3rd term = $x^2/2!$  = $(x^1/1!)(x/2)$ = (2nd term)  (x/2)

4th term = $x^3/3!$  = $(x^2/2!)(x/3)$ = (3rd term)  (x/3)


This should suggest an algorithm similar to that used in
calculating factorials.  This is the "trip value."  Stop
calculating terms for a particular value of x when the terms
of the series become less than $10^{-4}$.  The program should be
designed to calculate e to the x power for different
positive values of x until it encounters an x=-99.0.  Thus,
the last datum must be -99.0.

Input: Read in the following values of x: 3.5, 0.0, -2.31,
and 0.13; do not forget to include the trip value.

Output: For each x, write, on the same line, the value of x,
the value of e to the x power and the number of terms in
the series that were used in the calculation.

\* \* \* \* \* \* \* \* \* \* \* \* \* \* \* \* \* \* \* \* \* \* \* \* \* \* \* \* \* \*

LABORATORY PROBLEM 24 - A Hairy Problem

Problem: Compute the mass, volume, and surface area of an
average head of human hair.  Do some library research to
determine the probable number of hairs, the diameter of
a hair shaft, and the density of hair.  Assume each hair
shaft is a cylinder of length 10 cm (about 4 inches).
Assume further that each hair has been cut at 90 degrees
to the shaft so that the end surface of the hair shaft
is a circular disk.  Calculate the surface area as the
total area of the cylindrical part of each hair shaft
plus the area of the end.

# LABORATORY PROBLEM 25 - Compound Interest

Problem: Compute and print out a table for money in a
savings account where the interest is compounded
annually, semi-annually, quarterly, and daily (assume
365 days per year).  Assume all of the principal is
deposited at the beginning of the first year.

Procedure: The needed equation is the general compound
interest formula:

$$An = P \bullet ( 1 + i/m )^{m \bullet n}$$

where

An is the amount at the end of n years
P  is the principal
i  is  the annual interest rate expressed as a
decimal fraction such as 0.06
n  is the number of years
m  is the number of times per year  that
interest is compounded

Input: Several pairs of values of P and i.  The end of the
data will be identified by a negative value of P.  This
last value is not to be used in calculations.

Supply four data cards punched as follows:

| | |
|---|---|
| 500.00 | 0.05 |
| 1000.00 | 0.13 |
| 13000.00 | 0.045 |
| -1.00 | 0.0 |

Output: For each set of data, print P and i.  Then print n
and An for each of the four methods of paying interest.
Let n take on the values 1, 2, 3, . . . , 10.

LABORATORY PROBLEM 26 - Scanning an Array

Problem: Given a set of INTEGER numbers, find the value
    closest to the average (arithmetic mean).  There will be
    fewer than 100 numbers.  Your program should also
    determine how many times each distinct number occurs in
    the input.  Also required as output is a list of the
    different numbers and the frequency of occurrence of
    each.


Input: The data item is a two-digit number, which specifies
    the number of values which follow.

LABORATORY PROBLEM 27 - Array Manipulation

Problem: Write a TIPS program which will read in an array of
m (m<100) numbers (X[n]), n=1 to m) and which will then
write out the following five lists:

1. The m numbers and their subscripts as they were read.

2. The 1st, 3rd, 5th,. . . numbers (i.e., the numbers
   with odd subscripts) and their subscripts.

3. The m numbers and their subscripts in reverse order.

4. All the numbers that are divisible by 2 and their
   subscripts.

5. All the numbers that are greater than the number that
   follows them in the original list.

```
Input: The data are available from your instructor.

         1st record m
         2nd record X[1]
         3rd record X[2]
               .
               .
         m+1 record X[m]
```

Output: Print a descriptive heading on each of the five
lists and leave a blank line between lists.  Be sure to
leave several blank spaces between the number and its
subscript.

LABORATORY PROBLEM 28 - Numerical Inaccuracies

Problem: To demonstrate various arithmetic manipulations
which give rise to numerical inaccuracies.  (See Module
7.)

Procedure: Perform the following operations and produce the
indicated output.  Provide appropriate headings to
distinguish one answer from another.


1.  Add 0.1 fifty times and print out the sum.  Is the
answer 5.0?  If  not, why not?

2.  Find the sum of 1+1/2+1/3+.  .  .  +1/99 + 1/100.  (Add
the terms in the order indicated!)  Write the result.

3.  Find the sum of 1/100 + 1/99 + 1/98 +.  .  .  +1/3 +1/2
+ 1.  (Add the terms in the order indicated!)  Write the
result.  Are the answers to 2 and 3 the same?  If not,
why not?

4.  The value of the number e is given by the infinite
series,

$$e = (1/0!) + (1/1!) + (1/2!) + (1/3!) + (1/4!) + ...$$

where 0!  = 1! = 1, and
      4!  =  4•3•2•1

Implement the following flowchart to find the value of e.
Write c, t and e.  Since t never becomes zero, why does the
process stop?

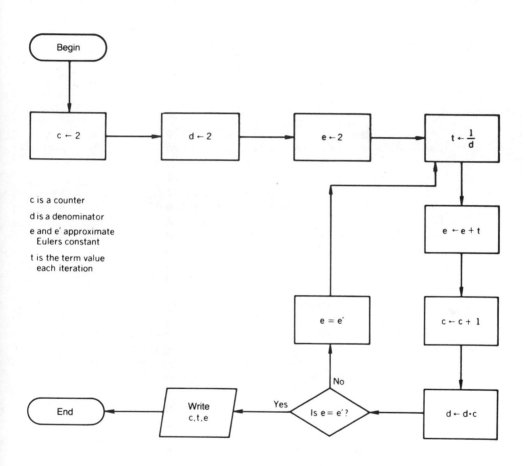

Begin

$c \leftarrow 2$

$d \leftarrow 2$

$e \leftarrow 2$

$t \leftarrow \dfrac{1}{d}$

$e \leftarrow e + t$

$c \leftarrow c + 1$

$e = e'$

$c \leftarrow c + 1$

$d \leftarrow d \cdot c$

Is $e = e'$?

No

Yes

Write
c, t, e

End

c is a counter

d is a denominator

e and e' approximate
 Eulers constant

t is the term value
 each iteration

LABORATORY PROBLEM 29 - Matrix Symmetry

An n by n matrix is symmetric if, for each r (1≤r≤n) and each s (1≤s≤n), the element a(r,s) is the same as the element a(s,r).

Problem: Write a program to determine, for a series of m matrices, whether or not each is symmetric.

---

Input: The data are available from your instructor, and are arranged as follows (each line constitutes one record):

```
    DATA

        m
        n        k
        a(1,1)   a(1,2)   a(1,3)   ... a(1,n)
        a(2,1)   a(2,2)   a(2,3)   ... a(2,n)
        .
        .
        .
        a(n,1)   a(n,2)   a(n,3)   ... a(n,n)
        n        k
        b(1,1)   b(1,2) ... b(1,n)
        etc.
```

where:

    m is the number of matrices in the series

    n is the order number of each matrix
        (n is ≤ 5); each matrix is square)

    k is the identification number of each
        matrix

    a(r,s),b(r,s) ... are the elements of the
        matrices

---

Output:   For each matrix print the message:

        MATRIX k IS SYMMETRIC
                or
        MATRIX k IS NOT SYMMETRIC

LABORATORY PROBLEM 30 - Sorting

Problem: To read in REAL numbers and sort them.

---

Input: Data are available from your instructor.
    Each record in the file contains one number.
    There are fewer than 500 numbers.

---

Output: Print n lines, one for each number, printing the
numbers in ascending order.

Procedure: Read all numbers into an array, sort the array
    into ascending order, and print the array.  Many sorting
    algorithms exist: two which sort in ascending order are
    shown below.  Both assume X is an array of values to be
    sorted, N is the number of elements in the array, and T
    is an element variable with the same attributes as the
    array X.

```
              (* SORTING METHOD 1 *)
         FOR I := 1 TO N-1 DO
             BEGIN
             FOR J := I+1 TO N DO
                 BEGIN
                 IF X[I]>X[J] THEN
                     BEGIN
                     T := X[I];
                     X[I] := X[J];
                     X[J] := T
                     END
                 END
             END
```

Another algorithm to do the same thing is:

```
              (* SORTING METHOD 2 *)
         FOR I := N-1 DOWNTO 1 DO
             BEGIN
             FOR J := 1 TO I DO
                 BEGIN
                 IF X[J]>X[J+1] THEN
                     BEGIN
                     T := X[J];
                     X[J] := X[I];
                     X[I] := T
                     END
                 END
             END
```

LABORATORY PROBLEM 31 - Loops or Logs

Problem: For every number x greater than 1 there corresponds
    a number n such that

$$2**(n-1) \leq x < 2**n$$
(where ** means "raised to the power")

Develop a program which would:

1. read a number m
2. read a number x
3. determine the value of n such that:  $2**(n-1) \leq x < 2**n$
4. write x and n
5. determine if m numbers have been processed.
6. if m numbers have not been processed, return to step 2.

Express  the  flowchart  as  a PASCAL program using data as
shown below.

---

Input: Available from your instructor.

    m

    the set of x's

---

Output: On the output device, display x as 20 digits with 8
    decimal places and each n as a 6 digit number.

Hint: this problem could be addressed either in terms of
    logarithms or iterative loops.

LABORATORY PROBLEM 32 - Gaussian Elimination (Matrices)
(Contributed by Dr. J. W. Atwood, Sir George Williams University, Montreal, Canada)

Background: Systems of equations frequently arise during the formulation or the attempted solution of various problems from the physical and biological sciences, engineering, applied mathematics and the social sciences. A solution to a set or system of equations is a simultaneous solution, in that it must satisfy each equation individually. Thus x=3 and y=-2 provide a solution to the system:

$$2x+y=4 \quad (1)$$
$$x+y=1$$

Linear systems of equations can usually be solved successfully either by hand or on a computer. A method that most people have met already is the Gaussian elimination technique. This is the method most frequently used to solve sets of linear equations and can easily be implemented on a computer. First a review of the method is given by showing the solution of a small problem, step by step, and following this a flowchart for implementing the general procedure on a computer.

Consider the system:

$$2X[1]+2X[2]-4X[3]=4 \quad (2)$$
$$X[1]- X[2]+2X[3]=4$$
$$4X[1]-2X[2]-2X[3]=20$$

The first stage of the method consists of eliminating X[1] from the second and third equations. This is accomplished by subtracting a suitable multiple of the first equation from the second and third equations. These multipliers are just the ratios of the coefficients of X[1] in each equation to the coefficient of X[1] in the first equation: in this case they are 1/2 and 2, respectively. Thus the system becomes

$$2X[1]+2X[2]-4X[3]=4 \quad (3)$$
$$-2X[2]+4X[3]=2$$
$$-6X[2]+6X[3]=12$$

The second stage of the method eliminates X[2] from the third equation. This involves only the second and third equations, and the necessary multiplier is (-6)/(-2)=3. The system is rewritten as

```
        2X[1]+2X[2]-4X[3]=4  (4)
             -2X[2]+4X[3]=2
                  -6X[3]=6
```

Thus, the third equation yields

$$X[3]=6/(-6)=-1$$
$$X[2]=(2-4(-1))/(-2)=-3$$
$$X[1]=(4+4(-1)-2(-3))/2=3$$

The solution (X[1],X[2],X[3]) to (2) obtained by back
substitution is therefore (3,-3,-1). The Gaussian
elimination method is thus a step by step triangularization
followed by a back substitution as the final stage.

An apparent pitfall for the method is the possible
occurrence of a zero coefficient of the first variable in
the first equation of the orginal system, or the second
variable of the second equation at the next stage, etc.
(Why?)

More specifically, in our example if either the coefficient
of X[1] in the first equation of (2) had been zero, or the
coefficient of X[2] in the second equation of (3) had been
zero, how could we have formed the multipliers necessary for
the eliminations? This problem can be avoided by simply
interchanging the first equation with any other equation for
which the coefficient of X[1] is not zero, and repeating
this process where necessary throughout the successive
stages of the method. Moreover, since any computer program
for Gaussian elimination must include this safeguard
feature, you are required to make a row interchange wherever
necessary to ensure that the coefficient with largest
absolute value is always employed when forming the
multipliers for that stage. Thus in the example above the
first and third equations of (2) should be interchanged so
that the coefficient 4 is used to form the multipliers for
the first stage. This modification improves the accuracy of
the elimination method when it is implemented on a computer,
since the overall effect of rounding errors can thereby be
reduced for most problems.

The general system of n linear equations is:

```
 A[1,1]•X[1]+A[1,2]•X[2]+...+A[1,n]•X[n]=B[1]  (5)
 A[2,1]•X[1]+A[2,2]•X[2]+...+A[2,n]•X[n]=B[2]
    •
    •
 A[n,1]•X[1]+A[n,2]•X[2]+...+A[n,n]•X[n]=B[n]
```

You should invent an algorithm or make a search of existing algorithms or flowcharts for the solution of the general system (5) by Gaussian elimination.

Write a program to solve a system of up to 20 equations. Then enter the data and solve the following two systems for the values of the X's:

```
    X[ 1] +2•X[ 2] +3•X[ 3] +4•X[ 4 ]=30     (A)
   -X[ 1]    +X[ 2]    -X[ 3]     +X[ 4 ]= 2
           10•X[ 2] +2•X[ 3] +8•X[ 4 ]=58
              X[ 2]    -X[ 3] +6•X[ 4 ]=23

     X[ 1]+ 2X[ 2 ]+0 X[ 3 ]= 25              (B)
    2X[ 1]-  X[ 2 ]-3X[ 3 ]=-45
    6X[ 1]-3X[ 2 ]+ X[ 3 ]= 15
```

LABORATORY PROBLEM 33 - Monte Carlo Technique

Problem: Suppose you have a sewing needle of length x.
    Suppose also you are in a room with a hardwood floor and
    the width of each board in the flooring is length 2x.
    Suppose further that you need to know the value of pi.
    No difficulty.  You simply drop the needle on the floor
    a few times and note how many times the needle crosses
    the lines between the flooring.  In particular, if you
    drop the needle n times and it crosses a line m times,
    the quantity n/m will approach pi as n approaches
    infinity.  Write a program to simulate the dropping of
    the needle on the floor.


Procedure: You will need two REAL random numbers for each
    toss of the needle: one for the position of one end of
    the needle and one for its angle with respect to the
    flooring.  Your instructor will tell you how to get
    random numbers on your computer.


Output: Drop the needle 1000 times; print out the
    approximation of pi after each 100 trials.

# LABORATORY PROBLEM 34 - Markov Chain

General: Since businesses either thrive or die depending
upon the soundness of decisions, there is a driving
force to preview the future whenever possible. Often,
through mathematical models, businessmen attempt a peek
ahead in time. One factor of interest to many firms is
brand share, that is, the percentage of market sales
captured by the firm. These companies study their share
of the market and the phenomenon known as "brand
switching." As an approximation to reality, firms
develop brand switching models that attempt to abstract
from reality and describe brand share in future time
periods. One such model is known as a Markov chain. It
is an iterative matrix technique, simple in construction
and although limited in predictive ability, it is
believed useful enough by some firms to warrant their
consideration.

The Markov chain consists of 3 arrays: a one-dimensional
array (current brand share), another one-dimensional
array (next period brand share) and a two-dimensional
array (transition matrix). The current share array is
simply the fractional share of the market currently held
by each firm. Suppose that five firms in a market
possess the following share of sales. The current array
would appear:

|        |      |
|--------|------|
| firm 1 | 0.20 |
| firm 2 | 0.15 |
| firm 3 | 0.10 |
| firm 4 | 0.30 |
| firm 5 | 0.25 |

The transition matrix contains one row and one column
for each firm (in this case five rows and five columns).
Each cell in the matrix contains a probability: the
probability that a consumer will switch from brand "i"
to brand "j" during one time period, where "i" is the
ith row and "j" is the jth column. The transition
matrix is determined after an extensive brand switching
consumer survey.

One such transition matrix is:

PROBABILITY THAT A CONSUMER WILL SWITCH--

TO BRAND j

|  | | 1 | 2 | 3 | 4 | 5 |
|---|---|---|---|---|---|---|
| | 1 | 0.57 | 0.03 | 0.13 | 0.16 | 0.11 |
| FROM | 2 | 0.15 | 0.47 | 0.15 | 0.08 | 0.15 |
| BRAND | 3 | 0.09 | 0.06 | 0.55 | 0.15 | 0.15 |
| i | 4 | 0.07 | 0.01 | 0.14 | 0.64 | 0.14 |
| | 5 | 0.10 | 0.05 | 0.14 | 0.19 | 0.52 |

The entry in row 1, column 1 shows that there is a 0.57 chance that a consumer will not switch from brand 1 (no switch - he remains loyal) in one time period. Row 2, column 1 indicates that there is a 0.15 chance that a consumer will switch from brand 2 to brand 1 in one time period.

If we multiply the first cell in the current share array by row 1 column 1 of the transition matrix (0.20 x 0.57), we find that 0.114 of the consumers will remain loyal to brand 1 during one time period. (0.15 x 0.15)=0.0225 of the market will have switched from brand 2 to brand 1 during one time period. If we multiply each cell in the current share array by each cell in the first column of the transition matrix, and add these together, the sum we get is the share of the market held by firm 1 after the first time period. We can do the same for each of the other firms. After the first period we find that the following is the new brand share array:

```
firm 1    0.1915
firm 2    0.0980
firm 3    0.1805
firm 4    0.2985
firm 5    0.2315
```

If we again perform the necessary arithmetic using the above new current array and the transition matrix, we get the brand share for the third period.  By continually repeating this procedure, we eventually find an equilibrium condition where a new iteration does not change any share value by as much as 0.0001

Problem: Write a program to compute the brand share of these five firms at equilibrium.

Input: Available from your instructor: There are two records; the first is the current share record (in order) which contains 5 two-digit numbers. The first number is firm 1 share, the second firm 2 share, etc.  The second record is the transition matrix consisting of 25 two-digit numbers representing the cells in order row-wise; that is row 1, column 1; row 1, column 2; row 1, column 3; etc.

Output: Print the results as follows, including the alphabetic information:

    EQUILIBRIUM REQUIRES XXXX PERIODS

        FIRM      SHARE
         1        x.xxxx
         2        x.xxxx
         3        x.xxxx
         4        x.xxxx
         5        x.xxxx

LABORATORY PROBLEM 35 - Inventory Application I

Problem: The purpose of this program is to record inventory
transactions.  Your company maintains inventory for 40
types of gaskets.  For simplicity we identify them as 1,
2, 3,...40.  Each day a computer run is made in which
all orders and inventory receipts are processed.

Assume that this day your firm starts with 10,000 of
each of the 40 types of gaskets.  Orders and receipts
are read from data supplied by your instructor and
inventory is "updated."  Orders and receipts are
interspersed in the input stream.

---

Input: Each record contains three numeric fields:

Columns    1    Transaction type. 0 (zero)
                means this is a customer order,
                1 means gaskets received.
           3-4  indicates the type of
                gasket involved (1-40)
           6-9  indicates the number of
                gaskets received or shipped

---

Procedure: As each record is read, either add to or subtract
from the inventory of the appropriate gasket type.  At
the end of the run, for each of the 40 types of gaskets,
print the gasket type and the number of gaskets left in
inventory.

Output: (40 lines of output)

        Columns 1- 3  gasket type
               10-20  number of gaskets on hand

LABORATORY PROBLEM 36 - Calendar Model (Contributed by Dr.
J. W. Atwood, Sir George Williams University, Montreal,
Canada)

Input: A punched card contains a four-digit positive integer
    n (indicating a year such as 1989), a two-digit month
    number m and a number x of value 1 through 7.  The
    number x indicates that January 1 of year n falls on
    weekday x.

Problem: Using this information, write a program to print a
    calendar for year n, month m.  A typical calendar should
    look like this:

```
┌──────────────────────────────────────────────────┐
│                                                    │
│                    JUNE 1984                       │
│                                                    │
│    Sun    Mon    Tue    Wed   Thur    Fri    Sat   │
│  ──────────────────────────────────────────────── │
│                                                    │
│                                         1      2   │
│                                                    │
│     3      4      5      6      7      8      9     │
│                                                    │
│    10     11     12     13     14     15     16     │
│                                                    │
│    17     18     19     20     21     22     23     │
│                                                    │
│    24     25     26     27     28     29     30     │
│                                                    │
└──────────────────────────────────────────────────┘
```

The program should take into account that February has
29 days if either

  1) n modulo 4 = 0 and n modulo 100 <> 0, or
  2) n modulo 400 = 0

Modulo means the remainder after dividing by a value.
For example, 25 modulo 4 would be 1 since 25 divided by
4 is 6 with 1 remainder.

LABORATORY PROBLEM 37 - The Automatic Change Maker
(Contributed by Dr. J. W. Atwood, Sir George Williams University, Montreal, Canada)

Procedure: We frequently observe the cashier "make change"
    as we pay our bill at a restaurant or shop, taking for
    granted the actual process of making change.  The
    computer can be programmed to simulate a cashier in the
    process of making change.  In this simulation the act of
    handing the cashier the customer's bill together with
    the cash payment is the input, and the cashier handing
    over the change containing a minimum number of bills
    and/or coins is the output.

Problem: Write and test a computer program which will
    perform the following steps:

    (1)  Accept any number of sets of two data
            items per set of parameters.  (The
            amount of a customer's bill and the
            cash payment.)

    (2)  For each pair compute the number of
            each denomination in the change
            returned to the customer.  Use ten
            common U.S. currency values (penny,
            nickel, dime, quarter, half-dollar,
            dollar bill or coin, five-dollar
            bill, ten-dollar bill, twenty-dollar
            bill, and fifty-dollar bill).  These
            ten values should be stored in an
            INTEGER array.

Output: For each set of data print out the amount of the
    customer's bill, cash payment and change on one line,
    followed by a list of denomination type and number.  For
    example, if the bill was $1.35 and $5.00 was tendered,
    the output would appear as follows:

                135      500      365
                  3      100
                  1       50
                  1       10
                  1        5

    If the change is negative (i.e., if an insufficient
    amount of money is paid to the cashier), simply print
    out the bill, cash payment, and change (negative).

244                    Laboratory Problems

At the outset of this book we outlined ten steps which you might follow to have a computer solve a problem for you. We now present the same section again, with considerable embellishment. What follows is an informal checklist of ideas, advice, and reminders. Most of the items mentioned will relate to matters we have dealt with in the text. Not all of the steps will be appropriate for every program. And there will be items which we have omitted. We have left some blank space at the end of each of the ten steps so that you may write in your own items as you think of them or as you discover which ones are important to you.

In most instances we assume that TIPS or PASCAL is the computer language which is being used. However, the ideas embodied are of a broader nature. This section of the book is designed not just for this part of the course nor even for this course; it is designed to see you through the first several years of your involvement with computers. For example, even though you are learning PASCAL from this course, part of this Reprise encourages you to look at other languages, and further, to look at already written programs which might solve your problem. Don't be disturbed, therefore, if we mention issues we haven't discussed before. As your experience grows you will come across them. We have marked sections which contain unfamiliar terms or concepts by using a * instead of a period following the section number.

As with most attempts to divide up knowledge or ideas into little packages, there are overlaps among many of the steps which follow. Further, the process of developing a computer program entails a lot of feedback: you get to a certain point and discover you must change something in an earlier step. Be that as it may, if you try to use these steps, you may avoid some of the errors others have made -- and save yourself the pain of their discoveries.

I.  Formulate the problem.

    A. Is the problem really one for a computer to solve?

        1. Is the problem large enough for the computer to be useful? Will the same program be run often enough to make the cost required to instruct a computer to do it worthwhile? To simply add 10 numbers together can be more economically performed on an adding machine or hand calculator.

        2. Is the problem too large to be solved? Do you have the facilities (time, assistance, etc.) for dealing with large quantities of data, putting them in machine-readable form, and insuring their accuracy? The number of operations required to do some problems is so great that even a computer may take years to solve them.

        3. Is the problem a well-defined one? Is it a problem which may be solved by a step-by-step manipulation of discrete symbols? If you had millions of years, pencils, and reams of paper could you do the problem yourself, or are there areas in the solution where the algorithmic approach is not appropriate? For example, the problem of determining whether there is intelligent life in the universe is too vague to be computerized.

    B. Do you really understand the problem?

        1. Are you sure that the inputs you plan to use can be manipulated in such a way as to produce the outputs you want?

        2. Are you sure that you are solving the right problem?

            a. If you are writing a program for someone else, do you understand completely what is to be done? Has it been written down for you? Do you understand what the person really wants or what he or she claims to want? Do you understand the context in which the problem is being solved and is the problem

really appropriate in that context, or should
you be dealing with a larger or different
problem? After you've finished the problem,
is the person going to suggest additions
which lead to patched, patched-on and
patched-up programs? How can you minimize
such requests for modifications?

b. If you are writing the program for yourself,
have you asked the questions immediately
above, pretending that you, yourself, are the
client?

c. Are you trying to use the computer to solve
more of a problem than you really need?
Would it be better (more economical or cost-
effective) to use the machine simply to solve
a subset of your problem and deal with the
rest of it by some other means?

d. On the other hand, are you solving enough of
the problem? Are there other parts you might
consider including for processing by
computer? Do you plan to do calculations by
hand or by calculator after you get the
computer results? Why?

e. Talk to someone about the problem. Can you
describe accurately what is to be done?

f. Are you altering the problem to fit the
computer? What concessions have you made to
the computer?

C. Write a problem statement that describes what the
problem is.

1. Don't restrict yourself to the computer portion
of the matter, but include everything which lies
between what you know now and what you want to
know that relates to the problem.

2. Now, consider that the computer is a symbol
manipulator: it takes in symbols you provide and
produces symbols which, you hope, increase
knowledge. Think of your problem in that larger
sense. The issue is what you have relative to
what you want.

D. Start a folder or notebook on the project. Make
the problem statement you just wrote the first
item. As the problem statement changes, make
additions or corrections. Plan to be surprised at
how much the problem statement will change in the
course of the project. Keep all the materials
related to the project: your scrappy notes, all
computer output, card decks, files on disk or tape.

II.  Decide on a method for solving the problem.

A. Before you try to develop your own algorithm and
   data structure ask: "Has someone else solved the
   problem or one close to it?"

   1* Have you looked in the program library or
      procedure library of your computing center?
      (For explanation of 1* see the introductory
      material to this section.)

   2. Have you checked with colleagues in the field to
      see if they have programs which might be used?

   3. If you do find an already written program, will
      it run on the machine you plan to use?  Is it in
      a language you understand in case you want to
      modify or check it?  Are your data already in
      machine-readable form and, if so, is the data
      format going to create difficulties with a
      borrowed or otherwise-acquired program?  What
      assurances do you have as to the correctness of
      the program?

   4. If you can't find a complete program to solve
      your problem, are there procedures available
      which you might use?

   5* If you can't find, can't use, or don't want to
      use previously written programs to solve your
      problem, consider examining available
      algorithms.  Search the literature in the field.
      Check the certified algorithms published by
      professional organizations such as the
      Association for Computing Machinery.

B. What computing resources do you have available?
   E.g., a fast machine, limited memory, computer
   terminals, slow turnaround?  How do these factors
   influence your choice of an algorithm and data
   structure?  Weigh the issues of computer time cost
   against programming time cost against program
   maintenance cost.  What is the cost of running the
   computer you plan to use--for time, printed lines,
   etc.?  Are there other machines available?  Should
   your program run in interactive or batch mode?
   Think about the balance between elegance and
   efficiency as it relates to the various costs.

C. Think of the input you have available.  Think about
   the output you want to produce.  How would you do
   the problem if you were going to do it by hand?
   Can you think of other ways to solve the problem
   which take advantage of the things the computer
   does quickly and well which would suggest a
   different approach than you would use manually?
   Reread the problem statement.

D. Determine the approach you will use.

   1. To help organize your thinking, write a general
      statement about what the program will do.  But,
      write the statement as though the program
      already existed.  This will give you confidence;
      also you can use the statement in the
      introduction to the documentation you write
      later.

   2* Computers can deal with immense amounts of data.
      For large, complicated problems most of these
      data will have underlying themes or
      commonalities.  You will probably want to group
      such data into structured aggregates.  The
      aggregate you know about already is the array.
      But there are many others: lists, files, sets,
      and records to name the ones we will take up in
      Part III.  Give considerable thought to the data
      structures that are appropriate for your
      problem.  This part of the process can be just
      as important as the algorithm development.

   3. Now break the job you have defined into a series
      of major tasks.  Give some thought to what the
      most logical, natural segments of the problem
      are.  Describe each of these major tasks
      together with a stepwise solution (algorithm) to
      the task.  Now take each major task and
      subdivide it into subtasks.  Continue the
      process of breaking complicated tasks into
      simpler ones until you have an algorithm
      composed of a hierarchical set of easily
      understood tasks and their associated
      algorithms.  Each of these will become a
      procedure in your program.

   4. Consider each subtask as a simple but complete
      problem to be solved.  It will have inputs and

outputs. Concentrate on one subtask at a time, being confident that the subtasks will fit together to solve the overall job.

5. Decide on those values which will be constant Decide on those values least likely to change. Do you want to bring them in early? Many values in the algorithm, while "dimensionless" as far as the machine is concerned, denote real world quantities--inches, people, etc. Are the units you are assuming for these values consistent with each other?

6. What output do you really want? Not considering the intermediate results for testing purposes, are you planning more output than you need? How will the output be used? Will some of it be processed further? By hand or machine?

7. Now that you've decided on all the subtasks which form your algorithm, do you have a clear idea of the ways in which they are linked? Consider the relationships between the various modules and the data structures you will use to store the values the program is to work with.

E. Is your algorithm flexible enough to allow changes if the problem statement should change somewhat, as it probably will? Where have you unduly restricted yourself?

III. Begin to formalize the algorithm with a Program Development Scroll.

A. Draw a master flowchart showing how the modules of the algorithm relate. Realize that the major reason for flowcharting is to aid your thought processes. Document the things you do and things you decide. Documentation helps as you go along. It helps later too.

B. Develop a Program Development Scroll of each task.

1. Include a separate sheet or section defining the use of every variable in the Program Development Scroll (PDS) or flowchart. Add it to the documentation.

2. Have you decided to use only the canonical forms of structured programming? (If you are using TIPS, you have no choice; you must.) If not, you must be doubly careful to follow up every decision the program makes. Try to keep the branches "localized."

3. Is the task you are developing getting too complex, running off the page? Can you break it into subparts, each of which becomes a task itself?

4. Have you set up some standardized way of handling errors caused by bad data (or bad logic, for that matter)? Consider using a procedure or preprocessing program that does nothing but service or detect errors. Also, consider a procedure to perform the initialization of variables, produce output, or do calculating.

C. Look over each refinement you have developed. Ask yourself some questions:

1. Can you make your most complicated expressions simpler by computing them in steps? Print out these intermediate steps for checking.

2. Have you written efficient procedures? Remember, every operation takes time and/or memory space. Examine the highly iterative

parts of your program--the ones that eat up all the time. Concoct ways to avoid using subscripted variables in these areas, if very large numbers of iterations are involved. Avoid doing processes within loops that could be done outside.

3. Examine the implications of your procedures in terms of the machine's memory. Don't use an array when one isn't needed. For instance, it is easy to think of an average in terms of an array: the sum of Xi divided by n. Don't get carried away! Use arrays when you need them; otherwise, save the time and memory space.

4. Assume your procedures were followed faithfully by a machine which left answers and garbage strewn around the memory. Is your "housekeeping" such that the procedures could be reexecuted? Did you take care to initialize every appropriate variable before using it the first time? The second time?

5. Think about a person who comes after you to fix the program--can he easily see what you've done? Or does your approach employ "neat" tricks to save a few microseconds or memory locations and thus use logic that is hard for a human to follow?

D. Do a desk check. Trace the algorithm through with a very simple set of data. It's amazing what you can find that way.

IV.  Complete the program development process by assembling
     the comments and computer instructions.

   A. Decide on a computer language to use.  The ones you
      know are doubtless the heavy favorites, but you
      might look around--there are dozens of languages.
      Are you doing simulation, list processing, text
      analysis?  Is there a better language for your
      application?  You might have to redevelop the
      algorithm or change algorithms.  It might be worth
      it.

   B. As you begin coding, have a copy of the language
      specifications with you.  Also obtain a manual of
      the particular compiler you will use and a
      "Programmer's Guide" for the machine and language
      if one is available.

   C. Properly declaring and "commenting" variable names
      is half the battle, since this is the area about
      which the Program Development Scroll says the
      least.

      1. Be careful to select variable names that are
         unique and meaningful.  Mind your spelling.
         Avoid trite names, keywords, built-in function
         and procedure names.  Keep a list of all the
         names you use and what each means; plan to
         include the list in the documentation.

      2* Do you use the declaration statement or other
         "static" methods to initialize values of
         variables?  Don't--if the program changes the
         variable later.  Use variables or the PASCAL
         "CONST" declaration (to be discussed in Part
         III) for the more "complicated" constants such
         as pi or e.  Set them early in the program.
         Look at each one intently, three times.
         Consider computing such constants. (e.g., pi is
         ATAN(1.0)*4. and e is EXP(1.0); they are easy to
         remember, deduce, check and/or convert to
         extended precision.)

      3* Is the precision of the variables sufficient to
         do the job?  Is the machine going to be able to
         store all you need it to?  Consider alternate
         length possibilities.  Ask yourself, in general,
         about the type you've selected for each

variable. Also, can you safely reuse some
memory space for another variable or array?

D. What differences are there between mathematical or
flowchart language and the computer language you've
chosen which are going to give you problems?
Fractions vs. integers?   Mixed types?
Input/output problems?   Conventions in computing
expressions?

E. Include comments to indicate what the general
function of each module is.   Include comments to
document any differences between the formal process
of the algorithm and the program.   Include comments
to describe differences between the flowchart and
the program necessitated by the computer language
syntax.   Include comments on the use of each
variable or a reference to where the variable
description can be found.

F* Will the program be writing out information just to
read it in again later?   (The PASCAL FILE type,
covered in Part III, may be useful here.)   Consider
the format (or lack of same) you might use for such
data and the devices on which you might store it.

G. Allow yourself the luxury of putting in
intermediate output statements for testing purposes
even if they aren't on the Program Development
Scroll.   Mark them well so you can remove them
later or put them on a "switch" so you can
deactivate them.   Consider turning them into
comments when "pretty sure" the program works and
taking them out when "very sure".   Plan to print
identifying information with each computer run:
program name, date, time, data identification, etc.

H. You are printing out (echoing) all input, aren't
you?   If not, how do you know what problem the
answer sheet will refer to?   How do you know the
input went in correctly?

I. Do you make the computer check for obvious errors?
Input data out of range?   Division by zero?
Subscripts too large or too small?   Input data set
not exhausted?   Do you have a good system for
identifying errors--a simple procedure perhaps?

J. Avoid nonstandard instructions.  Follow
conventions.  Assume somebody who is not so good at
programming as you are will have to read and modify
your code.

K. Do a desk check.  Trace the program with simple
data.  Find the bugs now!

V. Assemble the data the computer is to use in solving the problem.

A. Put together some packages of test data first.

    1. What input do you have access to for which you know the answers? Are there certain combinations of input values for which answers are known or which produce trends in sets of answers? Are there some simple analytical tests or ways to check results against each other? Are there data which should produce some known intermediate answers even if you don't know the final answers? Do the test data you've selected exercise at least the principal paths of your program, if not all paths? See that each path will do the right thing if you give it the right data and won't try to fake it with the wrong data.

    2. Plan to test in at least two different sets of runs. In the first, see if the machine will give you the right answers under the most favorable conditions. Next try to break the program. Test its digestion by purposely giving it incorrect parameters.

    3. Ask the meanest person you know to develop some test data for you. Make a contest out of the testing phase--your program against his or her data.

B. Assemble the actual data.

    1. Do you trust your sources? What bothers you most about the data? Investigate it. Are the data in the format you want them in? If not, what errors might occur in transforming them?

    2. Now that you've looked more closely at the data, are there things in the program which might be worth changing? Are there some obvious limits to the values which the program could check for? Are there attributes of some of the data which would improve processing, e.g., no fractional values, so that you can use integer (fixed-point) storage?

3. Do you mark the end of each set of data in the way the program expects it? Could the method you use for marking the end ever be confused with an actual datum?

4. What are the differences between your test data and the real McCoy? Quantity of data is an obvious one that can cause trouble. Are there other differences?

VI.  Prepare the written program and the assembled data so
     that they are in machine-readable form.

     A. This is one of the few places you may have to let
        the process get out of your control.  Are you going
        to let someone else type or punch for you?  One
        compromise is to prepare the program yourself while
        someone else prepares the data.  It is hard to say
        which is more critical: errors in program typing or
        in data typing.  Errors in programs are more
        devastating but also more likely to be caught.

     B. Have legible copy to type from.  Be very precise
        about what you want.  Consider using standardized
        coding forms for the program and data.  The only
        thing in the world more literal-minded than a
        computer is a data entry operator.  And he should
        be.  Differentiate carefully between I and 1,
        between letter O and zero, between ( and C, between
        2, 7, and Z, and between 5 and S.

     C. Are you going to type or punch the program
        yourself?  Take advantage of the event to examine
        each statement carefully.  Picture in your mind
        what each statement does, in the context of your
        program before you type or punch it.  When you are
        satisfied it is right, concentrate on typing or
        punching it correctly.  Use a card to mark your
        place on the coding sheet to avoid skipping or
        repeating sections of code.  Only punch into cards
        you are sure are fresh.  Find out how to use a drum
        card on a keypunch to reduce the likelihood of
        misplaced columns.

     D. If you entrust your program or data to someone else
        to be typed, ask that it be machine verified.  If
        it can't be, obtain a printed listing of all data
        for a visual check.  Let one person read aloud
        while another scans the listing.  Count lines and
        spaces.  Look for extra lines or cards left in the
        deck.  Apply any feasible cross checks you can
        think of.

     E. Regardless of the method of preparation, put
        identification numbers and card codes on all
        program and data cards.  Your program should check
        these during input as well.  Find a box that is the
        right size for your program if more than 200 cards

        Problem Solving With a Computer--Reprise        259

are involved.  If you opt for an unboxed deck, use
several rubber bands--not one that strangles (and
mangles) the cards.

F.  Data center clerks, machine operators, and even
computer card readers have been known to permute or
truncate card decks.  Consider writing a small
program to put your input on disk or tape.  Make
the necessary sequence checks.  There is less
likelihood of getting records out of order if they
are on disk or tape!

G.  Obtain a listing of all cards and store it away in
your folder.  What problems will you have if a
listing is lost, original data sheets disappear, a
card deck is dropped or a disk file is accidentally
erased?  Make provisions for these possibilities
with backups.

VII. Submit the machine-readable form of the program and the test data to the computer.

A* Examine the compilers you might use for your testing runs. Choose one which does a lot of error checking. Ignore object time efficiency--you shouldn't be using enough data to really be concerned with it initially.

B* Is it possible to test some or all modules separately? If you must test the entire package, consider printing out an indicator in each module to indicate when it is active. Also, are you printing out intermediate values as control goes from module to module so you can track down the locations of any errors? Does the compiler you are using have a trace feature?

C. Carefully follow the procedures for submitting programs specified by your computing center. If you are to run the computer or terminal yourself and must learn how, do so using a program that is known to work rather than the one you just wrote.

D* Do you have money in your computing account? Have you used the current password? Have you used the job control language properly for the compiler, I/O devices, and options you want? Have you examined the options which are available to help you decide if everything is working properly? Cross reference listings? Attribute list? List of machine coding? Have you given the machine operator the written information he or she needs to run the job?

VIII. Look at the results.  Debug program or data if
      necessary.

   A* Was your job cancelled by the system because it
      took too long?  Because it asked for a tape or disk
      you hadn't told the operator you were going to use?

   B. Did the program fail to compile?  Did you make any
      syntax errors?  (If so, go back to square one.)
      Why?  Careless?  Don't know the language?  Didn't
      desk check?  Consult the error message; fix the
      immediate problem.  Don't resubmit the program yet!
      Go over the entire program with a fine-tooth comb
      without the aid of the machine.  If you let a
      syntax error slip by, you probably have logic
      errors as well.

   C. Did the program fail in execution?  How far did it
      get?  Did it print out some of the intermediate
      results you were careful to include as part of the
      output?  Which module did it fail in?  Did that
      module get the correct data to work with?  What
      techniques for debugging are offered by your
      computing center or by the compiler you are using
      to help you find a really difficult bug?  Can you
      add special program statements to help you isolate
      the problem?  If you go over it 20 times and can't
      see the problem, ask someone else.  Don't tell him
      or her what the program is supposed to do. Let him
      or her tell you what it will do.  Plan not to be
      surprised if he or she looks at it for 30 seconds
      and points right at the problem.

   D. Are the answers there?  If so, don't assume they
      are right.  Compare them with the test data answers
      you worked out ahead of time.  Do they match?  If
      not, where is the first hint of trouble?  (Errors
      are like shopping carts in a grocery store parking
      lot.  They seem to breed and multiply.)

   E. Even if everything seems perfect, sit down in a
      quiet place with the listing and a pencil.  Write
      down each important idea you have about the results
      before the next thought blows it away.

IX.   Document the program.

   A. This step is out of place; but there is really no
      place to put it because documenting should be going
      on all during development.  Documentation is really
      a process as much as a product.  If you've
      developed the program properly much of the
      documentation will be in the program.

   B. Consider including the following items in the
      documentation:

      1. The context within which the program resides. A
         person with no understanding of computers or the
         problem itself ought to be able to understand
         the context-setting paragraph.

      2. The problem statement.

      3. Descriptions of the methods used, with
         references.

      4. The overall logical structure of the modules and
         the function of each.

      5. Operating instructions, machine requirements,
         memory requirements, language(s) used, input
         forms, etc.

      6. Programmer name, address, organization, dates of
         writing, testing, release.  Dates of
         modifications and their nature.

      7. Illustrated test run input and output.

      8. Examples of running time requirements--test
         data, other runs.

      9. A disclaimer, saying that, although you've done
         your best, you aren't responsible for any
         mischief caused by errors in the program.

      10. A program name--some darling acronym you come up
          with when you are tired of thinking seriously
          about the whole business.

      11. The program listing.

12. Line drawings to explain concepts for which English doesn't seem appropriate.

C* Just as the program is subject to modifications, the documentation is also. Consider using a text processing program to allow machine readable storage of the documentation.

X.    Use or release the program.

A* Remove any extra statements you inserted for
   debugging.  Be careful.  Rerun the program with
   test data and check the results.  Get a fresh card,
   tape, or disk copy of the source program for a
   back-up copy.  If you use cards and your deck is
   not sequence numbered to suit you, reproduce it
   with a sequence number adding program.  Save a
   listing of all cards.

B* Consider getting an object program with an
   execution time-efficient compiler.  Rerun your test
   data with the newly compiled version.  Match
   against prior test runs.  Any discrepancies are as
   serious as a cat in a sandbox.  Find the
   difficulty.

C. How sophisticated will the program's user be?  Are
   you assuming knowledge that he or she might not
   have?  Find a person willing to test run the
   program for you.  Give him or her the program,
   documentation, and some data.  Watch him or her
   struggle with it but don't help.  (You won't be
   around when a person 1500 miles away tries to use
   the program.)  Why does he or she have problems?
   What changes are suggested?

D. Now that you've been through all these steps,
   doesn't it seem reasonable that a carefully
   written, tested, documented, and working program
   can cost about $35 per statement?

# part III

# PASCAL
# DATA
# STRUCTURES

If you went through Parts I and II, you know enough
program structure to describe almost any algorithm. What
could be left to know? To give you a hint, Dr. Niklaus
Wirth, the esteemed designer of the PASCAL language, wrote a
book with an explicit title: <u>Algorithms</u> + <u>Data Structures</u> =
<u>Programs</u>. This should lead you to the belief that a large
part of the PASCAL language (and its popularity) is
concerned with the ways in which data can be represented and
operated on by PASCAL. The major concern will be with the
PASCAL concept of TYPE, but we'll warm up with a few other
things about data which you should know.

From this point in the book, we will discuss PASCAL, not
TIPS. Many companies sell PASCAL systems. Each system is
somewhat different and can be thought of as a different
"version" of PASCAL which might contain different features
from others. But all language features that work in TIPS
will work in any PASCAL.

## The Declaration Section

The declaration section of a PASCAL PROGRAM or PROCEDURE
may consist of six sections. You've come in contact with
two of them: VAR and PROCEDURE. Shortly we will introduce
CONST and TYPE. In PART IV we will describe LABEL and
FUNCTION. Because the order of the six sections is
specifically required by PASCAL syntax, we will give it to
you here, now, so you can refer back to it if you need it.

```
LABEL

CONST

TYPE

VAR

PROCEDURE and/or FUNCTION
```

Each of these delimiter words may appear in the declaration section of any PASCAL PROGRAM or PROCEDURE, but only in the order shown; any may be omitted but those present must be in the proper order.


## A Shortcut with VAR

In TIPS we always showed at least one line being used in the declaration of a variable. Thus we might say:

```
VAR
     I: (* LOOP COUNTER *)  INTEGER;
     J: (* LOOP COUNTER *)  INTEGER;
     K: (* LOOP COUNTER *)  INTEGER;
```

In PASCAL, you are allowed to say:

```
VAR I,J,K: (* LOOP COUNTERS *)  INTEGER;
```

or even

```
VAR I,J,K: INTEGER;
```

if you want to. We hope, usually, you won't want to. In any event, do make your choice based on what you think is the most readable rather than on the fact that you can save a few keystrokes by using this newly allowed technique.


## Declaring Constant Identifiers

Often it is useful to have an identifier stand for a number in a program. Suppose you needed the value of pi in several different places. Rather than write 3.14159 over and over again--with, of course, the attendant possibility of getting it wrong occasionally--you would like to have an identifier stand for the value.

There are two ways to do this. The one you know about is just the assignment statement:

```
PI := 3.14159
```

But there is a better way. It is to use a synonym for a constant. This feature allows the programmer to give an identifier a value and to assure that the value will not be changed in the course of the program. This feature is the

CONSTant declaration and has a number of uses. First, let's look at how it is accomplished.

In the declaration section of the program, you use the instruction CONST. The form of CONST is

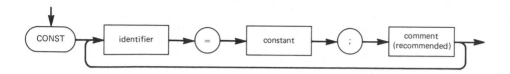

An example is:

CONST PI=3.14159; (* CIRCUMFERENCE/DIAMETER RATIO *)

With this definition, whenever the identifier PI is used in the action part of the program it will have the value 3.14159. What is the advantage of using a constant identifier rather than a variable? Declared as a CONSTant, PI is immune to tampering. Thus a statement--a misstatement really--such as

READ (PG,PH,PI)

would produce an error message, not an accidental change in the value of PI.

Another virtue of using CONST is that it puts the constants which are going to be used in the program right up front where they can be easily checked and where their meanings can be presented by comments. The CONST declaration comes just after the LABEL declaration so it is either the first or second item in the PASCAL program. Notice that, in the declaration itself, the identifier and the constant are separated by = rather than := to suggest that the identifier is really equal to the value of the constant. Here is what a constant declaration section for three natural constants might look like:

CONST
    PI=3.14159; (* CIRCUMFERENCE/DIAMETER RATIO *)
    E=2.71828; (* EULER'S CONSTANT *)
    G=1.61803; (* THE GOLDEN MEAN *)

Constant identifiers can also be used to stand for character strings.  For example,

```
CONST
     TOTALED=' THE FINAL TOTAL IS ';
     STARS=' *****************'; (* SECTION SEPARATOR *)
```

With these constant identifiers the programmer could achieve economies in WRITELN statements, particularly if the character strings were to be printed several times.

As with other instructions in the declaration section, the delimiter word CONST may appear only once.

A further advantage of CONST is that the value of the CONST may be used in other declarations.  For example, in the program MEDIAN of Part II (on the Program Development Scroll) we could have said:

```
CONST
     NUMBER=50;
VAR
     VALUES: ARRAY [1..NUMBER] OF REAL;
```

In summary, the advantages of this feature are: first, you don't have to write a particular numeric value each time you use it, which reduces the chance for error; second, while you could use a variable for the value, with CONST you avoid the risk of accidentally changing it and not being told of the error; third, CONSTants are declared right at the beginning of the program, making them quite obvious; fourth, we can use CONST in VAR (and TYPE) declarations, adding understandability to the program and reducing the number of changes required if the problem definition changes.

---

There is a CONST supplied with each version of

PASCAL; its name is MAXINT, and it is the maximum

value an INTEGER variable may take on.  Its value

for your machine is _____.

---

Many representations of data are allowed in PASCAL.  A
class of representation is called a TYPE.  You have met
three TYPEs so far: the pre-defined TYPEs (1) REAL, and (2)
INTEGER, and (3) the structured TYPE ARRAY which was based
on the two TYPEs REAL and INTEGER.

In this section you will be exposed to several more
TYPEs; some of them will seem pretty bizarre.  And sometimes
you may have difficulty distinguishing just what is meant at
a particular time by a particular construction.  It is
important to hold onto the idea that you will be dealing
with three different concepts: TYPE, variable, and value.
With the TYPE REAL, for example, you could have a variable
ABC and it could have a value 1.23456.  With the TYPE ARRAY
[1..5] OF INTEGER you could have a variable named DEF and it
could have five different values at the same time (e.g.,
4,0,-45,18,10101); the correct value would be indexed by a
subscript.

As we start describing new TYPEs you may find yourself
confusing these three concepts.  When that happens, go back
to basics and ask yourself about each entity: is this a
TYPE, variable, or value?


Baptism by Fire: All the TYPEs at Once

Just so you know what you're getting into, here's a
little picture of all the TYPEs.  You will not be able to
comprehend it fully now.  It's here so you can come back to
it occasionally and get your perspective.  An extensive
picture of the relationships among the TYPEs may be found at
the back of the book on the back of the fold-out sheet. (See
Note 1 at the end of Part III.)

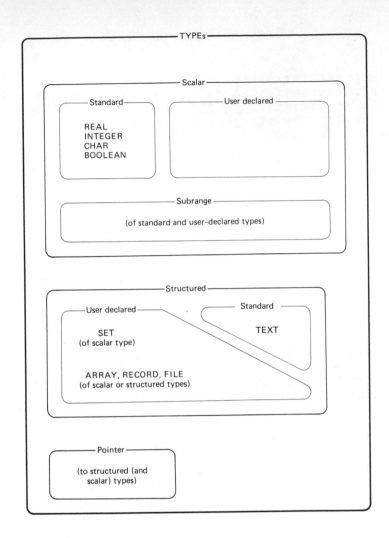

TYPEs, Variables, and Values

A scalar TYPE must have a name. Any number of variables
may be declared to be of a given TYPE. Each of those
variables may, at any given time, have a single value. The
range of values that a particular scalar variable may take
on depends on the TYPE of that variable.

The paragraph above is very important; read it again.

There are three classes of scalar TYPEs.

1)    user-defined

2)    standard (supplied by PASCAL)

3)    subrange (of the user-defined and standard TYPES)

## User-Defined TYPES (See Note 1 at the end of Part III)

To declare a scalar TYPE you select an identifier (e.g.,
up to eight characters in length, the first alphabetic).
Then you specify, explicitly, also using identifiers, (which
are not variable names), the values which variables of the
TYPE may take on. The order in which you specify the range
of values is important; the first will be considered the
least value; the last will be considered the greatest.

For example,

```
TYPE
        DAY=(MON,TUE,WED,THU,FRI,SAT,SUN);
```

This declaration of TYPE says that variables may be declared
to be of the TYPE DAY and that any variable so declared may,
at a given time, take on one of the values MON, TUE, etc.

For example,

```
VAR
      JULY4TH: (* 4TH OF JULY OF THE GIVEN YEAR *) DAY;
      NEWYEARS: (* JANUARY 1 OF THE GIVEN YEAR *) DAY;
      SOMEDAY: (* ANY DAY *) DAY;
```

Now it is possible to write such statements as:

```
JULY4TH := WED;
NEWYEARS := SAT;
SOMEDAY := SUN
```

Here's another example:

```
(* WHO GETS THE HIGH CARD WHEN TWO CARDS ARE DRAWN? *)
(* PLAYERS ARE PLAYER 1 (FSTPLR) & PLAYER 2 (SNDPLR) *)
PROGRAM HIGHCARD (INPUT, OUTPUT);
    CONST
        ONEWINS=' THE WINNER IS PLAYER NUMBER 1';
        TWOWINS=' THE WINNER IS PLAYER NUMBER 2';
    TYPE
        SUIT=(CLUB,DIAMOND,HEART,SPADE);
        RANK=(TWO,THREE,FOUR,FIVE,SIX,SEVEN,EIGHT,NINE,TEN,
                JACK,QUEEN,KING,ACE);
    VAR
        FSTPLRSU: (* SUIT DRAWN BY FIRST PLAYER *) SUIT;
        SNDPLRSU: (* SUIT DRAWN BY SECOND PLAYER *) SUIT;
        FSTPLRRK: (* RANK DRAWN BY FIRST PLAYER *) RANK;
        SNDPLRRK: (* RANK DRAWN BY SECOND PLAYER *) RANK;
BEGIN
(* SUBTERFUGE SECTION *)
(* IT'S REALLY A CROOKED GAME--AND WE'RE BETTING ON PLAYER 2 *
    FSTPLRSU := CLUB;
    FSTPLRRK := TWO;
    SNDPLRSU := SPADE;
    SNDPLRRK := ACE;
(* STRAIGHT SECTION *)
    WRITELN (' AND NOW THE CARDS HAVE BEEN DRAWN');
    IF FSTPLRRK <> SNDPLRRK THEN
        IF FSTPLRRK > SNDPLRRK THEN
            WRITELN (ONEWINS)
        ELSE
            WRITELN (TWOWINS)
    ELSE
        IF FSTPLRSU <> SNDPLRSU THEN
            IF FSTPLRSU > SNDPLRSU THEN
                WRITELN (ONEWINS)
            ELSE
                WRITELN (TWOWINS)
        ELSE
            WRITELN (' THERE IS A TIE--AND A BAD DECK')
END.
```

It was all so simple before. You had a TYPE, like REAL, whose name you could memorize; you had variable names that you could make up and keep track of; and you had values which looked "honest" like 38.98 or, at the worst, -22.555E-04.

Now you've got TYPEs like SUITS, variables such as FSTPLRSU, and values such as DIAMOND. And you can make up the names for all of them. It's the same principle as before--but you shouldn't get too unhappy if you become confused at times.

There is nothing you can do with user-defined scalar TYPEs that you can't do with the TYPE INTEGER. But after you become familiar with user-defined scaler TYPEs you may find the programs are more readable, and that you are spared the problem of remembering whether you programmed 5 to mean Thursday or Friday.

Here are a number of points relative to user-defined TYPEs.

1.  If a value is declared to be a member of one TYPE it may not be of any other. It is illegal, then to have

        TYPE
            COLOR=(RED, ORANGE, YELLOW, GREEN, BLUE, VIOLET);
            FRUIT=(APPLE, ORANGE, PLUM);
            FLOWER=(PANSY, VIOLET, DAISY);

    ORANGE and VIOLET are the trouble makers.

2.  The arithmetic operators do not work with user-defined TYPEs. But the assignment operator works. E.g., FSTPLRRK := TWO.

3.  The comparison operators work with user-defined variable TYPEs. The card drawing program illustrated that.

4.  Three new FUNCTIONs operate with variables of user defined TYPEs: ORD, SUCC, PRED.

        ORD(value) returns an INTEGER value which indicates the position of the user-defined scalar value in the list. The first member of the list is numbered zero, the second is one, and so forth. (This habitual misnumbering of things by computer-nuts is a carryover from the days when people who used computers at their most elementary level (the only level there was thirty years ago) got in the habit of numbering locations in memory by the bizarre scheme of calling the first location zero; the second, one; and so on. They did this for much the same reason the telephone people counted the tenth position on the dial as zero: they didn't want to waste any digits. The authors are not immune either; notice the number of the first laboratory problem in this book.)

SUCC(value) has the value of the SUCCessor. E.g., SUCC(TUE) has the value WED. The last value, e.g., SUN, has no succeeding value.

PRED(value) has the value of the PREDecessor. The first value has no preceding value. What is ORD(PRED(PRED(SNDPLRRK)))?

5. Before you get too excited about using TYPEs you define yourself we have some bad news: you cannot, in standard PASCAL, read in or write out the values of variables as such. That is, it is not legal to say:

WRITELN(FSTPLRSU)

and have CLUB written out of the machine. You may say

WRITELN(ORD(FSTPLRSU))

which prints out an INTEGER "0". But that takes the fun--and a lot of the usefulness--out of user-defined TYPEs.

6. The cardinality of a given TYPE is the number of values which a variable of the TYPE may take on. The cardinality of the TYPE SUITS is 4.

7. You can use a value of a user-defined scalar type as a subscript. For example if a program began

TYPE DAY = (MON,TUE,WED,THU,FRI,SAT,SUN);
VAR S: ARRAY[DAY] OF REAL

then S would consist of seven elements: S[MON], S[TUE], S[WED], S[THU], S[FRI], S[SAT], S[SUN].

8. You may use a user-defined TYPE in the FOR-DO statement (and other statements, covered later) where you used the

TYPE INTEGER before.  For example:

```
FOR SOMEDAY := SAT DOWNTO MON DO
        statement
```

## Exercise

A university uses the following table in coding student classifications:

| CODE | CLASSIFICATION |
|------|----------------|
| 0 | NON-DEGREE |
| 1 | FRESHMAN |
| 2 | SOPHOMORE |
| 3 | JUNIOR |
| 4 | SENIOR |
| 5 | GRADUATE |
| 6 | PROFESSIONAL |

a.  Write a definition for a TYPE called CLASTYPE which includes identifiers  for each Student Classification above.
b.  Define a variable named STUCLAS, which can take on any of the values in CLASTYPE. Define another variable named STUCODE which can assume the Code values.
c.  Write statements to assign to STUCLAS the value corresponding to the value of STUCODE.

```
+-----------------------------------------+
|     SUGGESTED LABORATORY PROBLEM        |
|                 51                      |
+-----------------------------------------+
```

There are four standard TYPES which PASCAL recognizes: REAL, INTEGER, CHARacter, and BOCLEAN.  Any PASCAL program will behave as though its author had, in the TYPE declaration instruction, written:

```
TYPE
    REAL=(-_____E+_____,-98.7653,...0.0, 0.000001,
         0.000002,...5.86124E+08..._____E+_____);

    INTEGER=(-MAXINT,..,-54,-53,..-1,0,1,2,3,4,..MAXINT);

    CHAR=(



                                                      );


    (By writing a program, described shortly, you will
    learn the sequence of each printable character such
    A,B,C,0,1. Then write the "collating sequence" above.)

    BOOLEAN=(FALSE, TRUE);
```

(Well, it's almost like that.  You can't use ORD, SUCC, and PRED on REAL numbers.  And if you use ORD on INTEGER values--who knows why you would do that?--some implementations pretend that only the non-negative integers are the permitted values.)

The four standard TYPEs are gifts to you from the compiler.  You already know about INTEGER and REAL.  Let's talk about CHAR.


The CHARacter TYPE

A scalar variable of the TYPE CHARacter may take on a value which is one of the letters, digits, or special characters allowed by the particular machine you are using.

So if we say

```
VAR
      ANYCHAR: (* COMMENT *) CHAR;
```

the variable ANYCHAR may take on the value "A" or "B" or "C"
or "1" or "2" or "3" or "$" or "-" or ")". Further, as with
all scalar variables, the values are ordered so that A is
smaller than B which is smaller than C etc. And "1" is
smaller than "2" which is smaller than "3". But there
things stop being neat. Is "1" smaller than "A"? Is "$"
smaller than "%"? It depends on the machine you are
using--almost on the whim of the person(s) who designed it.
Oh, there are standards--several of them, in fact.

How can you find out what CHARacters are available on
your machine and the order they are considered to be in?
You could look in the manual for the computer. Your
instructor could tell you. But the surest way, which is
also the most fun and educational, is to write a program
whose output will reveal the truth.

Here are some things you should know--both to write the
program and in general:

1.  You already know about the ORD, PRED, and SUCC
    functions. Since they work with all scalar data TYPEs
    (except REAL) they work with CHAR. When you use a
    value of the TYPE CHAR in a program you should surround
    it with apcstrophes. Thus if you want to produce the
    result of the ordinal function for the CHARacter
    constant Q you could write

```
      J := ORD('Q');
      WRITELN (J)
```

    If you wanted to use the ordinal function on
    a CHARacter variable such as ANYCHAR declared above you
    would simply say

```
      J := ORD(ANYCHAR);
      WRITELN (J)
```

    What effect would

```
      J := ORD ('''')
```

    have?

2. There is another function which relates to the use of
the CHARacter variable: CHR(n) where n is an INTEGER
constant variable or expression. The result is the
CHARacter which corresponds to the internal integer
representation value of n. It would be valid to say

        ANYCHAR := CHR(ANINT)

provided the value of ANINT, an integer, actually
corresponded to some character or other in the machine.
(If ANINT does not have a value which corresponds to a
valid character you may get an error.) What would

        ANYCHAR := CHR(ORD('G'))

do?

3. Most machines have character sets with integer
equivalent values of 0 to 63, 0 to 127, or 0 to 255.

4. Some of the "characters" in a machine may be
unprintable. An example is the BELL character which on
some terminals and microcomputers rings a bell or makes
a beep when "written."

We've left the next page blank so you can write in (or paste
in) the results of your program(s).


Exercise

Given:

    VAR
        ANYCHAR: (* VARIABLE WHICH CAN TAKE ON ANY
            PRINTABLE CHARACTER VALUE *) CHAR;

What's the difference between:

    ANYCHAR := C    and    ANYCHAR := 'C'

# Strings

Now we come to a construction in PASCAL which is something of a "half standard." You can imagine that you could define a CONSTant of the CHARacter TYPE by merely saying

```
CONST
    ELL='L';
```

And you certainly can. You can then say

```
WRITELN(ELL)
```

and the single character L will be written out, without surrounding apostrophes.

What's surprising is that you can declare

```
CONST
    SENTENCE=' HERE''S A BUNCH OF CHARACTERS.'
```

and if you say

```
WRITELN (SENTENCE)
```

you'll get the lot of them printed out. This suggests that there must be some variable TYPE that relates to a sequence of characters. Such a group is called a string.

There is no standard data TYPE string but you can manufacture string TYPEs by saying:

```
VAR
    ASTRING: (*   *) PACKED ARRAY [1..12] OF CHAR;
    BSTRING: (*   *) PACKED ARRAY [1..12] OF CHAR;
    SHORT: (*   *) PACKED ARRAY [1..2] OF CHAR;
```

Then it would be correct to say

```
ASTRING := 'ABCDEFUVWXYZ';
SHORT := 'AZ';
BSTRING := 'ABCDEFGHIJKL'
```

Character strings must be contained on one line. The word PACKED must be used here to allow assignment statements as shown above; PACKED places each character next to the next one in the memory of the computer and therefore economizes on storage space at the expense of execution time.

Although a string is simply a PACKED array of characters it has some properties that arrays do not normally have. (See the earlier definitions of ASTRING, BSTRING, and SHORT.)

1) You can say

WRITELN (' ',SHORT)

and the entire array (2 elements) will be written out. That is, strings can be written out. You can also specify the number of output columns used in writing out a string. For example if you wrote

WRITELN (' ',SHORT:8)

the output would appear with six blanks to the left of it (since SHORT is two characters and the field width is eight).

2) You can compare the value of one string with another:

IF ASTRING >= BSTRING THEN

The condition in this case would be true because the two strings differ in their seventh position (look at them carefully) and the ordinal value of G is smaller than the ordinal value of U.

The number of characters, including blanks, in a string is its length. Some high level languages allow strings of the same TYPE to have varying lengths; PASCAL doesn't. When you compare two strings in PASCAL you must be sure they are declared to be of the same length. If you have trouble because of this restriction, it may make you feel better to know that the requirement for fixed length strings is regarded as one of the (few) major failings of PASCAL.

For example, it would be illegal to write

IF ASTRING >= SHORT THEN

## Input of Character Strings

Instructing a computer to read a group of characters is somewhat more complicated than instructing it to read a number. The reason is simple: Standard PASCAL can only read one character at a time. Therefore to read a group of characters, one reads each character into an array of CHAR. Blanks are used to separate numbers. So we may say READ (NUM1,NUM2,NUM3) and be assured that, as long as the numbers to be read are in the proper sequence (and no number is split between lines), they will go in properly. They might be on one line:

55.3  -99E-08  888

or on more than one line

```
55.3
      -99E-08
  888
```

The READ procedure is smart enough to know that, since blanks may not be part of a number, it may read continuously until it finds a non-blank character and such a character will signify the beginning of a number.

But a blank is a valid CHAR so we may not rely upon it to separate CHARacters. If we want to read a character string, we can do the following:

```
VAR
     CSTRING: (*  *) PACKED ARRAY [1..7] OF CHAR;
     K: (* LOOP COUNTER *) INTEGER;
BEGIN
FOR K := 1 TO 7 DO
     READ(CSTRING[K])
```

The above program will read seven characters into the array CSTRING.

If character strings are separated by blanks, you could write a sequence of statements to read them. Specifically, suppose you want to read SAMPLE (defined as PACKED ARRAY [1..5] OF CHAR) and it is preceeded by an unknown number of blanks. You might write:

```
SAMPLE[ 1] := ' ';
WHILE SAMPLE [ 1] = ' ' DO
    READ (SAMPLE[ 1]);
FOR J := 2 TO 5 DO
    READ (SAMPLE[ J])
```

The problem of reading character strings becomes compounded if the strings might be on successive lines, rather than on the same line. We discuss this issue in greater detail later in this Part.


## UCSD STRING TYPE

The University of California San Diego (UCSD) PASCAL, which is implemented on many computers, contains an additional data TYPE called STRING, which is a group of characters. STRING variables are not part of standard PASCAL. To declare a STRING variable, one writes

           VAR name: (*    *) STRING[ n ];

This establishes "name" as a variable which can take on a value consisting of a sequence of "n" characters. If a specific length is not specified, length 80 will be assigned by default. For example,

           VAR ADDRESS: (*    *) STRING;

declares ADDRESS to be a character STRING of length 80. If we wanted to create a variable named ADDRESS as a STRING of 99 characters in length, we would write

           VAR ADDRESS: (*    *) STRING[ 99 ];

A STRING variable may be read, written, and compared with other STRING variables. To access the Nth character in ADDRESS you could simply write

           ADDRESS[ N ]

For example, suppose that the STRING variable ADDRESS contained the value

           409 LAREDO COURT

Then ADDRESS[ 3 ] would be 9 and ADDRESS[ 16 ] would be T.

We can also create arrays of STRINGS.  To do this we could declare

VAR CITIES:(*      *) PACKED ARRAY[1..100] OF STRING;

In this case, we have created an array of 100 variables, each of which is an eighty-character STRING.


## Exercise

If the STRING NAME contained the value MIKEANDMARTY what would be the value of

a. NAME[3] b. NAME[6] c. NAME[9] d. NAME[12] e. NAME[13]

To access a specific character in an element of a STRING array, simply reference the array element first followed by a comma followed by the character number desired.  For example, if ADDRESS[2] contained the value

1050 ELMENDORF

then to reference the sixth character one would write

ADDRESS[2,6]

which would reference the character E.

To determine the length of a STRING, we can use the LENGTH function which returns the number of characters, including blanks, in the variable.  In the example above, if we executed the statement

N:=LENGTH(ADDRESS[2])

the value of N would become 14.


## Exercise

If two STRINGS named B[1] and B[2] contained UNIVERSITY and KENTUCKY respectively, what would be the value of

1. B[1,4] 2. B[2,4] 3. B[1,7] 4. B[1,1] 5. B[2,2] 6. B[1,9]

## The READLN PROCEDURE

The READLN instruction operates exactly as does READ, except that, when the last variable in the READLN list has been defined, READLN "disposes" of the rest of the data on the line, so that the next READ or READLN begins reading at the beginning of the next line.  This can facilitate input; it can also cause problems.

For example, to use NUM1, NUM2, and NUM3 again, if you wrote

```
READ(NUM1);
READ(NUM2);
READ(NUM3)
```

and the data were

55.3   -99E-08   888

everything would work out fine because each READ picks up where the preceding one left off.  The effect is the same as

READ(NUM1,NUM2,NUM3).  However, if you wrote

```
READLN(NUM1);
READLN(NUM2);
READLN(NUM3)
```

you would lose the second two numbers; they would have been disposed of by the first READLN.

The way READLN facilitates the reading of character data is to let the programmer bring up a new line, "flushing" any reminants of a previous line which might contain blanks or other unwanted characters.  In general, if you want to start at the beginning of a line when reading character or string data, use a READLN to complete the reading of the previous line, whether you were reading numbers or characters.

There is a fourth procedure, WRITE, which performs in a manner similar to READ in that it does not complete a line but allows the values of variables from several WRITE instructions to be placed on a single line.  We describe it in detail later.

```
┌─────────────────────────────────────────┐
│        SUGGESTED LABORATORY PROBLEMS      │
│                 39, 58                    │
└─────────────────────────────────────────┘
```

## The BOOLEAN TYPE

You've met the BOOLEAN idea before.  A BOOLEAN
expression is one that is either false or true.  You've used
BOOLEAN expressions in IF--THEN statements and in WHILE--DO
statements.  Now we add the concept of a BOOLEAN variable:
one which may take on either the value FALSE or the value
TRUE.

A BOOLEAN constant is represented in a program as either
the delimiter word TRUE or as the word FALSE.  These words
may be used in a program in a parallel way with other
constants such as -18 or 56.78.  But, while there are many
REAL and INTEGER constants, there are only two BOOLEAN
constants.  ORD(FALSE) is zero and ORD(TRUE) is one.
BOOLEAN is one of the four standard, scalar TYPES.

BOOLEAN variables are declared in the VAR instruction of
the declarations section of the PASCAL program.  For
example,

```
VAR .
    .
    .
    FIRST: (* TRUE IF SUBJECT WAS IN FIRST PLACE *)  BOOLEAN;
    BAD: (* TRUE IF THE INPUT NUMBER WAS BAD *)  BOOLEAN;
    WINNER: (* TRUE IF OTHER PLAYER FAULTS *)  BOOLEAN;
```

A BOOLEAN variable may be assigned the values TRUE or
FALSE by an assignment statement:

```
    FIRST := TRUE;
    BAD := INPUTVL > 99
```

In the first case, FIRST is given its value directly by
use of the constant TRUE.  In the second statement, BAD is
given the value TRUE if the numeric value of INPUTVL is
greater than 99.  Otherwise BAD is given the value FALSE.
The second statement illustrates that a BOOLEAN variable can
take on the value of a logical expression of the sort you
met in TIPS  WHILE--DO and IF--THEN--ELSE statements.

Recall the sample problem in Part II on the Program Development Scroll. We needed a switch to indicate whether the number of values in the list was odd or even. We used an INTEGER variable named ODDVAL to which we assigned either a zero or a one. We could have used a BOOLEAN variable declared as

```
VAR
     TRULYODD:(* TRUE IF LIST LENGTH IS ODD *) BOOLEAN;
```

Then we might have said

```
TRULYODD := N MOD 2 = 1
```

The BOOLEAN expression N MOD 2 = 1 would be TRUE if and only if N was odd.

You can write (but cannot read) the values of BOOLEAN variables directly. We illustrate this feature, and a couple of others, by showing three sets of statements which are entirely equivalent in the output each produces.

```
1)   IF TRULYODD=TRUE THEN
          WRITELN (' TRUE')
     ELSE
          WRITELN (' FALSE')

2)   IF TRULYODD THEN
          WRITELN (' TRUE')
     ELSE
          WRITELN (' FALSE')

3)   WRITELN (TRULYODD)
```

To read in values of BOOLEAN variables requires some programming. Probably it is best just to write a little internal procedure which reads an F or T into a CHARacter variable and sets a BOOLEAN variable as a result.

Variables of the BOOLEAN type may be operated upon by either relational or logical operators. The relational operators are: =, <>, <=, <, >, >=, IN. (The IN operator is covered later under the SET type). The logical operators, in order or precedence, are:

```
┌─────────┐
│ NOT     │
│ AND     │
│ OR      │
└─────────┘
```

The "NOT" operator simply reverses the truth value of a
BOOLEAN variable.  That is, if P is TRUE, then

                        NOT P

is FALSE.

The truth table for the <u>AND</u> logical operator is shown below.

<u>Value of P</u>              <u>Value of Q</u>              <u>Result of Expression</u>
   TRUE        AND        TRUE                   TRUE
   TRUE        AND        FALSE                  FALSE
   FALSE       AND        TRUE                   FALSE
   FALSE       AND        FALSE                  FALSE

In short, only in the case where both P and Q are TRUE is
the expression, "P AND Q", TRUE.

The truth table for the <u>OR</u> operator is shown below.

<u>Value of P</u>              <u>Value of Q</u>              <u>Result of Expression</u>
   TRUE        OR         TRUE                   TRUE
   TRUE        OR         FALSE                  TRUE
   FALSE       OR         TRUE                   TRUE
   FALSE       OR         FALSE                  FALSE

In short, only in the case where both P and Q are FALSE, is
the expression, "P OR Q", FALSE.

For example, if P and Q are both TRUE and R and S are both
FALSE then

        P OR S AND Q OR NOT R          is   TRUE

First, "NOT R" is evaluated as TRUE.  Next "S AND Q" is
evaluated as FALSE.  Since "P" is TRUE, the evaluation boils
down to

Standard Scalar TYPEs

1) $\underbrace{\text{TRUE OR FALSE}}$ CR TRUE

2) $\underbrace{\quad\text{TRUE}\qquad\quad\text{OR TRUE}}$

3) TRUE

## Exercises

1. If P and Q are both TRUE and if R and S are both FALSE, then what is the value of each of the expressions below?

    a. P OR R
    b. Q OR R
    c. P AND R
    d. P < S
    e. P = S
    f. P <> S

2. For the values of P, Q, R, and S above, evaluate the following expressions as true or false:

    a. P AND Q OR S OR NOT P
    b. P OR Q OR S AND NOT R
    c. (S < Q) OR (R = S) AND P OR NOT Q AND S
    d. (S = P) AND NOT R

## Functions Yielding BOOLEAN Results

Three BOOLEAN functions are predefined in PASCAL. They return the value TRUE or FALSE depending upon which condition is TRUE. The first of these functions is

$$\text{ODD}(X)$$

If the INTEGER X is odd, the function returns the value TRUE. Otherwise, it returns the value FALSE. You would have used this in the program MEDIAN (on the fold-out Program Development Scroll). Where? (Two other functions related to the structured TYPE FILE, to be discussed in detail shortly, are EOLN and EOF. The function

$$\text{EOLN}(F)$$

returns a TRUE if an end of line condition has occurred on TEXTfile F. The function

returns the value TRUE if an end of file condition exists on
the file named F.)


## Exercise

If P and Q are TRUE, and R and S are FALSE, what are the
values of the following expressions?

a. P OR Q AND S OR NOT (P > S) AND ODD(12)
b. NOT ODD(2) AND (P >= S) OR (R <= P) OR S
c. ODD(1) OR S AND P AND (S > P)
d. S OR Q AND P OR NOT R AND P
e. P > S > Q > P < Q >= R


## Subrange TYPE

A subrange TYPE is a scalar TYPE which is built
completely on another scalar TYPE.  The TYPE on which a
particular subrange is built may be either user-defined or
standard (supplied by PASCAL).  A subrange is just that: a
TYPE whose variables may take on values which lie within a
reduced range of another TYPE.  A subrange TYPE may, because
of its reduced size (that is, reduced number of constant
members), be more useful.

To define a subrange you simply name the constants of
the associated scalar TYPE which are the smallest and
largest of the new TYPE you want to form.  The concept can
be shown by example:

```
TYPE
     FRSTHALF = 'A'..'M';
     LSTHALF = 'N'..'Z';
     MONTHDAY = 1..31;
     FULLWEEK = (MON,TUE,WED,THR,FRI,SAT,SUN);
     WEEKEND = SAT..SUN;
```

The declaration above defines five new TYPEs, four of
which are subranges.  FRSTHALF is a subrange of the built-in
TYPE CHAR and may take on values only of the first half of
the alphabet: 'A','B', . . . 'M'.  MONTHDAY is a subrange of
INTEGER and is restricted to thirty-one values: 1 through
31.  WEEKEND may take on only the values SAT and SUN.

You may have the sneaking suspicion that you've seen
this construction before.  Where?  In the VAR declaration of
a subscripted variable.

```
VAR
     DAYNUM: (* ARRAY OF 31 MEMBERS *) ARRAY[1..31] OF REAL;
```

Now, if you prefer, you may define the TYPE MONTHDAY as
above and say

```
VAR
     DAYNUM: (* SAME AS ABOVE *) ARRAY[MONTHDAY] OF REAL;
```

In general, you may use the name of the subrange TYPE (e.g.,
MONTHDAY) or the definition of the subrange TYPE (e.g.,
1..31) interchangeably in the program.

     The value of the subrange (beyond the fact that a
subrange of INTEGER is a convenient way to indicate the
number of elements of an array) is that it provides a way to
limit automatically the range of values which a variable may
take on.  This is particularly useful when you want to use
only selected values of the TYPE INTEGER.  If you know, for
example, that variables LIFT, PULL, SHOVE, PUSH, and TWIST
and the variables of an ARRAY named L should only take on
the values −1, 0, and 1 you can assure yourself that the
computer will sound an alarm if they get outside that range.
You simply declare a TYPE, say TRICHOT, as

```
TYPE
     TRICHOT = -1..1;
```

and then declare variables as

```
VAR
     LIFT: (* A TRICHOTOMOUS VARIABLE *) TRICHOT;
     PULL: (* ANOTHER ONE *) TRICHOT;
     SHOVE, PULL, TWIST: (* THREE AT ONCE *) TRICHOT;
     L: (* *) ARRAY[1..5] OF TRICHOT;
```

Or you can omit the explicit TYPE TRICHOT.  For example, for
the array L you could say

```
VAR
     L: (* SAME AS ABOVE *) ARRAY [1..5] OF -1..1;
```

     You may use a variable of the subrange TYPE in any place
in the program where you might use a variable of its
associated scalar TYPE.

Remember:

1. The constant defining the lower bound must be less than the constant defining the upper bound.

2. Subranges of the TYPE REAL are not permitted.

It is a good idea, whenever you are using a variable of scalar TYPE to ask yourself: are there any values which, if assigned to this variable, constitute an error?  If the answer is yes, you should examine the possibility of declaring the variable to be of a subrange TYPE.  For example, if TTPP represents the total number of people in a population, a negative number is probably a mistake. So you might declare TTPP as

```
VAR
     TTPP: (* TOTAL POPULATION *) 0..MAXINT;
```

instead of declaring it simply INTEGER.

In some versions of PASCAL the matter of checking whether a value is within its proper subrange is an option.  Not checking subranges will make the program run faster.  It will also leave you open to a disaster caused by bad data.

If the variable must be of the TYPE REAL you are stuck with doing the checking yourself.  And you should do it.

## ARRAYs Revisited

You know a lot about ARRAYs by this time.  We are going to use your knowledge to give you an understanding of the concept of structured TYPEs.  Structured TYPEs are built using other TYPEs.

You have declared ARRAYs in the following way:

```
VAR
    ABC: (* COMMENT *) ARRAY[1..5] OF REAL;
    DEF: (* COMMENT *) ARRAY[1..5] OF REAL;
```

In so doing you have used a TYPE (namely, ARRAY[1..5] OF REAL).  You could also use an explicitly identified TYPE. For example,

```
TYPE
    FEW=ARRAY[1..5] OF REAL;
VAR
    ABC: (* COMMENT *) FEW;
    DEF: (* COMMENT *) FEW;
```

Using what you have learned about CONST, you might better write:

```
CONST
    FEWMAX=5;
TYPE
    FEW=ARRAY[1..FEWMAX] OF REAL;
VAR
    ABC: (* COMMENT *) FEW;
    DEF: (* COMMENT *) FEW;
or
CONST
    FEWMAX=5;
TYPE
    FEWRANGE=1..FEWMAX;
    FEW=ARRAY[FEWRANGE] OF REAL;
VAR
    ABC: (* COMMENT *) FEW;
    DEF: (* COMMENT *) FEW;
```

In general the form is

```
TYPE
     identifier=ARRAY[type1] OF type2
```

where type1 may be a <u>subrange</u> of INTEGER or other scalar
type, or may be any scalar TYPE (except REAL and INTEGER).

The designation type2 refers to any TYPE, either built
into PASCAL or previously declared.

Since type2 may be of any TYPE, it may be a structured
TYPE (e.g., itself an ARRAY).  If you wanted a two-
dimensional ARRAY, then

```
TYPE
     •
     •
     FEWBYFEW=ARRAY[FEWRANGE] OF ARRAY[FEWRANGE] OF REAL;
VAR
     GHI: (* COMMENT *) FEWBYFEW;
```

would declare GHI as a variable which could be referenced as

```
     GHI[I][J]
```

Our purpose here is to show that you may declare a
structured TYPE of a structured TYPE.  For the ARRAY, the
shorthand declaration is preferred.  You declare

```
TYPE
     FEWBYFEW=ARRAY[FEWRANGE,FEWRANGE] OF REAL;
VAR
     GHI: (* COMMENT *) FEWBYFEW;
```

and the shorthand method of referring to an element of the
multidimensional ARRAY is

```
     GHI[I,J]
```

Set theory is about one hundred years old; it was given to us by mathematician Georg Cantor.  In addition to providing a new and startling basis for mathematics, set theory is also a lot of fun.  Children of young age grasp the principles immediately; even adults can understand them once they overcome their fear.  PASCAL nicely implements the set aggregate as a structured TYPE.

A set is a well-defined collection of distinct objects; the objects are called "elements" or "members" of the set. For example, your text books form a set.  All the positive integers do as well, although this set has infinitely many members.

In PASCAL the members of a SET are either specific identifiers, specific integers, or specific characters. SETs in PASCAL are always finite; sometimes the number of members allowed in a SET is small.

---

In your version of PASCAL a SET may have a maximum

of _____ members.

---

To use the PASCAL SET TYPE you choose a _universal_ SET which contains all the objects you might want to consider. This universal SET is called a _base_ TYPE in PASCAL.

```
      TYPE
           COLOR=(RED,YELLOW,BLUE,GREEN,ORANGE,VIOLET);
           COLORSET=SET OF COLOR;
```

COLOR is a scalar TYPE which serves as the base TYPE for the structured TYPE COLORSET.  The TYPE instruction declares COLORSET to be a SET and says that _each_ _variable_ of the TYPE COLORSET, _once_ _defined_, contains all, or any number, or none of the six members RED, YELLOW, etc.  Let's declare some variables to work with:

```
      VAR
           PRIMARY,THIS,THAT,SOME,FEW,OTHER: (*  *) COLORSET;
           INDEX: (*  *)COLOR;
```

Here six SETs are declared (INDEX is a scalar variable, not a SET).  If we want the SET variable PRIMARY to consist of the elements RED, YELLOW, and BLUE we can write:

        PRIMARY := [ RED,YELLOW,BLUE ]

or we can take advantage of the fact that RED, YELLOW, and BLUE are in a sequence within the definition of COLOR and, using the subrange concept, write

        PRIMARY := [RED..BLUE]

    The <u>union</u> of two SETs is a third SET whose members are in either (or perhaps both) of the first two SETs. Graphically we show the union of SETs A and B below.  (A pictorial representation such as this is called a Venn diagram.)  The union of the two SETs is shown unshaded.

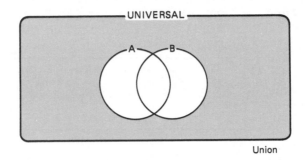

Union

    Using this concept, we can show you still another approach to defining PRIMARY, which demonstrates the SET operator <u>union</u>, denoted by a plus sign (+):

        PRIMARY := [RED]+[ YELLOW ]+[ BLUE ]

or

        PRIMARY := [RED]+[BLUE,YELLOW]

    Or we could say

        FEW := [ RED,BLUE ];
        PRIMARY := FEW+[ YELLOW ]

Now, you might ask, why did we enclose YELLOW in brackets but not FEW? Because brackets mean "the SET consisting of thus and such" where the elements themselves are members of the scalar variable which forms the universal set. FEW, however, is a SET (note its declaration) and if we put brackets around it we'd be saying "the SET consisting of the SET consisting of FEW" which would be incorrect.

For recreation and education, let's consider yet another way to generate the SET PRIMARY using the union operator. To do so we say that a SET consisting of no elements is still a SET. It is called the null SET and in PASCAL it is shown as [ ].

```
PRIMARY := [ ];
FOR INDEX := RED TO BLUE DO
    PRIMARY := PRIMARY+[INDEX]
```

Another SET operator is difference which is shown below as SOME-OTHER. The resulting SET consists of all the elements of SOME except for those members of SOME which are also members of OTHER. Graphically,

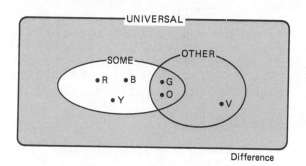

Difference

the SET SOME-OTHER is shown unshaded.

To generate the SET PRIMARY we could say

```
SOME := [RED..GREEN]
OTHER := [GREEN..VIOLET]
PRIMARY := SOME-OTHER
```

Still another way of defining the SET PRIMARY involves the intersection operator (*). The intersection of two SETs is defined to consist of those elements which exist in both SETs. Graphically,

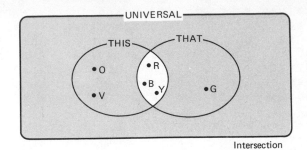

Intersection

the intersection of THIS and THAT is shown unshaded, given
that

```
    THIS  := [ORANGE,VIOLET,BLUE,RED,YELLOW];
    THAT  := [RED,GREEN,BLUE,YELLOW];
    PRIMARY := THIS*THAT
```

   As with the arithmetic operations, any degree of
complexity is possible using SET operands and the SET
operators (*,+,-). The intersection operation has
precedence over the other two, but you should probably use
parentheses to indicate the order in which you want the
operations performed.

   There are also relational operators which operate on
SETs. If we want to know if two SETs are identical we can
write the BOOLEAN expression: THIS=THAT. If the SET THIS
contains exactly the same elements as the SET THAT, and no
other elements, the expression will be true. We could say:

```
    WHILE THIS=THAT DO
```

The operator <> may also be used to produce the opposite
question.

   One can also ask if one SET is included completely
within another. Graphically, assuming the previous
definitions of PRIMARY, SOME, and OTHER,

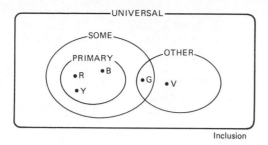
Inclusion

PRIMARY is included in SOME but OTHER isn't.

The operator used for determining SET inclusion (i.e., determining if one SET is a subSET of another) is <= and is called "is a subSET of." Thus, given the SETs pictured above, the BOOLEAN expression PRIMARY<=SOME is true; OTHER<=SOME is false. (The operator >= (we call it "contains") would give the same result as <= if the order of the operands were reversed.)

One more operator exists. It allows the programmer to ask if a value **which is not in a SET,** but which is a possible value for the associated or base TYPE of the SET, is a member of a given SET. The operator is the two letter delimiter word IN. To continue our example, one might form the BOOLEAN expression:

ORANGE IN PRIMARY

and the result would be false since PRIMARY consists of RED, YELLOW, and BLUE. It would also be possible to form the expression

[ORANGE] <= PRIMARY

The advantage of the IN operator, however, is that any value of the associated base TYPE may be used in the expression, whether it is a member of the declared universal SET or not. An example of the usefulness of this is in determining if some character is in the first half or last half of the alphabet. For example,

```
TYPE
    FIRST=SET OF 'A'..'M';
    SECOND=SET OF 'N'..'Z';

VAR
    F: (* FIRST HALF *) FIRST;
    S: (* SECOND HALF *) SECOND;
    IPCHAR: (* AN INPUT CHARACTER *) CHAR;
BEGIN
READ(IPCHAR);
IF IPCHAR IN FIRST THEN
    WRITELN(' FIRST')
ELSE
    IF IPCHAR IN SECOND THEN
        WRITELN(' SECOND')
    ELSE
        WRITELN(' NEITHER')
END.
```

If you don't see the advantage in checking IPCHAR against the two SETs as opposed to checking it without SETs write the program statements to do it in a more conventional way.

As an example which uses the SET TYPE let us suppose you are writing a program for a microcomputer which is to control a gymnasium scoreboard. (For simplicity let us say that the scoreboard displays only one digit which may be zero through nine.) The scoreboard display consists of seven "bars" arranged in two rhombuses. (Those of you with LED or LCD watches will be well familiar with the pattern.)

To form a given digit a certain SET of the bars are turned on. To make a three, for example, the bars TP (top), UR (upper right), MD (middle), LR (lower right), and BT (bottom) are on and the others off.

Our computer program interfaces with the scoreboard
through a PROCEDURE called LIGHTUP. The PROCEDURE LIGHTUP
uses two variables from the main program: the SET of bars
to be turned off (TURNOFF) and the SET of bars to be turned
on (TURNON). If we try to turn off a bar that is already
off or turn on a bar that is already on, the scoreboard
blows a fuse and we get fired. Also we may not turn a bar
off and turn it right back on. In other words, the computer
has to figure out which bars are on that have to stay on,
and leave them on. A program which will read a value (a
numerical digit in the range −1 to 9) and display that digit
(unless it is the trip value −1) is shown on the next page.
Determine how it works. Write comments for it. You may
assume that all the bars are off to begin with.

```
+-------------------------------------------+
|     SUGGESTED LABORATORY PROBLEM          |
|                  41                       |
+-------------------------------------------+
```

```
(* SET EXAMPLE *)
PROGRAM SCB(INPUT,OUTPUT);
    TYPE
        BARS = (MD,UL,TP,UR,LR,BT,LL);
        DIGIT = SET OF BARS;
    VAR
        S: (*                           *) ARRAY[0..9] OF DIGIT;
        LAST: (*                        *) DIGIT;
        NEXT: (*                        *) DIGIT;
        BLANK: (*                       *) DIGIT;
        TURNOFF: (*                     *) DIGIT;
        TURNON: (*                      *) DIGIT;
        SCORE: (*                       *) 0..9;
        BAR: (*                         *) BARS;
        INPSCORE: (*                    *) -1..9;
    PROCEDURE LIGHTUP;
        BEGIN (* LIGHTUP *)
        FOR BAR := MD TO LL DO
            BEGIN
            IF BAR IN TURNOFF THEN
                WRITELN (' OFF ',ORD(BAR));
            IF BAR IN TURNON THEN
                WRITELN (' ON ',ORD(BAR))
            END
        END; (* LIGHTUP *)
    BEGIN
    S[0] := [UL..LL]; S[1] := [UR,LR];
    S[2] := S[0]-[UL,LR]+[MD]; S[3] := [MD]+[TP..BT];
    S[4] := [UL,MD,UR,LR]; S[5] := [MD..TP]+[LR,BT];
    S[6] := S[5]+ [LL]; S[7] := [TP..LR];
    S[8] := [MD..LL]; S[9] := S[8]-[LL];
    BLANK := [ ];
    LAST := BLANK;
    NEXT := BLANK;
    INPSCORE := 0;
    WHILE INPSCORE <> -1 DO
        BEGIN
        READ (INPSCORE);
        IF INPSCORE <> -1 THEN
            BEGIN
            NEXT := S[INPSCORE];
            TURNOFF := LAST-(LAST*NEXT);
            TURNON := NEXT-(LAST*NEXT);
            LAST := NEXT;
            LIGHTUP
            END
        END
    END.
```

Structured TYPEs are made up of simple, base TYPEs. You can have an ARRAY of a given TYPE (e.g., VAR X: ARRAY [1...10] OF REAL). You can have a SET of a given, scalar TYPE (e.g., VAR Y: SET OF 'A'..'G').

The RECORD TYPE is also a structured TYPE made up of other TYPEs. But a RECORD may be made up of several base TYPEs instead of just one. For example, suppose you wanted to describe a particular model of automobile. For a given model you might want its weight, horsepower, number of doors, whether or not it has automatic transmission, and its manufacturer identification. Weight and horsepower might be REAL numbers, number of doors would be INTEGER, automatic transmission could be BOOLEAN, manufacturer's identification might be CHARacter. For example, if the variable name was CAR1, the value of the variable might be:

CAR 1

| 841.5 | 1998.8 | 3 | TRUE | G |
|:---:|:---:|:---:|:---:|:---:|
| WEIGHT | DISPL | DOORS | AUTOTRAN | MANFCID |

This would say that CAR1 weighs 841.5 kilograms, its engine has 1998.8 cubic centimeters of displacement, it has 3 doors, automatic transmission and was built by a manufacturer whose code was G. Another variable, say NEWAUTO, would have the same structure

NEW AUTO

| | | | | |
|:---:|:---:|:---:|:---:|:---:|
| WEIGHT | DISPL | DOORS | AUTOTRAN | MANFCID |

but different values for the elements of the RECORD.

How do you go about telling PASCAL that you want variables with such structure?  With a TYPE statement and a VAR statement:

```
TYPE
    CARDESCP = RECORD
        WEIGHT: (* IN KILOS *) REAL;
        DISPL: (* IN CC'S *) REAL;
        DOORS: (* NUMBER OF DOORS *) INTEGER;
        AUTOTRAN: (* FALSE IF MANUAL SHIFT *) BOOLEAN;
        MANFCID: (* STANDARD CODE *) CHAR
    END;
```

In the VAR section you would say

```
VAR
    CAR1: (* TESTED BEST *) CARDESCP;
    NEWAUTO: (* JUST ANNOUNCED *) CARDESCP;
```

The description of the RECORD which occurs between the delimiter words RECORD and END is called the _field list_; the elements of the record such as WEIGHT and DOORS are called fields.  To gain access to a field you use both the RECORD name and the field name, separated by a period.  Examples:

```
NEWAUTO.DOORS := 3
WRITELN (CAR1.WEIGHT,NEWAUTO.MANFCID)
IF CAR1.DISPL > 2000.0 THEN . . .
CAR1.DISPL := NEWAUTO.DISPL
```

If you want to duplicate _all_ of the values of one RECORD variable in another, you may simply use the assignment statement

```
NEWAUTO := CAR1
```

The RECORD TYPE, as it has been so far described, is more than just a naming convention--but not much more. After all, you could have a variable name such as CAR1DISP or, perhaps, NEWAUTODOORS.  With these, and several others, you could express the various scalar variables just as before.  The true advantage of the use of the RECORD comes when you recall the following fact:

Just as you may have structured TYPEs made up of simple TYPEs, you may have structured TYPEs made up of structured TYPEs.

Assume that the TYPE CARDESCP is declared as above.  In addition to being able to declare single variables as records we can also include in the VAR declaration

MODEL82: (* ALL U.S. MODELS *) ARRAY[1..80] OF CARDESCP;

Now it is permissible to write program statements such as:

```
      FOR I := 1 TO 80 DO
         IF MODEL82[I].WEIGHT > 3000.0 THEN
            •  •  • or

      WRITELN (MODEL82[45].DOORS)
```

> There are no variables of the complex TYPE in PASCAL.  But you could use the RECORD TYPE with two REAL fields to store complex numbers.  Another approach would be to make each complex number an ARRAY of two REAL elements.

## RECORD Variants

Each RECORD that we have seen so far contains a fixed number of fields; all RECORDS of a given TYPE are identical. PASCAL provides an additional flexibility in the design of RECORDs named the variant.  This feature allows the last part of a RECORD to be of varying constructs depending upon the content of the RECORD.  For example, a group of RECORDs is to contain information on employees of a company. The RECORDs are to contain name, social security number, salary, and department.  In addition, if the person is a supervisor, the RECORD is to contain the number of employees he or she supervises and the number of years that the person has been employed as a supervisor.  RECORDs of non-supervisory employees will not require these last two fields. Therefore, some employee RECORDs will have more fields in them than others.  This is called a variant RECORD and it is implemented by including a "CASE selector construct" before the variant portion of the RECORD.  Each field name in a given RECORD must be distinct from all other field names of that RECORD.

The program below writes a group of 100 such employee
RECORDs.  (The program uses identifiers of more than 8
characters; most PASCAL compilers allow this, but examine
only the first 8 characters for uniqueness.)

```
PROGRAM VARIANT(INPUT,OUTPUT);
    TYPE EMPLCYEERECORD = RECORD
        NAME: PACKED ARRAY[1..20] OF CHAR;
        SSNUMEER: INTEGER;
        SALARY: REAL;
        DEPARTMENT: CHAR;
        CASE SUPERVISOR: BOCLEAN OF
            TRUE: (NUMBEREMPLOYEES: INTEGER;
                    NUMBERYEARS: INTEGER);
            FALSE: ()   (*NULL CASE*)
    END;
    VAR R: EMPLOYEERECORD;
        I,SUPER,N: INTEGER;
        BEGIN
        FOR N := 1 TO 100 DO
            BEGIN
            FCR I := 1 TO 20 DO
                BEGIN
                READ (R.NAME,R.SSNUMBER,R.SALARY,
                    R.DEPARTMENT,SUPER);
                IF SUPER = 0 THEN
                    R.SUPERVISOR := FALSE
                ELSE
                    BEGIN
                    R.SUPERVISOR := TRUE;
                    READ (R.NUMBEREMPLOYEES,R.NUMBERYEARS)
                    END
                END;
            WRITELN (R)
            END
        END.
```

Notice that the field SUPERVISOR in the RECORD is
BOOLEAN and, as such, is either TRUE or FALSE.  Such a field
is termed a _tag_ field.  If it is FALSE, then that particular
RECORD will not contain the fields NUMBEREMPLOYEES or
NUMBERYEARS.

A RECORD may have only one variant part; it must follow
all the fixed parts.

The variant can consist of more than two cases.   The
example below shows four different variations of the same
RECORD.   The field EMPTYPE is INTEGER and should take on the
values 1, 2, 3, or 4.   If it is a 1, then the RECORD
contains the RECORD of the supervisory person as in the
previous program.   If EMPTYPE is 2, then only a merit rating
is recorded.   If EMPTYPE is 3, then previous supervisor and
previous rating is recorded and if EMPTYPE is 4, street
address and city are recorded.   Note that, as before, the
declaration of the CASE selecting variable is included
within the CASE selector.

```
TYPE EMPLOYEERECORD = RECORD
    NAME: PACKED ARRAY 1..20  OF CHAR;
    SSNUMBER: INTEGER;
    SALARY: REAL;
    DEPARTMENT: CHAR;
    CASE EMPTYPE: INTEGER OF
      1: (NUMBEREMPLOYEES: INTEGER;
          NUMBERYEARS: INTEGER);
      2: (MERITRATING: REAL);
      3: (PRIORSUPERVISOR: PACKED ARRAY[1..25] OF CHAR;
          PRIORRATING: REAL);
      4: (STREETADDRESS: PACKED ARRAY 1..40  OF CHAR;
          CITY: PACKED ARRAY 1..30  OF CHAR)
    END;
```

(What would be the danger if we had named
PRIORSUPERVISOR PREVIOUSUPERVISOR and PRIORRATING
PREVIOUSRATING?   Since they contain the same first eight
characters, these two variable names would not be unique in
most PASCAL systems.   That is, PASCAL would treat them as
the same variable.)

The RECORD variant is conceptually important because it
allows you to visualize a structured data TYPE with various
RECORD TYPEs.   The variant may not save space because, in
some versions of PASCAL, the amount of memory space used for
each RECORD is that of the RECORD which requires the most
space.

The RECORD variant can also be used in an ARRAY.   For
example, the variant could be employed as follows, given the
declaration of EMPLOYEERECORD above.

```
VAR
    R: PACKED ARRAY[1..100] OF EMPLOYEERECORD;
```

In this case, each of the 100 elements of R has the structure of EMPLOYEERECORD. Accessing an ARRAY element is done by writing the ARRAY name followed by a subscript followed by the field name in the RECORD. For example, to access the social security number of the fifth person's RECORD in the ARRAY one would write R[5].SSNUMBER

## Additional Considerations Concerning RECORDS

1.  You may have RECORDs within RECORDs. Suppose the RECORD OUTER has a field within it named MIDDLE, and MIDDLE itself is a RECORD containing a field named INNER. Then you could use the field INNER by writing OUTER.MIDDLE.INNER in any statement. For a complete discussion of RECORDs within RECORDs, see the PASCAL Usser's Manual and Report, 2nd Edition by Jensen and Wirth.

2.  Because it is cumbersome to mention the entire RECORD variable name, a statement is provided in PASCAL to remove the necessity of repeatedly naming the RECORD identifiers. In the case immediately above, if a statement made reference to OUTER.MIDDLE.INNER, you could preceed it by

    WITH OUTER,MIDDLE DO

    and then references just to INNER would be references to OUTER.MIDDLE.INNER. The statement preceded by the WITH could, of course, be a compound statement. Not only do you save time and space by not having to repeat the RECORD names, but you may enable the compiler to do a more efficient job of compiling your program as well. Again, if you want to use this feature, refer to the PASCAL User's Manual.

3.  It is possible to have a RECORD with a variant part but no tag field--in fact, no fixed part at all. The use of such RECORDs is generally not recommended although there are circumstances where it greatly simplifies programming. While an elaboration is beyond the scope of this text, consult the User's Manual.

```
SUGGESTED LABORATORY PROBLEMS
     46, 49, 50, 52, 54, 57
```

We have covered three TYPEs of structured variables in PASCAL: ARRAY, SET, and RECORD. Each TYPE represented an aggregate of data inside the memory of the computer. Here now is the fourth (and last) basic structured TYPE we will consider: the FILE. Unlike the other three TYPEs, a FILE may consist of more data than may be stored in the entire memory of the computer. This should suggest to you that the mechanism for storage of part of the data in a FILE may be outside the computer as well as inside it. In fact, you have already used the FILE TYPE without knowing it by that name. When you issued a statement such as READ you were telling the computer to get data from its INPUT FILE. And when you said WRITELN you were issuing an instruction for the machine to put information into its OUTPUT FILE. The FILEs you use in a PASCAL program are declared in the PROGRAM heading which is why the words INPUT and OUTPUT appear there.

As the programmer, you can define additional FILE variables with different names. The advantage of a user-created FILE variable is that large amounts of data may be placed in a FILE (written out on a FILE) and, later--perhaps even another day--that FILE may be retrieved (read in) by another PASCAL program and used as data. Thus, data contained in a PASCAL FILE variable may not only occupy more space than the entire data area of a PASCAL program, they may also continue to exist long after the PASCAL program that created them has ceased execution and been cleared from the memory of the machine. One mechanism outside the computer itself which makes the FILE TYPE possible is called a <u>magnetic</u> <u>tape</u> <u>drive</u>. It is shown in schematic form below:

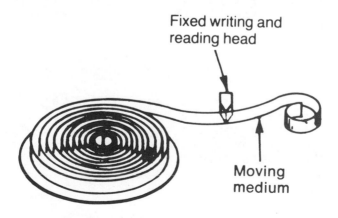

Fixed writing and
reading head

Moving

The magnetic tape drive has the ability to write data on and read data from magnetic tape in a way similar to that used by a cassette or reel-to-reel tape recorder for recording and playing back speech or music.  Further, it shares one of the same problems that music tapes have: only one selection (we'll call it a <u>component</u>) is available under the read-write head at any one time.  If you want a selection (component) further along the tape you have to roll the tape--sometimes quite a ways--to get it.  Contrast this with a side of a phonograph record where the selections are all about equally easy to get to.  (There do exist computer storage devices which are roughly similar to phonograph records--they are called disks or floppy disks or drums--but standard PASCAL does not have a FILE TYPE which uses them except as substitutes for tape.)

Now examine the steps which tell the computer to set up and generate a PASCAL FILE.  As with other TYPEs of variables (and we do consider a PASCAL FILE a variable although it can also be a method of external data storage) you must both declare the variable and then define its values.

Since a FILE may have portions both within the machine and outside it, the declaration is somewhat more involved than with other TYPEs.  The first mention of the FILE appears in the PROGRAM heading.  Suppose we wanted a program which would write a FILE of INTEGER variables; we'll call it JFILE.  In the PROGRAM heading we would say:

```
(*  FILE EXAMPLE  *)
PROGRAM FILEEXPL (INPUT,OUTPUT,JFILE);
```

This tells the computer that this PASCAL program is going to communicate with its environment by means of three FILEs: the two you have used all along, INPUT and OUTPUT, and another named JFILE.  Now, in the variable declaration section we need:

```
VAR
     JFILE: (* COMMENT *) FILE OF INTEGER;
```

Putting values into the file (or onto a tape) may be done with calls to two built-in PROCEDUREs: REWRITE and PUT. We use REWRITE first to set the tape so that the first component of the file may be written in the first position of the tape.  The PROCEDURE call:

```
REWRITE(JFILE)
```

rewinds the tape (if necessary) and prepares the machine to write on it.

Now we introduce the idea of a buffer variable whose purpose is to contain the data which is about to be written on the tape. It can be considered a window through which one can read from the file or write onto it. From physical considerations, you can see that, since the tape can only be at one position at one moment in time, only one component may be written at a time. The name used to indicate this component is the file name followed by an up-pointing arrow (in some PASCAL compilers, the @ sign is used as a substitute for the up-arrow). The buffer variable--with the strange appearance JFILE↑--is not declared. It is provided automatically, courtesy of the FILE declaration. Each FILE automatically contains its own buffer variable. In our example, then, the component to be written would be referred to as JFILE↑. In order to write an INTEGER number to the FILE we do two things: (1) define the value of JFILE↑, and (2) issue a call to PUT. For example:

```
JFILE↑ := 1024;
PUT(JFILE)
```

When PUT is invoked, it writes the value of JFILE↑ onto JFILE at the location which is under the read-write head, and then moves the tape so that the next position is available for writing. So if you later executed the statement

```
PUT(JFILE)
```

whatever value was then in JFILE↑ would be written to the file (tape) in the second location. In this way virtually any number of values may be written. Fifty million integers is not an unreasonable number of values to store on a tape. And since tapes may be exchanged by being mounted and dismounted from the tape drive unit, one might use several tapes for a single FILE. The point is: a FILE can be big.

Once a file has been written it may be read, either by the PROGRAM which wrote it or, if RECORDed externally on tape, by another PROGRAM at another time. For simplicity, let's assume that we want the file JFILE to be read back by the PROGRAM which wrote it out. We would use the procedures RESET and GET. The statement

```
RESET(JFILE)
```

will terminate the use of JFILE as a file which may be
written on and tell the computer to consider it as one which
may be read from.  If the file is a tape, a mark indicating
the "end of file" will be written and then the tape will be
rewound.  **If you accidentally REWRITE instead of RESETing
you may wipe out (erase) the file.**

The RESET procedure also defines the value of the buffer
variable (in our example, JFILE↑) as having the value of the
first component of the file.

So immediately after issuing RESET the program may use
the value of the first component:

SOMEINT := JFILE↑

The next component of the FILE would be accessed by

GET(JFILE)

which would redefine the value of JFILE↑ (leaving the values
of components in the FILE itself unchanged, of course).

But we've left something out.  Suppose we issue a
GET(JFILE) and there is no "next" component.  Or suppose we
issue a RESET and the file has no components.  Must we know
the number of components in a file ahead of time?  This
would certainly reduce the value of the FILE TYPE; one of
its advantages over the ARRAY is that, when we use it, we
don't have to know how many components are in it.

This difficulty is circumvented by PASCAL by providing
the programmer with a built-in BOOLEAN function named EOF
which indicates whether the End Of File has been
encountered.

If RESET(JFILE) is issued and the FILE is empty then it
is true that the end of the FILE has been reached, so
EOF(JFILE) becomes TRUE.  It is FALSE otherwise.  If
EOF(JFILE) is TRUE then JFILE↑ is undefined.

If the procedure GET(JFILE) is invoked and no more
components of the FILE remain, then JFILE↑ becomes
undefined; instead the EOF indicator is switched to TRUE.

To read properly from a FILE, then, one uses a set of
statements such as:

```
      RESET(JFILE);
      IF NOT EOF(JFILE) THEN
          BEGIN
          SOMEVAR := JFILE↑;
          (*  SOME PROCESSING *)
          GET(JFILE)
          END
```

If the FILE is empty then the IF statement skips the
program segment which processes JFILE.  Otherwise,
processing concludes immediately after an attempt to GET
from JFILE results in an EOF TRUE condition.


## To Summarize

For a file F, REWRITE(F) prepares the computer to write the
first component of the FILE.  It effectively erases any
components which were in the FILE before.  The EOF indicator
is set to TRUE.

PUT(F) appends (adds to the end) a component to the FILE,
whether the FILE is empty (after a REWRITE) or has other
components.  The component written to the file is F↑.  The
EOF(F) indicator remains TRUE.

RESET(F) prepares the computer to read the FILE from the
beginning.  If the FILE is empty then F↑ is undefined and
EOF(F) is set to TRUE.  If the FILE has one or more
components EOF(F) is set to FALSE and F↑ is defined to have
the value of the first component of the FILE.

GET(F) reads the next component from the FILE (provided
there is a next component) and stores the value as F↑; EOF
remains false.  If there is no next component, F↑ is
undefined by the GET(F) statement and the EOF(F) indicator
is set to TRUE.

In our example JFILE was a FILE OF INTEGER.  But a FILE
may be based on any legitimate TYPE.  FILEs of RECORDs are
particularly useful.  In this case, the buffer variable, F↑,
takes on the value of the entire RECORD component of the
FILE.

## All Is Not Roses

Input and output operations are the messiest of any the computer does. For one thing, there are many different devices which may be used; for another, techniques of representation of information differ between outside and inside the computer; and there are many ways and orders in which information can be arranged for input and output. Once data are in a computer, things become reasonably straightforward, if not easy. Internal operations, such as adding, are simple by comparison.

The techniques used by PASCAL to do input and output are extensions of the file-handling techniques. The approach is elegant. The trouble is, for input from and output to the real world--the world of people--it doesn"t work very well. Almost all high level languages have better ways of doing input and output than does PASCAL: less elegant, but better.

We aren't carping to you just because we're annoyed at the way PASCAL handles input and output. We are telling you because the chances are that the input and output techniques prescribed by standard PASCAL, and described in the next section, may well not be the ones in common use at your computing installation--because most PASCAL compiler writers have sought to improve on standard PASCAL. One reason for making changes in the specifications of the language is that different devices are available (e.g., disk drives which provide for random access). Another reason is so that the language can be used in an interactive (microcomputer or terminal) environment. Therefore what we have to say henceforth about input and output based on FILES may not be the way it is at your computing installation.

## Shortcuts using WRITE and READ

When you write to a FILE, say F, you find yourself using a statement combination such as:

```
F↑ := AVAR;
PUT(F)
```

By using the built-in PROCEDURE WRITE you can substitute

```
WRITE(F,AVAR)
```

Further, you can invoke the PROCEDURE WRITE with a variable
number of arguments and thus write out several variables:

```
WRITE(F,AVAR,BVAR,CVAR,DVAR)
```

If a filename is omitted, the OUTPUT FILE is assumed.

A similar shortcut may be used for reading a FILE.

```
READ(F,AVAR)
```

is equivalent to

```
AVAR := F↑
GET(F)
```

It is also true that

```
READ(F,AVAR,BVAR,CVAR,DVAR)
```

would be equivalent to

```
AVAR := F↑
GET(F)
EVAR := F↑
GET(F)
CVAR := F↑
GET(F)
DVAR := F↑
GET(F)
```

but you should be careful about using it because you cannot
check the EOF indicator after every GET.


## TEXTfiles

You can have a file of CHARacter just by saying
something like

```
VAR
     CFILE: FILE OF CHAR;
```

Such a FILE would consist of sequences of characters
followed by an indication that the end of file had been
reached.  But large sets of characters constructed by humans
often have a more definite format.  The characters appear as
groups (one to several characters, separated by blanks)

which we call words.  Further, the words also appear as
groups which we call lines.

Now a computer is perfectly capable of taking a FILE of
CHARacters and breaking it up into lines of words if you
just tell it the number of characters per line.  But
frequently you want to let the human who is composing the
lines make the determination as to when to begin a new line
(an example is a PASCAL program; another is a poem).  PASCAL
provides this capability by allowing the insertion of a
special character at the end of each line which is called,
appropriately enough, the End Of LiNe (or EOLN) character.
A FILE which allows this special character is called a
TEXTfile.

PASCAL provides the TEXTfile as a standard TYPE.  All
you have to do to define one (e.g., named TFILE) is to say

        VAR
            TFILE: TEXT;

and, of course, mention TFILE in the PROGRAM heading.

Assume that TFILE is a TEXTfile and SYMBOL is a variable
of the TYPE CHAR.  Then, to write the character in SYMBOL
onto TFILE, you simply say

        WRITE (TFILE,SYMBOL)

If you want the character to be the last character in a
line, you would say

        WRITELN (TFILE,SYMBOL)

or

        WRITE (TFILE,SYMBOL);
        WRITELN (TFILE)

WRITELN, then, generates a "mark" (called a line
separator) which indicates the end of a line.  If a FILE is
being written on tape, the mark is one which is peculiar to
the variety of equipment being used.  If the FILE is being
written on a printer or terminal, the mark is generally two
symbols called carriage return (CR) and line feed (LF).  (On
a typewriter terminal, the effect produced by a CR-LF
combination is to move the carriage so that the next
character will be printed at the left margin on the next

line down.  An analogous effect would occur on a CRT.  Think
about what the carriage return lever (or button) does on a
manual (or electric) typewriter.)  If the FILE being written
is in the form of cards, a new blank card would be readied
for punching.

There is also a built-in PROCEDURE READLN.

        READLN(TFILE,SYMBOL)

will skip the remaining portion (if any) of a line and
define SYMBOL to have the value of the first character of
the next line.

        READLN(TFILE);
        READ(TFILE,SYMBOL)

would have the same effect.

        READLN(TFILE)

by itself positions the file at the beginning of the next
line and defines the value of the buffer variable to be the
first character in that line.

Since the number of characters in a line of a TEXTfile
may be variable, and since WRITELN produces a mark to
separate the lines, you might imagine that there is some way
in which a programmer can instruct the computer to test for
the condition of an end of line.  There is; it is the
BOOLEAN function EOLN.  Basically, if READ is executed and
the character read is the last one in the line, the EOLN
function becomes TRUE.  Another READ at this point is
inappropriate; what is required is a READLN which positions
the FILE so that the next line may be read.

The EOLN function is different from the EOF function in
a subtle but important way.  EOLN becomes TRUE with the
reading of the last element of a line.  EOF becomes TRUE
when an attempt is made to READ an element of a file and no
more elements exist.

FILEs of REAL or INTEGER are also considered to be
TEXTfiles.  Therefore, numbers can be read and written as
can characters, as long as each adjacent pair of numbers.
is separated by at least one blank.

The way standard PASCAL handles input and output with TEXTfiles is illustrated below. Beneath this illustration we've left a box. Write the instructions which are appropriate for copying TEXTfiles on your computer.

```
(* COPIES TEXT FROM FILE SOURCE TO FILE OBJECT *)
PROGRAM COPY (INPUT,OUTPUT,SOURCE,OBJECT);
    VAR
        SOURCE,OBJECT: TEXT;
        SYMBOL:CHAR;
    BEGIN
    RESET(SOURCE);
    REWRITE(OBJECT);
        WHILE NOT EOF(SOURCE) DO
            BEGIN
            WHILE NOT EOLN(SOURCE) DO
                BEGIN
                READ(SOURCE,SYMBOL);
                WRITE(OBJECT,SYMBOL)
                END;
            READLN(SOURCE);
            WRITELN(OBJECT)
            END
    END.
```

A <u>list</u> in this section will refer to aggregates or clumps of information which have something in common but which are scattered throughout the memory of the machine. In this sense a list is different from an ARRAY, whose elements are stored consecutively. <u>List processing</u> refers to the techniques used in reading, manipulating, and writing information stored in list form.

When you use list processing techniques, the computer's memory is not partitioned into nice, neat parcels such as scalar (element) variables, ARRAYs, and the like. In fact, the allocation of space to numbers and symbols seems, at first blush, to be at least random if not totally chaotic. Under such conditions a person who is trying to understand what is going on must either become terribly rigorous and careful or, alternatively, become very relaxed, free, and easy going in order to fit in with the bizarre system. We will opt for the latter approach.

Let's suppose that Small Fry Play School decides to transfer the RECORDs of its doll collection to a computer. The RECORDs consist simply of the names of the dolls and their imaginary phone numbers. After careful consideration of the various approaches that might be used, the school's programmers decide to use the storage allocation techniques available in PASCAL to form what is called a <u>chained list</u> or simply a <u>list</u> of the information. Under such a scheme the programmer doesn't keep track of where he puts information in the conventional way. In one sense, he lets the data keep up with itself. When he has finally stored the information in the machine it might appear as shown in the following diagram.

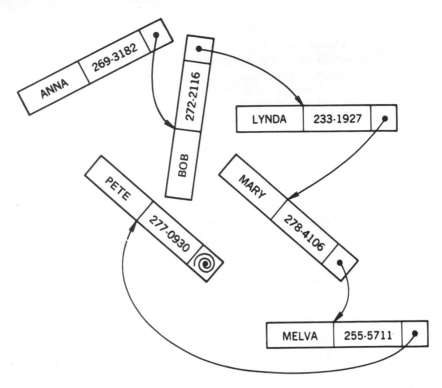

Here we have six "clumps" of information.  Each clump
consists of three items: a name, a telephone number, and a
special new gadget called a <u>pointer</u> whose function is to
point to the next "clump" of information.

As you might imagine, given the disorganized appearance
of the diagram, it is pretty hard to find a clump of
information unless you know the information in the preceding
clump.  And that's the way the whole scheme works: we know
where to find the first clump, the pointer within the first
clump allows us to find the next clump, and so on until the
last clump is found.  The pointer in the last clump doesn't
point anywhere else; it is defined to have a <u>NIL</u> value.

You might wonder, given all the neat ways known to
process information, why any sane person would elect such a
technique for data storage.  There <u>are</u> reasons but they
don't become obvious until we've gone a bit further.

Let's look first at the format for information in such a system.

Suppose we use the identifier DOLL to stand for all the names in the six clumps of information. In this sense DOLL is something like an ARRAY in that it is a single identifier which stands for several items of information. The question "which particular DOLL is being referred to at a particular time" is answered, not by a subscript, however, but by a pointer as we will demonstrate. We will assume that each of the six DOLLs is of the type

STRING10

where we have declared

TYPE
    STRING10 = PACKED ARRAY @1..10] OF CHAR;

We will use the identifier PHONE to designate the six telephone numbers stored; their identifier has been declared as STRING8.

And finally, we will use the name LNC to refer to the Location of the Next Clump of information. LNC is this new kind of variable called the pointer.

## Pointer Variables

If we write the instructions

```
PROGRAM SMALLFRY (INPUT,OUTPUT);
    TYPE
        STRING10 = PACKED ARRAY@1..10] OF CHAR;
        STRING8 = PACKED ARRAY@1..8] OF CHAR;
        APTR=↑CLUMP;
        CLUMP=RECORD
            DOLL:STRING10;
            PHONE:STRING8;
            LNC:APTR
        END;
    VAR
        FIRST:APTR;
        PREVPT:APTR;
        INDEXPT:APTR;
        ALP:APTR;
        FOUND:BOOLEAN;
        ABSENT:BOOLEAN;
        I:INTEGER;
```

we create a TYPE, APTR, whose variables (LNC, FIRST, PREVPT, INDEXPT, ALP) have the sole purpose in life of pointing to RECORDS of the name CLUMP. The contents of a pointer variable is an actual address of a location in the storage of the computer. The up-arrow preceding the name CLUMP in the program above designates APTR as a type of variable which points to CLUMP.

The programmer uses the pointer variable in somewhat the same way as he uses a subscript--to provide an index to the item of information he wants referenced. To use a pointer variable we write the name of the pointer and follow it with an arrow. Thus, to use the pointer FIRST to index another variable we would write

        FIRST↑variable

To illustrate the use of the pointer variable, assume that the variable FIRST has been defined to point to the first clump of information of the list in the preceding diagram; then to indicate that we wished to refer to the variable containing 'ANNA' we would write

        FIRST↑.DOLL.

(We don't say

        FIRST↑CLUMP.DOLL

because, FIRST is a variable whose TYPE, APTR, is "bound" to CLUMP.)

If we wanted to print out the telephone number associated with the first clump we could issue the statement

WRITELN (FIRST↑.PHONE)

and out would come 269-3182.

If we wanted to refer to the pointer LNC in the first clump of information (that pointer has the function of pointing to the second clump) we could write

FIRST↑.LNC

To refer to the variable containing 'LYNDA' we could write

FIRST↑.LNC↑.LNC↑.DOLL.

Pointer variables can be defined by the ordinary assignment statement. If we wanted a pointer variable named INDEXPT to have the same value as the pointer variable FIRST, we could simply say

INDEXPT := FIRST;

Both the quantity to the right and the quantity to the left of the := symbol must be pointer variables.

A pointer variable can be defined to point to nothing at all. An example of a pointer which doesn't point anywhere is the pointer associated with the last clump of information in our diagram. The NIL pointer is shown on the diagram by

If we had declared the variable NOPOINT as APTR and wanted it not to point anywhere, we would write the statement

NOPOINT := NIL

A programmer cannot do arithmetic with pointer
variables. However, he or she can, with an IF or other
statement, compare two pointer variables to see if they are
equal (i.e., if they point to the same clump.) He or she
can also compare a pointer variable with the keyword NIL to
ascertain if the pointer variable has been defined to point
nowhere.


## Retrieving Information

With this new knowledge of pointer variables in mind we
look at the problem of retrieving information from the list
in the diagram. Suppose that FIRST, INDEXPT, and the six
elements of LNC are of the pointer variety as shown in the
earlier TYPE and VAR declaration. We will assume that the
variable FIRST has already been defined to point to the
first clump of information. If we just wanted to print the
list we could say:

```
INDEXPT := FIRST;
WHILE INDEXPT <> NIL DO
    BEGIN
    WRITELN (' ',INDEXPT↑.DOLI,INDEXPT↑.PHONE);
    INDEXPT := INDEXPT↑.LNC
    END;
```

Follow through the logic of the program segment above.
INDEXPT := FIRST defines another pointer variable to point
to the first clump. After the execution of INDEXPT :=
FIRST, our diagram would look like this:

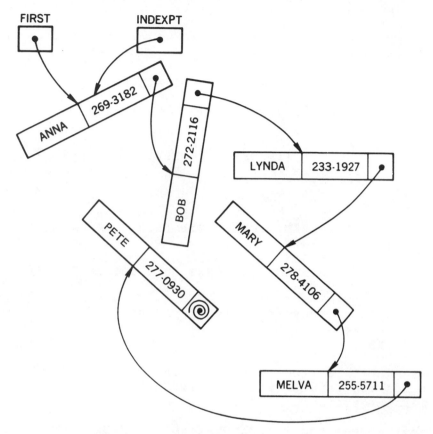

Our plan is to change the value of INDEXPT repeatedly to index the clump we want to print. First we initiate a loop which is to run until a clump is found in which the variable LNC is NIL. Each time through the loop the values of DOLL and PHONE are printed for each clump by the statement

WRITELN (' ',INDEXPT↑.DOLL,INDEXPT↑.PHONE)

The pointer, INDEXPT, is changed so as to point to the next clump by the statement

INDEXPT := INDEXPT↑.LNC

If you understand this statement you understand a good bit
of what list processing is all about.

Consider now a slightly more difficult problem: Find
MARY's phone number.  We can write

```
INDEXPT := FIRST;
FOUND := FALSE;
ABSENT := FALSE;
WHILE (NOT FOUND) AND (NOT ABSENT) DO
    BEGIN
    IF INDEXPT↑.DOLL = 'MARY       ' THEN
        BEGIN
        WRITELN (' MARY');
        WRITELN (INDEXPT↑.PHONE);
        FOUND := TRUE
        END
    ELSE
        BEGIN
        IF INDEXPT↑.LNC = NIL THEN
            BEGIN
            ABSENT := TRUE;
            WRITELN (' DARN! DOLL NOT IN LIST')
            END
        ELSE
            INDEXPT := INDEXPT↑.LNC
        END
    END;
```

Examine this program segment one step at a time.  We
first set the pointer variable INDEXPT to the same value as
the pointer variable FIRST.

Next we set two BOOLEAN variables, FOUND and ABSENT to
indicate that a clump containing 'MARY' has not, at this
point, either been found or declared to be absent.

Then we enter a loop which will continue until either a
clump containing 'MARY' has been found (NOT FOUND is FALSE)
or until a NIL pointer is encountered indicating that we
have checked all clumps without finding 'MARY' (NOT ABSENT
is FALSE).  If a match is found then we write 'MARY' and
then the phone number in the clump which is identified by
INDEXPT↑.PHONE.  But the first time through the loop there
will be no match because 'MARY' is not equal to 'ANNA'.  So
the ELSE branch will be taken.  Here we check to see if the
LNC of the clump is NIL (it isn't), so we proceed to the
statement INDEXPT := INDEXPT↑.LNC.  This statement says:

change the index pointer so that it points to the next clump
of information by setting the INDEXPT to the same value
(address) as LNC in the first clump.

The path through the program now returns to the top of
the loop, with INDEXPT redefined so that it points to the
second clump, and the process is repeated.

## Removing Information

So far we have not been able to do anything with the
information in the list that we could not have done if we
had stored our data in two ARRAYs, DOLL and PHONE, and had
indexed them with a subscript.

Now we consider a new wrinkle.  Suppose instead of
simply finding an item in the list, we wish to find and
delete the item.  If, for example, 'MARY' has come apart at
the seams and we want to remove her from the list, we can
modify the list so that it appears this way.

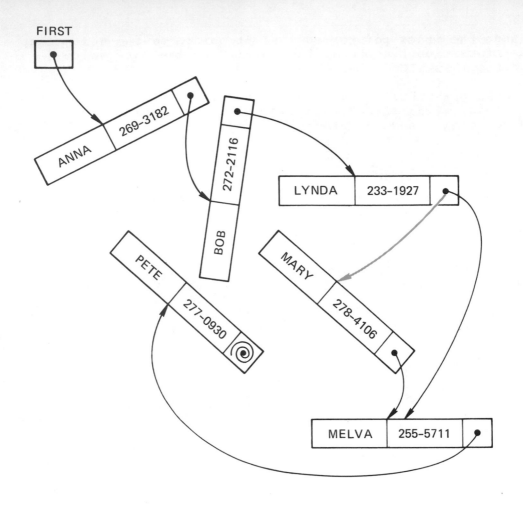

FIRST

ANNA 269-3182

BOB 272-2116

LYNDA 233-1927

MARY 278-4106

PETE 277-0930

MELVA 255-5711

To remove the clump containing 'MARY' from the list, we really need do only one thing: change the pointer in the clump containing 'LYNDA' so that it points to the clump containing 'MELVA'. Our six clumps of information, which we are about to reduce to five, form what is called a <u>unidirectional</u> chained list. Using such a list it is quite easy to process data going in one direction but almost impossible to process it going the other way. (If you have ever driven an automobile without an operable reverse gear you can understand the problem; one needs to plan carefully.) Thus we will use a new pointer variable, which we arbitrarily call PREVPT, whose function it is to point at the clump of information which precedes the one presently

being pointed at by INDEXPT.  We would modify our program so
that it appeared as follows.  (We will darken the additions
to the program which transform it into coding which will
remove rather than just find the information clump
containing 'MARY'.)

```
    INDEXPT := FIRST;
    FOUND := FALSE;
    ABSENT := FALSE;
    WHILE (NOT FOUND) AND (NOT ABSENT) DO
         BEGIN
         IF INDEXPT↑.DOLL = 'MARY        ' THEN
            BEGIN
            WRITELN (' MARY');
            WRITELN (' ',INDEXPT↑.PHONE);
            FOUND := TRUE;
(* IF CLUMP TO BE DELETED IS FIRST WE MUST CHANGE THE
   POINTER "FIRST" *)
            IF FIRST = INDEXPT THEN
                 FIRST := FIRST↑.LNC
            ELSE
(* CHANGE LNC IN CLUMP BEFORE "MARY"
   SO IT POINTS TO CLUMP AFTER "MARY" *)
                 PREVPT↑.LNC := INDEXPT↑.LNC
            END
         ELSE
            BEGIN
            IF INDEXPT↑.LNC = NIL THEN
               BEGIN
               ABSENT := TRUE;
               WRITELN (' DARN! DOLL NOT IN LIST')
               END
            ELSE
               BEGIN
(* PULL PREVPT ALONG *)
               PREVPT := INDEXPT;
               INDEXPT := INDEXPT↑.LNC
               END
            END
         END
```

   Carefully trace this revised program so that you
understand the functions of the new statements.

## Freeing Storage

We now come upon one of the advantages of list processing. If the clump of information containing 'MARY' had been part of one or several ARRAYs, we could easily delete the information from the clump, but the clump itself would still be taking up room in our ARRAY. We would have to note that the information had been removed. As you may have noticed, the clumps are in alphabetical order by DOLL and it would therefore be difficult to reuse the space in an ARRAY.

But by using the present system of data organization we can free the space previously occupied by the deleted clump and that space could later be reassigned to this or some other list. We can do this (in some implementations of PASCAL) by saying DISPOSE(INDEXPT↑CLUMP) after we've reassigned the pointer, LNC, associated with 'MARY'. (Different versions of PASCAL handle the issue of DISPOSE in different ways.)

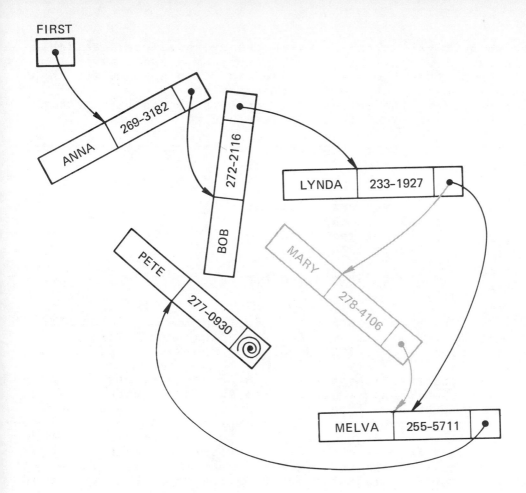

FIRST

ANNA 269-3182

BOB 272-2116

PETE 277-0930

LYNDA 233-1927

MARY 278-4106

MELVA 255-5711

## Allocating Clumps

If you have understood the program segments presented
thus far you have a pretty fair idea how one manipulates
information in a unidirectional chained list.  In order to
provide some insight into the more basic concepts involved,
we have ignored the question of how the clumps of
information are placed in the computer's storage so that
they can be operated on by the techniques we have described.
We now deal with that problem.

There are two classes of data storage in PASCAL: static
and dynamic.  In order to use variables in a list processing
situation--that is, variables which are located or indexed

by pointer variables--it is necessary to allocate variables
dynamically.  Variables which are dynamic are somewhat
different from those we are used to because space for them
is not reserved at the time they are declared.
Understanding the method of allocation begins with looking
at the declaration of the pointer and the "pointee."

   The declaration of pointers and the variables they point
to is fairly intricate:

```
TYPE
    pointertypename=↑clumpname;
    clumpname=RECORD
        clumpelement:type;
        clumpelement:type;
        etc;
        clumppointerelement:pointertypename;
    END;
```

   Compare this with the TYPE declaration of the SMALLFRY
program.  It is this declaraction which makes all the
variables of the TYPE APTR <u>bound</u> <u>to</u> the RECORDs of CLUMP.

   The statement which sets up storage locations so that we
can use them to store information is the standard PASCAL
procedure, NEW.  All we have to do to set up a new RECORD of
CLUMP is to invoke the PROCEDURE NEW using a variable of the
TYPE APTR as its argument.  It is best to set up a separate
variable of this type to do the allocation.  In our program
we call it ALP.  To tell the machine that we want it to set
up a clump of storage for our "Small Fry" problem, we would
write the statement

```
        NEW (ALP)
```

   Now a question might come to your mind: since there can
be several clumps, how do I know where the clump that has
just been allocated is?  Answer: it is pointed to by the
current value of ALP.  In general, when the NEW procedure is
executed, the appropriate storage is set aside and the
argument (a pointer variable, to which the allocated
variable is bound) points to the newly allocated storage.

   To put these recently learned ideas into play we now
look at a program segment which would set up the six
original clumps of information.

```
TYPE
    STRING10 = PACKED ARRAY@1..10] OF CHAR;
    STRING8 = PACKED ARRAY@1..8] OF CHAR;
    APTR = ↑CLUMP;
    CLUMP = RECORD
        DOLL: STRING10;
        PHONE: STRING8;
        LNC: APTR;
    END;
VAR
    FIRST: APTR;
    PREVPT: APTR;
    INDEXPT: APTR;
    ALP: APTR;
    FOUND: BOOLEAN;
    ABSENT: BOOLEAN;
    I: INTEGER;
BEGIN
FIRST := NIL;
WRITELN (' INPUT DOLL & PHONE');
FOR I := 1 TO 6 DO
    BEGIN
    NEW (ALP);
    READ (ALP↑.DOLL,ALP↑.PHONE) ;
    ALP↑.LNC := NIL;
    IF FIRST = NIL THEN
        BEGIN
        FIRST := ALP;
        PREVPT := ALP
        END
    ELSE
        BEGIN
        PREVPT↑.LNC := ALP;
        PREVPT := ALP
        END
    END;
```

You should thoroughly understand this program segment
before continuing.  Trace through the logic schematically,
with boxes to represent the storage locations and arrows
from pointer variables, if you are not certain what is
occurring.

One of the primary advantages of list processing is that
information can easily be added to a list while preserving
its order.  For example, it would be a simple matter to add
a new name to the set of DOLLs while maintaining the
alphabetical sequence.  If DOLLs were an ARRAY instead of a

list, then to insert a new DOLL one would have to move "down" all the elements of the ARRAY after the one to be inserted, to maintain the order in the ARRAY. This shuffling of data is unnecessary if the information is contained in a list.

## Exercise

Write a program segment which would read a DOLL and PHONE and insert them in the proper place in the list. Assume that the existing variables CLUMP, DOLL, PHONE, LNC, FIRST, INDEXPT, and ALP have all been appropriately declared, allocated, and/or defined. If you need any new variables you should make proper provision for them.

## Further Glimpses

What we have presented is enough list processing to let you catch the flavor of the technique. There is much, much more. For example, bi-directional lists could be formed which would contain pointers to both the previous and following elements. Lists without beginning or end, called rings, could be formed by making a pointer in the "last" clump point to the "first" clump.

Clumps could contain several pointers and could, therefore, belong to several lists although each clump contained the same basic information. For example, our doll RECORDs could be arranged in alphabetical order by DOLL name and, at the same time, arranged in numerical order by PHONE number in a second list without repeating the basic information. A second pointer element would have to be added to each clump.

Several lists, each containing different information, could be held in memory at the same time. Storage freed during the processing of one list could be allocated and used by another. The programmer can declare an ARRAY of pointer variables which could index the first elements of each of these lists. Most of the operations suggested above can be done with the knowledge the student has already learned.

List processing is a big subject all by itself; entire courses are built around it and other methods of storing data within a computer. Knowledge of the various methods of storing data allows the programmer to use the computer to do many exciting things such as text analysis, language translation, sorting, etc. PASCAL is not a language designed basically to do these functions, but it has the fundamental tools which allow them to be done.

---

```
SUGGESTED LABORATORY PROBLEM
              42
```

---

NOTE for Part III

Note 1:   There is a contradiction regarding simple and scalar TYPEs in the PASCAL USER'S MANUAL and REPORT.  It refers to simple types as (1) standard, (2) scalar (user-defined), and (3) subrange.  But it also refers to standard scalar types.  Our choice is to use scalar as the most general classification and to clearly specify which kind of scalar is meant in each instance.

# part IV

# PASCAL PROGRAM STRUCTURES

In this Part we continue our presentation of the features and statements of the PASCAL language which we omitted before in order to cover program development. In Part III we discussed different data types and different aggregates of data. Now, in Part IV, we describe additional statements which you may use to simplify your programs.

## MORE ON SELECTION

### The CASE Statement

The CASE statement allows the program to choose one (and only one) of several possible statements to execute, based on the value of an expression. You already know a statement which allows the program to choose from between two statements: the IF statement.

The CASE statement is structurally similar to the CASE selector in the RECORD variant. We give you an example first, then we'll explain.

```
(* CASE STATEMENT DEMONSTRATION *)
PROGRAM CASEDEMO(INPUT,OUTPUT);
    VAR
        K: (* A CASE SELECTOR *) INTEGER;
        A: (* INPUT *) REAL;
        B: (* INPUT *) REAL;
        C: (* ANSWER *) REAL;
        T: (* TERM VALUE *) REAL;
    BEGIN
    READ (K,A,B);
    CASE K OF
        1:   (* THE PRODUCT CASE *)
             C := A*B;
        2:   (* THE DIFFERENCE CASE *)
             C := A-B;
        3:   (* THE SERIES CASE *)
             BEGIN
             C := 0;
             T := A+B;
             WHILE ABS (T)>0.001  DO
                 BEGIN
                 C := C+T;
                 T := T*(A+B)
                 END
             END
    END;
    WRITELN (C)
    END.
```

If this problem looks familiar it's because you were
paying attention in Part I when we were telling you about
Algorithms and Design.  There we used two IF statements to
choose among the three mutually exclusive parts of the
program.  Here we use a single CASE statement.  The more
statements you have to choose among the better the CASE
statement looks.  For example, suppose DAY had a value of 1
or 2 or ... or 7 and we wanted to execute procedures MON or
TUE or ... or SUN depending on the value of DAY.  The seven
choices would take six IF statements:

```
IF DAY=1 THEN
     MON
ELSE
    IF DAY=2 THEN
        TUE
    ELSE
       IF DAY=3 THEN
            WED
       ELSE
          IF DAY=4 THEN
              THUR
          ELSE
             IF DAY=5 THEN
                 FRI
             ELSE
                IF DAY=6 THEN
                   SAT
                ELSE
                   IF DAY=7 THEN
                       SUN
```

Not only did our arm get tired from writing, we indented
ourselves half way across the page.  Write the CASE
statement equivalent of the foregoing mess.

Now that you've got the idea of the CASE statement you
should be aware of the following:

The flowchart structure which depicts the CASE statement
is:

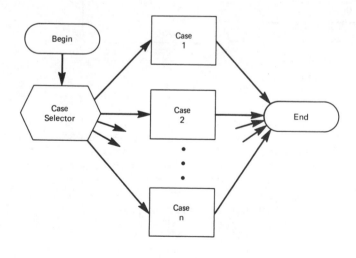

That is, the CASE statement will select for execution that statement, and only that statement, labeled by the value of the expression.

The gadget which precedes each statement (e.g., 2:) is called a case label list. In general, it can take on the form of any number of constants (they cannot be of the TYPE REAL), separated by commas, and followed by a colon. For example,

        18,11,-5,999: statement

indicates the statement to be executed if "expression" is 18, 11, -5, or 999. Order and magnitude of the constants in the case label list don't matter.

After a statement has been selected and executed, control passes to the statement following the END of the CASE statement. "END of the CASE statement? Say, where's the BEGIN?" Sorry, the paired keywords are CASE and END. Here's the whole syntax. Check it through; make sure you understand it.

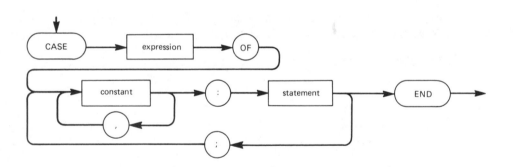

If the value of the expression is not equal to one of the constants in one of the case label lists, then you've got an error on your hands. Some versions of PASCAL generously skip the whole set of statements and go on past the END but you can't count on that. (The fact that you can't count on it is viewed by some as a design defect in PASCAL--but no language is perfect.)

Each constant in the case list must, obviously, be unique within a CASE statement. The expression may be of any complexity but must yield a value of the TYPE of the constants in the case label list. The constants may be values of any scalar TYPE except REAL. For example,

```
TYPE
    GEOSHAPE=(RECT,TRIANGLE,CIRCLE);
VAR
    FIGURE: (*  *) GEOSHAPE;
    AREA: (* AREA OF FIGURE *) REAL;
    HEIGHT, WIDTH, BASE, RADIUS:(*  *) REAL;
                    •
                    •
                    •
CASE FIGURE OF
    CIRCLE: (* RADIUS PREVIOUSLY DEFINED *)
        AREA := PI*SQR(RADIUS);
    RECT: (* KNOW HEIGHT, WIDTH *)
        AREA := HEIGHT*WIDTH;
    TRIANGLE: (* HAVE BASE AND HEIGHT *)
        AREA := BASE*HEIGHT/2.0
END (* CASE *)
```

The indentation convention we recommend is as shown. It does seem a little wasteful to devote a full line to a short case label list. But it allows a comment and our convention will always clearly show the relationships of the statements. You may want to devise your own.

The issue of efficiency comes into the decision of whether to use nested IF statements or a CASE statement.

In general, if the computer is to choose among several paths of action and each is about as likely as any other, use the CASE approach.

If, however, some cases are much more likely than others, use nested IF statements and arrange the program so that the most likely paths are encountered with the fewest number of comparisons.

Unless a very large number of loops are involved, this difference will be trivial.

## GOTO Escapes

You know how life is.  Sometimes you just want to give up and go south.  Writing a program can be like that.  There you are, up to your knees in nested IF statements and you realize that, if K is negative, you should really be in a part of the program that is further south.  Well, there's an escape hatch; it's called the GO TO statement.  An example will show how it works mechanically:  In your program you have the statement

        GOTO 54

and somewhere else in the program you have another statement

        54: statement

Then, if the statement GOTO 54 is executed, control immediately goes (jumps) to statement 54 and execution continues from there.

The constant "54" is called the statement label.  You have to declare the statement label as the first thing in the declaration section of the PROGRAM or PROCEDURE in which the label occurs. e.g.,

        LABEL
            54,871,999;

That tells the computer that statements labeled 54, 871, and 999 may be transferred to.

To show how the GOTO escape might be used, recall the program on the Program Development Scroll (the pullout at the back of the book).  Notice that the major portion of the program takes place as the second statement of an IF statement.  This major portion is all indented an extra four spaces.  This is because the test for error conditions occupied the first statement of the IF and the entire remainder of the program is the second statement of the IF. An alternative construction might have been:

```
PROGRAM FINDMEDN (INPUT, OUTPUT);
    LABEL
        9999;
    VAR
        . . .
    BEGIN
    IF (K<1) OR (K>50) THEN
        BEGIN
        WRITELN (' ERROR.  K=', K);
        GOTO 9999
        END;
    remainder of program
    9999: (* NULL STATEMENT *)
    END.
```

We wouldn't recommend this.  But you may find times when
the GOTO seems to simplify the programming greatly.  You
never _have_ to use it; any program can be written without it.
If you do elect to use it you should be aware that:

(1) You may never GOTO (jump) into another structure,
    such as the statements following a THEN, ELSE, DO,
    etc.

(2) You may not jump into a PROCEDURE although you may
    jump out of one in some versions of PASCAL.

(3) The statement label (nct to be confused with a CASE
    label list) must be an unsigned integer constant of
    not more than four digits.

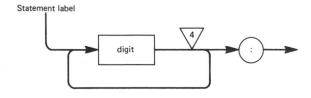

(4)  Some versions of PASCAL prohibit the use of the GOTO
     statement unless you specifically indicate
     otherwise.

The reason that we discourage the use of the GOTO
statement is that it introduces complexity into
understanding the flow and logic of a program.  It
makes a program hard to read and understand by
humans.  Therefore, it makes a program harder to
modify later, without error.

More on Selection

## REPEAT--UNTIL

In addition to WHILE-DO and FOR-DO there is another iteration structure: REPEAT-UNTIL.

Statically (syntactically), it looks like this

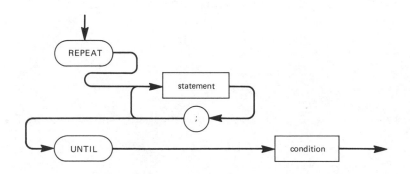

Dynamically (in execution), it works like this:

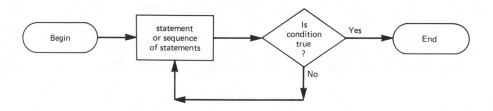

The REPEAT--UNTIL statement most resembles the WHILE--DO statement; there are three primary differences:

1.  If the form:  statement; statement; statement ... etc., is used the statement brackets BEGIN and END are unnecessary.  They are replaced by REPEAT and UNTIL.

2. The statement portion of the structure is executed
   once _regardless_ of whether the condition is true or
   false.  The condition isn't checked until the very
   last--that's why it appears syntactically at the
   end, after UNTIL.

3. Loop execution continues _up to the time_ (UNTIL) some
   expression becomes true, not _during the time_ (WHILE)
   some (other) expression is true as with the
   WHILE--DO.

For example, if a loop is to keep going until a zero is
calculated for Z, then you might use the form

```
REPEAT
     •
     •
   Z := something
UNTIL Z=0
```

The equivalent WHILE--DO loop would most sensibly be
written:

```
WHILE Z<>0 DO
    BEGIN
    •
    Z := something
    END
```

Notice that both loops are _identical_ except under one
condition: if Z is initially zero, the REPEAT loop will
execute once whereas the WHILE loop will not execute at all.
This

If you are willing to risk a headache in your quest for
understanding, you can tackle the following exercise.


## Exercise

Which of the following statements is true about the
first loop above?  About the second loop?

a. Looping will continue until Z is zero.

b. Looping will continue while Z is non-zero.

c. Looping will stop when Z is zero.

d.   Looping will continue when Z isn't zero.

If you breezed through that, make up your own questions
using this format:  Looping (will, won't) (continue, stop)
(while, when, if, until) Z (is, isn't) (zero, non-zero).

What can you do with this new structure that you
couldn't do with WHILE--DO?  The major useful difference is
that the first execution of the statement which is done
regardless with the REPEAT--UNTIL and conditionally with the
WHILE--DO.  After that, testing the condition really comes
at exactly the same point in the WHILE-DO and the REPEAT-
UNTIL: just before the loop is re-executed.  An example: You
are reading four values, A, B, C, and D.  You are looking
for the first set of values A, B, C, and D such that $A*B-C/D$
is exactly zero.  Using a REPEAT--UNTIL you are spared the
necessity of using two READ instructions.  Thus:

```
        REPEAT
            READ (A,B,C,D)
        UNTIL A*B-C/D = 0
```

could be substituted for

```
        READ(A,B,C,D);
        WHILE A*B-C/D <> 0 DO
            READ (A,B,C,D)
```


## GOTO Exits from Loops

In the preceding section we suggest that it's not too
important, usually, if you test at the beginning or end of a
loop.  Sometimes, however, it's helpful to be able to get
out of a loop in its middle.  The GOTO can be used for such
a mid-loop escape.

Because the GOTO, as previously covered, is an informal
statement, we'll adopt an informal approach to illustrating
its use.  Suppose a friend of yours has asked you to get
sums of the numbers which have already been punched out, one
to a card, by an archaic piece of laboratory equipment.
"I've got twenty sets of a hundred cards each," he tells
you.  "Just need the twenty sums."

So you write his program.

```
(*   SAM'S QUICK AND DIRTY SUMMING PROGRAM *)
PROGRAM SUMNUM (INPUT, OUTPUT);
    VAR
        I: (* CARD COUNTER *) INTEGER;
        J: (* CARD-SET COUNTER *) INTEGER;
        X: (* EACH VALUE *) REAL;
        S: (* SUM OF EACH SET *) REAL;
    BEGIN
    FOR J := 1 TO 20 DO
        BEGIN
        S := 0.0;
        FOR I := 1 TO 100 DO
            BEGIN
            READ (X);
            S := S+X
            END;
        WRITE (J,S)
        END
    END.
```

Having keypunched and checked your program you stroll confidently to the card reader, telling Sam how easy it all was--especially because you're learning from this great textbook.  You drop the cards in, smile,...and the program bombs: it ran out of data cards.

You recheck your program.  Then you ask, "Are you sure you got two thousand cards here?"

"Sure I am," he says.  And then a distant look appears in his eyes.  "Unless the machine malfunctions and punches a negative value.  Then it quits on that set and goes on to the next and in this case the sum is meaningless."

Muttering under your breath about the limits of friendship, you sit down to see what modifications must be made.  It seems that an overhaul may be required.

Actually, this thing is your fault, not his. Clients seldom give you a complete set of problem specifications unless you make a determined effort to get them.  Being thorough in the problem definition at the outset has two advantages: (1) it may keep you out of situations such as that depicted above, and (2) it usually generates a sense of

contrition on the part of the client when he changes
his mind about what he wants for his answers.

You could rewrite the whole thing as follows:

```
BEGIN
FOR J := 1 TO 20 DO
    BEGIN
    X := 0.0;
    I := 1;
    WHILE (X>=0.0) AND (I<=100) DO
        BEGIN
        READ (X);
        IF X<0.0 THEN
            WRITE (J,' BAD DATA')
        ELSE
            BEGIN
            S := S+X;
            I := I+1
            END
        END;
    IF X>=0.0 THEN
        WRITE (J,S)
    END
END.
```

You survey the damage: you've got to initialize X and I;
you've got to throw out your FOR--DO and replace it with a
more complicated WHILE--DO; you've got to check the value of
each "X" three times (once to see if you should add it, once
to see if you should print "S", and once to see if the loop
should keep going); you've got to increment "I" with a
statement rather than having it happen automatically.
There's probably a better way to write this thing but you
don't see it.

Then you remember the GOTO exit. You can just add eight
lines (shown in bold face) to your existing program.

```
LABEL  888;
other declarations
BEGIN
FOR J := .1 TO 20 DO
     BEGIN
     S := 0.0;
     FCR I := 1 TO 100 DO
          BEGIN
          READ (X);
          IF X<0 THEN
               BEGIN
               WRITE (J,' BAD DATA');
               GOTO 888
               END
          ELSE
               S := S + X
          END;
     WRITE (J,S);
     888: (* COME TO HERE IF X IS NEGATIVE *)
     END
END.
```

Notice that the statement label is attached to a comment
telling how the path of control got there.  The path of
control will normally go this way as well, but without
effect because the "statement" 888 doesn't do anything; it
is merely the escape hatch.  An "escape south" is the only
way we recommend using the GOTO in PASCAL.

Now you try the program again and it works beautifully.
You and Sam prepare to pack up your stuff and leave the data
processing area.  Then he says, "You know, it sure would
help if the machine could print out the sum of all the
sets--and the averages, hey, how about the averages."  We
leave the course of the ensuing dialogue and the ultimate
state of the friendship to your imagination.

You met PROCEDUREs first as part of TIPS. There we used a PROCEDURE to avoid repeating a set of statements in a PROGRAM. But there are several reasons to use PROCEDUREs, as this section will make clear. Among these reasons are:

1.  A large program can be written by various people if each person writes PROCEDUREs. (Take a look at Lab Problem 60, Magic Squares.)

2.  A large program can be tested and, if necessary, debugged more easily if it is written as a set of PROCEDUREs.

3.  PROCEDUREs often contain instructions that are to be executed many times. Rather than including these instructions in the PROGRAM each time the set is to be used, memory space can be conserved if these instructions are in the form of a PROCEDURE and reused each time.

4.  A program can be logically segmented into PROCEDUREs.

5.  Once a PROCEDURE is written, it can be reused later with another calling program.

First we do a bit of review on PROCEDUREs (or subroutines or subprograms, as they are sometimes referred to). In the statements below:

```
                    PROGRAM Q (INPUT, OUTPUT);
                    VAR
                        •
                    PROCEDURE R;
                        BEGIN (* PROC R *)
                        •
                        •
                        •
                        END; (* PROC R *)
                    BEGIN (* MAIN PROGRAM *)
                        •
                        •
                        •
                    END. (* MAIN PROGRAM *)
```

Procedures With Parameters                              357

Q is a main PROGRAM and R, which is totally contained in the declaration section of Q, is an internal PROCEDURE.  Q could contain one or more internal PROCEDURES in addition to R. And R could contain PROCEDURES as well.

Here is an example with specific PROCEDURES.  Let us create a program which requires the examination of numbers periodically to insure that the number stored in X is greater than zero, is less than 121, and is a whole number. If the number being examined conforms to these constraints, no action is taken; otherwise, the value of the variable, BADX, is set to TRUE.

```
(* PROCEDURE DEMO *)
   PROGRAM PROG2 (INPUT, OUTPUT);
   VAR
       X: (* VALUE TO BE CHECKED *) REAL;
       BADX: (* TRUE IF X IS BAD *) BOOLEAN;
   PROCEDURE CKVAL;
       BEGIN (* CKVAL *)
       BADX := FALSE;
       IF (X<0) OR (X>121) THEN
           BADX := TRUE
       IF TRUNC(X) <> X THEN
           BADX := TRUE;
       END; (* CKVAL *)
   BEGIN
   READ (X);
   CKVAL;
   IF BADX THEN
       WRITELN (' ERROR IN X');
      •
      •
      •
   X := something;
   CKVAL;
   IF BADX THEN
       WRITELN (' WOOPS')
```

Each time the PROCEDURE CKVAL is invoked, X is examined to determine if it is greater than zero and less than 121; if not, BADX is set to TRUE.  (A variable used in this way is called a flag; it signals some condition to be true or false.)  Next X is checked against TRUNC (X) whose value is X sheared of any fractional part.  If they are not equal, then X is not a whole number, and BADX is set to TRUE. Finally,

```
   END; (* CKVAL *)
```

returns control to the point of invocation. Notice that the PROCEDURE CKVAL is invoked twice during the execution of the program. Using a PROCEDURE saved the programmer from writing the equivalent statements twice.


## Another Example

What values are printed by the following program?

```
PROGRAM PRCG3 (INPUT, OUTPUT);
    VAR
        A: (* COMMENT *) INTEGER;
        B: (* COMMENT *) INTEGER;
        C: (* COMMENT *) INTEGER;
        D: (* COMMENT *) INTEGER;
    PROCEDURE ST1;
        BEGIN (* PROC ST1 *)
        A := A + 3;
        B := B + 4;
        C := C + 5
        END; (* PROC ST1 *)
    PROCEDURE ST2;
        BEGIN (* PROC ST2 *)
        D := D - 20;
        A := A - 1;
        B := 0
        END; (* PROC ST2 *)
    BEGIN (* PROG3 *)
    A := 0;
    B := 0;
    C := 0;
    D := 300;
    B := B + 1;
    ST1;
    ST2;
    WRITELN (A,B,C,D)
    END. (* PROG3 *)
```

The values of A, B, C, and D printed will be 2, 0, 5 and 280 respectively. If you have difficulty understanding the above program, examine the following table, which shows the values of the variables at each step, beginning with their initialization.

| STEP | VALUES OF VARIABLES | | | |
|------|------|------|------|------|
|      | A | B | C | D |
| 1 | 0 | 0 | 0 | |
| 2 | | | | 300 |
| 3 | | 1 | | |
| 4 | 3 | | | |
| 5 | | 5 | | |
| 6 | | | 5 | |
| 7 | | | | 280 |
| 8 | 2 | | | |
| 9 | | 0 | | |

## Exercises

1. What basic error exists in the program below?

```
PROGRAM EXER (INPUT,OUTPUT);
    VAR
        AA: (* COMMENT *) REAL;
        BB: (* COMMENT *) REAL;
    PROCEDURE AA;
        BEGIN (* PROC AA *)
        BB := SQRT(AA)
        END; (* PROC AA*)
    BEGIN (* EXER *)
    AA := 3;
    BB := 4;
    AA;
    WRITELN (AA,BB)
    END. (* EXER *)
```

## Variables and Internal PROCEDUREs

Up to this point, any variable declared in the invoking
PROGRAM or PROCEDURE was available (or known) to the invoked
PROCEDUREs. The invoked PROCEDURE could not use any
variable names which were not also known to the PROGRAM or
PROCEDURE which called it. But variables may also be
declared within a PROCEDURE. If a variable is so declared
(is considered local to that PROCEDURE), it is known to the
invoked PROCEDURE but not to the invoking PROGRAM or
PROCEDURE. This is true even if the same variable is
declared in each. Each variable represents a different
location in storage and hence each is treated separately.
For example, the program below prints the value 5 because

the variable X in the PROGRAM PGM is known to the PROCEDURE
SUB.

```
      PROGRAM PGM (INPUT, OUTPUT);
          VAR
              X: (* A MAIN PROGRAM VARIABLE *) INTEGER;
          PROCEDURE SUB;
              BEGIN (* SUB *)
              X := 5
              END; (* SUB *)
          BEGIN
          X := 0;
          SUB;
          WRITELN (X)
          END.
```

By contrast, in the program below, the variable X is
also declared in the PROCEDURE.  Therefore, the name X
represents two different variables--one in the main PROGRAM
PGM, and one in the PROCEDURE SUB.

```
      PROGRAM PGM (INPUT, OUTPUT);
          VAR
              X: (* A MAIN PROGRAM VARIABLE *) INTEGER;
          PROCEDURE SUB;
              VAR
                  X: (* KNOWN ONLY TO THIS PROCEDURE *) INTEGER;
              BEGIN (* SUB *)
              X := 5
              END; (* SUB *)
          BEGIN
          X := 0;
          SUB;
          WRITELN (X)
          END.
```

The value printed in the above program is zero.  The
assignment statement in the PROCEDURE SUB sets X, a variable
known to the PROCEDURE, to 5.  But since this X is declared
in SUB, it is a different variable from the X declared in
the main PROGRAM.  Therefore, the value of X in the main
PROGRAM is unchanged.

One advantage of declaring variables in the internal
PROCEDURE is that if you needed additional variable names
for intermediate calculations in the PROCEDURE, you needn't
worry about duplicating names in the invoking PROGRAM or
PROCEDURE.  Simply declare any extra variables you want--and

be assured that they will be separate.  However, variables "go away" when the PROCEDURE is not <u>active</u> (i.e., being executed) so you will have to redefine them at every execution of the PROCEDURE.  **A PROCEDURE cannot remember locally declared variable values from one execution to the next.**

> It is good programming practice to declare <u>every variable</u> used in an internal PROCEDURE <u>in that</u> PROCEDURE, unless you need that variable to communicate with the calling PROGRAM or PROCEDURE. And, soon, we'll see a better way to do that communication.

## Exercise

What values are printed by the program below?

```
PROGRAM PGM (INPUT,OUTPUT);
    VAR
        X:(* COMMENT *) REAL;
        Y:(* COMMENT *) REAL;
    PROCEDURE SUB;
        VAR
            Y:(* COMMENT *) REAL;
        BEGIN
        Y := 4;
        X := X+3;
        Y := Y+3;
        WRITELN (' FROM SUB',X,Y)
        END;
    BEGIN
    X := 10;
    Y := 10;
    Y := Y+10;
    SUB;
    WRITELN (' FROM PGM',X,Y)
    END.
```

## PROCEDURES with Formal Parameters

A not-too-obvious restriction is present in PROCEDURE use as it has been thus far described.  Suppose, for example, we want to do a calculation with A, B, and C; we decide to use a PROCEDURE to do the calculation, and write it so that it operates on A, B, and C. Now suppose that, at some later point in the PROGRAM, we wish to invoke the PROCEDURE, but the variables on which we now want it to operate are D, E, and F. There is no immense problem here; prior to invoking the PROCEDURE, we can simply supply three statements in the PROGRAM:

```
A := D;
B := E;
C := F
```

But it is clear that we have a potential nuisance on our hands. If the PROCEDURE is to be invoked several times by the main PROGRAM--and that's one reason for having a PROCEDURE--then the chances increase that we will want to have the PROCEDURE perform the same operations on different sets of variables.

This same general annoyance will crop up if we try to write a general PROCEDURE which might be used with several different invoking PROGRAMS or PROCEDUREs. We will likewise have trouble if we want to have someone else write a PROCEDURE for us while we write the invoking PROGRAM; the PROCEDURE writer would need to know what variable names we are using before he or she begins writing. Further, if a PROCEDURE was to operate on an ARRAY (or other data aggregate) with a different name in the PROGRAM than that in the PROCEDURE, we would have to transfer all the elements from that ARRAY to the one named in the PROCEDURE.

In short, the requirement that identical variable names be used in the invoking PROGRAM or PROCEDURE and in the invoked PROCEDURE is a drag. So we introduce a feature of PASCAL which allows us to "pass" information to a PROCEDURE through the use of <u>actual parameters</u>, which we term <u>arguments</u>, in the invoking (or calling) statement. Such arguments may be constants, variables or expressions.

For example,

```
SUB(F,G,H)
```

means that the PROCEDURE SUB will be invoked as before, but now we "pass" the variables F, G, and H to it.

In the PROCEDURE heading we list the <u>formal parameters</u> (which we refer to simply as <u>parameters</u>) which are to be associated with the arguments of the call. For example,

```
              PROCEDURE SUB  (VAR P,Q,R: REAL);
```

The parameters in the PROCEDURE statement inform the
computer which variable names in the PROCEDURE will be
associated with the argument names in the invoking PROGRAM
or PROCEDURE.   To illustrate graphically, assuming that F,
G, and H have been typed REAL in a main PROGRAM:

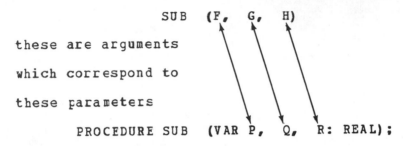

```
                    SUB  (F,   G,   H)
```

    these are arguments

    which correspond to

    these parameters

```
         PROCEDURE SUB   (VAR P,   Q,   R: REAL);
```

Now, anywhere in the PROCEDURE that we refer to P, we are
really referring to F in the invoking PROGRAM; likewise Q
and R in the PROCEDURE really refer to G and H respectively
in the invoking PROGRAM.  A better way to write the
PROCEDURE heading shown above is as follows:

```
     PROCEDURE SUB
          (VAR P: (* COMMENT *) REAL;
           VAR Q: (* COMMENT *) REAL;
           VAR R: (* COMMENT *) REAL);
```

    Note that VAR is repeated each time.  This may seem to
be a lot of trouble but it will pay off in readability,
especially when different TYPEs of parameters are used.
Please don't forget the parentheses!

```
PROGRAM PROG4 (INPUT, OUTPUT);
   VAR
      A: (* AN ARGUMENT FOR ADDEM *) REAL;
      B: (* ANOTHER ARGUMENT *) REAL;
   PROCEDURE ADDEM
      (VAR ALPHA: (* DESCRIPTION *) REAL;
       VAR BETA: (* DESCRIPTION *) REAL);
      BEGIN (* ADDEM *)
      ALPHA := ALPHA + BETA
      END; (* ADDEM *)
   BEGIN
   A := 12;
   B := 24;
   ADDEM (A,B);
   WRITELN (A,B)
   END.
```

In the program above the values printed are 36 and 24
because ALPHA, in the internal PROCEDURE named ADDEM,
actually refers to A in the PROGRAM named PROG4.   And BETA
in the internal PROCEDURE refers to B.   Therefore, when
ALPHA is incremented by BETA, A is really being incremented
by B.   The identity of the variable A is passed to the
PROCEDURE as the first argument which is associated with the
parameter ALPHA, and B is passed to the PROCEDURE as the
second argument which is then associated with the second
parameter, BETA.

Several points are important here.

1.   Variable names used in the calling or invoking
     statement are termed arguments or actual parameters.
     Variable names used in the internal PROCEDURE
     heading are termed formal parameters.

2.   The TYPE of each parameter in the internal PROCEDURE
     is declared within the parameter section of the
     PROCEDURE statement using a form of the VAR
     instruction.   In the example above, both parameters
     ALPHA and BETA, were declared as REAL.   The TYPEs of
     the declared parameters must match the TYPEs of the
     corresponding arguments in the invoking PROGRAM or
     PROCEDURE.   More than one TYPE may be declared in
     the PROCEDURE statement.   An abbreviated syntax
     diagram looks like this:

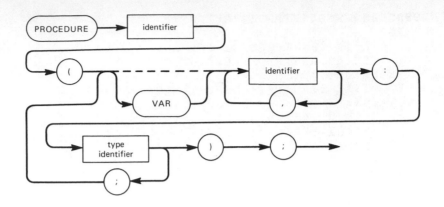

We'll describe the reason for the dotted line
shortly.

3.  Locally declared variables in an invoked PROCEDURE
    are different from and independent of variables in
    the invoking PROGRAM or PROCEDURE (except those in
    the calling statement), even if they have the same
    names.  In the example above, if the main PROGRAM
    had contained a variable named ALPHA as well as one
    named A, it would have been a different variable
    from the ALPHA in ADDEM.

Another example:

```
PROGRAM PROG5 (INPUT,OUTPUT);
    VAR
        W: (* COMMENT *) INTEGER;
        X: (* COMMENT *) INTEGER;
        Y: (* COMMENT *) INTEGER;
    PROCEDURE SUB
        (VAR U: (* W IN PROG5 *) INTEGER;
         VAR V: (* X IN PROG5 *) INTEGER;
         VAR W: (* Y IN PROG5 *) INTEGER);
        BEGIN (* SUB *)
        U := U+V*W;
        WRITELN (W)
        END; (* SUB *)
    BEGIN
    W := 5;
    X := 3;
    Y := 4;
    SUB(W,X,Y);
    WRITELN (W)
    END.
```

The value of W printed in PROG5 will be 17 while the value
of W printed by SUB will be 4, since the W in SUB really
refers to Y in PROG5.

Every algorithm of any complexity at all involves
decisions.  If you are drawing a flowchart or
writing a program and come to a point where the
machine must make a decision, then you too must make
a decision: which branch of the coding should you do
first?  If the branch you select also has a decision
in it, the problem is compounded.  One suggestion is
to code the shorter branch first--you are less
likely to forget the longer one.

     A situation in which one branch can be disposed
of quite quickly is when you are testing for an
error of some sort.  Presumably you want to display
or print out a signal, should an error occur.  One
technique for doing this is to write a PROCEDURE
similar to OUCH below:

```
PROCEDURE OUCH (VAR N:(* ERROR NUMBER *) INTEGER);
    BEGIN
    WRITELN (' YOU''VE MADE ERROR', N,' SHAME')
    END;
```

Now suppose you are at a point in the program
at which you want to signify an error if a variable,
WEIGHT, is negative.  You simply write

```
IF WEIGHT < 0 THEN
    BEGIN
    ERRNUM :=  23;
    OUCH (ERRNUM)
    END;
```

and dutifully write down on your documentation
notes, which are always by your side, that error
number 23 refers to a value of WEIGHT less than
zero.

Using internal PROCEDURE OUCH is not a perfect
solution, but it is vastly superior to reflecting
momentarily on the probable impact of WEIGHT being
negative and then saying, "Heck, that won't happen,"
because it's too much trouble to diagnose and
announce it.

PROCEDURE OUCH could, of course, have more
arguments, such as one telling it whether to assign
a special value to a variable in the calling program
(sometimes called setting a flag) to signify that an
error has occured.  A really sophisticated OUCH
could have ARRAYs of explanatory error messages.
But regardless of the form you choose to use, you
would be wise to employ some neatly packaged method
of dealing with errors which occur during the
execution of your programs.

A parallel exists between the headings of the PROGRAM
and the PROCEDURE.  The list in parentheses refers to the
way the PROGRAM or PROCEDURE communicates with its
environment.  The PROGRAM communicates by way of INPUT,
OUTPUT, and other FILEs.  The PROCEDURE may communicate by
way of variables in its parameter list.


## PROCEDUREs and Arrays

A subscripted variable name may be used as an argument
in a call to a PROCEDURE.  As with scalar variables, the
ARRAY must be declared in both the invoking PROGRAM or
PROCEDURE and in the invoked PROCEDURE.  And, as with scalar

variables, the programmer is again spared the necessity of using the same name to stand for the ARRAY in both the invoking and invoked PROCEDURE.  Take, for example, the program below.

```
PROGRAM PROG6 (INPUT, OUTPUT);
    TYPE
        ITEMS = ARRAY[ 1..4 ] OF INTEGER;
    VAR
        T: (* TOTAL OF ARRAY ELEMENTS *) INTEGER;
        BUNCH: (* ARRAY TO BE PASSED *) ITEMS;
    PROCEDURE SUB6
        (VAR TOT: (*  *) INTEGER;
         VAR SCONCH: ITEMS);
        BEGIN (* SUB6 *)
        TOT := SCONCH[ 1 ]* SCONCH[ 2 ]-SCONCH[ 3 ]*SCONCH[ 4 ]
        END; (* SUB6 *)
    BEGIN
    BUNCH[ 1 ] := 4;
    BUNCH[ 2 ] := 3;
    BUNCH[ 3 ] := 2;
    BUNCH[ 4 ] := 1;
    SUB6 (T, BUNCH);
    WRITELN (T)
    END.
```

It is mandatory that the number of dimensions and the number of elements in each dimension of the ARRAY in the called PROCEDURE be precisely the same as in the calling PROGRAM or PROCEDURE.

The call statement passes the address of the locations of T and the ARRAY BUNCH to SUB6 which relates the name TOT to T and the name SCONCH to BUNCH.  SUB6 computes the value of TOT as 10.0.  Since TOT is simply the PROCEDURE's name for the location called T in the PROGRAM, the PROGRAM prints the value 10.  The values originally stored in the ARRAY BUNCH in the PROGRAM are unchanged.  It is important to understand that only one ARRAY has really been declared; it is called BUNCH in the main PROGRAM and SCONCH in the PROCEDURE, but the identical four locations in computer memory are being referred to by each.

## Calling a PROCEDURE with Value Parameters Instead of Variable Parameters

Up to now we have said that an argument in an invoking statement is the name of some specific location of storage in the computer, and it is the location of that storage which is passed to the PROCEDURE. But it is not always wise to let a PROCEDURE know the address of particular locations within the calling PROGRAM or PROCEDURE. There is a concept--it's referred to as value parameter--which insulates the calling PROGRAM or PROCEDURE from the called PROCEDURE. It works by transmitting only the value the invoked PROCEDURE needs, but not the location of that value. It can only be used when a value is being transmitted from the calling PROGRAM or PROCEDURE. It is a safety feature which assures that a called PROCEDURE will not change values in the calling PROGRAM or PROCEDURE.

When you use a variable parameter (as you have up to now), only one location is used for a scalar variable; that location is in the calling PROGRAM or PROCEDURE; the called PROCEDURE may change the value in that location. So you should use a variable parameter if the PROCEDURE is expected to change the value of a variable in the calling PROGRAM or PROCEDURE. You may also use a variable parameter if you are simply transmitting information to the PROCEDURE but then you run the risk that an error in the PROCEDURE will make a change in that parameter which wasn't intended.

When you use a value parameter you insulate and protect the calling PROGRAM or PROCEDURE because only the value of the argument is transmitted to the invoked PROCEDURE. This means that the invoked PROCEDURE must set up a location within itself to accept the value. For scalar variables the extra storage requirement is generally a small price to pay for the added protection. If large ARRAYs or other structured aggregates of information are being transmitted, however, there may not be sufficient room to hold two copies of them: one in the calling PROGRAM or PROCEDURE and one in the called PROCEDURE. Even if there is room, running time for the program will be increased.

The way you use this technique is to treat the declaration of formal parameters in the PROCEDURE heading differently: you simply do not indicate them as VAR.

Parameters in the example below are ALPHA (an INTEGER value parameter), SWITCH (a BOOLEAN value parameter), RUGBY

(a REAL <u>variable</u> parameter), and ERIE (an INTEGER value
parameter). Also declared are INTERN and VITA; they are not
parameters but are declared as variables local to the
PROCEDURE.

```
PROCEDURE NAME
    (    ALPHA:(* COMMENT *) INTEGER;
         SWITCH:(* COMMENT *) BOOLEAN;
    VAR RUGBY:(* COMMENT *) REAL;
         ERIE:(* COMMENT *) INTEGER);

    VAR
         INTERN:(* COMMENT *) REAL;
         VITA:(* COMMENT *) BOOLEAN;
```

Note carefully the difference between the use of VAR in
the PROCEDURE heading and in the usual VARIABLE declaration.
In the PROCEDURE heading VAR must be repeated each time a
variable is to be used as a variable parameter. Contrast
this with previous usage of VAR.

Sometimes it is mandatory that you use a value
parameter. There are cases in which the location of the
storage will not possess a unique name in the invoking
program. For example, if we write the statement:

```
SOMESUB (18.5,A*B)
```

it is clear that neither argument in the invoking program
has a unique identifier (name) which refers to it. The
first argument is a constant and the second is an
expression. You could not legitimately begin the PROCEDURE
SOMESUB

```
PROCEDURE SOMESUB
    (VAR X: REAL;
     VAR Y: REAL);
```

because there are no variables in the calling PROGRAM which
correspond to X and Y. It is better, and sometimes
required, to use value parameters which have their own place
in the PROCEDURES:

Procedures With Parameters                     371

```
(* VARIABLE VS. VALUE INVOCATION *)
PROGRAM PROG7 (INPUT, OUTPUT);
    VAR
        E: INTEGER;
        F: INTEGER;
        P: INTEGER;
        Q: INTEGER;
        X: INTEGER;
        Y: INTEGER;
    PROCEDURE VARNVAL
        (VAR A: (* VARIABLE PARAMETER *)  INTEGER;
             B: (* VALUE PARAMETER *)  INTEGER;
             C: (* VALUE PARAMETER *)  INTEGER;
             D: (* VALUE PARAMETER *)  INTEGER);

        VAR E: (* NOT A PARAMETER *)  INTEGER;
        BEGIN (* VARNVAL *)
        A := B;
        B := B+150;
        E := 1;
        F := F*2;
        WHILE E<=C DO
            BEGIN
            A := A+D*E;
            E := E+2
            END
        END; (* VARNVAL *)
    BEGIN  (* PROG7 *)
    Y := 50;
    P := 8;
    Q := 80;
    E := -58;
    F := 33;
    VARNVAL (X,Y,7,P+Q);
    WRITELN (E,F,P,Q,X,Y)
    END. (* PROG7 *)
```

When you use a value parameter in a PROCEDURE, the corresp
argument in the calling PROGRAM or PROCEDURE is transferred
to a second location in the calling PROGRAM or PROCEDURE as it

PROG7 and its internal PROCEDURE VARNVAL are responsible
for setting up ten different locations in the machine.  Each
location can store one INTEGER value.  We hesitate to call
them all variables because three of them really have no name
which is known to the PROGRAM of which they are a part.

Let's assume we can take a snapshot of the situation just
before VARNVAL completes execution and returns control to
PROG7.  From the program you notice that X corresponds to A,
Y corresponds to B, 7 corresponds to C, and P+Q corresponds
to D.  Here is the snapshot:

|  | actual location of variable | name in PROG7 | name in VARNVAL | value just before return of control from VARNVAL |
|---|---|---|---|---|
| a) | PROG7 | E | not known | -58 |
| b) | PROG7 | F | F | 66 |
| c) | PROG7 | P | not known | 8 |
| d) | PROG7 | Q | not known | 80 |
| e) | PROG7 | X | A | 1458 |
| f) | PROG7 | Y | not known | 200 |
| g) | PROG7 | NONAME1 | B | 50 |
| h) | PROG7 | NONAME2 | C | 7 |
| i) | PROG7 | NONAME3 | D | 88 |
| j) | VARNVAL | not known | E | 9 |

Now we discuss each location.

a.  E at the top of the list.  It was given the value -58 in
PROG7 and retains that value throughout.  It is not
changed by the use of E in VARNVAL because another
variable E was declared in VARNVAL.  You see it at the
bottom of the list.

b.  F is known to both PROG7 and VARNVAL.  It was defined to
have the value 33 in PROG7 and its value was doubled in
VARNVAL.

c. P exists only in PROG7 where its value is 8.

d. Q also exists only in PROG7. Its value is 80.

e. X exists in PROG7; but VARNVAL also has access to it
   because it was declared in the parameter list with a VAR
   in front of it; VARNVAL knows it as A because X is the
   first argument and A is the first parameter in the
   calling sequence of VARNVAL.

f and g.  Y exists only in PROG7; when VARNVAL is invoked,
   the value of Y, (that is, 50) is transferred to a
   location in PROG7 which we will call NONAME1; VARNVAL
   knows this location as B; VARNVAL in fact changes the
   value of B, and hence of NONAME1, to 200, but the value
   of Y is unaffected even though Y and B correspond in the
   argument--parameter list.  It is vital for you to
   understand why X and Y are treated differently: X was
   indicated as VAR in the parameter list; Y was not.
   Therefore X can be changed by the PROCEDURE and Y
   cannot.

h. The third argument--parameter is 7 in PROG7 and C in
   VARNVAL.  But because C is a value parameter PROG7
   stores the value 7 in NONAME2.  If you are careless and
   allow a call with a variable parameter to occur with a
   constant, the program might even change the value of
   that constant in the program.  It would be as though you
   had written in a program

                    7 := 999;
                    X := 7;
                    WRITELN(X)

   and the program printed 999.  Probably all PASCAL
   compilers are protected against both of these disasters,
   but you should protect your program as well.

i. The value P+Q, that's 88, goes into NONAME3 where
   VARNVAL knows it as D.

j. E, finally, is a completely different E in VARNVAL than
   the E in PROG7 due to its declaration in VARNVAL.

   In general, use a variable parameter when the PROCEDURE
is going to return a value in that variable to the calling
PROGRAM or PROCEDURE.  Use a value parameter otherwise.

What values are printed by the program below?

```
PROGRAM PGM (INPUT,OUTPUT);
    VAR
        A:(* COMMENT *) INTEGER;
        B:(* COMMENT *) INTEGER;
        C:(* COMMENT *) INTEGER;
        D:(* COMMENT *) INTEGER;
        E:(* COMMENT *) INTEGER;
        F:(* COMMENT *) INTEGER;
    PROCEDURE SUB
        (VAR A: (* COMMENT *) INTEGER;
         VAR B: (* COMMENT *) INTEGER;
             C: (* COMMENT *) INTEGER;
             D: (* COMMENT *) INTEGER);
        VAR
            E: (* COMMENT *) INTEGER;
        BEGIN (* PROC SUB *)
        A := A+10;
        B := B+10;
        C := C+10;
        D := D+10;
        E := 10;
        F := F+10
        END;
    BEGIN (* PGM *)
    A := 1;
    B := 100;
    C := 3;
    D := 45;
    E := 5;
    F := 6;
    SUB (A,C,2,4);
    WRITELN (A,B,C,D,E,F)
    END.
```

responses to a questionnaire, or compute the FICA
(Social Security) tax on salaries, the chances are
pretty good that someone has faced the problem
before and may be able to hand you a program to do
it.  His or her program may not work, may not be
documented so that you can use it, or may not run on
your machine without modifications, but at least you
have more options than if you never asked yourself
the question: Am I re-inventing the wheel?

## Transfers and Internal PROCEDURES

While it is not possible to transfer or GOTO a statement
within a PROCEDURE from an invoking PROGRAM or PROCEDURE,
the reverse may be permissable: it is valid to GOTO a
statement in the invoking PROCEDURE from a point in an
invoked PROCEDURE.  For example, the GOTO statement below is
valid because it transfers from a statement within an
internal PROCEDURE to a statement in the main PROGRAM.   Not
smart, but it's legal.

```
PROGRAM BADNEWS (INPUT,OUTPUT);
   LABEL 9876;
       •
       •
   PROCEDURE SUB;
      BEGIN (* SUB *)
      IF X=0 THEN
         GOTO 9876
      •
      •
      END; (* SUB *)
   BEGIN (* MAIN *)
      •
   SUB;
      •
   9876: (* COMES FROM THE PROCEDURE SUB *)
   READ (NEWX)
      •
      •
   END. (* MAIN *)
```

On the other hand, the transfer below is invalid because
it transfers control from the PROGRAM to the internal
PROCEDURE.

```
PROGRAM WORSE (INPUT,OUTPUT);
    LABEL 1234;
        •
        •
    PROCEDURE SUB;
        BEGIN (* SUB *)
            •
            •
        1234:(* TRIES TO COME FROM PROGRAM WORSE *)
        X := X+Y
            •
            •
        END; (* SUB *)
    BEGIN (* MAIN *)
        •
        •
    IF Y>X THEN
        GOTO 1234
        •
        •
    END. (* MAIN *)
```

## Summary of Internal PROCEDUREs

1.  An internal PROCEDURE is invoked (or activated or
    called) by the use of its name as a statement.

2.  The invoking statement must possess the same number
    of arguments (sometimes called actual parameters) as
    the PROCEDURE heading possesses formal parameters.
    That number may be zero.

3.  If the invoking statement uses arguments, the
    locations of the variables used as arguments are
    "passed" to the PROCEDURE if its formal parameters
    have been designated with VAR.  If its formal
    parameters have not been designated by VAR, the
    values of the arguments are passed.

4.  All variable names used in the invoking PROGRAM or
    PROCEDURE are known and available to the internal
    PROCEDURE provided that those names are not also
    declared in the internal PROCEDURE.

5.  Statement labels in the invoked PROCEDURE are not
    known or available to the invoking PROGRAM or
    PROCEDURE.

6.  When the final END statement of a internal PROCEDURE
    is encountered in execution, control is returned to
    the statement in the invoking PROGRAM or PROCEDURE
    which directly follows the calling statement.  Any
    values in the subprogram (i.e., (1) declared
    variables, and (2) value parameters) are forgotten.

7.  Each internal PROCEDURE must be contained entirely
    within the declaration section of its invoking
    PROGRAM or PROCEDURE.

8.  An internal PROCEDURE must be called before it can
    become active.

9.  Internal PROCEDUREs may, themselves, contain
    internal PROCEDUREs.  For example, PROCEDURE A may
    contain PROCEDURE B which may contain PROCEDURE C.
    PROCEDURE A may invoke PROCEDURE B; PROCEDURE B may
    invoke PROCEDURE C.  However, PROCEDURE A may not
    invoke PROCEDURE C directly.

10. It is possible to use PROCEDURE names as arguments.
    We do not cover that feature in this text.

11. Some versions of PASCAL allow external PROCEDUREs
    which are not part of the main PROGRAM but may be
    invoked by it.  We do not cover this feature in this
    text.

## Designing Solutions vs. Solving Problems

By this time you know well what an algorithm
is: a step-by-step procedure used to solve a
problem.  If the problem is in terms of symbols,
then we can write instructions to a symbol
manipulator (computer) to follow the algorithm and
give us the answer.  But while the solution of such
a problem takes place in a stepwise (algorithmic)
fashion, it is not appropriate to plan the
construction of an algorithm in a stepwise manner.
Most planning, indeed most human conceptualization
of complex matters, takes place in quite another way
which we call hierarchical.  We consider the overall
schema or idea first.  Then we consider parts of it.
If we are careful we look at subparts of each part.
At some point we fill in the details.

This isn't to say that you can never plan the solution to a problem in a single-step-at-a-time fashion, but that such a process frequently leads to a technique of trial and error.  If you have the alternative of an overall examination and plan, your chances of success are considerably increased. There is no ready-made step-by-step approach for designing a step-by-step approach to solve a problem.


## Hierarchical Form

There is evidence to suggest that a person can keep in mind only three or four ideas at once.  To avoid argument let us say that it is extremely unusual for a person to be able to deal with more than eight thoughts at a time; the more usual number for most of us would be half that.  (Try, for example, to hold the names of all five American Great Lakes in your mind at the same time.)

Careful consideration of this fact again suggests breaking a complex "thing" down into simpler elements which are related in some hierarchical manner.  An example which is familiar to most of us is the theme "outline" we were asked to produce in high school English classes.  It had a title, some main ideas usually indicated with Roman numerals, some secondary ideas indicated with capital letters, etc.

The outline is indeed a helpful structure in constructing a piece of writing.  It imposes structure in at least two ways: (1) by relating ideas in a hierarchical manner, and (2) requiring uniformity of structure.

Consider the same principle applied to the construction of computer programs.  First, the title tells what the program is about. Next, we determine, on a gross level, the principal parts. Then we look at each of these parts and reapply the principle, determining again the constituent parts. This approach lets us focus our attention on parts of the program, at different levels, with the assurance that all the parts will relate to each other when we finish.

## Program Modules

Now that we have beaten you over the head with the preceding two sections regarding hierarchical problem solving, we come to an admonition: Do not write any but the simplest programs as a single, start to finish, sequence of statements.

It is difficult to quantify exactly what is meant by the simplest program. (The question is similar to asking, "What is the maximum number of words a sentence should contain?") A prevalent view is: if the statements you use in a program or subprogram won't all fit on a single page then the program or subprogram is probably attempting to do too much. Consider breaking it up into smaller pieces or modules. Obviously, examples counter to this suggestion can be generated. But we feel "only one page per program" is still a good rule of thumb.

The technique by which programs can be partitioned or broken up into sensibly sized modules, each with its logical task to perform, is to use subprograms. Subprograms were originally developed to reduce the amount of computer memory required to solve a problem. (E.g., if you need the area of a triangle at three different points in a program, why put the code in three separate times or, alternatively, fuss with making the path of control such that it arrives at the appropriate code at the appropriate time?)

It has become apparent that the use of subprogram modules is as useful in the production of better programs as it is in saving memory. Subprogram modules should be used even if the code they contain is executed only once by the invoking PROGRAM. The slight additional time and memory it takes to generate the necessary linkage to the subprogram is a small price to pay for isolating the essential logical elements of a program.

```
SUGGESTED LABORATORY PROBLEMS
        53, 55, 59, 60
```

Procedures With Parameters

You are familiar with functions. You've used SQRT and
SQR. Maybe even LN and EXP. Such functions are provided by
PASCAL and are called predefined functions. But you may
write your own FUNCTIONs and have the advantage of invoking
them just as you do the predefined ones by using the name of
the FUNCTION, followed by arguments in parentheses, in a
PASCAL expression.

To give an example of a user-written FUNCTION, let us
assume we need a FUNCTION which will calculate the area of a
triangle, given the lengths of its three sides. To recall
high school geometry, the area is

$$\sqrt{s\,(s-a)\,(s-b)\,(s-c)}$$

where a, b, and c are the lengths of the three sides and s
is the semi-perimeter: (a+b+c)/2. The FUNCTION we would
write, together with an invoking PROGRAM, might appear as
follows:

```
(* TRIANGLE FUNCTION DRIVER *)
PROGRAM PROG8 (INPUT, OUTPUT);
    VAR
        A,B,C: (* THE THREE SIDES OF A TRIANGLE *) REAL;
        H: (* SOME VARIABLE *) REAL;
    FUNCTION TRIAREA (X,Y,Z: REAL): REAL;
        VAR
            S: (* THE SEMIPERIMETER *) REAL;
        BEGIN (* TRIAREA *)
        S := (X+Y+Z)/2.0;
        TRIAREA := SQRT(S*(S-X)*(S-Y)*(S-Z))
        END; (* TRIAREA *)
    BEGIN (* PROG8 *)
        •
        •
        •
    H := TRIAREA(A,B,C)-12.0*TRIAREA(A/2,A/3,A/4);
```

Look at the FUNCTION definition heading. It shows some
similarities to, and some differences from, the PROCEDURE
definition heading we discussed previously. Differences
include:

1. The word FUNCTION is used.

2.   The parameters are value parameters.   (This is not
     mandatory but it is a good idea.)

3.   The FUNCTION name, itself, is declared to be REAL.
     Actually, the FUNCTION name serves two purposes.
     First, it is the name used to invoke the subprogram,
     as with a PROCEDURE.   Second, it is the identifier
     with which the single, scalar value which is
     computed by the FUNCTION, is made known to the
     invoking PROGRAM or PROCEDURE.   That is, the name of
     the FUNCTION serves as a variable in that it takes
     on the value to be returned; therefore, the name
     must have a TYPE.

   Within the FUNCTION we have pretty much what you might
expect: a declaration of a local variable, S; and a
BEGIN--END pair to encompass the action part of the program.
What you might not expect is the statement which says:
TRIAREA := SQRT(S*(S-X)*(S-Y)*(S-Z)).   **Before the execution
of the FUNCTION terminates, the identifier which is the name
of the FUNCTION must have been assigned the value to be sent
back to the invoking PROGRAM or PROCEDURE.**

   Now look at the PROG8.   We invoke TRIAREA twice.   Once
we use a straightforward call involving A, B, and C.   Then
we invoke the FUNCTION using three expressions.   In each
case, the value for TRIAREA is calculated, returned to the
invoking PROGRAM, and then control passes back to the main
PROGRAM.

   In general, a FUNCTION itself bears strong resemblance
to a PROCEDURE.   The differences are:

1.   The FUNCTION returns a single scalar value to the
     invoking PROGRAM or PROCEDURE.   The TYPE of the
     value returned is known to the invoking PROGRAM or
     PROCEDURE by the FUNCTION heading.

2.   The FUNCTION is invoked by using its name in an
     expression.

3.   The FUNCTION "sends back" a value and transfers
     control to the invoking PROCEDURE by storing the
     value in an identifier, which is the FUNCTION name,
     and terminating normally.

## Another Example

```
(* ANOTHER FUNCTION EXAMPLE *)
PROGRAM PROG9 (INPUT, OUTPUT);
    VAR
        N,P:(* ARGUMENTS FOR FACT ROUTINE *)  INTEGER;
        ANS: (*  *) REAL;
    FUNCTION FACT (VAL: INTEGER): INTEGER;
        VAR
            Q: (* FACTORIAL INITIALIZATION *)  INTEGER;
            K: (* LOOP INDEX AND FACT MULTIPLIER *)  INTEGER;
        BEGIN (* FACT *)
        Q := 1;
        FOR K := 2 TO VAL DO
            Q := Q * K;
        FACT := Q
        END; (* FACT *)
    BEGIN (* PROG9 *)
        •
        •
    N := 12;
    ANS := FACT(N)/FACT(2*N-1);
        •
        •
        •
    READ(P);
    ANS := FACT(TRUNC(SIN(P)/COS(P)))+3.14159
        •
        •
    END. (* PROG9 *)
```

You might ask: why did you use the variable Q in the
routine FACT?  Couldn't you just have written:

```
            FACT := 1;
            FOR K := 2 TO VAL DO
                FACT := FACT*K
```

The answer is you can't use the name FACT <u>as a variable</u> <u>name</u>
<u>in an expression</u> in the routine named FACT, and FACT*K is an
expression.

The reason: a FUNCTION name may not be declared as a
variable.  The FUNCTION name is <u>treated</u> as a variable only
in that it may have a value assigned to it.  If the FUNCTION
name FACT appears as a variable in an expression, it is
considered to be another invocation (or call) of the
FUNCTION FACT.  Since this would be in the FUNCTION FACT, it

would try to call itself. Such an invocation of a FUNCTION
by itself, if you intend it, is termed a recursive call; if
you don't intend it, it is termed a mistake.

FUNCTIONs are designed to return a single, scalar value
to the invoking PROGRAM or PROCEDURE. They should not
change the value of <u>any</u> variable in the invoking PROGRAM or
PROCEDURE. To assure that they don't:

1.  Always use the value parameter form of the parameter
    list to insulate the calling arguments from change.

2.  Declare, with a VAR instruction in the FUNCTION, all
    variables used in the FUNCTION which aren't in the
    parameter list.

These two steps insulate the calling PROGRAM or
PROCEDURE from the internal PROCEDURE and avoid the strange
side effects which can occur if a FUNCTION is able to change
something you didn't intend for it to.


Exercises

1.  What values are printed by the program below? The
    WRITELN statement in POWERUP is legal. Why?

```
(* RAISE A REAL NUMBER TO A NON-NEGATIVE INTEGER POWER *)
PROGRAM POWERUP (INPUT,OUTPUT);
    VAR
        X: (* FIRST BASE *) REAL;
        NX: (* POWER OF X *) INTEGER;
        Y: (* SECOND BASE *) REAL;
        NY: (* POWER OF Y *) INTEGER;
    FUNCTION RAISE (BASE:REAL;EXPON:INTEGER): REAL;
        VAR
            I: (* LOOP INDEX *) INTEGER;
            TEMP: (* COMPUTED VALUE *) REAL;
        BEGIN (* FUNCTIONRAISE *)
        TEMP := 1.0;
        FOR I := 1 TO EXPON DO
            TEMP := TEMP*BASE;
        RAISE := TEMP
        END; (* FUNCTION RAISE *)
    BEGIN
        X := -5.5;
        NX := 3;
        Y := 1.01;
        NY := 10;
```

```
        WRITELN (RAISE(X,NX),RAISE(Y,NY))
    END.
```

2.  Rework Lab Problem 03 Revised by writing the five
    subprograms needed by the driver below.  Do not use
    the variable name HEIGHT in any subprogram.

```
PROGRAM LAB03RR(INPUT,OUTPUT);
    VAR
        HEIGHT:(* COMMENT *) REAL;
        WIDTH:(* COMMENT *) REAL;
        AREA: (* COMMENT *) REAL;
(* SUBPROGRAMS GO HERE *)
    •
    •
    •
    •
    BEGIN (* MAIN *)
    INPUT(HEIGHT,WIDTH);
    IF(HEIGHT<WIDTH/2.0)THEN
        WOOPS(HEIGHT,WIDTH)
    ELSE
        BEGIN
        AREA := RECT(HEIGHT,WIDTH)-SEMI(WIDTH);
        OUTGO(HEIGHT,WIDTH,AREA)
        END
    END. (* MAIN *)
```

You need three PROCEDURES:  INPUT, WOOPS, and OUTGO; you
need two FUNCTIONS:  RECT and SEMI.  Test it on a computer.

## Elegance vs. Efficiency

There are, unfortunately, no good rules
governing whether a particular programming shortcut
should be taken in programming an algorithm.
Clearly, there are times when it is inappropriate to
follow the formal expression of a problem solution
exactly.  On the other hand, many programmers write
horrendous sections of code which bear little or no
resemblance to the formal process they are supposed
to depict except that (one hopes) they provide
equivalent answers.

Now that we've thrown out the two extremes we
are left with a more difficult problem.  What are

the appropriate actions of a programmer who must
compromise between elegance (following the formal
process) and efficiency (conserving memory or time)?
Basically, the answer is simple. You document what
you have done, starting with the formal description
of your computation, and then you detail those
techniques used to make the process more efficient.

Unless the explanation is terribly involved, a
very good place to do this is right in the program
listing itself. If there are reasons not to put
such explanations in the listing, then the listing
should certainly contain a complete reference to the
document in which the explanation occurs.

## Starting Over

Sometimes it happens. You've analyzed the problem,
decided on an approach, designed the algorithm,
started programming, and even done some debugging.
And nothing seems to be going right. Maybe the
problem definition has changed. Maybe you made some
assumptions that turned out to be false. Or maybe
fifty other things. There does come a time when
it's best to just start over. Lay the old stuff
aside (don't throw it out yet); take a deep breath
(or go for a walk, and get a good night's sleep), go
back, and take it from the top, again.

```
SUGGESTED LABORATORY PROBLEMS
38, 40, 43, 44, 45, 47
```

If an operating television receiver is connected directly to a TV camera whose lens is then pointed at the receiver, an image of the receiver will <u>recur</u> on its screen. Then, of course, since the TV camera is pointed at a TV set showing a TV set, that must appear on the screen as well. The effect of this on many people is an eerie new comprehension of the idea of infinity.

But a TV isn't necessary to generate the idea of infinite <u>recursion</u>. Four other examples are:

1. Two mirrors set across from each other will generate the recursive effect graphically.

2. Years ago a salt company used a label on their table salt box showing a girl carrying an identical table salt box. You couldn't see the next recursion, but you knew it was there--and the millions after that as well.

3. The syntax diagram for a TIPS statement includes a "statement" within it.

4. As a final example (this is fun, but we're supposed to be concerned with problem solving here) each cell of a living thing, yourself included, contains the structure by which it can be replicated. Recursion is responsible for life itself!

Something is recursive if it, directly or indirectly, includes or implies or replicates itself or a portion of itself. In mathematics, a function is recursive if it is defined in terms of itself. As a simple example, recall the idea of the factorial of a positive integer n.

$$n! = n * ((n-1)!)$$

But this does not satisfactorally complete the definition. You must also be told something else: that 0! has the value 1. The implication is that, if a recursive entity is to be useful, rather than just mind expanding, its definition must include at least two parts: (1) a definition of it in terms of itself, and (2) a concrete value for itself at some point.

A PASCAL PROCEDURE or FUNCTION is recursive if it can, directly or indirectly, invoke itself. An example of a routine which directly invokes itself is the FUNCTION to calculate factorials which follows:

```
PROGRAM FINDNFAC(INPUT,OUTPUT);
    VAR
        N,F: INTEGER;
    FUNCTION FACTRECU(N:INTEGER): INTEGER;
        VAR
            ANS: INTEGER;
        BEGIN (* FACTRECU *)
            WRITELN (' FACTRECU CALLED TO FIND FACTORIAL
                      OF',N);
            IF N<2 THEN
                ANS := 1
            ELSE
                ANS := N*FACTRECU(N-1);
            WRITELN(' FACTRECU FINDS ANSWER OF ',ANS);
            FACTRECU := ANS
        END; (* FACTRECU *)
    BEGIN (* MAIN *)
        READLN(N);
        F := FACTRECU(N);
        WRITELN(' ANSWER IS ',F)
    END. (* MAIN *)
```

In the function FACTRECU above, FACTRECU continues to invoke itself until M-1 becomes less than 2. If the program above read the number 4 for N the output would appear as below. Notice that the PROCEDURE FACTRECU calls itself several times before it is completed or returns any value to the invoking program.

```
FACTRECU CALLED TO FIND FACTORIAL OF          4
FACTRECU CALLED TO FIND FACTORIAL OF          3
FACTRECU CALLED TO FIND FACTORIAL OF          2
FACTRECU CALLED TO FIND FACTORIAL OF          1
FACTRECU FINDS ANSWER OF                      1
FACTRECU FINDS ANSWER OF                      2
FACTRECU FINDS ANSWER OF                      6
FACTRECU FINDS ANSWER OF                     24
ANSWER IS 24
```

The function has both prerequisites for being a useful recursive procedure: it is defined in terms of itself and,

for some argument, it produces a result other than in terms
of itself.

Notice the output from the program.  Each time the
function was executed it interrupted itself by calling
itself--until the last time when it called itself requesting
the factorial cf one.  Then it returned the value of 1!
which enabled it to return the value of 2! and so on.  It
was able to do this because, each time it called itself it
stored away a value for N for later use.  And, when the
process was reversed, it recalled a value of N each time as
it "unwound."

Contrast this routine (FACTRECU) with the FACT routine
of the last section (on user-written FUNCTIONS).  Here we
use the name FACTRECU in an expression--

        N*FACTRECU(N-1)

--but not as a variable, rather as a function name.)

## Recursive Procedure "Efficiency"

A more complicated recursive procedure might
have many variables with which it operated.  Each of
them would have to be stored away each time the
procedure called itself.  You can see that a lot of
memory space could be used if a routine called
itself a lot of times.  Further, each storing takes
time, as does the invoking of any procedure or
function.  You are left with the conclusion that
recursive procedures can be pretty inefficient both
in terms of computer storage and computer time.
(For an example, work Lab Problem 48.)  Because a
problem may be couched in terms of recursion does
not imply that it should be solved that way.  The
factorial problem is more directly and efficiently
solved by iteration as we showed in the previcus
routing FACT.

## Mutually Recursive PROCEDUREs

We said something could be recursive by indirectly
implying or replicating itself.  An example from the
physical world is two mirrors set opposite each other so
that when you looked at one you see it and its reflection in

the other.  In PASCAL, indirect recursion might occur if
function "g" invoked function "h" . . . and function "h"
invoked function "g".

    For example, consider an interesting geometric figure:
the Golden Rectangle.  Its sides have proportions of about 1
to 1.618035.  One distinguishing property it has is that, if
a square is removed from one end of the rectangle, a second,
smaller golden rectangle remains at the other end.  This
property suggests a progression which might look graphically
like

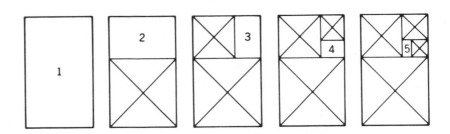

And the progression suggests a question: if we know the
dimensions of the left-most rectangle (the "parent"), what
is the area of the i'th rectangle?  You could write a
program which would do this by iteration, but let's do it
with recursive procedures.

    If the length of the long side of any Golden Rectangle
is L, the length of the short side is L/1.618035.  Thus the
area of a Golden Rectangle is L*L/1.618035.  From the
diagrams it is clear that the long side of any given
rectangle is the same as the length of the short side of the
next larger rectangle.

    Suppose we want a program which will calculate the area
of the i'th Golden Rectangle when the largest parent
rectangle is 1" by 1.618035".  We will write a driving
program which will compute the area of the desired
rectangle, say number 4, from the length of its longer side.
To get this longer side we use a PROCEDURE called LS.  LS
computes the longer side by finding the length of the
shorter side of the preceeding rectangle (number 3.)  It
does this with another FUNCTION, SS.  SS computes the

shorter side of a Golden Rectangle on the basis of its own
longer side and hence invokes LS again.  This recursive
process continues until one routine or the other finds a
side length of the parent rectangle.  Here is a program
which does this.

```
(* CALCULATE AREA OF GOLDEN RECTANGLE *)
PROGRAM AREAGLD (INPUT,OUTPUT);
    VAR
        I: (* RECTANGLE IDENTIFIER *) INTEGER;
        AREA: (* AREA OF I'TH GR *) REAL;
        SIDE: (* LENGTH OF SIDE OF I'TH GR *)  REAL;
    FUNCTION LS(N: INTEGER): REAL; FORWARD;
(* COMPUTE SHORT SIDE OF M'TH RECTANGLE *)
    FUNCTION SS(M: INTEGER): REAL;
        VAR
            SSLENGTH: REAL;
        BEGIN (* FUNCTION SS *)
        WRITELN(' SS ENTERED WITH M=',M);
        IF M=1 THEN
            SSLENGTH := 1
        ELSE
            SSLENGTH := LS(M)/1.618035;
        WRITELN(' SSLENGTH=',SSLENGTH:10:5);
        SS := SSLENGTH
        END; (* FUNCTION SS *)
(* COMPUTE LONG SIDE OF N'TH RECTANGLE *)
    FUNCTION LS;
        VAR
            LSLENGTH: REAL;
        BEGIN (* FUNCTION LS *)
        WRITELN (' LS ENTERED WITH N=',N);
        IF N=1 THEN
            LSLENGTH := 1.618035
        ELSE
            LSLENGTH := SS(N-1);
        WRITELN(' LSLENGTH=',LSLENGTH:10:5);
        LS := LSLENGTH
        END; (* FUNCTION LS *)
    BEGIN (* MAIN *)
    READ(I);
    SIDE := LS(I);
    AREA := SIDE*SIDE/1.618035;
    WRITELN(' I=',I,'    AREA=',AREA:10:5)
    END. (* MAIN *)
```

```
Carefully study          LS ENTERED WITH N= 4
the output in order      SS ENTERED WITH M= 3
to determine the         LS ENTERED WITH N= 3
flow of control          SS ENTERED WITH M= 2
through the program.     LS ENTERED WITH N= 2
                         SS ENTERED WITH M= 1
                         SSLENGTH= 1.00000;
                         LSLENGTH= 1.00000;
                         SSLENGTH= 0.61803;
                         LSLENGTH= 0.61803;
                         SSLENGTH= 0.38197;
                         LSLENGTH= 0.38197;
                         I=       4    AREA= 0.09017;
```

You probably noticed the declaration

FUNCTION LS(N:INTEGER):REAL;FORWARD;

This declaraction is called a _forward reference_. It is the
FUNCTION heading for the FUNCTION LS; this FUNCTION heading
is separated from the block of LS which you will find after
FUNCTION SS. The block of FUNCTION LS is preceeded by the
dummy heading: FUNCTION LS;. Why this bizarre arrangement?
Well, LS invokes SS; and SS invokes LS; there's no way we
can place each physically inside the other. Further, the
PROGRAM AREAGLD also invokes LS so that the parameter
sequence and TYPE must be available to AREAGLD--not hidden
away in FUNCTION SS. The way out of this tangle is just to
use a separate heading for LS with the word FORWARD. This
gives the compiler the hint that it can't handle the
FUNCTION (or PROCEDURE) calls in its usual, neat, nested
manner.

## A Warning

The examples we have shown you on recursive procedures
are _not_ the kinds of problems you should use them for. We
showed you the examples so you could understand the concept.
The only time you should allow yourself the luxury of using
recursive procedures is when you find the idea of recursion
more conducive to solving the problem than is iteration.
You know this has happened when you cannot see a
straightforward solution to the problem but you can see a
way to transform the problem into a very similar problem
which is simpler or littler in some way.

## A Last Example

Here's a problem that yields more easily to a recursive approach than an iterative one: Find all permutations of n consecutive integers.  If n is 3, the permutations are:

```
123
213
132
312
321
231
```

Now suppose we wanted the permutations of 1 2 3 and 4. One way to approach this problem is through recursion: note that if we simply append a "4" to the six permutations of 1, 2, and 3, shown above, we've solved part (one fourth) of the problem.

```
1234
2134
1324
3124
3214
2314
```

The other thing to note is that if we swap the "4" with the "3" in the six permutations above we'll get another six permutations:

```
1243
2143
1423
4123
4213
2413
```

Swapping the "4" with the "2" and with the "1" will complete the process.

Here's a recursive procedure which solves the problem. Trace it through.  If you have difficulty run it on your computer and follow the output listing.

Recursive Functions and Procedures                393

```
(* RECURSION EXAMPLE *)
PROGRAM PROG199(OUTPUT);
    TYPE
        SEQARRAY=ARRAY[1..4] OF INTEGER;
    VAR
        E: (* THE ARRAY *) SEQARRAY;
        Z: (* NUMBER OF ITEMS *) INTEGER;
        J: (* COUNTER *) INTEGER;
    PROCEDURE PERMUTE
            (    M:INTEGER;
             VAR E:SEQARRAY);
        VAR
            I,J: (* COUNTERS *) INTEGER;
            D: (* TEMPORARY STORAGE *) INTEGER;
        BEGIN (* PROC PERMUTE *)
        WRITELN(' PERMUTE ENTERED WITH M=',M:2);
        IF M>1 THEN
            BEGIN
            PERMUTE(M-1,E);
            FOR I := M-1 DOWNTO 1 DO
                BEGIN
(* SWAP E SUB M WITH E SUB I *)
                D := E[M];
                E[M] := E[I];
                E[I] := D;
(* FIND LOWER ORDER PERMUTATIONS *)
                PERMUTE(M-1,E);
(* SWAP BACK *)
                D := E[M];
                E[M] := E[I];
                E[I] := D
                END
            END
        ELSE
            BEGIN
            FOR J := 1 TO Z DO
                WRITE (E[J]);
            WRITELN
            END;
        WRITELN(' PERMUTE EXITED WITH M=',M:2)
        END; (* PROC PERMUTE *)
    BEGIN (* MAIN *)
    Z := 4;
(* SET UP ARRAY *)
    FOR J := 1 TO Z DO
        E[J] := J;
(* GET PERMUTATIONS *)
    PERMUTE(Z,E)
    END. (* MAIN *)
```

# part V

# MODULES ON COMPUTERS AND COMPUTING

A digital computer system accepts a set of instructions (called a program) and executes these instructions quickly, faithfully, and precisely.

A computer system is composed of three basic types of components:

    a.  Main Storage (or memory),
    b.  Central Processing Unit (CPU, consisting of the Control and Arithmetic Unit)
    c.  Input and Output Devices.

## Main Storage

Main Storage is a set of storage locations, each of which possesses a unique address. Each storage location can hold information. The storage locations might be visualized as a set of post office boxes.

| | | |
|---|---|---|
| 0 | 1 | 2 |
| 3 | 4 | 5 |
| 6 | 7 | 8 |
| 9 | 10 | 11 |

Two types of information are placed in the storage locations of a computer: instructions and data.

Module 1: Fundamentals of a Computer System     397

A programmer writes instructions in some computer language and these instructions are entered into computer storage. The computer then begins executing the instructions one after another until an instruction specifies a halt or branch to another instruction.  As the instructions are executed, data are brought into storage by read instructions; the data are placed in storage locations not occupied by instructions.

Data are any items of information other than the instructions to the computer.  The data in storage are later accessible for computation, inspection, or output.

The storage locations are general in that any location can be used for data or instructions.  Once an instruction is placed in a specific location, that location is not then generally available to hold data.  The converse is also true.

Some computers possess a small number of storage locations; others have a large number.  The price of the computer is somewhat dependent upon the storage size, rented or purchased.  The price is also somewhat dependent on the number of instructions the computer can execute in a second.

Normally, all or a portion of computer storage is available to a "job" or program (set of instructions) while that program is in operation.  When that program finishes, another program gains control of storage.  The contents of storage are generally obliterated between jobs.  So if the programmer wants some specific quantity in memory, he must arrange, through his programming, to put it there.

## Central Processing Unit

The Central Processing Unit (CPU) contains control circuitry which interprets the instructions which are in storage and sends electrical impulses to the proper places in the computer system.  Also contained in the CPU is the arithmetic unit which performs arithmetic operations.

Instructions tell the computer what to do and the sequence in which the operations are to be carried out.  The computer can understand various types of instructions such as:

    a.  arithmetic (add, subtract, multiply, divide)

    b.  input (read information into storage)

c.    output (write information out of storage)

d.    branch (take next instruction from specific
      storage location)

e.    logic (is a value greater than another value, less
      than another value, or equal to another value?)

## Input and Output Devices

Input devices allow information which is stored on some
external medium, such as punched cards, (or the tips of your
fingers) to be placed in computer storage. Output units
allow information from computer storage to be duplicated on
some external medium such as paper. Several types of input
and output units are described below. Devices such as those
described below are sometimes called "peripheral devices" or
"peripherals".

Card Reader - transforms information punched on
tabulating cards into electronic signals and sends these
signals over a cable into the storage of the computer.
Performs input only.

Typewriter Terminal - typewriter connected to a
computer, frequently via telephone lines. Typing is
performed in a conventional way except that data is sent
into computer storage or from computer storage. Performs
either input or output.

Line Printer - device for printing out information from
the machine a line at a time rather than a character at a
time. Principle advantage over typewriter terminals is
speed. Performs output only.

Cathode Ray Display - interprets information from the
storage of a computer and displays letters, numbers--and
perhaps lines and shapes in color--on the face of a TV-like
cathode ray tube. With an attached keyboard, information
can be typed and sent to computer storage. Performs output.

Card Punch - transforms signals coming from storage over
a cable into holes in punched cards. Normally performs
output only.

Magnetic Tape Unit - reads information from or writes
information onto magnetic tape. This unit is similar to a

home tape recorder except that it records onto half-inch-wide tape instead of quarter-inch tape and it records characters and digits instead of sound. Performs either input or output. Can store 6,000 or more characters per inch of tape; tapes are commonly 2400 feet long or shorter.

Magnetic Disk Unit - records information onto or reads information from a magnetic disk, which is similar in geometry to a phonograph record. Its advantage over magnetic tape is that it can be read from or written on beginning anywhere on its disk surface rather than operating in a sequential mode. Performs either input or output. Millions of characters may be stored on a single, interchangeable disk pack.

Magnetic Ink Character Reader (MICR) - Interprets numbers printed with special magnetic ink (e.g., characters at the bottom of bank checks) and sends the information over a cable to the storage of a computer. Performs input only.

Optical Character Reader - Interprets print or type on a paper page and sends information over a cable into the storage of a computer. Performs input only.

Optical Mark Reader - Interprets horizontal or vertical marks on a paper page (for example, test scoring sheets) and sends information over a cable into the storage of a computer. Performs input only.

X-Y Digitizer or Data Tablet - an electronic drafting board which can continually send the X and Y (Cartesian) coordinates of a pen or cursor applied to its surface. By allowing the user to automatically specify series of points, it can transmit graphic entities (lines, dots, curves) to a computer. Performs input only.

Plotter - Interprets information from computer storage consisting of x-y coordinates and other control information and draws graphs, charts, or diagrams with a pen on paper, or with laser or light beam on film. Performs output only.

# A Diagram of a Computer System

The diagram below shows the most rudimentary kind of computer schematic.  The solid arrows indicate flows of information; the dashed arrows indicate that one device controls another.

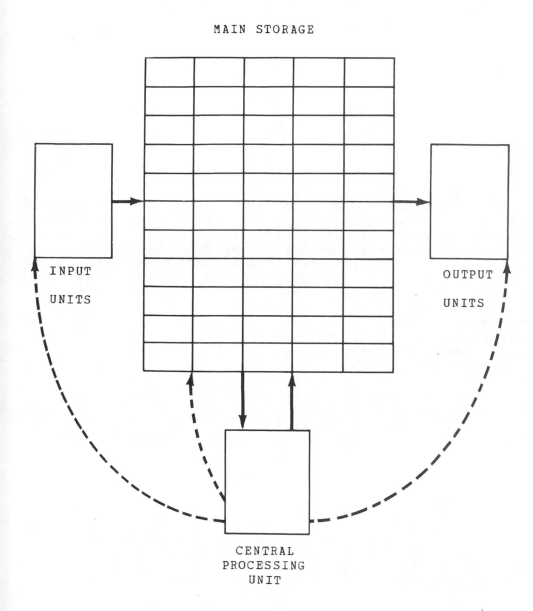

MAIN STORAGE

INPUT

UNITS

OUTPUT

UNITS

CENTRAL
PROCESSING
UNIT

## Binary Storage

A storage location in a computer is composed of electronic components which can store binary digits called bits. A bit can take on either the value zero or the value one. A series of bits can then represent a number. To show this the decimal and binary equivalents for the numbers zero through ten are represented below.

| | |
|---|---|
| 0 | 0 |
| 1 | 1 |
| 2 | 10 |
| 3 | 11 |
| 4 | 100 |
| 5 | 101 |
| 6 | 110 |
| 7 | 111 |
| 8 | 1000 |
| 9 | 1001 |
| 10 | 1010 |

Storage locations in a computer are composed of bits and can be used in several ways. To illustrate, we describe the bit structure of the IBM System /370 computer. Bits can be grouped to represent a number, a series of numbers, or alphabetic characters. When representing alphabetic characters, bits are logically grouped into 8-bit segments which are called bytes. A byte can contain one alphabetic character. If one refers to a 32-bit location, it is customary to speak of it as a computer word. Therefore one word consists of four bytes, each of which consists of eight bits. A word can store an INTEGER or REAL number or up to 4 alphabetic characters.

The size of a computer's storage or memory is sometimes defined in terms of computer words and sometimes in terms of bytes of storage. Whichever term is used, in the IBM System 360/370 computer, a word is 32 bits and a byte is 8 bits or one-fourth of a computer word.

## The Compiling Process

TIPS or PASCAL is not the "natural" or machine language (ml) of any computer. Every computer that understands TIPS or PASCAL must first translate a program in that language into its own language. Thus the TIPS or PASCAL program is transformed into a machine language program. The computer then solves the problem by following the steps in the machine language program.

When a computer follows a machine language program to solve a problem, the process occurs in the manner schematically illustrated below.

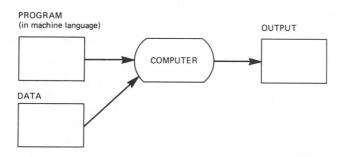

PROGRAM
(in machine language)

OUTPUT

COMPUTER

DATA

A program (written in the machine's own language) is put into the computer. Under control of this program the computer reads in data (or input).  The computer manipulates these data and produces answers (or output).

In solving a problem in which the program is written in PASCAL, this principle is applied two or more times.  See the diagram and explanation below.

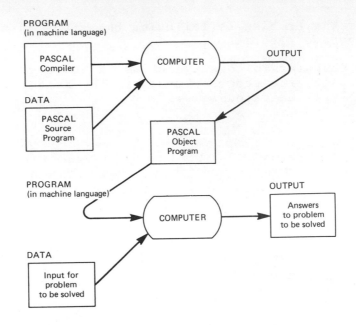

PROGRAM
(in machine language)

PASCAL
Compiler

DATA

PASCAL
Source
Program

COMPUTER

OUTPUT

PASCAL
Object
Program

PROGRAM
(in machine language)

COMPUTER

OUTPUT

Answers
to problem
to be solved

DATA

Input for
problem
to be solved

First a machine language program (called a PASCAL
compiler) is put into the machine. Under control of this
program, data are read, but the data are of an unusual kind.
They are PASCAL language instructions of the kind you write,
called a source program. The computer manipulates these
data to produce "answers" which are also of an unusual kind.
The output is the machine language equivalent to the PASCAL
program that was read in. Thus the PASCAL source program is
the input and a machine language program (called an object
program) is the output. It is usually placed on magnetic
disk (or, in some earlier computers, on tape or even cards)
or is stored away in another part of the memory for later
use. Now to solve the original problem, the object program
and the data for that problem are read in, manipulated, and
answers are produced.

With many compilers it is possible to compile a PASCAL
source program and obtain an object program on disk so that
it may be used immediately and/or be kept and used later.
The advantage of keeping the object program (which is in
machine language) is that there is no need to repeat the
compiling process when you or someone else wants to reuse
the program.

# Compiling and Baking: An Analogy

Suppose you are given a recipe for a pie--but there is a catch: the recipe is written in French and you only read English.  To use the recipe you proceed to (1) translate it into English and then (2) obey the instructions of the English recipe to make the pie.

One might make a loose analogy between using a computer to produce a solution to a problem and making the pie from a recipe written in French.  Here are the equivalent elements:

| Using a Computer | Baking a Pie |
|---|---|
| 1) The computer. | You. |
| 2) The PASCAL Language. | French. |
| 3) Machine language. | English. |
| 4) A PASCAL compiler. | A book about French grammar and a French to-English dictionary. |
| 5) A program made up of PASCAL instructions. | The recipe written in French. |
| 6) Compiling PASCAL into Machine language. | Translating the recipe from French to English. |
| 7) A computer program equivalent to item 5, made up of Machine Language statements. | The recipe after it's translation from French to English. |
| 8) The data for the problem. | The ingredients for the pie. |
| 9) Executing the Machine Language program. | Following the instructions of the English recipe. |
| 10) The answers. | The pie. |

The parallel processes are:

1)  You take the recipe (written in French) and use your
    ability, the grammer book and dictionary, to translate
    the recipe into your own language (English).  Now you
    follow the instructions of the translated recipe,
    combine the ingredients, and produce the pie.

2)  The computer takes the source program (written in
    PASCAL) and, using it's circuitry and the PASCAL
    compiler, translates the program into an object program
    in its own language (Machine Language).  Now the
    computer follows the instructions of the translated
    program, manipulates the data, and produces the answers.

A microcomputer is a self-contained unit.  When you use
one you do not (usually) share its use with anyone else.
The cost, size, and operating expense of a microcomputer is
so small that it is not unreasonable that much of its
computing power is wasted while you sit in front of it and
decide what you want to do next.  A microcomputer is a big
brother to a hand held calculator--which also has
considerable calculating power--which waits patiently while
you key in the numbers you want it to work with.

There are many microcomputers on the market today.  All
are based on "microprocessor chips"--tiny complex,
electronic devices which can be produced and sold for a few
dollars each.  If you have a digital watch the chances are
good that it has such a microprocessor chip in it.  A
microcomputer is, of course, more than just the chip which
lies at its heart, so microcomputers cost considerably more
than a dollar or so.  But a microcomputer can be otained for
a few hundred dollars.  The prices go up from there
depending on the peripherals (see Module 1) which you attach
to them.

The microcomputer we used in testing the programs in
this text is an APPLE II PLUS.  It has forty-eight thousand
characters of memory (in computer lingo, 48K bytes), a
television monitor for output, and a keyboard for input.  It
also has some auxilary storage in the form of "floppy disks"
which can be inserted into the two disk drives attached to
the computer.  Each floppy disk can store about 50,000 bytes
of information.  We programmed our Apple using PASCAL; the
compiler which came with the machine was UCSD (University of
California at San Diego) PASCAL.  Some microcomputers which
offer PASCAL as a programming language use the UCSD
compiler.  Further, the methods of operation for different
microcomputers are similar once the UCSD operating system is
invoked.  Therefore, we will describe the procedure for
using the APPLE in the PASCAL environment.  Probably the
experience you have with your machine will not be much
different.

## Booting PASCAL

In the last century a man who made a success of himself starting from humble beginnings was said to have "pulled himself up by his bootstraps."  It is comical illusion to the difficulty of lifting oneself off the ground by pulling on one's shoe laces.  The issue is "how do you start from nothing and get something."  That is also an issue when you start with a computer which has nothing in its memory. Since (1) a computer operates by executing instructions which are in its memory, and (2) in order to put something in its memory it normally has to execute input instructions, it is clear that something extraordinary has to happen at the beginning.  A program or method which starts the process off is called a bootstrap.

With the APPLE II the process of booting PASCAL happens quite simply.  You simply select the floppy disk with the PASCAL operating system and compiler on it, put it into a disk drive, and turn on the computer's power switch.  The computer then automatically reads a portion of the information on the floppy disk, stores that information in it's memory, and then begins executing the instructions which just went into it.  Part of the information is displayed on the video screen indicating that the computer is now ready for you to type commands to it.  The display looks something like this:


COMMAND:E(DIT,R(UN,F(ILE,C(OMP,L(INK,X(EXUTE,A(SSEM,D(EBUG?


and is called a "menu" from which you select what you want.


## The UCSD Monitor

When you first type a letter on the APPLE's keyboard you are giving a command to the primary or master program in the computer's memory.  This program is called a monitor and all other programs are executed "under" or "within" it.  Some of the programs which may be selected are the Editor (type an "E"), the Filer (type an "F"),or the PASCAL compiler (type a "C").  You may also execute another program of your choosing (type an "X") provided that program is on a floppy disk in a disk drive.  Briefly,

1)  The Editor allows you to construct a file consisting of
    lines; the lines consist of characters which are typed
    from the keyboard.  The editor has a menu which lets you
    select whether you want to add lines, delete characters,
    or do a host of other functions.  One of the reasons to
    have the Editor is so that you can construct PASCAL
    programs.  Further, if the program you construct doesn't
    operate properly, you can use the Editor to modify it.

2)  The Filer allows you to manage the files which are on
    floppy disks.  For example, you might want to take a
    file which you just constructed with the Editor, give it
    a name, and place it on a floppy disk.  Then you could
    come back the next day and retrieve that file from the
    floppy disk using the Filer program.

3)  The Compiler translates the PASCAL instructions which
    you typed in under the auspices of the Editor into
    machine language instructions which can be executed by
    the APPLE central processing unit (CPU).  This machine
    language form of the program is called an object program
    and can be stored on floppy disk along with the original
    PASCAL form which is called a source program.

    Learning to use the Editor, the Filer, and the Compiler
is not too complicated but it requires "hands-on"
experience.  Regardless of the microcomputer and PASCAL
version you use, your instructor will provide you with the
particular information for your installation.  But the basic
ideas--that you must somehow put the program into the
machine and have the ability to modify it, that it must be
compiled into machine language (or some other, intermediate
language), and that there must be some way to store it on
disk (or perhaps magnetic tape)--are unchanged.  In this
section we have tried to give you a brief overview of the
process and the important elements--important ideas that
sometimes get lost when a process contains many details.

A terminal consists of a keyboard and some kind of
display. It can send and receive information over a
communication channel. Some terminals display information
on paper like ordinary typewriters. Other terminals display
information on TV-type screens. The terminals described
here are not computers or calculators but are simply
vehicles for transmitting to receiving information from a
central computer.

## Operating Modes

There are two operating modes for most terminals: LOCAL
and LINE.

When in LOCAL mode, the terminal cannot be connected to
the computer, but can be used like a typewriter. This mode
can be used for practicing, or for spacing and paper or
clearing the screen before connecting to the computer.

The terminal must be in LINE mode before it can be
connected to the computer.

## Major Parts of the Terminal

Terminals have four major parts or control devices:

1. The Keyboard
2. The Set Controls
3. The Display
4. The BREAK or ATTENTION Control

## The Keyboard

The keyboard is usually similar to an ordinary
typewriter keyboard. The keys that you might use in your
first terminal session are the alphabetic keys, the number
keys, the RETURN key, the BACKSPACE key, and the LF (LINE
FEED) key.

The alphabetic keys are in the same location as on a typewriter. Some terminals have both uppercase and lowercase letters while others have only uppercase.

The locations of the number keys vary among terminals. The RETURN key serves the same purpose as on a typewriter: it returns the carriage to the beginning of the next line; it also serves as a line delimiter, telling the computer that you have finished a line and wish to either begin a new line or get a response from the computer. You must press the RETURN key after you have typed a line.

The BACKSPACE key is used to correct errors in a line. Unfortunately, the backspace is usually considered to be a special symbol (like $, ¢, or /.) You may have to specify that you really want the backspace key to cause backspacing. You would do this at the time you logged on according to the procedure provided by your instructor. If, before pressing the RETURN key, you find that you have made an error, you may backspace to the error and retype the remainder of the line. Although your original line may still show on the paper or screen of a terminal, each letter, number, or symbol that you backspace over is erased from the memory of the computer. For this reason, you must retype all characters over which you have backspaced. If you have already pressed the RETURN key and notice that you have made an error, you will have to retype the entire line correctly.

The LINE FEED key simply moves the lines on the screen or paper up one by one. Pressing the LINE FEED key does not insert a blank line as far as the computer is concerned.

There is a PAPER ADVANCE key on some terminals for rapid spacing. On terminals that use screens to display information, rapid spacing can be done by holding down the LINE FEED key.


The Set Controls

The set controls are used to turn the terminal on and off, and to put it into the LOCAL and LINE modes described earlier. Some terminals have a single button or control to put the terminal in each mode while others have a combination of switches and controls. Some terminals do not have a LOCAL mode but instead have a single switch to turn the terminal on and off. The locations of the various set controls vary among terminals.

## The Display

Your typing and the computer's responses are displayed on paper or on a screen. Terminals that use paper to display information are called hardcopy terminals. Terminals that use screens for a similar display are called CRT (Cathode Ray Tube) terminals. The type of terminal you use will depend on availability and personal preference.

The advantage of using hardcopy terminals is that you have a paper copy of your terminal session for future reference. If you have difficulties during a computer session and need assistance, a listing of your session would be valuable to the consultant. Because of this, a beginner should use a hardcopy terminal, if there is a choice.

The advantage of using CRT terminals is that they are quieter and sometimes faster. With this terminal you will have no printed record of what you did in your session with the computer.

Sometimes we use the term "cursor" when talking about CRT terminals. The cursor indicates the next data entry point. The cursor usually appears as a bright block. Some terminals use a single or double underline for a cursor.

Regardless of which type of terminal you use, remember that the characters you see on the screen or paper are sometimes printed differently on the system high-speed printer.


## The BREAK or ATTENTION Control

The BREAK or ATTENTION control is a special key or button on a terminal. Its name and location will vary from one type of terminal to another. Most manufacturers label the control BREAK, but some use ATTN or ATTENTION. It serves the same function regardless of the label. You use this control to stop whatever the computer is doing. When you press this key, you get a response from the computer such as READY. This indicates that the computer has stopped what it was doing and is ready for you to have it do something else. You may also press this key in the middle of the line you are presently typing if you want the whole line deleted.

## Communicating with the Computer

As we stated earlier, the letters, numbers, or symbols that you type are transmitted to the computer and its responses are transmitted back to your terminal. The communication is accomplished in one of several ways, including:

    1. Direct Connection
    2. Telephone Connection


## Direct Connection

Direct connection is the simplest method, since it only involves connecting four wires from the terminal to the computer. This method is used for terminals which are physically close to the computer to which they are connected.

For terminals farther away an extra unit near the terminal may be used to amplify the signals.


## Telephone Connection

It is also possible for the terminal and computer to communicate via telephone. This requires the use of a translation device called a modem (modulator-demodulator) which changes the electrical signal generated at the terminal (when you type a letter, number, or symbol) to a sound signal which can then be sent through a standard telephone to the computer. A similar device is also required on the computer end of the line to translate the sound signal back to an electrical signal so that the computer can understand the information.

To turn the modem on, push the switch on the modem to the ON position. When this is done, some lights on the front panel of the modem will come on. The modem must be turned on before you can connect the terminal to the computer. To turn the modem off, push the switch on the modem to the OFF position. The lights on the front panel will go out.

There are usually two other switches located on the modem. One switch is labeled H on one side and F on the other. The effects of this switch depend on the type of

terminal being used.  The other switch is labeled CPLR on
one side and LINE on the other.  Your instructor will advise
you on the positions of these switches when he or she
describes the logon sequence to you.  We have left space
below for you to place the logon instructions applicable to
your machine.

Logging On Your Computer

The punched card, Hollerith card, or IBM card, as it is
variously known, is a paper device for storing information
in a form which a machine can read. The card is 7 3/8" wide
by 3 1/4" deep by 0.007" thick. Information is stored "in"
the card by punching small rectangular holes in it. The
device which punches these holes is called a keypunch; it
has a keyboard which resembles a typewriter keyboard. The
keypunch is discussed later in this module.

The card is defined to have 80 vertical columns numbered
1 through 80 across its width. The card is also defined to
have 12 horizontal rows designated from top to bottom as 12,
11, 0, 1, 2, 3, 4, 5, 6, 7, 8, 9. The punching positions
are defined to be the points at which the rows and columns
intersect. Thus in each of the eighty columns there are
twelve punching positions. By punching in one, two, or
three of these twelve positions many different characters
can be represented. If no punches are present in a column,
the character stored there is called a blank. One punched
card can, therefore, store eighty characters of information;
the characters may be in any order. The coding for each of
the possible characters which may be created using a
standard keypunch machine is shown below. The keypunch also
prints the punched characters at the top of the card so a
person can easily read the characters punched.

## Simplified Keypunch Instructions

The numbers in parentheses which follow relate to the numbered components of the diagram of the IBM 029 keypunch on the next page.

a.  Load the hopper (1) with cards.  Any type card, regardless of color or corner cuts, will work.

b.  Turn machine on if it is off.  The switch (2) is located at right under the table.

c.  Press down the right side of switch (3) so that the contacts are raised away from the drum (the contacts may be seen through the window (4)).

d.  Turn all four center switches (5) up.

e.  Push FEED button twice.  A card is now ready to be punched.  Use as a regular typewriter for lower order characters or letters.  For upper order characters (i.e., numbers and special characters) hold down NUMERIC.

f.  The numbered wheel (6) indicates the number of the next column to be punched.

g.  When finished with the punching of a card, press REL.

h.  The next fresh card is now ready for punching.

i.  If the keyboard locks (buttons have no effect), press the ERROR RESET.

j.  When finished (or to clear the machine) flip the CLEAR switch (8).

k.  It is possible, using the DUP key, to reproduce information which is in one card into another. Experiment with this feature to see how it works.

If you keypunch your own programs or data, you may find that you want to make use of some of those piles of "blank" cards which are inevitably left lying around keypunch machines. To do so is folly unless you check each card very carefully for punches. Someday, after you have saved $.42 worth of cards, you may ruin a $30 computer run and waste half a day of your time because a card wasn't quite blank.

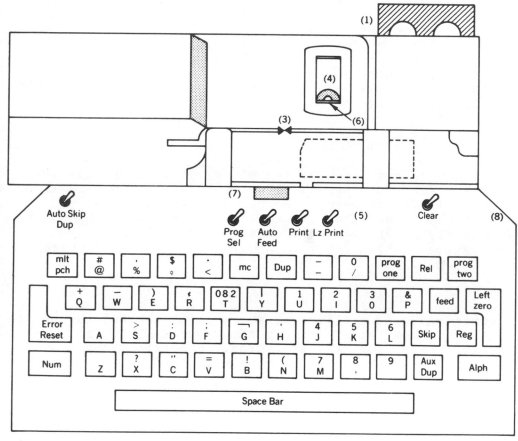

(2) not shown; switch
under table on right
hand side

An algorithm is a procedure to solve a problem in a stepwise manner. It implies a sequence of operations or steps which will take place one after another in time.

A flowchart is a two-dimensional description of an algorithm which uses basic elements to describe both the operations of the algorithm and the order in which they take place. A flowchart is not a computer program but rather provides a convenient base from which a computer program (which is essentially a one-dimensional description of an algorithm) can be explained. A flowchart, like a program, is an explicit set of instructions which describes a procedure for solving a problem. In this text we use flowcharts to illustrate graphically the sequences of steps used during the execution of an algorithm.

## Elements of Flowcharting

We now define a set of symbols which will provide a shorthand for describing an algorithm for solving problems which deal with numbers. The basic set of symbols constitute a flowchart language. A collection of these symbols may be arranged to constitute the flowchart description of the algorithm or, more simply, a flowchart.

## A Warning:

When you draw a flowchart you must be careful to use the three logic-control structures discussed in Part I: sequence, selection, and iteration. Otherwise your flowchart will not be implementable in TIPS.

## Terminal Block

A terminal block is used wherever the solution to a
problem starts or stops.   The block has either "begin" or
"end" written in it.   A particular flowchart has exactly one

Begin

block and at least one

End

block.

Flow Arrow

——————————>

The flow arrow indicates the sequence in which the steps
described by the flowchart are to be executed.   The shortest
possible flowchart is

If a flow arrow changes directions several times, then
several additional arrowheads should be used, e.g.,

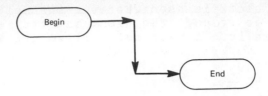

## Variable

   A variable is usually a letter of the English or Greek alphabet which stands for a number.

## Expression

   An expression in flowchart language is made up of previously defined variables (those that have had numbers--or other values-- assigned to them) and operators. Any time a variable appears in an expression it must have been previously defined to have a particular value. There are two basic ways of defining the value of a variable: the "becomes" symbol and the "read" verb.

## The "Becomes" Symbol

   The symbol "<—" means "becomes" or "is replaced by." The symbol must always have a variable on its left and an expression on its right. Any variables used in the expression must have been previously defined. For example, suppose that T is to be the total of x, y, and z. To put it another way, T becomes x+y+z or, in our new notation, T<—x+y+z. Anytime the "<—" symbol is encountered it means to compute the value of the "expression" on the right of the symbol (e.g., x+y+z) and to assign the value of that result to the variable (e.g., T) to the left of the arrow. This is the first of the two ways in which the value of a variable can be defined.

   For example, consider

$$w \longleftarrow t + a * 6$$

   In the expression above, t, a, and of course, 6 are quantities which have been previously defined to have

values.  The "becomes" symbol indicates that these
quantities are to be combined, as indicated by the
arithmetic--or other--operators, and the resulting value
assigned to the variable w, which may or may not have been
previously defined.  If w had been previously defined, the
original value would be replaced by the new one.


## Processing Block

This symbol contains the computations used to solve the
problem.  The "becomes" symbol is usually used in
conjunction with the processing block.  A processing block
should have exactly one "in" flow arrow and exactly one
"out" arrow.  For example,

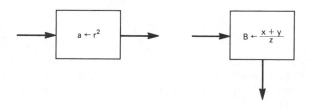

## Input-Output Block

This symbol is used whenever information is read into or written out of the computer.  For example,

implies an instruction which tells the machine to "read" a number and call it "x".  This is the second way in which a variable can be defined.  The word "write" can also appear in the input-output block and it instructs the machine to move information out of the system.  For example,

would cause the value of "s" to be duplicated on some medium outside the memory of the machine.  Of course, "s" must have been previously defined for the box to mean anything.  An input-output block should have one "in" arrow and exactly one "out" arrow.

## Decision Block

The decision block surrounds a question which can be answered "yes" or "no".  The question is asked in terms of variables already defined in the flowchart.  For example,

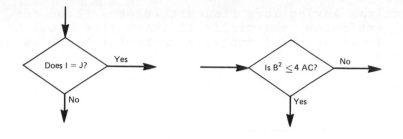

A decision block should have one "in" arrow and exactly two "out" arrows.

## Looping Block

In this text a composite flowchart block is used to indicate looping through a set of blocks.

A detailed discussion of it appears in Part I in the section which covers the FOR-DO statement. This flowchart symbol is explicitly designed to represent the FOR statement and, unlike the other symbols shown here, is not a standard flowchart symbol.

## Connector

Sometimes having long flow arrows on a flowchart produces confusion, especially if these lines have to cross others. To solve this problem a connector block is used, as illustrated below.

This

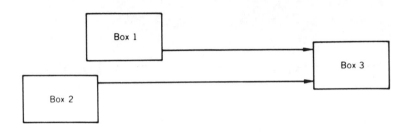

can be replaced by this

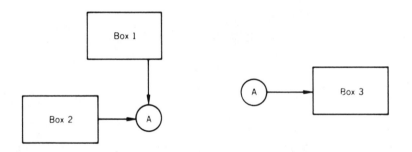

## Off-page Connector

When a flowchart consists of more than one page, an off-page connector may be used to connect flowchart boxes on different pages, as shown below.

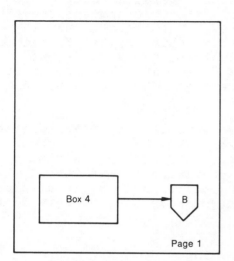

Page 1

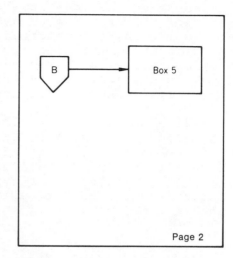

Page 2

Humans, at least in the western world, do arithmetic in the "base ten" (decimal) number system. Computers use the "base two" (binary) number system. But the student may have heard some computers referred to as "base eight" (octal) or "base sixteen" (hexadecimal). Why are there different number systems, what makes them different, what are their various advantages? Before these questions are answered let us put forth a fundamental idea:

There is basic meaning in •••• or aaaa or ****, whether it is called 4, four, 100, &&, or ugh. It has a basic meaning to an intelligent being regardless of its name or even lack of name. You will probably find that your principal difficulty in studying number systems is divorcing yourself from the number system you have used "forever": the decimal system.

## Dissecting the Decimal System

We begin by taking the decimal system apart. Examine the decimal number 348.72 for example. It means

$$
\begin{array}{rl}
3 \times 100 = & 300.00 \\
+\ 4 \times 10 = & 40.00 \\
+\ 8 \times 1 = & 8.00 \\
+\ 7 \times 1/10 = & .70 \\
+\ 2 \times 1/100 = & .02 \\
\hline
& 348.72
\end{array}
$$

or put another way:

$$
\begin{array}{rl}
3 \times 10^2 = & 300.00 \\
+\ 4 \times 10^1 = & 40.00 \\
+\ 8 \times 10^0 = & 8.00 \\
+\ 7 \times 10^{-1} = & .70 \\
+\ 2 \times 10^{-2} = & .02 \\
\hline
& 348.72
\end{array}
$$

or still another way:

| $10^2$ | $10^1$ | $10^0$ | $10^{-1}$ | $10^{-2}$ |
|:---:|:---:|:---:|:---:|:---:|
| 100 | 10 | 1 | 1/10 | 1/100 |
| 3 | 4 | 8 | 7 | 2 |

but this is really the starting point again.

The rule for determining the value of a base ten number is clear. For each digit in the number multiply that digit by ten raised a power dictated by the number of "positions" the digit is from the units position. Ten is the number raised to the power because there are ten characters in the system:

```
0
1
2
3
4
5
6
7
8
9
```

Each of these characters means something. For example 3 means ••• and 8 means ••••••••.

But when all of the characters have been used, say in a counting process, something must happen to mark the event. What happens is that the position immediately to the left of the column of characters already written is changed. For example,

```
           0
           1
           2
           3
           4
           5
           6
           7
           8
           9
         ─────
          10
          11
          12
          13
          14
           .
           .
           .
          19
         ─────
          20
          21
           .
           .
           .
          97
          98
          99
         ─────
          100
```

Why did humans select ten symbols instead of, say, 2 or 14?  The number of "digits" on one's hands might provide a clue.  The French have the vestiges of a system based on twenty (no shoes perhaps); some warlike tribes whose men frequently carried a weapon in one hand have a base five system.  At any rate the link between a herder counting sheep on his fingers, then throwing a rock on a pile each time he ran out of fingers and our present number system doesn't seem too implausible.

## Base Four

What do other number systems look like?  Here is counting in base four.

| Base Four | Base Ten |
|:---:|:---:|
| 0 | 0 |
| 1 | 1 |
| 2 | 2 |
| 3 | 3 |
| 10 | 4 |
| 11 | 5 |
| 12 | 6 |
| 13 | 7 |
| 20 | 8 |
| 21 | 9 |
| 22 | 10 |
| 23 | 11 |
| 30 | 12 |
| 31 | 13 |
| 32 | 14 |
| 33 | 15 |
| 100 | 16 |

Note the repeated use of four symbols:  0, 1, 2, 3.  Note that there is no single symbol "four" in a base four number system just as there is no single symbol "ten" in a base ten system.

A base four number such as 312 can be converted to base ten by simply using the same positional procedure shown earlier, and doing arithmetic in base ten:

| $4^2$ | $4^1$ | $4^0$ |
|:---:|:---:|:---:|
| 16 | 4 | 1 |
| 3 | 1 | 2 |

$$3 \times 16 = 48$$
$$1 \times 4 = 4$$
$$2 \times 1 = 2$$
$$\overline{\phantom{xxxx}}$$
$$54$$

The doubting student can continue the "correspondence counting," shown above, which compared base four and base ten if he or she is not convinced.

## Base One

What would a base one system be like?  It would have only one symbol which could not be zero.

| base ten | base one | | | | | | | |
|---|---|---|---|---|---|---|---|---|
| | $1^7$ | $1^6$ | $1^5$ | $1^4$ | $1^3$ | $1^2$ | $1^1$ | $1^0$ |
| 0 | | | | | | | | |
| 1 | | | | | | | | 1 |
| 2 | | | | | | | 1 | 1 |
| 3 | | | | | | 1 | 1 | 1 |
| 4 | | | | | 1 | 1 | 1 | 1 |
| 5 | | | | 1 | 1 | 1 | 1 | 1 |
| 6 | | | 1 | 1 | 1 | 1 | 1 | 1 |
| 7 | | 1 | 1 | 1 | 1 | 1 | 1 | 1 |

It could not represent zero except by "nothingness."

It would represent a number by the total number of times the symbol (in this case 1) was used, so its impracticality (and fundamentality) is obvious.  It is a "degenerate" system and will not be described further.

## Base Two

Is a base two system more useful?  Yes!

| base ten | base two | | | | |
|---|---|---|---|---|---|
| | $2^4$ | $2^3$ | $2^2$ | $2^1$ | $2^0$ |
| 0 | | | | | 0 |
| 1 | | | | | 1 |
| 2 | | | | 1 | 0 |
| 3 | | | | 1 | 1 |
| 4 | | | 1 | 0 | 0 |
| 5 | | | 1 | 0 | 1 |
| 6 | | | 1 | 1 | 0 |
| 7 | | | 1 | 1 | 1 |
| 8 | | 1 | 0 | 0 | 0 |
| 9 | | 1 | 0 | 0 | 1 |
| 10 | | 1 | 0 | 1 | 0 |
| 11 | | 1 | 0 | 1 | 1 |
| 12 | | 1 | 1 | 0 | 0 |
| 13 | | 1 | 1 | 0 | 1 |
| 14 | | 1 | 1 | 1 | 0 |
| 15 | | 1 | 1 | 1 | 1 |
| 16 | 1 | 0 | 0 | 0 | 0 |
| 17 | 1 | 0 | 0 | 0 | 1 |

The system seems inefficient in that it takes five
positions (or columns) to represent the number seventeen
when the decimal system requires only two positions.  But
efficiency is not always accomplished by more different
symbols and fewer positions.  If it were, perhaps man should
consider a base eighty-five system, or a base four billion
system.  Or, better yet, a character for every possible
number.  The point here is that there are trade-offs between
using fewer positions and more characters, and vice-versa.
Humans, it seems, have little difficulty working with ten
symbols.  Computers can most easily work with two characters
or "states" such as on and off, yes and no, clockwise and
counter-clockwise, or current flowing and current not
flowing.

Thus at present, it is more economical to have the
computer manipulate a large number of bi-stable (two-state)
devices than to use fewer devices which can have more than
two states.

To illustrate the economics involved, you might consider
a panel with lightbulbs on it.

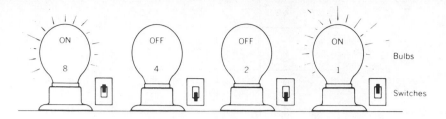

Here you can clearly represent any integer, between 0 and
15, just by turning switches. (The number 9 is shown.) If
you are given two bulbs and told to do the same job by
varying the intensity with which each bulb burns you have
two immediate problems: more sophisticated equipment than
switches is required to vary the light intensity and you
must be able to recognize the varying intensities. You save
on light bulbs but is it worth it?


## Binary Arithmetic Operations

The rules for arithmetic operations between binary
numbers are simple--much more so than the rules for
operations between decimal numbers. You may recall that you
memorized addition and multiplication tables for base ten
numbers. Memorizing the binary addition and multiplication
tables is vastly easier. Probably a good thing, too, since
our abilities for rote memorization seem to decline with
age. Here's the add table:

```
        0   1
    ┌────────
  0 │ 0   1
    │
  1 │ 1  *0
```

The * beside the 0 in the "1 plus 1" position indicates a
carry. 1 plus 1 is 10, which is the binary representation
for the base ten quantity 2. As an example, consider

```
      10110    (which is 22 base ten)
    + 01101    (which is 13 base ten)
     100011    (which is 35 base ten)
```

It's ridiculously easy to do. If you want more practice,
invent some arbitrary binary numbers and add them; check
your results by converting everything to base ten.

The multiplication table is even easier.

```
      0   1
   ┌─────────
 0 │  0   0
   │
 1 │  0   1
```

Take, for example, 101 times 011.

```
       101
       011
      ─────
       101
       101
      000
     ───────
     01111
```

It should be pretty clear why computers have such an easy
time with base two. Multiplying is simply a matter of
writing down the multiplicand in the appropriate position
each time there is a 1 bit in the multiplier. We leave it
to the you to develop the techniques for subtraction and
division if you're interested.


## Octal and Hexadecimal

If the binary system is so basic, what about octal and
hexadecimal computers? Actually there is no machine which
truly uses an octal or hexadecimal base. Scratch the
surface of any present-day computer and you find a binary
machine underneath. But binary converts easily to base
four, eight, sixteen, and hence the use of these bases has
advantages.

In general, a number of a system of base-n can be
converted to its equivalent in a system of n-raised-to-the-
power-m quite easily. (For example, base 2 can be easily
converted to base $2^3$ or 8.) One simply arranges the base-n
number into sets of m digits beginning at the decimal point.
These sets of m digits are then each individually converted
from base-n to base-n-to-the-m. The resultant set of digits
is the number in base-n-to-the-m. To convert a base-n-to-
the-m number tc a base-n number one simply applies the
process in reverse.

For example, the binary number 100111110101 is the octal (base eight) number 4765. The doubting student can convert both to base ten to assure himself. Here is the simple conversion from binary to octal, obtained by simply grouping the binary digits in threes since 8=2³.

| $8^3$ | $8^2$ | $8^1$ | $8^0$ | |
|---|---|---|---|---|
| 1   0   0 | 1   1   1 | 1   1   0 | 1   0   1 | binary |
| 4 | 7 | 6 | 5 | octal |

What is the base ten value of 4765 (base eight)?

This sort of intermediate number system turns out to be useful to humans who go at least goggle-eyed if not smack out of their minds by looking at a number like

100111110101

Octal numbers look reasonable if one ignores the lack of 8's and 9's. In fact, they look so reasonable that they are sometimes taken for base ten numbers, with unhappy results.

Hexadecimal (base sixteen) goes like this, assuming we use the beginning letters of the alphabet for the six needed symbols:

| Base Ten | Base Sixteen |
|---|---|
| 0 | 0 |
| 1 | 1 |
| 2 | 2 |
| 3 | 3 |
| 4 | 4 |
| 5 | 5 |
| 6 | 6 |
| 7 | 7 |
| 8 | 8 |
| 9 | 9 |
| 10 | A |
| 11 | B |
| 12 | C |
| 13 | D |

Module 6: Number Systems

```
14          E
15          F
16          10
17          11
18          12
19          13
20          14
```

It is useful also as an intermediate base for computer-human conversation, since $16=2^4$.

For example, the binary number which was octal 4765 becomes hexadecimal 9F5 with the conversion as shown below.

| $16^2$ | $16^1$ | $16^0$ | |
|---|---|---|---|
| 1  0  0  1 | 1  1  1  1 | 0  1  0  1 | binary |
| 9 | F | 5 | hexadecimal |

What is the base ten value of 9F5 (base sixteen)?

In all the number systems we have considered, if the first two symbols in a number system are 0 and 1, the base of the system itself is always written as

10

That is, ten in a base-ten system is 10, two in a base-two system is 10, sixteen in a base-sixteen system is 10.

```
┌─────────────────────────────────────┐
│   SUGGESTED LABORATORY PROBLEMS      │
│             19, 56                   │
└─────────────────────────────────────┘
```

REAL Storage Technique

    INTEGER numbers are represented simply as a set of
binary digits in a computer word.  For example, the number

43

or, as it might be written to show it as a base ten number,

43 (ten)

would be represented in a 32 bit machine as:

00000000000000000000000000101011 (two)

    A number represented in this form can be quickly
manipulated arithmetically by the computer.  Unfortunately
its maximum magnitude is quite limited.  The largest value
which can be represented in this form (donating a bit for
the sign) is $2^{31}-1$ or 2,147,483,647, or somewhat more than 2
billion.  But many things are larger than that: the number
of atoms in a pin, diameter of the solar system in miles,
the national debt, etc.  Clearly, a general purpose computer
needs to be able to handle numbers of greater range.

    This is accomplished by dividing the computer word into
two parts.  One of these parts is used to store the
significant digits (mantissa) of the number while the other
stores a scale factor (base two exponent).  For example,
envision a ten bit computer word.  In INTEGER form the
largest number which could be stored is

+111111111(two) = +511(ten)

if one bit is donated for the algebraic sign.

But if the word is divided into two parts a much larger
number can be represented.  For example,

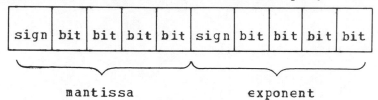

Now, if the decimal point is assumed to be at the
extreme left-hand end of the mantissa, the largest number
which can be stored is the number


$$+0.1111 \ \bullet \ 2^{1111} \quad \text{(represented in binary)}$$
$$= (1/2+1/4+1/8+1/16) \ \bullet \ 2^{15} \quad \text{(represented in base ten)}$$
$$= 15/16 \bullet 32,768$$
$$\text{or } 30,720$$

Thus the range has been vastly increased by sacrificing
some significance in the numbers which can be represented.
(For example, a 32 bit computer word is required to
represent the quantity two billion in integer.  In the
IBM/370, INTEGER numbers have a magnitude of about 2 x 10 ,
while REAL numbers range to more than $10^{75}$.

Usually more bits of the computer word are donated to
the mantissa portion of the word than to the exponent.

The admittedly sketchy discussion of REAL storage was
presented to allow you an understanding of the section which
follows, which might be entitled: "Why computers don't
always tell the truth."


Inaccuracy of REAL Representation

It may alarm you to discover that a computer
occasionally does not provide the correct answer even when
no mistake has been made in the programming.

There are several sources of such errors.  Some of these
sources will be discussed below.

## Representational Error

The computer would flunk the following test:

```
(* DEMO OF REPRESENTATIONAL ERROR *)
PROGRAM FLUNK(INPUT,OUTPUT);
    VAR
        S: (* COMMENT *) REAL;
        P: (* COMMENT *) REAL;
        I: (* COMMENT *) INTEGER;
    BEGIN
        S:=0;
        P:=0.1;
        FOR I:=1 TO 100 DO
            S:=S+P;
        WRITELN(S)
    END.
```

The result will be something like

$$9.9999974$$

rather than 10. Why? Because 0.1 cannot be represented exactly in the binary number system as a finite number of digits although it can be so represented in the decimal number system.

For the REAL number P the computer uses the form

(a binary mantissa (which is < 1 in absolute value))
times
(2 raised to a binary exponent)

where the binary mantissa is of the form

| $2^{-1}$ or 1/2 | $2^{-2}$ or 1/4 | $2^{-3}$ or 1/8 | $2^{-4}$ or 1/16 | $2^{-5}$ or 1/32 |
|---|---|---|---|---|
| bit | bit | bit | bit | bit |

Unfortunately, it is impossible to represent the number 1/10 by adding together a finite number of powers of two.

Asking a binary computer to solve this problem exactly
is similar to asking a human to solve the problem

$$1/3 + 1/3 + 1/3$$

in the decimal number system.

The human must proceed:

```
.33333
.33333
.33333
_____
.99999
```

and it is clear that since a finite number of digits is
involved, the answer of "one" will not be found.


## Normalized Form

General laws of mathematics sometimes fail to hold when
the arithmetic is performed by computers.  To illustrate,
instead of using a REAL representation of

    (a binary mantissa (which is < 1 in absolute value))
                          times
           (2 raised to a binary exponent)


a similar system of

    (a base ten mantissa (which is < 1 in absolute value))
                          times
           (10 raised to a base ten exponent)


will be used.  The general effect is the same.

Assume that a computer can store three decimal digits
for the mantissa and one decimal digit for the exponent.
For example,

$$2.39 = .239 \times 10^1 = \quad .2 \; 3 \; 9 \; \{1\}$$

and

$$-.00531 = -.531 \times 10^{-2} = -.5\ 3\ 1\ \{-2\}$$

where the quantity in brackets is the base ten exponent.

It can therefore represent numbers along the real number line in the range

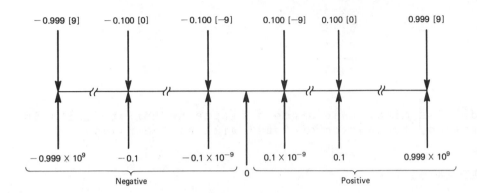

One additional rule for the storage of REAL numbers is that the left-most digit of the mantissa may not be zero unless the entire number consists of zero digits.  That is,

$$.0\ 3\ 8\ \{5\}$$

is not a legal representation of $.038 \times 10^5$ but

$$.3\ 8\ 0\ \{4\}$$

is.  This latter form is called the normalized form of the number.

Since only three significant digits can be stored, some calculations will be subject to <u>truncation</u> <u>or</u> <u>roundoff</u> error.  Two examples are illustrated below.

## The <u>Cancellation</u> <u>Law</u>

The cancellation law of mathematics says

$$a+e=a \text{ implies that } e=0$$

(i.e., if "a" and "e" are added together and the sum is equal to "a" this implies that "e" is zero).

This law does not hold for computers and consequently surprising results sometimes occur.   The effect will be illustrated using the three-digit-mantissa computer.

Suppose a=222. and e=.333 and these numbers are stored as

$$a=.2\ 2\ 2\ \{3\}$$

$$e=.3\ 3\ 3\ \{0\}$$

Assume an <u>accumulator</u> (a separate location in memory where arithmetic operations are conducted) can hold numbers of any length.

To add "a" and "e" the number "a" is moved to the accumulator

.2 2 2 {3} ⎯⎯⎯⎯⎯⎯⎯⎯⎯⎤

and "e" is added

.3 3 3 {0}
⎣⎯⎯⎯⎯⎯⎯⎯⎯⎯→

```
                              222.000
                                .333
                              ────────
                              222.333
```

giving the proper answer.

Now the answer is stored back into some other location in the machine, say location "b".

.2 2 2 {3} <⎯⎯⎯ 222.333

But in this "storing back" process only the most significant three digits are kept.   Thus the effect is that the addition of a+e really failed to take place because "e" was small relative to a.   Thus, while e was not zero, a+e=a.

To illustrate this, write a program according to the following flow chart:

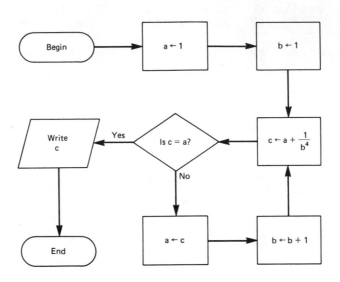

The fact that the computer is not "hung up" in an infinite loop and does indeed print c is proof of the proposition that

a+e equals a does not imply that e is zero

if a computer is doing the addition.

## The Associative Law

Another law of mathematics which fails to hold for computers is the associative law for additon.  The law is

$$(a+b) +c=a+ (b+c)$$

or, in words, the order in which three quantities are added does not affect their sum.  Computers, not having been

properly educated, sometimes fail to comply.  For example,
assume a=421., b=11.7 and c=11.7.

Evaluating (a+b)+c first:

```
"a"      .4 2 1 {3} ────> 421.00
"b"      .1 1 7 {2} ────>  11.70
                         ───────
                          432.7C
```

which is stored back in some location as

.4 3 3 {3} <────

if rounding is assumed.

The second addition then takes place and produces

```
         .4 3 3 {3} ────> 433.00

"c"      .1 1 7 {2} ────>  11.70
                         ───────
                          444.70
```

which is stored back as

.4 4 5 {3} <────

giving the result (a+b)+c.

Now evaluating a+(b+c) in a similar manner:

```
"b"      .1 1 7 {2} ────> 11.70
"c"      .1 1 7 {2} ────> 11.70
                         ──────
                          23.40
```

.2 3 4 {2} <────

```
                    ────> 23.40
"a"      .4 2 1 {3} ────>421.00
                         ──────
                          444.40
```

.4 4 4 {3}<────

which disagrees with the first result of .4 4 5 {3}.

The results would also disagree with each other if truncation, instead of rounding, were assumed.

The preceding examples were presented chiefly to demonstrate that you should not expect exact results from a computer when you are using any form of REAL representation in any compiler language, PASCAL included.

For example, it would be inadvisable to write a program containing

```
VAR A: REAL;
     .
     .
A:=4;
     .
     .
IF SQRT(A)=2 THEN
     .
```

because the chances are quite good that SQRT(A) will come out as 2.0000001 or 1.999993 rather than 2.000000.

You should say something like

```
IF ABS(SQRT(A)-2.0)<0.00001 THEN
     .
```

instead.

A better way to test for "equality" is to decide what relative difference you are willing to accept rather than the absolute difference.  If G1 and G2 are supposed to be equal you could ask

```
IF ABS(G1-G2) < G1*0.01 THEN
```

and get a TRUE result if G1 and G2 were within 1% of each other, regardless of the absolute values involved.

## Moral

"Do not do arithmetic on REAL numbers and expect exact answers."   Many involved and carefully written programs have been "bugged" because their authors did not heed this warning.

```
┌─────────────────────────────┐
│   SUGGESTED LAB PROBLEM      │
│            28                │
└─────────────────────────────┘
```

There are two branches of the computer family: digital
and analog.  A digital computer obtains answers by
manipulation of discrete quantities.  These quantities might
be beads on a stick (as in an abacus), magnetized spots on
magnetic tape, electrical pulses, etc.  Analog computers
obtain answers by making some continuous physical analog of
mathematical quantities.  The physical quantity might be
length (as with a slide rule), pressure, voltage, etc.

This module, indeed this book, deals solely with digital
or discrete computers as opposed to analog or continuous
computers.  But the dichotomy between discrete and
continuous phenomena is so interesting on so many levels
that we might take a moment to reflect on it.  The Western
world seems to be making a move toward the use of discrete
systems and away from continuous ones.  Some examples: (1)
Programs have been written for digital computers to instruct
them to simulate analog computers.  (2) The pocket-sized
digital electronic calculator has replaced that genesis of
analog computing devices, the trustworthy sliderule.  (3)
Musical recordings are being made with digital technology.
(4) Digital clocks and watches seem to be shoving their
analog counterparts toward antiquity.

(An interesting liability to society created by the move
to digital time pieces was illustrated to the authors
several years ago by observing a seven year old.  She could
"tell time" just fine, but terms such as clockwise and two-
o'clock position meant nothing to her.  We may have to come
up with some new concepts.)

Below in the briefest possible form we describe what
seem to us to be the major events in the development of
digital computing as it exists today.

Year                Event or Machine

circa          Abacus comes into use - inventor unknown.
600 B.C.

1642 A.D.      Blaise Pascal of France builds the first adding
               machine.

1694        Gottfried Wilhelm Leibnitz completes "stepped
            reckoner" - an adding machine which "carries"
            automatically.

1786        J. H. Muller conceives idea of an automatic
            computer - never built.

1801        The first successful machine to operate from
            punched cards was built in France by Joseph Jacquard.
            The machine, a loom, could weave decorative designs
            into cloth according to instructions given by the
            punched cards.

1822        Charles Babbage of England builds a small model
            of a "mechanical difference engine" for
            computation of logarithm and similar tables; he
            persuades the British government to spend a
            million dollars in its development; engine not
            completed during his lifetime.

1830        Babbage conceives an "analytical engine" which
            has many characteristics of modern day computers
            even though it is mechanical and not electronic
            in design.  This machine is never completed but
            involves brilliant parallels to modern computers.

1842        The first computer program was written by Ada
            Augusta, Countess of Lovelace, for computing
            Bernoulli numbers.

1890        Herman Hollerith uses a forgotten Babbage idea
            and develops the punched card and a battery of
            equipment to process data stored on it: sorter,
            tabulator, etc.  The U.S. Census Bureau, which
            discovers it isn't going to get the 1880 census
            published before 1890, sponsors the work.  The
            Hollerith card, now also referred to as the
            punched card or IBM card, is the same size as the
            U.S. currency of that day.

1930        International Business Machines Corporation (IBM)
            markets its 600 series of calculating card
            punches which use relays as memory units - not
            computers except in the most rudimentary sense.

1938-1944   Various people and organizations invent, build,
            and experiment with electro-mechanical components
            and computers which take instructions from cards
            or magnetic tape and perform arithmetic

operations.

Important, among others, are George R. Stibitz, Samuel B. Williams, and E. G. Andrews of Bell Telephone Laboratories who develop the "ballistic computer" and the Mark 22 Error Computer. The largest electro-mechanical computer ever to be built is the Harvard Mark I computer developed under the direction of Howard Aiken with the help of IBM.

1945     John von Neumann, working with J. P. Eckert and John Mauchly, proposes EDVAC (Electronic Discrete Variable Computer) which uses its memory to store both numbers and instructions for the operations it is to carry out. Thus the idea of the "stored program" is born.

1946     ENIAC (Electronic Numerical Integrator and Calculator) is completed by Mauchly and Eckert at the University of Pennsylvania; ENIAC is the first large scale electronic digital computer. The ENIAC contains 18,000 vacuum tubes, weighs 30 tons, and occupies a space 30 by 50 feet. The computer has 200 digits of memory.

1947     The Association for Computing Machinery is founded.

          A computer is built at Manchester University in England, using an electrostatic storage memory system called the Williams tube and a rotating magnetic drum for auxilary storage.

1948     The IBM CPC (Card Programmed Calculator) is developed by Northrup Corporation and IBM.

From 1949 on the history is largely related to the introduction of information processing systems by various groups and manufacturers. Some of the more important are listed below because of technical innovation, popularity, or because they represent a manufacturer's entry into the field. Adjectives describing a machine as large, fast, or popular apply to the state of the art at the time the machine was introduced.

1949     EDSAC (Electronic Delay Storage Automatic Calculator) - first computer to utilize the stored program concept - completed in Cambridge,

England, under the direction of Maurice Wilkes.

BINAC (Eckert and Mauchly Computer Company) - sponsored by the Bureau of the Census.

1950    SEAC (Standard Eastern Automatic Computer) - first stored program computer operating in the U.S. - at the Bureau of Standards.

Whirlwind I, developed at MIT - uses a magnetic core memory also developed at MIT.  Jay W. Forrester directs the project.

UNIVAC 1101 - ERA 1101; Eckert-Mauchly merge with Engineering Research Associates and a rotating magnetic drum machine is produced.

Digital plotting equipment makes its debut; later to be connected to computers, this equipment will make it possible to draw graphs and pictures - and a picture is worth more than 1024 words.

1951    SWAC (Standards Western Automatic Computer) - UCLA.

UNIVAC I (Universal Automatic Computer) - Eckert-Mauchly Computer Corporation - first installed at the Bureau of the Census.  Features include a magnetic tape system whose operation is overlapped with arithmetic computation.

Whirlwind at MIT has attached to it a Cathode Ray Tube (CRT) as an output device.  This innovation is to be supplemented a year later when a "light gun" or "light pen" is attached allowing the user to manipulate information on the TV-like screen and in the memory.

1952    MANIAC I - Los Alamos.

ORDVAC - University of Illinois.

EDVAC is finally finished at the University of Pennsylvania.

IAS COMPUTER - stored program computer using a cathode ray tube memory - (Institute for Advanced Studies, Princeton) - is completed by von Neumann.

ILLIAC (Illinois Automatic Computer) – University
of Illinois.

1953      ORACLE (Oak Ridge Automatic Computer and Logical
          Engine) at the Atomic Energy Commission
          installation in Oak Ridge, Tennessee.

          IBM 701 – Defense Calculator.

          UNIVAC 1103 – powerful scientific computer with
          cathode ray storage and parallel arithmetic.

1954      JOHNIAC – named for John von Neumann – built at
          Rand Corporation.

          DATATRON – Electro Data Corporation – machine
          features hardware index registers, hardware
          floating point, and a random access magnetic strip
          storage scheme.

          IBM 650 – highly popular scientific machine with
          a high speed magnetic drum memory and auxiliary
          magnetic disk memory, RAMAC.

Late in 1954 Philco Corporation develops the surface barrier
transistor; vacuum tubes will soon be on their way out as
computer components.  The change from tubes to transistors
will mark the beginning of second generation computing
equipment in about three years.

1955      NORC – giant IBM computer built for the
          U.S. Naval Weapons Laboratory.

          BENDIX G-15 – popular small scale drum computer.

          IBM 705 – first large scale computer to use a
          magnetic core memory.

1956      IBM 704 – popular, large, scientific machine.
          IBM and some of its customers write an algebraic
          compiler or formula translator called FORTRAN for
          the IBM 704.  High level computing languages thus
          become part of the computing scene, opening up
          computer use to people in many fields.

          BIZMAC – RCA's entry into the computing field.

          LGP 30 – popular, small drum computer by
          Librascope Corporation.

E101 - Burroughs' first marketed computer.

1957    UNIVAC II produced by Remington-Rand; it has core
memory.

TX-0 is produced by Lincoln Laboratories - it
uses Philco's surface barrier transistor.  The
second generation cf computing equipment has
dawned.

DATAMATIC 1000 is produced by Honeywell and,
indirectly, by Raytheon.

1958    IBM 709 is marketed - large scientific computer
with tubes, core memory.

PHILCO 2000 - features include transistors, tape
drives and data channels.

BURROUGHS 220 - last major vacuum tube computer.

UNIVAC solid state 80/90 - medium-sized second
generation drum machine.

A general high level language, ALGOL-58, is
introduced.  Though never in as wide use in this
country as FORTRAN it is more elegant and has a
profound effect on the development of future high
level languages, including PASCAL.

1959    IBM 1620 - highly popular, small scientific
machine of the second generation.

ATLAS design is completed at Manchester
University in England; time-shared machine using
a paging concept.

NCR 304 - earliest second generation business
machine.

IBM 7090 - large, fast, highly popular scientific
machine - a solid state IBM 709.

RCA 501 - business machine featuring a Common
Business Oriented Language compiler (COBOL).

GE 210 - marks General Electric's entry into the
computing field.

1960                CDC 1604 – first machine by Control Data Corporation - fast, solid state.

UNIVAC LARC – giant computer built by Remington-Rand for the Atomic Energy Commission.

IBM 7070 – popular, large business computer.

CDC 160 – popular business-oriented machine.

PDP 1 – first major machine by Digital Equipment Corporation.

IBM 1401 – highly popular, medium-sized business machine.

HONEYWELL 800 – features a multiprogramming system – business machine.

IBM develops a major remote terminal system for handling passenger reservation for American Airlines: SABRE.

1961                RCA 301 – popular small business machine.

IBM STRETCH (7030) – giant second generation machine built for the Atomic Energy Commission.

University of Waterloo produces an 11,000 statement-per-minute FORTRAN compiler called WATFOR. This development brings the cost of educating large groups of students in programming within reason.

1962                B-5000 – Burroughs' large scientific machine featuring hardware to accommodate the algorithmic language ALGOL.

Dartmouth College begins use of a teaching language they devised: BASIC.

1963                IBM 7040 – popular medium-sized scientific computer similar to the IBM 7090 in its instruction set.

CDC 3600 – large scientific machine – very fast.

The third generation of computing equipment begins to dawn at about this time. It is characterized by microcomponents, monolithic integrated circuits, or sheer, blinding speed. Time-sharing also begins to come of age. Manufacturers begin to introduce compatible series of machines.

1964        HONEYWELL 200 - popular business machine using some of the instructions of the second generation IBM 1401.

            CDC 6600 - the fastest computer available for several years to come - it contains one half million transistors - several satellite processors share and direct the central processor.

            BURROUGHS B-5500 - a third-generation version of the B-5000.

            GE 600 series is introduced - its circuitry is composed of micro-components.

            General Electric announces a major time-sharing computer, the GE 645; it is ordered by MIT's time sharing PROJECT MAC (Machine Aided Cognition) and by Bell Labs.

            IBM commits itself to the development of a New Programming Language called NPL; some farsighted soul will soon prevail and the name will be changed to Programming Language One or PL/1.

1965        UNIVAC 1108 II - a popular, large, fast, scientific machine of the third generation.

            IBM 360 models 40 and 30 constitute the first two models of the 360 series - the several models, though different in design and speed, operate with essentially the same instruction set. Time-sharing is not included among the features of the original series. Features do include "read-only" storage and "emulation." The series is intended to serve both scientific and business needs.

            IBM markets the 1130 - a relatively small machine which is not compatible with the 360 series. It, along with its process-control sister, the 1800, becomes very popular.

| 1966 | IBM 360/67 - IBM's first major time-sharing product. |
|------|------|
| | SDS Sigma 7 - third generation machine by Scientific Data Systems. A separately priced COBOL compiler for the Sigma 7 is also announced by SDS. Now there is precedent for breaking the established hardware-software package up and the software industry begins to blossom. |
| | PDP 9 - medium sized scientific computer featuring cathode ray graphic capability. |
| | RCA Spectra 70 series is introduced. It uses monolithic integrated circuits and has an instruction set similar to the IBM 360 series. |
| 1967 | "Desk top" or "mini" computers begin to make their debut as large batch systems get further from the user and time sharing proves expensive. |
| | Burroughs gets the contract to build the processors the ILLIAC IV. |
| | Optical scanners begin to come on the market in force; some read marks, others read machine or even hand written characters. |
| | Computers which direct other machines (process control computers) become a large industry in their own right; more than 1000 are in operation. |
| | Commercial Time Sharing firms begin to appear en masse. With a Teletype, password, and lots of money you can call up several computers. |
| 1968 | Wide interest develops in the area of Computer Aided Instruction (CAI). Special languages are developed. |
| | Burroughs markets the B6500 series - most models have a new kind of memory: thin film instead of magnetic core. |
| | NCR announces a self compatible line of computers: the Century series. |
| | Goddard Space Flight Center puts the "supercomputer" IBM 360/91 into service. The IBM |

360/85 is the fastest generally available IBM computer.

The possibilities of large data banks of information about individuals becomes a national concern; questions regarding invasion of privacy are asked increasingly by Congress and the public.

1969            Control Data Corporation markets the CDC 7600.

IBM "unbundles" - the future holds corporate divisions of hardware, software, service, etc. A more or less single industry has split up.

1970            Scientific Data Systems (SDS) and Xerox get together to form Xerox Data Systems (XDS).

IBM markets System 3 - a small, completely different line of computers - incompatible even down to a different punched computer card.

Honeywell buys General Electric's computer effort.

IBM announces System 370. Features include error correction circuitry, micro coding, and CPU identification hardware.

1971            The PASCAL language makes its formal debut--its designer is Niklaus Wirth.


For those interested in details of the historical development of computers we recommend the following from which we drew heavily in preparing this chronology:

Saul Rosen's superb article, "Electronic Computers: A Historical Survey," in the ACM journal Computing Surveys, March 1969.

Mathematics and Computers by George R. Stibitz and Jules A. Larrivee, McGraw-Hill, 1957.

Both of these works and the references they contain will allow the interested student to look long and deeply into the past. We don't include information on the last decade; it will be some time before the truly significant events of

that period can be put into perspective.  But you might
peruse the monthly magazine, "Datamation."  As for the
future, we invite you to join with us and watch.  Or,
perhaps, participate.

# part VI

# LABORATORY PROBLEMS

Twenty-three laboratory problems to be run on a computer are included in this part. There are four general sections. The Lab Problems are of interest to students in mathematics and science areas and business areas as well. There are also some miscellaneous--and fun--problems.

After a student has learned programming fundamentals, a "real life" problem can be one of the most interesting. The student is encouraged to select problems from other sources for his particular area of study and write programs to solve them.

A very good additional source of provocative problems is the RAND Corporation publication Problems for Computer Solution by Fred Gruenberger and George Jaffray. Although PASCAL is not the featured language, the student might also examine the IBM Manual PL/ONE for Scientific Problem Solving, and Scientific and Engineering Problem Solving with the Computer by William Ralph Bennett, Jr.

Problem: Given a, b, and c as the lengths of the three sides
of a triangle, the area (A) of the triangle is given by

$$A = \sqrt{s\,(s-a)\,(s-b)\,(s-c)}$$

where s is the semi-perimeter

$$\frac{(a+b+c)}{2}$$

Procedure: Write a function to compute the area of the
triangle and return this value. Write a main program to
read in the lengths of the sides, call the function, and
print the results.

LABORATORY PROBLEM 39 - Character String Manipulation

Problem: A secret message written in code has been received.
    You are to write a program to decode this message.  The
    message may include all 26 letters of the alphabet and
    special characters.  The special characters are to be
    left unchanged.  The letters are to be decoded as
    follows:

| Letter in Message | A | B | C | D | E | F | G | H | I | J | K | L | M |
|-------------------|---|---|---|---|---|---|---|---|---|---|---|---|---|
| Decoded Letter    | R | C | G | U | I | A | D | W | X | T | H | N | M |

| Letter in Message | N | O | P | Q | R | S | T | U | V | W | X | Y | Z |
|-------------------|---|---|---|---|---|---|---|---|---|---|---|---|---|
| Decoded Letter    | P | B | Z | L | E | Q | S | Y | K | O | J | V | F |

Input: Your instructor will inform you of the location of
    the data for this problem. The first record is a three-
    digit integer which specifies how many records make up
    the message.  The rest of the records make up the
    message itself, with 30 characters per record.

Output: Write the original message as read.  Then write the
    decoded message.  Put 30 characters on each line.
    Provide appropriate titles for each message.


* * * * * * * * * * * * * * * * * * * * * * * * * * * * * *


LABORATORY PROBLEM 40 - Quadratic with Square Root Function

Problem: Solve the quadratic equation using a function for
    square roots.

Rewrite Lab Problem 5 for solving the quadratic equation,
using a PROCEDURE to calculate the square root of $b^2-4ac$.
The method used for calculating the square root is to be the
iteration method used in Lab Problem 16.  Do not use the
SQRT built-in function in this program.

Use the same input you used for Lab Problem 5.

LABORATORY PROBLEM 41 - Matching Schedules

Problem: You wish to get the faculty of your school (no more
    than 100 people) together at an all school meeting to
    discuss student complaints.  You want to pick a time
    when all the faculty can be present.

Procedure: The registrar has given you permission to scan
    the file on which is located a record for each faculty
    member.  The records contain the social security number
    and information concerning whether the faculty member
    has a class at a certain hour.  Classes may begin at ten
    times during each of the five week days: 8AM, 9AM, 10AM,
    11AM, etc.

Input: The information for each faculty member consists of 6
    records.  Your instructor will inform you of the
    location of the data for this problem.  The first record
    for each faculty contains his or her social security
    number.  Following that is a set of five records, one
    for each day of the normal work week.  The format of
    each faculty member's information is as follows:

first 9 cols of record 1 - social security number

first column of record 2 - a one or a zero indicating
    whether or not this person has an 8AM Monday class
    scheduled.

next column - blank

next column - a one or a zero indicating whether this
    person has a 9AM Monday class scheduled.

next column - blank

next column - etc.

first column of record 3 - a one or a zero indicating
    whether this person has an 8AM Tuesday class
    scheduled.

next column - blank

next column - a one or a zero indicating whether this
    person has a 9AM Tuesday class scheduled.

next column - blank

next column - etc.

Output: Write a program which will select the hours during
the week when none of the faculty have classes.  If no such
times exist, find the hours at which the fewest faculty have
classes and print those times and days along with the number
of faculty free at that time.


* * * * * * * * * * * * * * * * * * * * * * * * * * * * *


LABORATORY PROBLEM 42 - List Processing

Problem: Write a program to expand the "Small Fry" example
    at the end of Part III.  The program should have the
    capability of building the list, adding information to
    it, deleting information from it, and finding a
    requested item of information.  The clumps of
    information should be in alphabetical order by name and
    also in numerical order by phone.  This implies that
    each clump of information will have to have two pointers
    in it.

Input: Write the program so that it will accept card input
    containing the information to be stored or deleted; the
    indication of whether a particular datum is to be added
    or deleted should be on the data card itself.  Invent
    your own test data for the problem.

Output: After a mix of addition/deletion cards has been
    input, write out two lists: the information in
    alphabetical order by name and in numerical order by
    phone.

LABORATORY PROBLEM 43 - Dot Product

Problem: Write a function to calculate the scalar product of two vectors (one-dimensional arrays).

The scalar product is

$$S = \sum_{i=1}^{N} A[i] \bullet B[i]$$

Use REAL for A and B and INTEGER for N.

The function should have 3 arguments: the names of the two arrays and the number of numbers in each. For example, assuming the name SCALAR for the function,

SCALAR (A,B,N)

the function should be able to accept a value of N as large as 40.

Label your output with the following:

SCALAR PRODUCT =

The data to be read by the calling program are:

| N=12 | A | B |
|---|---|---|
| | -14.012 | 360.000 |
| | 200.013 | 88.555 |
| | -200.132 | -777.777 |
| | 11.111 | 3.333 |
| | 21.212 | 6.667 |
| | .001 | 9.999 |
| | 10.345 | -0.010 |
| | -60.789 | -1.712 |
| | 3.141 | 1024.255 |
| | 57.322 | 550.055 |
| | -2.782 | -1.872 |
| | 999.314 | 11.412 |

LABORATORY PROBLEM 44 - Polynomial Evaluation

Problem: Write a FUNCTION to evaluate the polynomial
function


$$y = a0 + a1*x + a2*x^2 + a3*x^3 + \ldots + an*xn$$


Where x, the coefficients (ai), and n are to be given.


Procedure: Write a program to compute the value of the
polynomial by considering it in factored form. That is,
taking a third degree polynomial for example,

   a0+x(a1+x(a2+x*a3))

which is equivalent to

   $a0+a1x+a2x^2+a3x^3$

Using the factored polynomial for computation is better
for two reasons: speed and accuracy.


Input: Your instructor will inform you of the location of
the data for this problem. The first record contains x
and n. Following this record are n+1 records in order,
each containing a coefficient (a).


Output: Return the answer y. Print out the data and the
answer from the calling program.

# LABORATORY PROBLEM 45 - Integration

Problem: Find the area under a curve between two values X=A
and X=B, using the trapezoid method.  Given are the
beginning point A, the ending point B, and N, the number
of small trapezoids into which that area is to be
divided.  Write a FUNCTION to calculate the area.  The
mathematical function used in this problem will be

$$X^2+25X+3$$

Input: A, B, and N.

Procedure: The trapezoid algorithm is given below:

```
H := (B-A)/N;
X := A;
S := 0;
FOR I := 1 TO N+1 DO
    BEGIN
    IF I=1 OR I=N+1 THEN
        W := 0.5
    ELSE
        W := 1.0;
    S := S+(X*X+25*X+3)*W;
    X := X+H
    END;
S := S*H;
```

In the algorithm above the larger the value of N, the closer
is the approximation to the true area under the curve, but
at the same time, the more costly is the computer run.
Notice that this algorithm can be used with functions of
your own by substituting the function expression within the
parentheses above.

LABORATORY PROBLEM 46 - The Registrar's Problem

Problem: The Registrar's Office has a tabulating card for
    each student. Write a program to count the total number
    of students, the number of each gender and the number
    from each state. Although only a small set of data may
    be provided, write the program so that it could process
    a data set of any size.

Input: The data cards from the Registrar's Office are
    punched as follows:

        cols.       1- 5      student ID number
                    7         gender code
                              (0=female,1=male)
                    9-10      state code (ranges
                              from 1-50)

    The last card will be a trip card with a negative ID
    number. For this program, punch an input data deck as
    follows:

            31625     0     21
            68261     1     15
            53812     1      7
            12953     0     21
            68532     0     49
            73861     1     15
            26385     0     21
            63998     1     33
            82138     1     50
            93189     0      1
               -1     0      0


Output: Print the total number of students on the first line
    and the number of males and the number of females on the
    second line. On each following line, print the state
    code and the number of students from that state if the
    number of students from that state is non-zero. Be sure
    to label your output.

Problem: Write a FUNCTION that will return a given value in the sequence of Fibonacci numbers.  A Fibonacci sequence is one in which each term in the sequence is equal to the sum of the previous two terms, given that the first two terms are 0 and 1.  The beginning terms would, therefore, be

0,1,1,2,3,5,8,......

For example, the number 0 is the 0th term and the number 8 is the 6th term.

Procedure: Write the function to have one argument.  This argument is the number of the term that you wish to be returned.

Output: Write the function such that the first time it is invoked, it will generate the first 40 terms and store them in an array and return the term specified by the argument.  On subsequent calls the function will only require that the term be locked up from the array of numbers.

In the main program write out the number M given by

$$M=(F[n-1]*F[n+1])-F[n]^2$$

for n ranging from 2 to 39, where F[n] refers to the nth term in the sequence of Fibonacci numbers.  Put appropriate labels on the output.  Each of the 38 lines of output should have 4 numbers printed: first M, then F[n-1], F[n+1], and finally F[n].

LABORATORY PROBLEM 48 - Recursion

Problem: The Fibonacci sequence consists of terms F such
   that

   F[n] = F[n-1] + F[n-2]

   F[0] is given as 0, and F[1] is given as 1.

   The first few terms are therefore

   0,1,1,2,3,5,8,13,21,34,...

      Write an internal recursive procedure called FIB
   which has as its argument the desired term number, n,
   and which returns the appropriate Fibonacci number.  The
   procedure should compute a Fibonacci number based on
   only the two previous numbers or the first two numbers,
   0 and 1. Write a procedure to call the subprogram.  For
   example, if the procedure contained the statement

   WRITELN (FIB[8]);

   the value printed would be 21.

      Now write a similar routine which produces
   Fibonacci numbers by iterative rather than recursive
   means.  Figure out a way to "race" the two routines
   under identical circumstances.  Form some impression of
   the relative efficiencies of recursion vs. iteration.

# LABORATORY PROBLEM 49 - Questionnaire Analysis

Complete the following questionnaire by filling in the
blanks at the right with the appropriate numbers or numeric
code.  Notice that each blank has a number below it.  After
filling in the questionnaire, keypunch your responses in the
card column indicated by the number under the line.  As an
example, punch your age in card columns 1 and 2, punch your
sex code in column 3, etc.  Submit the punched card to your
instructor who will provide further instructions on the
input for your program.  Write a PASCAL program to tabulate
the responses as outlined below.

1.  Age

$$\overline{\phantom{XX}}\ \overline{\phantom{XX}}$$
$$\;1\quad\;2$$

2.  Sex (female=1, male=2)

$$\overline{\phantom{XX}}$$
$$4$$

3.  Academic year (fr=1, soph=2, jr=3, sr=4, grad=5,
    special student=6)

$$\overline{\phantom{XX}}$$
$$6$$

4.  Overall grade point average

$$\overline{\phantom{X}}\ \overline{\phantom{X}}\ \overline{\phantom{XX}}\ \overline{\phantom{XX}}$$
$$8\quad9\quad10\quad11$$

For Questions 5-11, no=0, and yes=1

Have you taken or are you currently taking:

5.  Two years of high school algebra or a year of
    college algebra?

$$\overline{\phantom{XX}}$$
$$13$$

6.  First semester calculus?

$$\overline{\phantom{XX}}$$
$$15$$

7.  Second semester calculus?

$$\overline{\phantom{XX}}$$
$$17$$

8.  Third Semester calculus?

$$\overline{\phantom{XX}}$$
$$19$$

9. Differential equations?

$$\overline{\phantom{xx}}_{21}$$

10. Applied calculus?

$$\overline{\phantom{xx}}_{23}$$

11. Had you ever written a computer program before enrolling in this class?

$$\overline{\phantom{xx}}_{25}$$

12. What grade did you receive in plane geometry? (Write A, B, C, D, or E; if you didn't take plane geometry, write X.)

$$\overline{\phantom{xx}}_{27}$$

Problem: Tabulate the responses to questions on the class questionnaire.

Input:

   1st record: m (number of records following)

   2nd through m+1 record:  (punched cards that were turned in by students answering the questionnaire)

Output: Prepare a report tabulating the totals for each question and response.  Use appropriate headings to identify results.

LABORATORY PROBLEM 50 - Grade Reports

Problem: Write a program to process final student grades.
    For each student print a grade report.

Procedure: Grade point standing= $c[i]*w[i]/c[i]$ where $c[i]$
    is credits for the i'th course and $w[i]$ is the weight
    for the grade (4 for A, 3 for B, 2 for C, 1 for D, and 0
    for E).  If a grade is blank, the student is auditing
    the course; do not include credits for an audited course
    in the sum of credits.  If the sum of credits for a
    student is zero, print zero for the grade point average.

Input: For each student, up to ten records may exist.  All
    of the records for any one student are together in the
    input stream.  Each record indicates a course, credits
    and grade, and is written in the following form:

    Columns: 1-9      social security number
             11-12    credit hours for course
             14-16    course id (numeric)
             18       grade (A,B,C,D,E)

    The end of the entire data set is indicated by a trip
    record which contains a social security number which is
    all zeros.

Output: For each student print a report as follows:

    First line: social security number

    One line for each course: identification, credits, grade

    Last line: total credits for semester, total credit hours,
        semester grade point standing

LABORATORY PROBLEM 51 - Counting Students

Problem: Search a data file for specific information.  The
    problem here is to find out how many full-time freshmen,
    sophomores, juniors, seniors, and graduate students are
    listed.

Input: Your instructor will inform you of the location of
    the data for this problem.  An undetermined number
    (fewer than 500) student records are recorded.  Each
    student record contains:

            Cols. 1- 5    Student number
                  7- 9    Home town code (disregard this)
                  11      Full-time, part-time code.
                          0 = part-time student and
                          1 = full-time student.
                  13-15   Overall grade point average.
                  17      Classification:
                          1  freshman
                          2  sophomore
                          3  junior
                          4  senior
                          5  graduate student

Procedure: Search the file, counting the number of full-time
    freshmen, sophomores, juniors, seniors, and graduate
    students.  You can disregard part-time students.

Output: Print in columns:

            1-10    the number of full time freshmen
            11-20   the number of full time sophomores
            21-30   the number of full time juniors
            31-40   the number of full time seniors
            41-50   the number of full time graduate students

LABORATORY PROBLEM 52 - Inventory Application II

Problem: To program a system that will retain inventory
    records, write invoices and reorder merchandise.  The
    XYZ Wholesale Company maintains an inventory of ten
    different types of gaskets (serial numbers 5, 8, 19, 21,
    35, 66, 81, 82, 83, 98).

Input: Your instructor will inform you of the location of
    the data for this problem. The data file contains ten
    status records.  Each record contains:

| Columns | | |
|---|---|---|
| | 1- 2 | gasket serial number |
| | 4- 8 | inventory on hand at beginning of run |
| | 10-13 | retail price of this type of gasket (dollars and cents) |
| | 15-18 | reorder point |
| | 20-23 | reorder quantity |

Following these records is an unknown number of customer
orders.  Each customer order contains:

| | | |
|---|---|---|
| | 1- 4 | customer code |
| | 6- 8 | number of gaskets ordered |
| | 10-11 | type of gasket |

Procedure: First, after creating the current status of the
    inventory of the firm, process customer orders.  As each
    is read, the computer must decide whether the inventory
    is sufficient to ship the goods.  If sufficent inventory
    is available, write an invoice and reduce inventory--if
    not, write an invoice for the goods on hand and a
    backorder for the remainder.  If no inventory is on
    hand, write a backorder for the entire order.  Second,
    after all customer orders have been processed (and all
    invoices and backorders have been written), write one
    reorder line for each type of gasket whose inventory is
    below the reorder point.

Third, print the current status of each gasket.

Invoice:
    columns
| | | |
|---|---|---|
| | 1- 5 | customer code |
| | 15-20 | number of gaskets shipped |
| | 25-30 | price per gasket |
| | 35-40 | amount due in dollars and cents |
| | 50-52 | type of gasket |

Status Report:
    columns
        3- 5   gasket type
        7-12   gaskets on hand
       14-19   number of gaskets backordered
               (excluding orders)
       28-38   number of gaskets shipped
       48-58   $ sales of gaskets shipped

Backorder Report:
    columns
        1- 4   9999
        5-14   blank
       15-20   number of gaskets backordered
       25-30   price per gasket
       40-42   type of gasket

Reorder Report:
    columns
        1- 4   8888
           5   blank
        6-11   number of gaskets
       14-16   gasket type

LABORATORY PROBLEM 53 - Inventory Simulation
                         (Random number generator needed)

Problem: Given 3 reorder-point, reorder-quantity
    combinations, determine the cost of each inventory
    policy using simulation.

Data: For each day's demand, generate a random number
    uniformly distributed between 0 and 50.

Information: Assume the following:

a. Each re-order placed costs $50.
b. Each unit of inventory costs $.50 per day for storage
    (insurance, deterioration, etc.).
c. Each unit out of stock when it might have been sold
    creates ill will worth $1 per unit plus the $3 net
    income that would have resulted in its sale, or a total
    of $4 per unit.
d. There is a 3-day lag between the time merchandise is re-
    ordered and received.
e. Initial inventory is 100 units.
f. Lost sales are lost forever; they cannot be backordered.
g. Initially, no merchandise has been ordered for stock.


Policies: The three policies to be tested are:

| Reorder-point | Reorder-quantity |
|---------------|------------------|
| 10            | 20               |
| 10            | 50               |
| 10            | 80               |

Procedure: Start the simulation at day 1.  Determine whether
    today's demand can be filled or partially filled from
    inventory on hand.  Add costs of today's transactions to
    total cost; then determine whether inventory is above
    the reorder-point.  If not, place an order (to be
    delivered three days hence).  Repeat this procedure
    until 50 days' simulation is complete.  Use the same 50
    random numbers for each of the three simulation runs.


Output: Print, for each of the three inventory policies:

| columns | item             |
|---------|------------------|
| 1-11    | reorder-point    |
| 13-23   | reorder-quantity |
| 25-35   | cost             |

LABORATORY PROELEM 54 - Simplified Payroll

Input: Your instructor will inform you of the location of
    the data for this problem.  There is cne parameter
    record that indicates the number of employee records to
    be processed.

    Employee Records--one for each employee (these records
    follow the parameter record).

    | Columns | Information in these columns |
    | --- | --- |
    | 1- 6 | employee number (no decimal) |
    | 8- 9 | number of dependents |
    | 11-14 | number of hours this employee worked this week (fractional hours possible) |
    | 16-20 | hourly pay for this worker (in dollars and cents;e.g. 5.25) |
    | 22 | insurance code.  A one denotes that $2.22 is to be deducted.  A zero denotes no deduction. |

Procedure: For each employee ccmpute gross pay and net pay.
    Gross pay = hours worked times hourly pay.  If the
    employee has worked more than 40 hours, he receives time
    and one-half for these excess hours.

        Deductions:
        Federal Tax=(gross pay-(13* dependents))*.14
        FICA = gross pay * .052
        City Tax = gross pay * .0125
        Insurance = $2.22 or nothing

Output: For each employee print:

    | Printer Cols. | Information |
    | --- | --- |
    | 1- 7 | employee number |
    | 8-19 | gross pay (pay before deductions) |
    | 20-30 | net pay (pay after deductions) |

    After all employee records have been processed, print:

    | | |
    | --- | --- |
    | 1-20 | (2 decimals) average gross wages |
    | 21-40 | (2 decimals) average net wages |

    Notes: 1) Do not worry about rounding.
           2) If Federal Tax turns out to be negative,
              set it equal to zero and proceed.

LABORATORY PROBLEM 55 - Waiting Line Model
                         (Needs random number generator)

Problem: In some economic activities waiting lines (or
    queues) form because more demanders appear than can be
    served in one time interval.  The solution to such a
    problem generally involves the determination of the
    optimum number of servers (that is, the number of
    servers that minimize cost or maximize profit).

    Here we analyze a supermarket waiting line.  We will
    determine the optimum number of checkout counters to
    install in the following manner: simulate 50 minutes of
    activity with one clerk (checkout counter), then
    simulate 50 minutes with two clerks, then three, etc.,
    each time computing and printing the costs.  As soon as
    the cost of N clerks is greater than the cost of N-1
    clerks, discontinue the simulation.  (In reality we
    would simulate many more minutes of activity, but
    because of computer cost limitations, we arbitrarily
    choose 50.)

Assumptions:

1.  At most, one customer can arrive in any one minute.
2.  Four minutes are required to check out one customer.
3.  Each minute that a customer waits in line costs the
    store 80 cents in lost future purchases.
4.  Each clerk receives 4 cents per minute salary.
5.  There is a 0.3 probability that a customer arrives in
    line in any one minute.  There is a 0.7 probability that
    no customer arrives in line in any one minute.
6.  When a customer arrives in line, he remains in line
    until he is served.
7.  Initially, 2 customers are waiting.
8.  A customer will join the shortest line.

Procedure:

1.  Generate 50 one-digit random numbers.
2.  Each simulated minute, look at the next random number.
    If it is a zero, one, or two, another customer enters a
    waiting line.  If the random number is  greater than
    two, no new customer enters a waiting line.


Output: For each simulation run, print the number of clerks
    and the total cost.

LABORATORY PROBLEM 56 - Counting Binary Digits

Problem: Each card in a deck contains one positive number in
    card columns 1-10. For each input card print one line
    with the number of one-bits contained in the binary
    representation of the number; print also the hexadecimal
    representation of the number. For example, if the
    number punched into a card were 29, the binary
    representation of the number would be 11101 and,
    therefore, the number of one-bits would be 4. The
    hexadecimal representation would be 1D.



* * * * * * * * * * * * * * * * * * * * * * * * * * * * * *



LABORATORY PROBLEM 57 - Alphanumeric Sorting

Problem: A deck of cards (200 or fewer) contains names and
    salaries of workers in a company.

Output: The president of the company wants two lists: the
    first a list of all employees in alphabetical order by
    last name, showing name and salary; the second a list of
    employees in order by salary (descending order), showing
    name and salary. Each card contains the employee's
    salary in columns 1-6 (whole numbers only) and the
    employee's last name in columns 8-20.

LABORATORY PROBLEM 58 - Parsing I

Problem: Data lines contain various character information
    between columns 1 and 72 (inclusive). Your task, as a
    programmer, is to write a computer program to search
    through the lines looking for the following words:

| | | |
|---|---|---|
| ARRAY | END | OR |
| EEGIN | FOR | PROCEDURE |
| DIV | IF | PROGRAM |
| DO | MOD | THEN |
| DOWNTO | NOT | VAR |
| ELSE | OF | WHILE |

Procedure: After searching through all of the data lines,
    print a list of each of the words with the number of
    occurrences of each beside it. In this problem, words
    cannot be split between data lines and words cannot
    contain imbedded blank characters. Now run the program
    using the program itself as data.

* * * * * * * * * * * * * * * * * * * * * * * * * * * * * *

LABORATORY PRCELEM 59 - Parsing II

Problem: You are to write a program which uses as input data
    a TIPS program. For each instruction, print a line
    consisting of the instruction and the corresponding
    description if it is one of those shown below:

        PROGRAM
        VAR
        READ
        WRITELN
        arithmetic assignment
        FOR
        END

    If it is not one of the above, print "OTHER".

Data: Run the program using some of the TIPS programs you
    wrote previously as data.

LABORATORY PROBLEM 60 - Magic Squares (A problem for three
    students; contributed   by   Dr. J. W. Atwood,  Sir George
    Williams University, Montreal, Canada)

Background: A Magic Square consists of a number of integers
    arranged in the form of a square, so that the sum of the
    numbers in every row, in every column, and in each
    diagonal is the same.   If the integers are the
    consecutive integers from 1 to $n^2$, the square is said to
    be of the nth order, and the sum of the numbers in every
    row, column and diagonal is equal to $n(n^2+1)/2$.

    Thus the first 25 integers, arranged in the form of
    Figure 1, represent a magic square of the fifth order.

| 17 | 24 | 1  | 8  | 15 |
|----|----|----|----|----|
| 23 | 5  | 7  | 14 | 16 |
| 4  | 6  | 13 | 20 | 22 |
| 10 | 12 | 19 | 21 | 3  |
| 11 | 18 | 25 | 2  | 9  |

Figure 1
Magic Square

The formation of these squares is an old amusement, and
in times when mystical ideas were associated with
particular numbers it was natural that such arrangements
should be studied.  Magic squares were constructed in
China before the Christian era; their introduction into
Europe appears to have been due to Moschopulus in the
early part of the fifteenth century.  A magic square
engraved on a silver plate was sometimes prescribed as a
charm against the plague.  The mathematical theory of
the construction of these squares was taken up in France
in the seventeenth century, and since then it has been a
favorite subject with writers in many countries.

A magic square of the nth order, where n is odd (i.e., n=2m+1, where m is an integer), can be constructed as follows. First, the number 1 is placed in the middle cell of the top row. The successive numbers are then placed in their natural order in a diagonal line which slopes upwards to the right, except that

1) when the top row is reached, the next number is written in the bottom row, one column to the right;

2) when the right-hand column is reached, the next number is written in the left-hand column, one row up;

3) if a number, say k, is written in the upper right hand cell, the number k+1 should be written in the cell immediately underneath it; and

4) if a number, say j, cannot be written n a cell because the cell is occupied by another number, then j should be written in the cell immediately beneath the cell containing the previous number j-1.

A check of Figure 1, showing the construction of a square of the fifth order, should make the rules clear. Magic squares of the nth order, where n is even and n=2(2m+1)--i.e., n is twice an odd number--can also be constructed by a rule. Determine m by the formula m=(n/2-1)/2. Divide the square into four equal quarters: A, B, C, D, as in Figure 2. Construct in A, by the method above for an odd n, a magic square with the numbers 1 to $u^2$, where u=n/2.

| A | C |
|---|---|
| D | B |

Figure 2
Subdivision of Magic Square

Construct by the same rule, in B, C, D, similar magic squares with the numbers $u^2+1$ to $2u^2$, $2u^2+1$ to $3u^2$, and $3u^2+1$ to $4u^2$. The resulting composite square is magic in columns only (see Figure 3).

| 8 - | 1 | 6 | 26 | 19 | 24 |
|---|---|---|---|---|---|
| 3 | 5 - | 7 | 21 | 23 | 25 |
| 4 - | 9 | 2 | 22 | 27 | 20 |
| 35 -- | 28 | 33 | 17 | 10 | 15 |
| 30 | 32 -- | 34 | 12 | 14 | 16 |
| 31 -- | 36 | 29 | 13 | 18 | 11 |

Figure 3
Initial Quarter-Squares

In the middle row of A take the set of m cells next but
one to the left-hand side; in each of the other rows of
A take the set of m cells nearest to the left-hand side.
The numbers in these cells are underlined in Figure 3.
Now, interchange the numbers in these cells with the
numbers in the corresponding cells of D.

Next, interchange the numbers in the cells in each of
the m-1 columns next to the right-hand side of C with
the numbers in the corresponding cells of B. Of course,
the resulting square remains magic in columns, and it is
now also magic in rows and diagonals as seen in Figure
4.

| 35 | 1 | 6 | 26 | 19 | 24 |
|----|----|----|----|----|----|
| 3 | 32 | 7 | 21 | 23 | 25 |
| 31 | 9 | 2 | 22 | 27 | 20 |
| 8 | 28 | 33 | 17 | 10 | 15 |
| 30 | 5 | 34 | 12 | 14 | 16 |
| 4 | 36 | 29 | 13 | 18 | 11 |

Figure 4
Final Square, n=6

In the example of Figure 3 and Figure 4, m=1, so m-1=0
and therefore no interchanges were made between blocks C
and B. In general, however, there would be interchanges
of the corresponding m-1 columns on the right-hand side
of blocks B and C. For instance, when n=14, then m=3
and m-1=2, so that the two most right-hand columns of
block B must be interchanged with the two corresponding
columns of block C.

Procedure: Write an internal PROCEDURE to compute a magic
square of any order. Call the subprogram MAGSQR.
MAGSQR should call a second PROCEDURE to compute the
magic square of any odd order. Call this subprogram
ODDSQR. Write a driving program to call MAGSQR, print
the results, and print checks of the sums of the rows,
columns and diagonals. The driver should be able to
handle a magic square of order 15.

Three students should cooperate on this project. One
writes the driver, one writes MAGSQR, and one writes
ODDSQR.

# part VII

# APPENDICES

# APPENDIX A:
## RESERVED WORDS IN PASCAL

| | | | |
|---|---|---|---|
| AND | END | NIL | SET |
| ARRAY | FILE | NOT | THEN |
| BEGIN | FOR | OF | TO |
| CASE | FUNCTION | OR | TYPE |
| CONST | GOTO | PACKED | UNTIL |
| DIV | IF | PROCEDURE | VAR |
| DO | IN | PROGRAM | WHILE |
| DOWNTO | LABEL | RECORD | WITH |
| ELSE | MOD | REPEAT | |

# APPENDIX B:
## STANDARD IDENTIFIERS IN PASCAL

Constants:

| FALSE | TRUE | MAXINT |

Types:

| INTEGER | BOOLEAN | REAL |
| CHAR | TEXT | |

Files:

| INPUT | OUTPUT |

## Functions

| NAME | ARGUMENT | RESULT | FUNCTION |
|---|---|---|---|
| ABS(X) | REAL or INTEGER | REAL or INTEGER | Absolute Value |
| ARCTAN(X) | REAL or INTEGER | REAL | Inverse Tangent |
| CHR(X) | INTEGER | CHAR | Character defined by ordinal value of parameter |
| COS(X) | REAL or INTEGER | REAL | Cosine |
| EOF(X) | FILE | BOOLEAN | End of File Indicator |
| EOLN(X) | FILE | BOOLEAN | End of Line Indicator |
| EXP(X) | REAL or INTEGER | REAL | e to the x power |
| LN(X) | REAL or INTEGER | REAL | Natural logarithm |
| ODD(X) | INTEGER | BOOLEAN | Returns TRUE if parameter is an odd number |

| ORD(X) | CHAR, BOOLEAN or User defined Scalar | INTEGER | Ordinal value of X |
|---|---|---|---|
| PRED(X) | Scalar (not REAL) | Scalar (not REAL) | Predecessor of X |
| ROUND(X) | REAL | INTEGER | X rounded |
| SIN(X) | REAL or INTEGER | REAL | Sine |
| SQR(X) | REAL or INTEGER | REAL or INTEGER | X squared |
| SQRT(X) | REAL or INTEGER | REAL | Square root |
| SUCC(X) | Scalar (not REAL) | Scalar (not REAL) | Successor of X |
| TRUNC(X) | REAL | INTEGER | X truncated |

## Procedures

| NAME | DESCRIPTION |
|---|---|
| DISPOSE(P) | Returns the space used by P to the available space pool. |
| GET(F) | Reads the next component in file F and stores it in F↑ |
| NEW(P) | Allocates a new storage location pointed to by pointer variable P |
| PACK(A,N,B) | Packs array A starting with subscript N and stores the packed array in B starting at the first location |
| PAGE(F) | Allows the next line to be printed at the top of a page |
| PUT(F) | Writes the contents of F↑ onto file F |
| READ(F,...) or READLN(F,...) | Reads from file F |
| RESET(F) | Rewinds file F to the beginning |

| | |
|---|---|
| REWRITE(F) | Creates a new empty file F and positions it at the beginning |
| UNPACK(B,A,N) | Unpacks array B beginning at the first position and places it into array A starting at subscript N |
| WRITE(F,...)<br>or<br>WRITELN(F,...) | Writes information onto file F |

| OPERATOR | | OPERANDS | RESULT |
|---|---|---|---|
| + | Addition | REAL or INTEGER | REAL or INTEGER |
| | Unary | REAL or INTEGER | REAL or INTEGER |
| | SET Union | Any SET Type | Any SET Type |
| − | Subtraction | REAL or INTEGER | REAL or INTEGER |
| | Unary | REAL or INTEGER | REAL or INTEGER |
| | SET Difference | Any SET Type | Any SET Type |
| * | Multiplication | REAL or INTEGER | REAL or INTEGER |
| | SET Intersection | Any SET Type | Any SET Type |
| / | REAL Division | REAL or INTEGER | REAL |
| DIV | INTEGER Division | INTEGER | INTEGER |
| MOD | Modulus | INTEGER | INTEGER |
| NOT | Logical Negation | BOOLEAN | BOOLEAN |
| OR | Logical Disjunction | BOOLEAN | BOOLEAN |
| AND | Logical Conjunction | BOOLEAN | BOOLEAN |
| <= | Implication | BOOLEAN | BOOLEAN |
| | SET Inclusion | Any SET Type | BOOLEAN |
| | Less than or equal | Any Scalar Type | BOOLEAN |
| = | Equivalence | BOOLEAN | BOOLEAN |
| | Equality | Scalar, SET or POINTER | BOOLEAN |
| <> | Exclusive OR | BOOLEAN | BOOLEAN |
| | Not equal | Scalar, SET or POINTER | BOOLEAN |
| >= | Set Containment | Any SET Type | BOOLEAN |
| | Gr than or equal | Any Scalar Type | BOOLEAN |
| < | Less than | Any Scalar Type | BOOLEAN |
| > | Greater than | Any Scalar Type | BOOLEAN |

| IN | Set Membership | Left Operand: Any Scalar Right Operand: Its SET Type | BOOLEAN |
|----|----------------|-------------------------------------------------------|---------|
| := | Assignment | Any (Except FILE) | |

| Punctuation | Meaning |
|-------------|---------|
| , | Separates Items in a List |
| ; | Separates Statements |
| : | Separates Variable Name and Type |
| ' | Delimits character strings, separates format items |
| . | Program Terminator, Decimal point |
| .. | Subrange Specifier |
| ( | Start Parameter List or nested Expression |
| ) | End Parameter List or nested Expression |
| [ | Start Subscript List or Set Expression |
| (. | Start Subscript List or Set Expression (Alternate Form) |
| ] | End Subscript List or Set Expression |
| .) | End Subscript List or Set Expression (Alternate Form) |
| { | Start a Comment |
| (* | Start a Comment (Alternate Form) |
| } | End a Comment |
| *) | End a Comment (Alternate Form) |
| ↑ | Denotes a Buffer or a Pointer Variable |
| @ | Denotes a Buffer or a Pointer Variable (Alternate Form) |

APPENDIX D:
ANSWERS

Page 19
The following are invalid identifiers:
    c.  does not begin with a letter
    e.  contains a blank
    f.  too many characters
    g.  "=" and "+" are not valid in a variable name
    i.  "=" is not valid in a variable name
Page 20
The following delimiter words were used in LAB Problem 00:
    PROGRAM
    VAR
    BEGIN
    END

Page 28
1.  The following are invalid TIPS numbers:
    c.  includes a blank
    e.  includes a "*"
    f.  includes a letter
    g.  includes two decimal points
    h.  includes two algebraic signs
    j.  includes a "/"
    k.  includes a ","
    l.  begins with a decimal point
    m.  ends with a decimal point
    n.  ends with a decimal point
    o.  begins with a decimal point
    p.  includes a ","

2.  END, NOT, IF, PROGRAM, DIV

Page 31
The block of the PROGRAM EASY is:

    VAR A: REAL;
        B: REAL;
        X: REAL;
    BEGIN READ (A,B);
    X := A/B+1.5;
    WRITELN (X:10:2,A:10:2,B:10:2)
    END.

Page 33

Declaration section of the program named ORWELL:

```
(* PROGRAM DESCRIPTION OR PURPOSE *)
PROGRAM ORWELL (INPUT,OUTPUT);
    VAR
        PIG: (* DESCRIPTION OR USE OF PIG *) REAL;
        COW: (* DESCRIPTION OR USE OF COW *) REAL;
        HORSE: (* DESCRIPTION OR USE OF HORSE *) REAL;
        DUCK: (* DESCRIPTION OR USE OF DUCK *) REAL;
```

Page 36
CAT:  -777.2
DOG:     0.0098

Page 38
Question: KRK would be printed out as bb15.3.

Page 43
1.  6.66666E+02      -7.10000E+00        3.00000E-04

2.  0.0055           -5500.0

3.  a.      6.50000E+00
    b.      6.50000E+00
            1.00250E+03
            2.50000E-01
            2.50000E-01

4.  WRITELN

5.  Comments are:
        Delimited by "(*" and "*)";
        Printed in the program listing only.
    Character Strings are:
        Delimited by single quotes;
        Printed in the program listing,
            and also during program execution
            with the rest of the output.

6.  WRITELN (' THE WEIGHT MUST BE',EXER:5:1,
            ' OR WE''RE IN TROUBLE!')

Page 51
1.  a.  6           g.  16
    b.  -2          h.  16
    c.  2           i.  0.25
    d.  8           j.  1

494                     Appendix D: Answers

```
        e.    5             k.    9
        f.    2             l.    1

2.    a.    W + X - Y
      b.    W - X * X
      c.    W * X - Y
      d.    W - X * Y
      e.    W - X * Y + Z
      f.    W * X * Y + Z
      g.    W / Z + X
      h.    W - X -Z
      i.    W / Y  +   X / Z
      j.    (W / X ) * (1 / Z)
      k.    (W + X ) / (Y + Z)
      l.    W - (X * Y) / 2


3.    a.    3           f.    -0.2
      b.    49          g.    -2.0
      c.    8           h.    3
      d.    -0.6        i.    - 12
      e.    -0.2        j.    -38.5


4.    b.    B is not a variable name
      c.    More than one operator between operands
      d.    More than one operator between operands
      e.    '*' required between BB and '('
```

Page 56, 57
Question: AZ will have the value 18

```
1.    a.    13
      b.    14
      c.    11
      d.     1.25
      e.    27
      f.    25
      g.    51
```

Question: How many multiplications would you save?
$n*(n+1)/2 - n = n*(n-1)/2$

```
2.    1.60000E+00

3.    C := A;
      A := B;
      B := C;
```

4.
```
PROGRAM CONVERT1 (INPUT, OUTPUT);
(* PROGRAM TO CONVERT A FAHRENHEIT
   TEMPERATURE TO CELSIUS *)
   VAR
        F: (* FAHRENHEIT TEMP *) REAL;
        C: (* CELSIUS TEMP  *) REAL;
   BEGIN
   READ (F);
   C:= (F-32)*(5/9);
   WRITELN (' FAHRENHEIT = ',F,' CELSIUS = ',C)
   END.
```

Page 59

Question:
The general method of attack is to compute area of the
rectangle and subtract the area of the semi-circle.
"r" represents the area of the rectangle, and "s" the
area of the semi-circle.

Page 66
Question: The other appropriate compound statement is
```
      BEGIN
      WRITELN (' YOU BLEW IT--FIGURE IS DEGENERATE');
      WRITELN (' WIDTH ',WIDTH,' HEIGHT ',HEIGHT)
      END
```

Page 71, 72
1.  a.  False
    b.  True
    c.  True
    d.  True

2.  a.  IS GREATER THAN is not a valid comparison operator
    c.  => is not a valid comparison operator (>= is)

3.  The = symbol may be preceded by a colon (:=), to
    mean "replaced by", or it may be used alone, as a
    comparison operator.

4.  C IS LITTLE

5.
```
(* PROGRAM TO CONVERT FAHRENHEIT TO
   CELSIUS OR CELSIUS TO FAHRENHEIT,
   DEPENDING ON CODE *)
PROGRAM CONVERT2 (INPUT, OUTPUT);
   VAR
```

```
        X: (* TEMPERATURE INPUT *) REAL;
        F: (* FAHRENHEIT TEMPERATURE *) REAL;
        C: (* CELSIUS TEMPERATURE *) REAL;
        FTOC: (* FAHRENHEIT TO CELSIUS
                CONVERSION FACTOR *) REAL;
        CTOF: (* CELSIUS TO FAHRENHEIT
                CONVERSION FACTOR *) REAL;
        CODE: (* FAHRENHEIT--CELSIUS CODE *)  INTEGER;
    BEGIN
    FTOC := 5/9;
    CTOF := 9/5;
    READ (X,CODE);
    IF CODE = 3 THEN
        BEGIN
        F := X*CTOF+32;
        WRITELN (' CELSIUS TEMP = ',X,
                 ' FAHRENHEIT TEMP = ',F)
        END
    ELSE IF CODE = 6 THEN
            BEGIN
            C := (X-32)*(FTOC);
            WRITELN (' FAHRENHEIT TEMP = ',X,
                     ' CELSIUS TEMP = ',C)
            END
        ELSE
            WRITELN (' ERROR IN CODE .. ERROR VALUE IS '
                     ,CODE)
    END.
```

6.  A, B, AND C ARE   8     8     10

## Page 74

```
    IF A > B THEN
        WRITELN(A)
    ELSE
        WRITELN(B)
```

## Page 75

```
    IF A > B THEN
        BEGIN
        WRITELN(A);
        IF C > D THEN
            WRITELN(C)
        ELSE
            WRITELN(D)
        END
    ELSE
```

```
WRITELN(E)
```

```
IF A > B THEN
    BEGIN
    WRITELN(A);
    IF C > D THEN
        WRITELN(C)
    END
```

## Page 76

```
IF A > B THEN
    BEGIN
    WRITELN(A);
    IF C > D THEN
        WRITELN(C)
    ELSE
        WRITELN(D)
    END
```

```
IF A > B THEN
    BEGIN
    IF C > D THEN
        WRITELN(C)
    END
ELSE
    WRITELN(B)
```

## Page 77

```
IF A > B THEN                        IF A > B THEN
    IF C > D THEN                        IF C <= D THEN
        (* NULL *)        or                WRITELN(D)
    ELSE                                 ELSE
        WRITELN(D)                           WRITELN(E)
ELSE
    WRITELN(B)
```

## Page 81
Question:
444 is divided by the sine of EEE and added to CCC.
The square root of this value is multiplied by BBB
and the result is stored in AAA.

1.  a.  4
    b.  0
    c.  15.5
    d.  12.3137

    e. An error would result

2.  a.  "A,B" is not a valid arithmetic expression.
    c.  The argument of SQRT is not enclosed in
        parentheses.
    d.  The argument of SQRT is not enclosed in
        parentheses;
        "OF C" is not a valid arithmetic expression.

3.  2.70000E+01

Page 84
Question:
  box 1 one time
  box 2 one time
  box 3 four-hundred times
  box 4 three-hundred-ninety-nine times
  box 5 three-hundred-ninety-nine times
  box 6 three-hundred-ninety-nine times

Page 85
Question:  The loop in the square root program
  terminated because the value of X increased each
  time Y was computed.  In this way Y eventually
  got to be greater than 20.

Page 88
1.  a., d., e., and g.

2.  a.  7  0
    b.  Nothing--endless loop

Page 95
  (* PROGRAM TC CONVERT SECS TO HOURS, MINUTES, SECONDS *)
  PROGRAM CONVSECS(INPUT,OUTPUT);
      VAR
          SECS:     (* NUMBER OF SECONDS INPUT *)  INTEGER;
          HRS:      (* NUMBER OF HOURS IN SECS *)  INTEGER;
          MINS:     (* NUMBER OF MINUTES IN SECS *)INTEGER;
          REMSECS:  (* NUMBER OF SECONDS REMAINING
                       IN SECS *) INTEGER;
      BEGIN (* CONVSECS *)
      READ (SECS);
      (* COMPUTE HOURS AND REMAINING SECONDS *)
      HRS := SECS DIV 3600;
      REMSECS := SECS MOD 3600;
      (* COMPUTE MINUTES AND REMAINING SECONDS *)
      MINS := REMSECS DIV 60;
      REMSECS := REMSECS MOD 60;

```
        WRITELN (' ',SECS,' SECONDS =',HRS,' HOURS,',
                 MINS,' MINUTES',
                 REMSECS,' SECONDS')
      END.
```

Page 96, 97
1.  a.  8
    b.  102


Page 102
Question: -18 in both cases


Page 103
```
 (* PROGRAM TO CONVERT 10 PAIRS OF
    NUMBERS FROM FAHRENHEIT TO CELSIUS
    OR FROM CELSIUS TO FAHRENHEIT, DEPENDING ON CODE *)
 PROGRAM CONVERT3 (INPUT, OUTPUT);
    VAR
        X:(* TEMPERATURE INPUT *) REAL;
        F:(* FAHRENHEIT TEMPERATURE *) REAL;
        C: (* CELSIUS TEMPERATURE *) REAL;
        FTOC: (* FAHRENHEIT TO CELSIUS
                 CONVERSION FACTOR *) REAL;
        CTOF: (* CELSIUS TO FAHRENHEIT
                 CONVERSION FACTOR *) REAL;
        CODE: (* FAHRENHEIT/CELSIUS CODE *) INTEGER;
        I: (* INDEX OF DO LOOP *) INTEGER;
    BEGIN
    FTOC := 5/9;
    CTOF := 9/5;
    FOR I := 1 TO 10 DO
        BEGIN
        READ (X,CODE);
        IF CODE = 3 THEN
            BEGIN
            F := X*CTOF+32;
            WRITELN (' CELSIUS TEMP = ',X,
                     ' FAHRENHEIT TEMP = ',F)
            END
        ELSE IF CODE = 6 THEN
                BEGIN
                C := (X-32)*(FTOC);
                WRITELN (' FAHRENHEIT TEMP = ',X,
                         ' CELSIUS TEMP = ',C)
                END
            ELSE
                WRITELN (' ERROR..CODE= ',CODE)
        END
    END.
```

Question:   How might you easily compute
            BVAR to the 16th power?

```
    (* COMPUTE BVAR TO THE 2ND POWER *)
    RESULT := BVAR*BVAR;
    (* COMPUTE BVAR TO THE 4TH POWER *)
    RESULT := RESULT*RESULT;
    (* COMPUTE BVAR TO THE 8TH POWER *)
    RESULT := RESULT*RESULT;
    (* COMPUTE BVAR TO THE 16TH POWER *)
    RESULT := RESULT*RESULT;
```

Or

```
    RESULT := BVAR*BVAR;
    FOR I := 1 TO 3 DO
        RESULT := RESULT*RESULT;
```

Page 144
Question: The path of control splits at b
    and rejoins at exit;
    BUT there is a forbidden crossover from e to c.

Page 148
Question: There is no (INPUT,OUTPUT).

Page 164
    X(3) = 287

Page 166, 167
1.  VAR

        EXER: (* SCALAR VARIABLE *) REAL;
        CISE: (* ARRAY VARIABLE *) ARRAY [1..100] OF REAL;

2.  a.  The numbers in the VAR declaration indicating
        the lowest and highest subscripts must be
        constants;
    c.  The word "ARRAY" is missing.
    d.  The word "ARRAY" is missing;
        Also the declaration of an array requires both
        the lowest and highest subscripts;
    f.  This is an assignment statement, not an array
        declaration.

3.  The array X was declared to have "1" as its lowest
    subscript.

4.  7 locations would be reserved for the array RULEONE.
    They would be referred to as RULEONE[-6], RULEONE[-5],

Appendix D: Answers

501

RULEONE[-4], RULEONE[-3], RULEONE[-2],
RULEONE[-1],RULEONE[0].

Page 169, 170
1. 14.5

2. 3.85

3. TEST[4] is referred to in each.

Page 172
Questions:

| | |
|---|---|
| 1 | 1 |
| 2 | 0 |
| 3 | 2 |
| 4 | 1 |

A variable which appears on the right side of an
assignment statement must be previously initialized.

Page 173
```
(* CONVERT FAHRENHEIT TO CELSIUS USING TABLE *)
 PROGRAM CONVERT4 (INPUT, OUTPUT);
     VAR
        F: (* FAHRENHEIT TEMPERATURE *) INTEGER;
        C: (* CELSIUS TEMPERATURE (CURRENT) *) REAL;
        CPREV: (* CELSIUS TEMPERATURE (PREVIOUS) *) REAL;
        FTOC: (* FAHRENHEIT TO CELSIUS CONVERSION
                FACTOR *) REAL;
        FIRST: (* FIRST-TIME-THRU-PROCEDURE
                 SWITCH *) INTEGER;
        CELSIUS: (* CONVERSION TABLE *) ARRAY [-40..212]
                                       OF REAL;
        FAHRX: (* INDEX FOR CELSIUS ARRAY *) INTEGER;
        AVECEL: (* AVERAGE OF CURRENT AND PREVIOUS CELSIUS
             VALUES *) REAL;
     PROCEDURE CONVERT;
        BEGIN (* CONVERT *)
        IF FIRST=0 THEN
             BEGIN
 (* INITIALIZE CELSIUS ARRAY *)
             FOR FAHRX := -40 TO 212 DO
                 CELSIUS[FAHRX] := (FAHRX-32)*FTOC;
             C := CELSIUS[F];
             WRITELN (F:6,C:12:2);
 (* RESET SWITCH *)
             FIRST := 1
             END
        ELSE
             BEGIN
 (* SAVE PREVIOUS TEMPERATURE *)
```

Appendix D: Answers

```
              CPREV := C;
      (* LOOKUP CURRENT TEMPERATURE IN TABLE *)
              C := CELSIUS[ F ];
      (* AVERAGE PREVIOUS AND CURRENT TEMPERATURES *)
              AVECEL := (CPREV+C)/2.0;
              END (* CONVERT *)
          END;
      BEGIN
      (* INITIALIZE CONSTANTS AND SWITCHES *)
      FTOC := 5/9;
      FIRST := 0;
      WRITELN (' FAHREN  CELSIUS   AVE CELSIUS');
      (* INPUT AND PROCESS FAHRENHEIT VALUES *)
      READ (F);
      WHILE (F<>999) DO
          BEGIN
          IF (F<-40) OR (F>212) THEN
              WRITELN (' INPUT TEMP IS OUT OF RANGE: ',
                       F,' ****')
          ELSE
              CONVERT;
              WRITELN (F:6,C:12:2,AVECEL:12:2)
          READ (F)
          END
      END.
```

Page 184
Question:   Yes, this would produce the same result.


Page 187
a.  missing "ARRAY";
    the limits of the array should be given
    on the right side of the colon;
b.  nothing wrong;
c.  1 is not within the subscript limits of the PAY;
d.  Nothing wrong;
e.  PAY requires two subscripts;
f.  Nothing wrong.


Page 202
Question:  Median is 2.5


Page 202
Question: Zero coefficients would result in division by zero
   in forming the multipliers.


Page 221
Question:   $(n+1)^2$ lines.  The printed digits, when taken
   together form the first $(n+1)^2$ numbers of that system

starting the counting with zero.

Page 230
See Module 7 (cn the cancellation law)

Page 278
Question:   10.

Page 279
a.
```
   TYPE
       CLASTYPE=(NONDEG,FRESH,SOPH,JUNIOR,SENIOR,GRAD,PROF);
```
b.
```
   VAR
       STUCLAS:(* STUDENT'S CLASSIFICATION *)   CLASTYPE;
       STUCODE:(* STUDENT'S CODE *) INTEGER;
```
c.
```
       TEMPCLAS:(* TEMPORARY CIASSIFICATICN *) CLASTYPE;
   IF (STUCODE<0) OR (STUCODE >5) THEN
       WRITELN (' BAD STUDENT CODE',STUCODE)
   ELSE
       BEGIN
       FOR TEMPCLAS := NONDEG TC PROF DO
           IF STUCODE = ORD(TEMPCLAS) THEN
               STUCLAS := TEMPCLAS
        END
```

or

```
       TEMPCLAS:(* TEMPORARY CIASSIFICATION *) CLASTYPE;
   IF (STUCODE<0) OR (STUCODE >5) THEN
       WRITELN (' EAD STUDENT CODE',STUCODE)
   ELSE
       BEGIN
       STUCLAS := NONDEG;
       WHILE STUCODE <> ORD (STUCLAS) DO
           STUCLAS := SUCC(STUCLAS)
       END
```

Page 281
Question:   J wculd have the value of the ordinal function
            for a single quote.

            ANYCHAR would have the value "G".

Page 282
ANYCHAR := C will assign to ANYCHAR the same value as C,
another variable of TYPE CHAR.   ANYCHAR := 'C' will assign
to ANYCHAR the value 'C', a character string.

a.  K     b.  N     c.  A     d.  Y     e.  invalid

1.  V     2.  T     3.  S     4.  U     5.  E     6.  T

Page 293
    1.  a.  TRUE
        b.  TRUE
        c.  FALSE
        d.  FALSE     (ORD(FALSE)=0, ORD(TRUE)=1)
        e.  FALSE
        f.  TRUE

    2.  a.  TRUE
        b.  TRUE
        c.  TRUE
        d.  FALSE

Page 294
    a.  TRUE
    b.  TRUE
    c.  TRUE
    d.  TRUE
    e.  TRUE

Page 338
```
    VAR
        INSERT:ECOLEAN;
(* PROGRAM SEGMENT TO INSERT DOLL *)
    WRITELN (' INPUT DOLL & PHCNE');
    NEW(ALP);
    READ (ALP↑.DOLL,ALP↑.PHONE);
    INDEXPT := FIRST;
    PREVPT := FIRST;
    INSERT := FALSE;
    WHILE  (NOT INSERT) DO
        IF INDEXPT=NIL THEN
            INSERT := TRUE
        ELSE
            IF  (INDEXPT↑.DOLL>=ALP↑.DOLL) THEN
                INSERT := TRUE
            ELSE
                BEGIN
                PREVPT := INDEXPT;
                INDEXPT := INDEXPT↑.LNC
                END;
    ALP↑.LNC := INDEXPT;
    IF PREVPT=FIRST THEN
        FIRST := ALP
```

```
     ELSE
          PREVPT↑.LNC := ALP;
```

## Page 345
Question:  IF ... THEN ... ELSE
```
     CASE DAY OF
          1:   MON;
          2:   TUE;
          3:   WED;
          4:   THU;
          5:   FRI;
          6:   SAT;
          7:   SUN;
     END;
```

## Page 352
All four statements are true about both loops.

## Page 360
The PROCEDURE has the same name as a variable in the PROGRAM

## Page 362
FROM SUB  13    7; FROM PGM   13   20

## Page 375
11   100    13    45    15    16

## Page 384
1.  -166.375          1.10462
Because expressions are legal arguments of the WRITELN
procedure.  But we try to hide the fact because it's a bad
idea to use an expression in an output statement.

2.
```
PROGRAM LAB03RR (INPUT, OUTPUT);
    CONST
        PI=3.14159;
    VAR
        HEIGHT:(*   *) REAL;
        WIDTH: (*   *) REAL;
        AREA:(*   *) REAL;
(*  SUBPROGRAMS GO HERE *)
    FUNCTION RECT
        (VAR H: REAL;
        VAR  W: REAL): REAL;
        BEGIN
        RECT := H * W
        END;
    FUNCTION SEMI
```

```
            (VAR W: REAL): REAL;
        BEGIN
        SEMI := PI * W * W / 8.0;
        END;
    PROCEDURE INTAKE
        (VAR H: REAL;
        VAR W: REAL);
        BEGIN
        READ (H,W)
        END;
    PROCEDURE WOOPS
        (H: REAL;
        VAR  W: REAL);
        BEGIN
        WRITELN (' YOU BLEW IT -- FIGURE IS DEGENERATE');
        WRITELN (' WIDTH ',W,' HEIGHT ',H)
        END;
    PROCEDURE CUTGO
        (H: REAL;
        VAR  W: REAL;
        VAR  AREA: REAL);
        BEGIN
        WRITELN (' INPUT VALUES H AND W:', H,  W,
                 ' AREA=',AREA)
        END;
    BEGIN (*  MAIN  *)
    INTAKE (HEIGHT,WIDTH);
    IF (HEIGHT<WIDTH/2.0) THEN
        WOOPS(HEIGHT,WIDTH)
    ELSE
        BEGIN
        AREA := RECT(HEIGHT,WIDTH)-SEMI(WIDTH);
        OUTGO(HEIGHT,WIDTH,AREA)
        END
    END. (*  MAIN  *)
```

Page 432
Hardly!

Page 434
2549

Page 435
2549 also

The error codes shown here are the standard codes for
almost all versions of PASCAL. Your instructor may give you
additional codes for the particular version of PASCAL that
you may be using.


```
 1:   error in simple type
 2:   identifier expected
 3:   'PROGRAM' expected
 4:   ')' expected
 5:   ':' expected
 6:   illegal symbol
 7:   error in parameter list
 8:   'OF' expected
 9:   '(' expected
10:   error in type
11:   '[' expected
12:   ']' expected
13:   'END' expected
14:   ';' expected
15:   integer expected
16:   '=' expected
17:   'BEGIN' expected
18:   error in declaration part
19:   error in field-list
20:   ',' expected
21:   '*' expected


50:   error in constant
51:   ':=' expected
52:   'THEN' expected
53:   'UNTIL' expected
54:   'DO' expected
55:   'TO' or 'DOWNTO' expected
56:   'IF' expected
57:   'FILE' expected
58:   error in factor
59:   error in variable
101:   identifier declared twice
102:   low bound exceeds highbound
103:   identifier is not of appropriate class
104:   identifier not declared
```

```
105:    sign not allowed
106:    number expected
107:    incompatible subrange types
108:    file not allowed here
109:    type must not be real
110:    tagfield type must be scalar or subrange
111:    incompatible with tagfield type
112:    index type must not be real
113:    index type must be scalar or subrange
114:    base type must not be real
115:    base type must be scalar or subrange
116:    error in type of standard procedure parameter
117:    unsatisfied forward reference
118:    forward reference type identifier in variable
        declaration
119:    forward declared; repetition of parameter list not
        allowed
120:    function result type must be scalar, subrange or
        pointer
121:    file value parameter not allowed
122:    forward declared function; repetition of result type
        not allowed
123:    missing result type in function declaration
124:    F-format for real only
125:    error in type of standard function parameter
126:    number of parameters does not agree with declaration
127:    illegal parameter substitution
128:    result type of parameter function does not agree with
        declaration
129:    type conflict of operands
130:    expression is not of set type
131:    tests on equality allowed only
132:    strict inclusion not allowed
133:    file comparison not allowed
134:    illegal type of operand(s)
135:    type of operand must be Boolean
136:    set element type must be scalar or subrange
137:    set element types not compatible
138:    type of variable is not array
139:    index type is not compatible with declaration
140:    type of variable is not record
141:    type of variable must be file or pointer
142:    illegal parameter substitution
143:    illegal type of loop control variable
144:    illegal type of expression
145:    type conflict
146:    assignment of files not allowed
147:    label type incompatible with selecting expression
148:    subrange bounds must be scalar
```

```
149:   index type must not be integer
150:   assignment to standard function is not allowed
151:   assignment to formal function is not allowed
152:   no such field in this record
153:   type error in read
154:   actual parameter must be a variable
155:   control variable must not be declared on intermediate
       level
156:   multidefined case label
157:   too many cases in case statement
158:   missing corresponding variant declaration
159:   real or string tagfields not allowed
160:   previous declaration was not forward
161:   again forward declared
162:   parameter size must be constant
163:   missing variant in declaration
164:   substitution of standard proc/func not allowed
165:   multidefined label
166:   multideclared label
167:   undeclared label
168:   undefined label
169:   error in base set
170:   value parameter expected
171:   standard file was redeclared
172:   undeclared external file
173:   Fortran procedure or function expected
174:   Pascal procedure or function expected
175:   missing file "input" in program heading
176:   missing file "output" in program heading
177:   assignment to function identifier not allowed here
178:   multidefined record variant
179:   X-opt of actual proc/func does not match formal
       declaration
180:   control variable must not be formal
181:   constant part of address out of range
201:   error in real constant: digit expected
202:   string constant must not exceed source line
203:   integer constant exceeds range
204:   8 or 9 in octal number
205:   zero string not allowed
206:   integer part of real constant exceeds range
250:   too many nested scopes of identifiers
251:   too many nested procedures and/or functions
252:   too many forward references of procedure entries
253:   procedure too long
254:   too many long constants in this procedure
255:   too many errors on this source line
256:   too many external references
257:   too many externals
```

```
258:  too many local files
259:  expression too complicated
260:  too many exit labels
300:  division by zero
301:  no case provided for this value
302:  index expression out of bounds
303:  value to be assigned is out of bounds
304:  element expression out of range
398:  implementation restriction
399:  variable dimension arrays not implemented
```

# APPENDIX F:
## PASCAL SYNTAX DIAGRAMS

Syntax Diagrams:
Hierarchical or
Self-recursive

None of the thirteen syntax diagrams below
depends on a syntax diagram above itself for
its definition; thus they are in hierarchical
order except that (1) a syntax diagram may
include a reference to itself in its definition,
and (2) a diagram from the next section may
be needed.

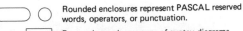

Rounded enclosures represent PASCAL reserved
words, operators, or punctuation.

Rectangles enclose names of syntax diagrams.

A triangle on a path means that there may be a
restriction on the number of times a path may
be traversed.

An asterisk indicates a feature in PASCAL not
covered in this book.

The syntax diagrams are taken, in modified form,
from the *PASCAL User's Manual and Report*, by
Jensen and Wirth, copyright 1973, Springer-Verlag,
with permission.

**program**

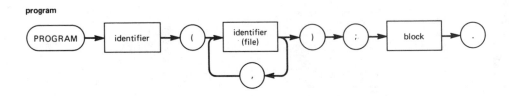

**block**

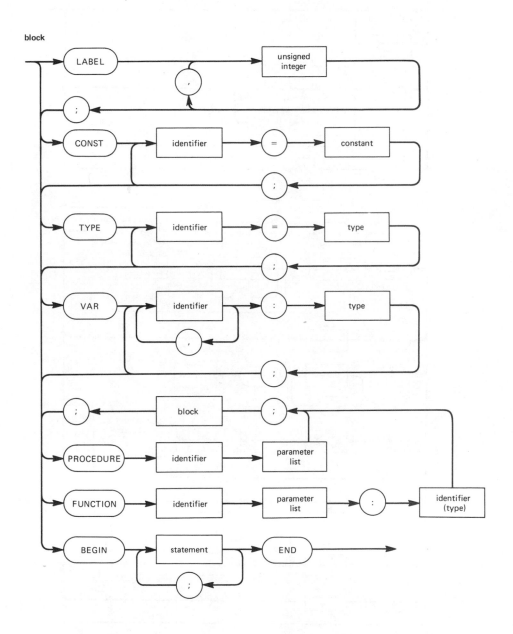

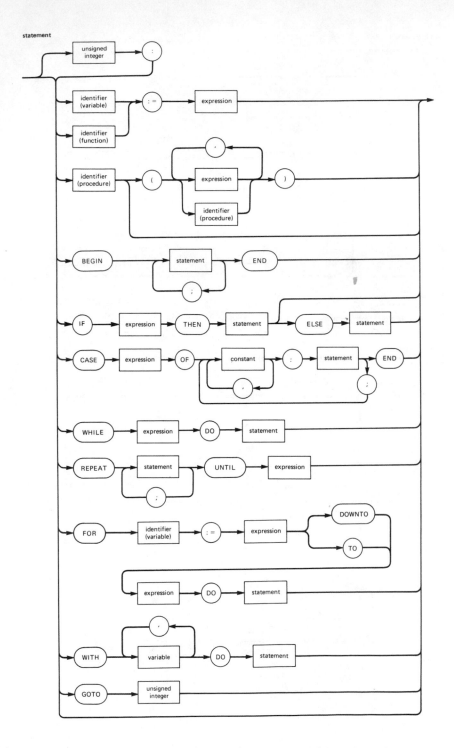

Appendix F: Pascal Syntax Diagrams

**parameter list**

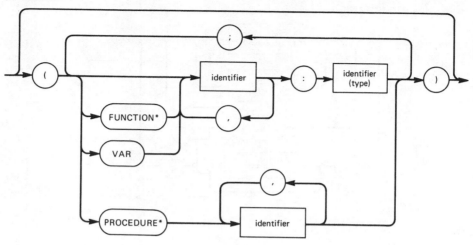

**simple type**

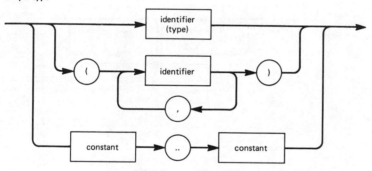

**constant**

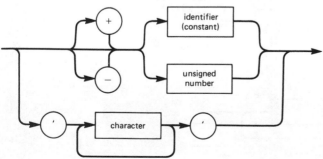

Appendix F: Pascal Syntax Diagrams          515

**unsigned constant**

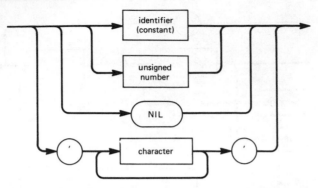

**unsigned number**

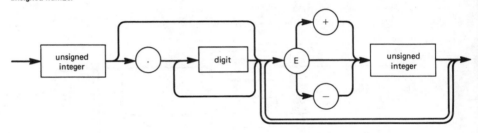

**identifier**

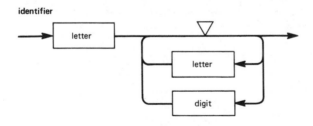

**unsigned integer**

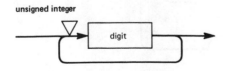

**character**

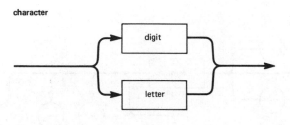

**digit**
(any of the ten digits: 0, 1, 2, . . . 9)

**letter**
(any of the twenty-six letters:  A, B, C, . . . , Z)

Syntax Diagrams:
Mutually Recursive

The seven syntax diagrams below (a group of
five followed by a group of two) may not be
placed in logical order because one diagram
may include a reference to a second diagram
which, in turn, mentions the first.

**simple expression**

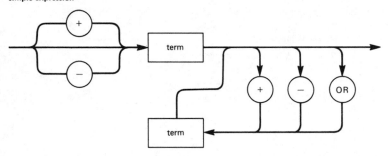

**term**

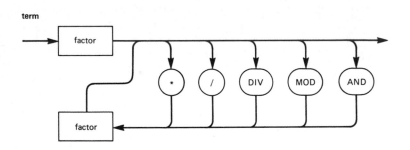

**factor**

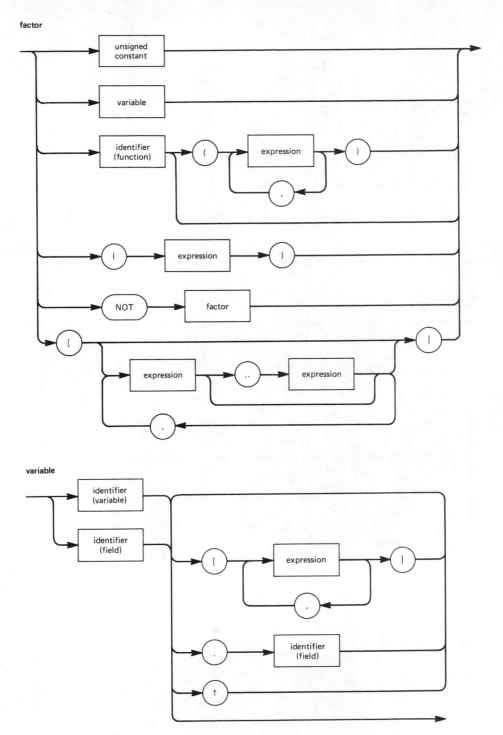

**variable**

**expression**

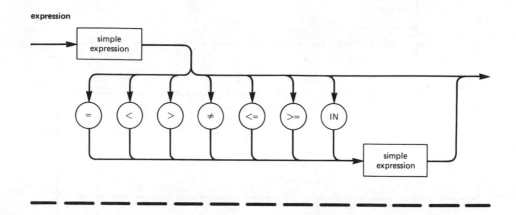

**type**

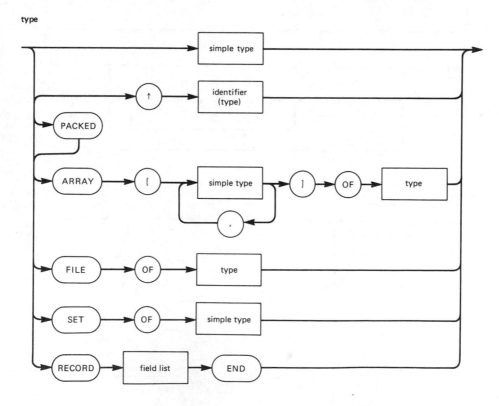

Appendix F: Pascal Syntax Diagrams

**field list**

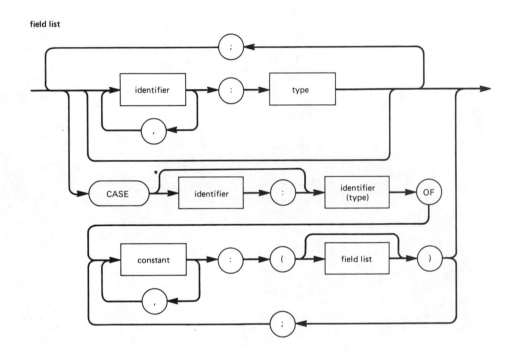

# INDEX

**This book contains a fold-out sheet as the last page. If the fold-out is missing, the book is incomplete.**